Thomas Nicolas Burke

Lectures and Sermons

Third Edition

Thomas Nicolas Burke

Lectures and Sermons
Third Edition

ISBN/EAN: 9783337201647

Printed in Europe, USA, Canada, Australia, Japan

Cover: Foto ©Lupo / pixelio.de

More available books at **www.hansebooks.com**

LECTURES AND SERMONS

DELIVERED BY THE

VERY REV. THOMAS N. BURKE, O.P.,

SINCE HIS DEPARTURE FROM AMERICA.

COMPILED AND EDITED, WITH INTRODUCTION,

BY THE

VERY REV. J. A. ROCHFORD, O.P.

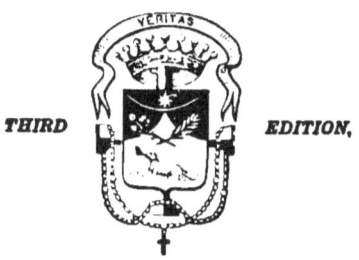

THIRD EDITION.

NEW YORK:
P. J. KENEDY,
EXCELSIOR CATHOLIC PUBLISHING HOUSE,
5 BARCLAY STREET.
1884.

Carefully considering the extraordinary merit of all the sermons and lectures of the renowned Father Burke, and thoroughly convinced of their immense value as reading matter to the American public, whether Catholic or not, I hereby most heartily endorse the efforts of my predecessor, Very Rev. J. A. Rochford, to give them as wide a circulation as possible. It is to be hoped that they will have a place in every Catholic household in the land ; and that they will serve to purify, enlighten, and elevate not only our generation but also generations unborn.

STEPHEN BYRNE, *Provincial O.P.*

St. Antoninus Vicariate, August 25, 1878.

CONTENTS.

	PAGE
INTRODUCTION,	7
PANEGYRIC ON PIUS IX.,	17
THE GRANDEUR OF POPE PIUS IX.,	36
"FOLLOW THOU ME,"	50
THE PONTIFICATE OF PIUS IX.,	70
EULOGY OF THE LATE CARDINAL BARNABO,	100
THE LIFE AND CHARACTER OF ST. DOMINIC,	111
ST. THOMAS AQUINAS,	121
ST. PATRICK,	131
ST. IGNATIUS,	145
ST. FRANCIS XAVIER,	151
ST. VINCENT DE PAUL,	160
ST. CATHERINE OF SIENNA,	169
ST. COLUMBKILLE,	177
THE CATHOLIC CHURCH IN AMERICA,	199
THE CATHOLIC CHURCH THE SAFETY, NOT THE DANGER, OF THE GREAT AMERICAN REPUBLIC,	225
THE CATHOLIC CHURCH AND EDUCATION,	239
THE CHURCH AND CIVIL GOVERNMENT,	251
THE CATHOLIC CHURCH AND THE AGE WE LIVE IN,	267
THE CATHOLIC CHURCH AND SCIENCE,	288
IRELAND'S CATHOLICITY, AND WHAT SAVED IT,	306

	PAGE
A Plea for Catholic Education, ...	316
The Music of the Church, ...	335
God our Father, ...	350
The Attributes of God, ...	362
The Mystery of the Incarnation, ...	376
The Sacred Heart of Jesus, ...	390
The Altar of the Sacred Heart, ...	398
The Virgin Mother, ...	411
The Feast of the Immaculate Conception, . . .	421
The Stations of the Cross, ...	430
The Passion of Our Lord, ...	444
The Cross the Sign of Salvation, ...	467
The Beauty of Divine Worship, ...	475

INTRODUCTION.

IN introducing to the public this new series of lectures of the Very Rev. Thomas N. Burke, we are actuated by an abiding hope that the Catholic truth so beautifully expounded therein will find attentive readers in every Christian family of America. Our country, so expansive in all commercial and political affairs, needs sadly the stable teachings of our holy mother the Church in order to perpetuate the blessings of equal liberty.

Ignorance is no offspring of Catholic faith. Penal enactments, it is true, against religion and education, have produced sad results among the children of Ireland; but the love of education, fostered by the Church, burns as warmly in the Celtic heart to-day as it did in the days of Erin's glory. Such iniquitous laws do not exist in the United States, and there is no reason why the children of Irish exiles should not enjoy all the blessings of education. Civil and religious liberty, and education, are the pet theories of our statesmen, and the Church not only does not object to them, but has nurtured them for centuries.

Torn from family and country by the relentless hand of despotism, Irishmen have found a generous welcome on the shores of Columbia. Nor have they been ungrateful.

They have settled in her cities and villages, and have performed no ignoble part in their destinies. With their axes they have entered her virgin forests, and made for their children reputable homes. They have ploughed her fertile valleys, and the God of abundance blessed them. They have dug her canals, built her railroads, and forwarded her productions to the uttermost limits of the earth. They have spoken with ability in her legislative halls, and sacrificed their blood with intrepidity in her defence. Ingratitude, indeed, is not their characteristic; for they nestle as fondly in the lap of their adopted mother as ever, praying and hoping for her glorious future. They have given their sweat and their blood; they must now give the *Faith*.

Prosperity is not always the harbinger of durability; nor is commercial activity an unfailing sign of success. The republics of ancient times flourished under the influences of virtue and simplicity, but died in the arms of luxury and prosperity. Virtue is the important element of society, without which governments have no lasting foundations. Hence the necessity of a *virtuous education*.

We have had our share in establishing the wealth and prosperity of the country; why should we not now wield an influence in disseminating the truths of the spouse of Christ, so that the *faith* which has lived on triumphantly amidst the vicissitudes of nineteen centuries, may find its way into the hearts of all our fellow-citizens, and cement the union of these States by a fellowship of Christian education which will make the Republic endure for ever!

Indeed, the Irish race has hitherto borne "the burdens

and the heats of the day," in building up the Church in America. It has not only planted the faith of Christ in every portion of America, but it has accomplished it under difficulties that would have daunted any other people under the sun. The sons and daughters of this race have listened with sublime patience to the truths of the Church, as expounded by the broken English of zealous missionary priests, and have not loved any the less the glorious faith of their forefathers. They have materially assisted the people of other nationalities in building their churches and chapels, but have never received in return that gratitude they so eminently deserved. The history of their sacrifices is unwritten on earth, although their love for religion, for education, and their adopted country is universally known.

Why may they not now bend all their energies to advance the education of their children ? Why should they not be aggressive in teaching the doctrines of the Church and the glories of their native land ?. They have won imperishable renown in the practice of moral and civic virtues. They will hereafter teach the faith of Christ to their non-Catholic fellow-citizens, and thus again contribute to the glories of the Republic.

To assist this worthy enterprise, we have taken great pleasure in compiling this new volume of lectures by the Very Rev. Thomas N. Burke. The people are clamorous for them. They are bread to those who hunger for truth. The volume consists of lectures almost exclusively given since the departure of the great orator from America. They form a reservoir of Catholic thought on most of the leading questions of the day, and, though the matchless declamation which accompanied their delivery be necessarily wanting, they still are wonderful productions, and must bring the light of wisdom to many minds now partially darkened by the want of faith.

A glance at the contents will show this volume to contain, probably, the most interesting course of lectures ever given in the English language. The panegyrics are splendid, though it is to be regretted that the stenographer, in a few of them, did not give a more copious report. Even these are worthy of the orator. To study them is to advance in Christian education. To meditate on them is to make hearts love obedience, chastity, and poverty. To produce these virtues is to establish the reign of Christ in America, and to nourish the roots of the tree of liberty.

The controversial discourses are, as already said, on the most interesting topics of the day. They are equally remarkable for simplicity of language and power of reason. They are particularly adapted to benefit the sceptical, and impart faith to the atheistic scientist.

The didactic discourses are exquisite portrayals of God's love for man. The rich will find in them reasons to bless the Author of their abundance, and will be charitable to the poor; and the poor, after reading them, will bless the providence of God, and abide with hope the imperishable riches of eternity. Thus the conflict between capital and labor might be averted, and civil society would find happiness and peace in the Sacred Heart of Jesus.

Before concluding this introduction we wish to inform

the public that we are indebted to the *Freeman's Journal*, of New York, for the copy of these valuable lectures. We wish also to publicly thank Mr. Eliot Ryder, of the New York *Sun*, who has given us much valuable assistance in this compilation. Nor shall we forget the kindness of the very reverend author of these lectures, who desired that this book should be supervised by us. In a letter dated the 30th of June, 1878, he writes: "I am glad it [the book] will have the benefit of your supervision, and I hope my American brethren will derive large profits from it." He also stated in a letter 2d February, 1878: "When I left America I handed over to our Fathers in New York all my interests in the sale of my lectures, and I am sorry that the *order has derived little or no pecuniary benefit* from the sale of them, whilst laymen have been making large sums by the same." The same letter also says: "If you wish to give the countenance of your honored name to Mr. Collier for my American lectures and sermons I need not tell you that I cannot hinder you, NOR WOULD I IF I COULD."

These statements would not be made, but that it has been very generally understood that the Dominicans have derived large sums of money from the sale of the lectures of Father Burke. This opinion, however, is so much at variance with the truth, that we deem it prudent to corroborate the extract from the above letter, and say that the pecuniary benefit to the *friars of Sixty-sixth Street, New York*, arising from the sale of said lectures, is infinitely less than they had a right in justice to expect. We think that *four hun-*

dred dollars, not in cash but on account, will more than cover the receipts, notwithstanding the fact that a committee of gentlemen of New York did offer twenty thousand dollars to the Fathers for the right of publishing the same lectures. The public need not think, therefore, that we are in any way indebted to it for kindness extended to the former publisher of Father Burke's lectures; though we do thank the public most cordially for its appreciation of the enterprise and integrity of Mr. P. F. Collier, who has been extremely generous to us, and who has abundantly established his claims to be the publisher of this volume.

With these few preliminary remarks, we unhesitatingly commit this new series of lectures to the careful reading of our fellow-countrymen, confident it will wield a salutary influence in the promotion of faith, liberty, and education.

J. A. ROCHFORD, O.P.

St. Dominic's Church,
Washington, D. C., 1878.

Panegyric on Pius IX.

On Thursday, February 7, 1878, Pius IX. breathed his last, and went, as is fondly believed, to the realms of infinite bliss, where, in the delights of the Beatific Vision, surrounded by the angels who had watched over his long and eventful pontificate, and in the blessed presence of the Holy Mother whom he delighted to honor, he enjoys the eternal reward of his constant and abiding love for the Spouse of Christ. The whole world mourned the loss of its beloved and holy father. Nowhere were the services of the Solemn Office and High Mass of Requiem more imposing and impressive than in the pro-cathedral, Marlborough Street, Dublin, where on Wednesday, February 13, Father Burke delivered his eloquent panegyric and fitly eulogized the good Pope, whom men of all beliefs loved and honored. A fierce storm of wind, rain, and sleet had prevailed from the night previous, yet the sacred edifice was not large enough to contain all who sought admission, hundreds being turned away. The cathedral was draped in the deepest mourning, and in the centre of the nave was placed a catafalque covered with black, relieved only by the papal insignia, and by silver scrolls, each bearing note of some great event in the life of the dead Pope. A hundred wax-lights surrounded the catafalque, and branches of drooping willow ornamented the bier, which was guarded by veterans of the Roman army in the uniform of Pontifical Zouaves, to which corps they belonged.

The Cardinal-Archbishop presided, attended by the Bishop of Ferns, the Coadjutor-Bishop of Kildare, the Bishop of Gadara, and about three hundred of the clergy.

As soon as the Cardinal had taken his seat the Solemn Office of the Dead began, and was recited with much impressiveness by the body of priests and prelates. The three psalms and lessons of the first Nocturn and the psalms of the Lauds were said, and it was not till the "Benedictus" at the Lauds that there was any noticeable singing. The singing of the exquisite canticle by the choir of priests in harmony was exceedingly beautiful and visibly impressed the entire congregation. At the conclusion of the Office High Mass was celebrated, the Most Rev. Dr. McCabe being celebrant; Rev. P. O'Neill, Adm., assistant priest; Rev. T. O'Reilly, deacon; Rev. S. Burke, subdeacon; and Rev. T. Farrell and Rev. M. Ryan being masters of ceremonies. The Very Rev. Dr. Woodlock and the

Very Rev. Canon Keogh were assistants at the archiepiscopal throne. At the conclusion of the Mass Father Burke ascended the pulpit and delivered the panegyric of the deceased Pontiff. He spoke as follows:

"HE was beloved of God and men, whose memory is in benediction. He made him like unto the saints in glory, and He magnified him in the fear of his enemies, and He sanctified him in his faith and meekness, and He chose him out of all flesh, and He gave him commandments before his face, a law of life and instruction, to teach Jacob His covenant and Israel His judgments."

These words, dearly beloved, are taken from the forty-fifth of Ecclesiasticus. May it please your eminence, my lords, reverend brothers, and dearly beloved, the inspired one tells us that it is better to go into the house of mourning than to the house of joy. There is something peculiarly holy in Christian sorrow; and you, dearly beloved, who so often enter into this house of God, generally find it a house of joy. To-day it is a house of mourning; to-day the Church has put on her recent widowhood; to-day her heart is made, as it were, desolate, and her grieving tears of sorrow are upon our mother's face; for the great father, the great guide, the great visible head of the Church of God has passed from his militant spouse here to his appointed place among the triumphant Church in heaven. And, as it was written of old, all earth mourneth. It is not like any other sorrow that falls upon the hearts of men; it is not a mere family affliction or a mere national sorrow; it is not like the mourning of old, when they mourned family and family apart, and their women apart; it is not like unto the mourning of the Israelites when for thirty days they wept when Aaron, the great priest, was taken away; it is not like the sorrow of the Israelites when for thirty days all Israel mourned on the plains of Moab for him, the great one, who had found his mysterious grave on the mountain summit; it is not a mere national grief, as when the great King Josias died in Jerusalem, and all Judea and Jerusalem mourned for him—it is not like these, because they were but partial griefs.

The outer world knew nothing of the sorrows of the Israelites as they wept for the death of Aaron, the high-priest; the nations around rather rejoiced than sympathized in the grief of the Israelites when they lamented for the great lawgiver. The enemies whom he had met at Magdala sent up shouts of joy while Jerusalem and Judea were weeping over the great king. But to-day sorrow has overspread the whole earth; a note of grief and lamentation comes forth from hundreds of millions of hearts. Wherever the sun shines there is found the Catholic Church, and everywhere it is afflicted. There exists to-day a universal sorrow, bounded only by the limits that circumscribe the whole world in which we live, ceasing only at the golden gates, where that which is for us a motive of such deep sorrow is, we believe and hope, the subject of a mighty joy. And why this universal sorrow? Because the head of the Church has been taken away from us. And why this deep sorrow? Because it is the sorrow of children mourning over their father—the deepest form, perhaps, that human sorrow can take; for the sorrow of a son weeping over his father is not a mere passing sentiment, but it is a sorrow that springs out of the very depths of the mind, out of the hidden and innermost chambers of the soul—a sorrow that is grafted upon the memory, recalling so many tender traits of paternal care and love and kindness.

Even such is our sorrow to-day as we stand mute around our mother, who is here grieving while she stands by the death-bed of Pius IX. In truth, my dearly beloved brethren, the occasion requires us to consider the position, the office, and the character of him who is dead, which brings us at once face to face with something that is a great mystery—namely, the Papacy, the Headship of the Catholic Church. Whether we consider the powers the Pope exercises, their extent, their greatness, or whether we consider the extent and limits of his jurisdiction, I consider his position is a most awful and mysterious one.

What are the powers that the head of the Catholic

Church exercises? O my dearly beloved! if we would know we must go back to that day when Christ said to Peter: "All power in heaven and on this earth is given me; and even as the Father sent me, so do I send you." We can only limit his powers by the eternal principles of law, justice, and sanctity, as they are in the mind of God; and, in so far as they are reflected in the legislation and the action of man, we must not limit the powers of the Christ, the Omnipotent, who was unlimited in His power, conferred so largely and so mysteriously. Every ecclesiastical law is under the immediate power of the Pope of Rome. There are divine institutions in this Church of God; the episcopacy is a divine institution, so is the priesthood; but no bishop can grasp his crosier with legitimate jurisdiction, no priest can preach or stand upon the altar lawfully, unless from Peter, the Pope of Rome, and from the Pope comes that blessing of communion and that faculty of jurisdiction. Consider, again, the extent of this enormous power. It extends wherever the Church is to be found upon earth; it is to be found active, living, and in the full exercise wherever a Catholic priest preaches, wherever a Catholic listens to the Word, wherever a Catholic altar is erected. Does this power stop here? Oh! no. Go out beyond this earth; pass the terrible portals of death; go down into the place of expiatory suffering—there the pontiff's power is still in the full exercise of its mercy—there the hand of the pope can touch the suffering souls, lift them out of their place of expiation, hasten their delivery, anticipate their joy, and send them—I was about to say before their time—into the presence of their God.

And now, dearly beloved, if you ask me what is the source, what is the origin, of this vast power—so great in itself that we almost fail to realize how it can be centred in one man; so great in extent, that the whole Christian world should submit to it, should accept and should obey it so joyfully; which is one of the most astounding miracles of God in this world, and one of the strongest proofs that the Church is the bride and spouse of God—if you ask me the origin and cause of all this, I answer: If we wish to understand what the visible head of the Church, the Pope, is, what he must be, what his functions and his office are, we must go back to consider the invisible Head of the Church, what He is in relation to His Church, what office He fulfils, what proofs out of the infinite treasury of His greatness he pours out of His love for her as her Head. And who is this Head? He who from all eternity was the very figure of that Father's substance and the splendor of His glory; He who came down from heaven, incarnate of the Holy Ghost and of the Blessed Virgin Mary, but still remaining God, true God, Infinite, Omnipotent, and Holy, living upon earth—the all-glorious and adorable Jesus Christ. He is the Head of the Church, and as such He enters into special relations with her. For among the privileges, if I may use the word, conferred upon Him by the Incarnation was this: that as man He became the Head of the Church. We know that as man He inherited the eternal priesthood—that He was a priest as soon as Mary spoke the fiat and God became man in her immaculate bosom. As man He was Head of the Church; and it is worthy of remark how often and how lovingly the apostle puts Him before us in this particular office as Head of the Church. To the Ephesians He says the Father of Glory hath subjected all things beneath His feet, and He has made Him Head over all the Church. To the Colossians again He repeated the same word. And now, dearly beloved, there are times and moments when the Headship—really abiding, unfailing, though invisible—comes out more emphatically and distinctly before us, and especially at such a moment as the present, when the Church has lost her visible head, and when Christ our Lord remains still the Head of the Church, so that this living body is not headless, for Christ is there. And what are these attributes that the Vicar of Christ, as head of the Church, brings out especially? Principally they are four. As Head of the Church, Christ, the Son of God, is the infallible Guide of the Church's teaching, preserving her in the truth, not permitting her to err in that teaching even by the slightest admixture of one iota of dogmatic error. " You shall know the truth," He said ; " I am the truth, and I am with you all days, even to the consummation of the world."

Dearly beloved brethren, when we consider that the purpose for which the Son of God instituted this Church was that man should be instructed in the truth—that truth without which there is no faith, and which should be known to all men—it follows of necessity that the Church which was to be the one teacher of that truth must be infallible, incapable of error, lest men might believe falsely concerning Him who is essential truth ; there is the first office of Christ as Head of His Church. The second office of the Lord as Head of the Church is that He is the wise, the prudent Guide of His Church in her government and in her administration. One of the popular errors of our day is to say that Christ is the God of truth indeed, and consequently that His Church cannot err, but that from time to time He allows this Church of His to do unwise things, to speak the truth at inopportune moments, to bring out some dogma or great truth or principle and give it a prominence when it would be wiser and more prudent, if not to compromise with error, at least for a while to hold back the stern, prominent announcing of that which is true. But those who thus think or speak seem to forget that Christ our Lord not only as the God of truth keeps His Church in eternal truth in her teaching, but that also as a God of infinite wisdom He guides His Church in the ways of wisdom in her administration and in her government. Do we not find Jesus Christ instructing His apostles, and saying to them : " If they persecute you in this city, fly to another " ; and again : " Whilst you are prudent as the serpent, you must still be simple as the dove " ; and elsewhere laying down rules for their management and government ? " When you are brought before kings and princes," He says, " do not think or meditate upon what things you shall say, for in that hour it will be given you what to say; for it is not you who speak, but the Spirit of the Father that speaketh in you." And, dearly beloved, the third office of the Saviour as Head of the Church is that He is the invincible defender and champion of His Church, and His omnipotent arm is for her like to a shield. "His truth and power shall surround you as a shield," exclaims the Psalmist; "thou shalt not be afraid of the things of the night." Terrible things of the night, terrible storms of persecution, terrible essays of all that this earth has of power, and all that hell has of malice—O my brethren! these terrible onslaughts may arise; there may be thick clouds over the sky, and the storm may lash the sea into fury; the angry waves may appear to cover the land; but He who is omnipotent is there, and it is the destiny, the fate of the Church to outlive all persecution, for the strength of God is her defence.

The fourth office the Son of God fulfils towards His Church is that of the true-hearted and faithful lover; for, as the apostle says, God loved His Church. And what proof did He give of His love for her? He never denied her the aid of His teaching and the guidance of His wisdom; He never held back any grace, any favor. He lived for her and He died for her. He gave Himself up for His Church. Behold, then, the four great relations of the invisible Head of the Church: the infallible guide in doctrine, infallible wisdom in government, omnipotence and power in defence, and love stronger even than death.

But, dearly beloved, if this be the invisible Head of the Church, then these four attributes must belong to him who represents Christ, who is the visible head of the Church; for this Church was founded among men for men. It was to appeal to the senses of men that the splendor of her ceremonial was established, every sense helped on by external action, external ritual; and therefore it was necessary that the invisible Head should be represented, and that Christ, who is the abiding, invisible Head of the Church, should have His vicar and viceroy governing her before the eyes of men. And He called St. Peter, as we know, among His apostles, and He conferred on him and upon his successor the sacred office of that headship in His Church, and all the powers that were necessary for it. All the faculties without which it could not adequately exist, all the honor that belonged—all these were conferred upon Peter in the day when Christ, having put him to the test, said to him: To thee, beyond all others, in its fullest and most special sense, do I give the keys of the kingdom of heaven. "Feed my lambs, feed my sheep." Nay, more, for what I am to the Church thou shalt be as my vicar and viceroy. Fear not for that faith. I have prayed for thee and will live in thee. A thousand may fall at thy left hand and ten thousand at thy right hand, but thou shalt not waver, much less perish, and thou shalt confirm thy wavering brethren.

The tradition of Peter's powers, of Peter's office, and of Peter's graces has passed on from pope to pope for nearly two thousand years. The hands that received this great depository were, some more, some less, worthy of it; but the deposit itself was never violated. Never did pope speak to his Church, in virtue of his office, one word of falsehood; never did pope refuse to defend the Church committed to him; never did pope neglect the administration and government of that Church; and let us hope never was pope found wanting in his love for the Church. But although that long and magnificent list brings before us the names of ome of the greatest saints that God ever gave to His Church—brings before us historic names, whom the world has even canonized with its own evanescent canonization of fame; even though the roll recalls a Gregory the Great and a Gregory perhaps still greater, an immortal Hildebrand; Boniface VIII., so magnificent in his triumph; Pius V., so terrible in his prayer, who commanded the elements on that dreadful day at Lepanto—yet, with all these, never, perhaps, in the annals of this Papacy has a name been written in brighter characters, both as a man and as Vicar of Christ, than the name that is inscribed on the catafalque in St. Peter's to-day—the name of Pius IX. Speaking of the Blessed Virgin, St. Bernadine of Sienna tells us that whenever Almighty God raises any being to any particular office or dignity in His Church, and imposes upon him any specific responsibilities, in His mercy He always gives graces in proportion to the work which is to be done. And, truly, when we look upon the days of our century, and recollect what is now history in the life of Pius IX. from his earliest day, we find a man to whom Almighty God had given graces to enable him to bear the mighty burden of the responsibilities and glories of the Papacy. He was born in 1792, and the nobility of his birth is but the least of the greatness and the beauties of his exalted life. He grew up from childhood into youth surrounded and protected by the blessing of sweetness; so that, when he presented himself in 1818 to be ordained a priest, he was found worthy of the priesthood, because he brought into the sanctuary of God a virgin heart unsullied for service, and virgin hands for consecration. He was distinguished in the schools as a theologian and canonist; but he was far more remarkable and distinguished for the tenderness of his piety, for the wonderful spirit of prayer which has been the secret, the soul of all his greatness, and for the gentleness and compassionate feelings of his heart. Of this he gave a proof immediately when he was ordained priest. His learning, the circumstances of his birth, his surroundings—all might have prompted in his young mind a career of office, of dignity, of nobility. What was the first act of Pius IX.? Upon being made priest he went into an obscure street in Rome; he found there a large orphanage, but recently founded; he entered there, selected a little room for himself, and for seven years remained teaching the orphans, providing for them, seeing to all their wants, and happy as their father. Behold how the career of this great priest began, and from what humble beginnings came such an uprising of glory. Who would have imagined that a heart that was satisfied with an orphan's love was destined one day to be dilated and to take in the love of the whole Christian Church? Who would imagine that the mind, cultured, highly trained as it was, yet so unambitious as to be willing to expend itself on the government of a small institute of orphans, was destined one day to be what the mind of Pius IX. has been for the last thirty-two years—the light of the world, the consolation, the strength, and the glory of the universal Church of God?

But he was not destined to remain in the quiet and prayerful calm of his orphanage. Troublesome times were coming; the nations were fermenting and disturbing themselves; the spirit of irreligion was beginning to appear abroad, and the Sovereign Pontiff of the day found it necessary to send a mission involving labor and danger far away to the state of Chili, in South America. The moment the office of danger and labor, the thankless office that involved residence in an unhealthy climate, banishment from home and friends, exile from his dear Italy that he loved so well, cutting off any prospect (if he entertained any) of promotion or dignity—the moment this difficulty offered and he was called upon he joyfully rose up, left his humble home, and went out upon that mission that was so heavy and dangerous, and actually before he reached the scene of his labors he was obliged, for the Church of God, to undergo imprisonment. Returning after two years, he was made Archbishop of Spoleto. The moment he reached the archiepiscopal see what was the first thing that Pius IX. did? There, close to his archiepiscopal palace, so that they might be under his eyes and hands, his first care was to build an orphanage. Five years later, translated to Imola, his first care again was to build two orphanages and to erect what was then almost unknown in Italy—refuges for fallen sinners. Thus, dearly beloved, the works of mercy multiplied under his hands, according as his facilities for being merciful increased. Arriving in Rome, he who was anxious to hide himself from all men, he who among the sons of Jesse seemed to be a very David, the least, the youngest of all—over him rested the Spirit of God and pointed him out; and then began the pontificate of Pius IX. That pontificate has closed to-day. A double record remains of it—the record that this world has taken of him and that the Church militant has preserved ; a record that may be read by future generations and called a history ; the record which, in the case of so many pontiffs who have gone before him, has been a strange and unequal mixture of a grain of truth and a bushel of calumnies— that history which loves to calumniate and find fault with them because they are popes.

But there is another record for that pontificate which has gone forth, and it is that which the hand of the dying Pontiff brought with him to his judgment, and which he submitted to the all-seeing eye of Jesus Christ, to stand or fall by the issue of it, to make it either his passport to heaven or to make it the condemnation of his own unworthiness. Which of these two records shall we take to-day in commemorating his pontificate ? I love the one which the Pope took to God—I love it. It was my privilege to know something personally of him, for twelve years to live almost under the light of his presence, to behold him in the moment of supreme trial as well as in moments of supreme glory ; to behold him when, kneeling before the altar of God, in the presence of Jesus Christ, he instantly, and apparently without any effort, fell into that wonderful abstraction of prayer, so that the very sight of him at prayer was a most vivid memento of him. Whilst I love the one I am not afraid of the other ; the world has spoken as well as the Church of this man ; the world has passed its judgment on him, and forth from the bitterest of his enemies has come the unwilling testimony of the virtues and greatness of Pius IX. Not a voice is heard in dissent, not a vice or a fault of the long catalogue of human weaknesses and errors have they been able to take and fix upon his escutcheon ; not a single day or act of that long and wonderful pontificate are they able to bring up as a reproach upon his memory. Yes, it is the special and peculiar glory of this man that after his pontificate, wonderful in its greatness and glory, even the world has canonized him by the voice of human praise. For, in truth, he fulfilled in a remarkable manner the four great offices and duties which belonged to him as the viceroy of the invisible Head. He was guide of the Church's doctrine, fearless in the assertion of the truth, clear and emphatic in the definition of her divine faith. His position was as head of the Church. It is well known it was the understanding and the mind of the Church since the day that the Council of Jerusalem heard Peter and acquiesced in his decisions, since the day that the Fathers of Ephesus cried out, "Peter has spoken; the cause is finished; Christ has spoken in Peter," that the action of the Church was ever governed by the great principle that her visible head was her infallible guide; that the only infallible witness to the Church's truth, the only infallible guardian of the deposit of her faith, was the Pope of Rome, who cannot err when he imposes his word upon the Church *ex cathedrâ* as her visible head on earth.

But, dearly beloved, although this great truth was recognized, laid down by every theologian, enunciated by every father, and acted upon in every age by the Church, yet the moment had not come when it was necessary to meet not only the dangers of the present but the wants of every future age, that the Church of God should speak out her mind, that she should give dogmatic testimony, that she should crystallize the truth and embody it in a formal diction of faith. This glory was reserved for Pius IX. One of the last acts of his pontificate, one of the most glorious, was on that day in July, 1870, when he rose up in St. Peter's, in Rome, with the whole teaching Church of God there around him, and the whole Church that was taught waiting, as the people were awaiting the decisions of Ephesus. Forth from that voice which was heard from end to end of the earth—forth from that voice there came, re-echoing and explaining the mind that was burdened with the very accents of the God of eternal truth, forth amid the acclamation and the joy of the Church of God came the definition of Peter's infallibility and of Peter's successors, so that wherever the successor of Pius IX. may be, wherever the wave of persecution may bear him, no matter how wild the shore, how far away the land, even if God destines for him exile, he will bear away with him that sign of God's protection.

He was, moreover, the wise governor of the Church of God. The government and administration of the Church of God, dearly beloved, is a very wonderful thing. It branches out into a thousand ramifications; it goes out and makes itself felt in the administration of every sacrament; it is brought home to every individual, to every house, to every parish; it ramifies all over the earth; but as a fruitful vine which, no matter how it extends itself here and there, still is derived from one root, from which it takes all its sap and richness, so the whole Church of God, even though it is extended, as I have said, yet gathers itself together and becomes one in the Pope of Rome, the head and centre of the Catholic Church. What wisdom, then, must be his whose words all men wait to hear, that they may be guided thereby! What knowledge and wisdom must he have who has to interpret the traditions of ages of learning and experience! What a vigilant eye must he have who is expected to see wherever the Church is from end to end of the earth! That wisdom, that vigilance, that laborious care was the life of the glorious Pontiff Pius IX. Behold the efforts of his wise administration in the midst of his own sorrows. In 1850, having just returned from exile, he does not forget to re-establish the hierarchy so long abolished and extinguished in England. Behold the Church of North America, with its dioceses amounting almost to one hundred, a glorious and flourishing Church. To whom, under God, does it owe all its glorious progress? Whose breath is it that gave life to that young giant Church that has risen up in the West? It was the care of him who established its parishes and bishoprics, and crowned that Church by giving it a prince-cardinal. His care went beyond, even to the ends of the earth. Far away in the Australian antipodes churches have sprung up and are flourishing. The cross of Christ is everywhere raised in glory. Under God all this is due to the fertilizing influence and the energizing hand of Pius IX. The history of his government of the Church of God will be one of the brightest pages in that Church's history, both for an unceasing, ever-vigilant care and for the profound wisdom and prudent courage with which he held the helm of the bark of Peter and guided it in such dark and fearful storms.

He also fulfilled the other duty which he derived as Pope from the invisible Head. His was the dauntless heart, the strong voice, the fearless, powerful arm that defended the Church since the day he was elected to be Pontiff before all men. Oh! how brave was that heart of the Sovereign Pontiff. When all were afraid he alone was fearless; when the air was thick with danger, revolution, and blood, he alone, like to his Divine Master when He rose from His sleep in the storm-tossed boat—he alone was calm; his faith never wavered, his voice never faltered when he uttered the words, "O ye of little faith! why are ye afraid?" When was that voice ever silent when the interests of the Church were imperilled? Every form of injustice rose up around him. He grappled with them all. The principal of the Catholic powers of Europe pressed upon him to come to some compromise with the loose principles and the dangerous maxims that are afloat in the present day. Ay, would he only extend his hand to injustice because it was in its mildest form of error, because it had put on its most plausible shape? The answer that came from the heart and the lips of the Pontiff was the immortal *Non possumus*, which were, perhaps, the grandest words that were ever uttered—"We cannot do it," as the apostles answered when they were told to cease preaching, and mention no more the name of the Nazarene; they answered, "We cannot do it; there is a power greater than man." Behold him almost upon his death-bed, as he turned those dying but fearless eyes of his and spoke with that unfaltering voice, with the hand of death already upon him, the crown of the temporal empire fallen from his brow, but the other crown remaining of which it is written: "Thou shalt be a crown of glory in the hands of the Lord and the diadem of the kingdom of God." But his temporal crown was gone, the sceptre stricken from his hand. And before him stood a mighty figure, an emperor at the head of countless legions flushed with glory; a man before whose nod all Europe was standing trembling; a man in whose eye all the nations could read their own destinies; a man who held, as he holds, peace or war, destruction or life, to thousands in the palm of his hand; a man no one dared to confront. One man alone rebukes him, convicts him of his treachery, and puts his falsehood before the whole world, and that man is the dying Pius IX.

He not only governed the Church of God, taught the Church of God, but he fought for the Church of God, and his name will go down not merely with the tiara of jurisdiction, ay, but with the higher crown of a life-long martyrdom on his brows.

He loved the Church with all the ardor of his great, tender, virgin heart; he loved the Church and the splendor of her glory. He might well say with David, "I have loved, O Lord! the beauty of Thy house, and the place where Thy glory dwelleth." How well he showed this love for the Church of God in the assiduous labors of so long a pontificate, in the delight and joy of his heart when he saw cardinals and bishops of the Church of God and the faithful children of the Church gathered around him! Of Jesse, the high-priest of old, it is written in his praise, and as the sign of his sanctity and love for the Church, that he delighted to see around him all the sons of Aaron; and so with Pius IX. Now to canonize a saint; again to celebrate the eighteenth centenary of the great first pope; again to take counsel for the affairs of the Church, Pius IX. loved to call his brothers around him, loved to see them around him, he towering above on his throne, as the cedar planted by the side of running waters. Oh! how he loved the Church of God. He gave a great and wise and deep proof of that love. He knew that

Mary, the Mother of Jesus Christ, was the most powerful of all God's creatures; he knew that her voice resounded, not without a tone of maternal command, where every other voice was but the humble whisper of a suppliant. He knew that she had claims such as no other creature could have upon God, and because he loved the Church he proclaimed Mary's glories, and he placed the whole Church of God under her peculiar protection in the mystery of the Immaculate Conception.

How he loved the Church! One of his devotions, flowing out of the mystery of the Incarnation, yet required to be developed. To bring that mystery in all its fulness, in all its greatness, in all the height of its mystic feeling, he brought all the abundance of its graces home to every heart in the devotion to the Sacred Heart. Out of that wonderful Incarnation flowed four great lights, two of them appertaining to Jesus Christ Himself—one the truth of His divinity, the second the truth of His humanity, which was assumed into the Godhead. The other two great lights that came forth from the Incarnation are the position of Mary His Mother and the position of Peter His vicar, both relating to Him in virtue of that humanity. The Church of God took thought for the defence of His divinity in the Council of Nice; the Church of God defended His humanity in the fifth General Council. Mary's position in relation to Him as Mother was defended at Ephesus, and there only remained the great dogmatic language of the Church of God which declared Mary fit to be Queen of the Church. This was the definition of the Immaculate Conception which was declared by Pius IX.

The fourth light that streams forth from the Incarnation is the perpetuity of that headship visible before men in the throne of St. Peter, and the glory of this definition was reserved for Pius IX. Oh! how he loved the Church. His heart was weighted with age; many a winter and stormy year had passed over his venerable head; his heart, so loving, was bruised and broken by ten thousand acts of ingratitude; his strong, natural sense of right was outraged by ten thousand forms of national as well as individual treason and falsehood. What sustained him? What made him pass beyond the mystic years of Peter, the first pope that ever crossed the sacred boundary? What sustained him during the seven years of his enforced imprisonment at the Vatican? What upheld him amid so many treasons? The same principle that enabled the Son of God to outlive the hours of agony on the cross—the same principle that enabled Mary to stand and, without dying, to witness the awful agony of her Son. Every other passion, every other influence, every other power fades away before death. At the sight of death the ambitious abandons the designs of his soul for ever. At the sight of death the successful man forgets his honors. At the sight of death the victor, even flushed with triumph, weeps when he beholds through how many waves of destruction he has waded on to glory. There is but one sentiment, one feeling, which the Holy Ghost declares to be as strong as death, and that feeling is love. It was his love for the Church that fed his great heart, that was the consolation of his mind when every other consolation was gone, that enabled him to spend seven years of such trial that the very fact of his outliving them so long made him the wonder of friends and enemies alike. And when he was dying, and the very agonies of death were upon him, forth from his dying lips came the words to the cardinals around him: "Guard the Church that I love."

Now he is gone. On earth he did not witness much of the Church's glory. Other pontiffs lived in different ages, and they saw the triumphs of the Church, sometimes in one country, sometimes in another. Pius IX. saw not its triumph anywhere; every hand was raised against him, every government had turned upon him, every element of the so-called progress of our day considered that it could not establish itself even as a scientific principle until it first denied his position. And he passed away in the midst of these sorrows. But,

O dearly beloved! what must have been his joy, as we hope and believe that joy is already his, when he beheld the glories of the Church triumphant, when he saw there all that he had already seen, exalted though he was, dimly as through the glass of faith on earth! Oh! what was his joy when every class of saint came forth to greet the great Pope. The martyrs of Japan and Holland, whom he had canonized, rose up to meet him. St. Mary Alacoque, the victim of love in the Sacred Heart, rose up and headed the holy virgins, for he had beatified her; St. Francis de Sales and St. Alphonsus Liguori, who had received at the hands of him who was approaching heaven's gates the bright aureola of their doctorship—they rose up to meet him. Mary, his Queen and Mother, met him who had proclaimed her glorious title of the Immaculate Conception. Peter and his glorious following of crowned pontiffs came to meet him. Every element of incidental glory heaven could administer seems to have been waiting him, and in the Sacred Heart of Jesus, the devotion to which he had awakened in every land, he found the essential glory of the beatific vision of the Lord. This we hope, this we believe; and, looking back upon that glorious life, we have every reason to be confident that he who was our father on earth now enjoys endless glory with the Father in heaven.

The Church's sorrow, dearly beloved, must soon change to joy. The Church cannot remain long without her visible head; she never remained for an instant without her invisible Head. The Church's councils of the world will assemble in the halls of the most venerable palace on earth, the Vatican. And there—there among those who will have to decide the solemn and the grand question—there will the Irish race and this poor down-trodden people find a voice; for, for the first time in any papal conclave, an Irish cardinal goes out from Ireland to take a part in its decisions, and have a voice in the election of a sovereign pontiff. This also did he do in that love for his Church; this also did he do from the same love that prompted

him to empty his already scanty treasury that the people
of Ireland, famine-stricken, might be relieved and fed in
their misery ; this also did he do as a crown and testimony
of love that he gave to his people, for one of his latest utterances when he was approaching his end was his answer
to the Irish deputation, when he said : " In all my afflictions Ireland has been always faithful to me and has never
deserted me." O father ! wherever thy spirit is this day—
whether, as we hope and believe, shining in the bright light
of God, or, perhaps, expiating by a brief purgatory some
little fault, some little spot or stain that may be upon thy
soul, that suffered so much—wherever thou art, Pius IX.,
the heart of Ireland follows thee to-day in grief and in
mourning, and that Ireland which was so faithful to thee
and all thy predecessors before thee will await in joy the
appearance of thy successor, and bow down in love at his
feet !

The Grandeur of Pope Pius IX.

This lecture of Father Burke has been delivered many times. It is one of the best pen-portraits of the grand old Pope which have ever been given to the world. It teaches us that we may overcome the greatest trials and difficulties if we only keep in our hearts the grace of our Lord and Saviour. This grace we can only obtain by prayer and meditation. Let us ponder on the goodness and greatness of Pius IX. His was a s'ormy and perilous journey o'er the sea of life in this world. He died a conqueror, and " great is his reward in heaven."

THIS nineteenth century has been called, and not without reason, a wonderful age ; and amongst its many admirers, it may seem strange to your ears to hear there is not one, perhaps, more ardent or more sincere in his admiration of the age in which we live than I myself, a representative of the old mediæval period. I am proud of the nineteenth century—proud of its spirit, proud of the great results of its scientific knowledge and resources, proud of the age which has annihilated space, which has grasped the whole world in its scientific hand, which has caught the very lightnings of heaven, crushed them down, and made them the faithful messengers of man from end to end of the earth. Yes, I am indeed proud of the wonders and glories of this nineteenth century.

But I hold that the most wondrous and most glorious thing in it is the pontificate of Pius IX., Pope of Rome. For in all the other triumphs of the nineteenth century we behold the traces of man—wonderful triumphs of human invention and human genius, the developments of nature's powers, the discovery of nature's hidden laws. But when we contemplate the man who now for nearly thirty years has been at the head of the Catholic Church, and filled the mighty and awful position of Vicar of Christ amongst His people on this earth, it is no longer the mere energy of man, the mere resources of human genius, or the strength of human character that we contemplate, but we see realized in this Pontiff the highest and most glorious promises that God ever made to his Church. (Applause.) I am not come here to speak this evening of the personal character of Pius IX. The subject of my lecture is not the Pope personal and individual. If this were my theme I might feel it a grateful and fruitful one. Yes, I have knelt before the man when in my early youth. I received the blessing of our Holy Father in the prime of his glorious manhood, and I have gone again and again and knelt before him when I saw his sorrows bowing him down and whitening his hair, and marked the lines of care on that manly and once so fair face ; and the record of these times would make the personal history of the Pope fruitful to me. But I have not to deal with it, but with his pontificate ; I am not to speak to you of the individual, but of his long reign with which Almighty God has blessed His Church. I have not to speak to you of a temporal king unthroned and uncrowned, but of a Pontiff whose throne can never be shaken and whose crown can never be torn from his brow ; for his throne is founded on a rock and his crown set on his head by Jesus Christ.

It is of the Sovereign Pontiff, the supreme head of the Holy Roman Catholic Church, the Vicar of God on earth, the visible head and governor of God's Church, the man who joins in himself the fulness of apostolic power and jurisdiction, the man whose hand is on the helm of the bark of God, to steer her safe through every storm and bring her forth triumphantly from every wild sea—it is of this man, in his papal, spiritual character and pontificate as such, that I have come to speak to you this evening. And I will lay down this proposition, which I will endeavor to prove, that since the day when Christ laid His hand on the head of Peter and said, "Thou art Peter, and on this Rock I will build my Church, and the gates of hell shall not prevail against it: I have prayed for thee, O Peter! that thy faith fail not"—since that day when Peter received his high commission and the keys of the kingdom of heaven, although his successors exhibit a list of names to many of which the world has appended the title of great, there never was a greater pope than Pius IX., or a greater pontificate than his. His pontificate is a theme not only of joy but of sadness. When we look on the majestic figure of this uncrowned king, but still crowned, imperishable Pontiff, our hearts are filled with Catholic joy, but yet our eyes are full of tears of sorrow. But it is not with our sorrow that I have come here to deal this evening, nor with a good man persecuted in his old age, and life made bitter to him when he is anxious to be with God. It is not of this sorrow I am going to speak to you, but of the imperishable worth that cannot pass away, of titles that cannot be forfeited, of a pontificate in which, as head of the Church, Pope Pius has shown himself one of the most truly glorious pontiffs who ever wielded the sceptre of Peter.

And now, to put this thesis clearly and intelligibly, I must ask you to consider what are the real glories of a pope's reign or pontificate. You know that there must be a given standard by which we can measure the worth and true glory of this man's reign. We must see how far he has come up to that standard. We must also see how far his natural character, combining with divine grace, has led him to the complete fulfilment of the duties and the accomplishment of the glories of his high position in the Church of God.

What is that standard? Well, the first standard is—and you will, perhaps, smile to hear it—the first rule by which we must measure the greatness of any pope is the hatred the world has for him. Is he well hated? Is he well abused? Is he detested? Are men sighing and longing for his death? Are bad men trembling if his life should be prolonged? If these things be so, it is a sure sign that he is a very great man. You remember that O'Connell, the immortal Liberator, used to say of himself that he was the best-abused and the best-hated man in the House of Commons; and he made that one of his great titles to the consideration of the people. Well, the world outside the Catholic Church is one of her greatest enemies. The more faithfully a man serves his God the more the world detests him; and therefore the Apostle Paul said: "If I please men I am no longer a servant of Christ." In the long line of martyr popes, where so many fell victims to the world's hatred and suffered exile or death, there is not one so hated by the enemies of the Church as Pius IX. (Applause.) Nay, more, whatever the secret of it is, he has managed to make himself more feared, as well as hated, than any of his predecessors.

At this moment the strongest man in the world is Bismarck, a man of supreme ability and genius, and successful in all that he has undertaken. He has an empire behind him to back him up with nearly three million armed men. He is not afraid of any one; he need not be. He can put his foot on the neck of France, he has humbled Austria, he has crushed down everything that came before him. Surely that man knows no fear. There is not a man or a nation that he is afraid of, save one. He is afraid of the old Pope of Rome. (Laughter and applause.) Bismarck is afraid of his life of the Pope. (Laughter.) He is always crying out, "Oh! save me from that dreadful man. I must get three or four million more men. God knows what he intends to do with me! I must stick more bishops into jail. When is he going to die?" And then he writes letters to the different cabinets of Europe, saying: "When he dies you must join with me in seeing after his successor." And all this while the grand old Pope sits in his chamber in the Vatican and says, "I will not die."

I asked a poor laboring man I met on the road if he heard the news.

"Oh! yes," said he, "I read the papers."

I said: "Is it not a wonderful thing how long the Pope is living?"

"Begorra it is," said he.

"Why is he living so long?"

"The Lord lets him live so long," said he, "to deprive Bismarck of his appetite." (Great laughter.)

But this is not the real standard by which we are to measure the greatness of Pius IX. and his pontificate. There is one far higher. It is this: the more any pontificate or reign of a pope brings out and proves the highest attributes of God's Church, the more glorious that pontificate is; and never, in the long line of Roman pontiffs, has any pope brought out so strongly the highest attributes of the Church of God as Pius IX. during his pontificate of wellnigh thirty years. What are these divine attributes of the Catholic Church, and how have they come out under the glorious guidance of this wonderful man? My friends, any man, Catholic, Protestant, or unbeliever, who reads the new law must come to the conclusion that, whoever Christ was, He intended to found a Church. He is always speaking of it, telling what kind of a thing it is to be, describing it as His kingdom, His city, His place. He gathers together His apostles, and He tells them that they are His Church. No matter who or what He is, He intended to found a Church. But we know and believe He is the Son of God. If He came to found a Church, and if He founded that Church, it is of God, and it must be for ever and for ever, as the Son of God has intended it to be. (Applause.)

Now, He has set certain marks on that Church which make it the Church of Christ. They belong to her supernaturally, as they come to her from God, and they belong to her imperishably. They are unity, sanctity, apostolicity, strength, and immortality. Christ made His Church one; He made it holy; He made it apostolic; and He made it the strongest thing that the hand of God ever built up in heaven or on earth. (Applause.) And He not only made His Church all this, but He took good care that all these gifts should be ensured to her and remain with her. As to her sanctity, he guaranteed it to her through the sacraments which belong to the faithful.

The sanctity of the Church is scattered by the hand of God over the universe. The same Omnipotent hand that gave the Church her sanctity gave her the other three gifts. He made Himself the centre of her unity; He made Himself the fountain-head of her apostolicity; He made Himself the guardian of her strength and immortality. Listen to His words at the Last Supper when He prayed: "O God, Father in heaven! keep them one, let them be one. I have given them my word. Let them be one in unity, as I and thou, the Father, are one." Thus He made Himself and His union with the Father the centre of His Church's union.

Secondly, He made Himself the fountain-head of her apostolicity, for He said to the apostles: "The Father in heaven sent me, and I send you. Go, therefore, teach all nations, and tell them all the things I have told you." Therefore He made Himself the fountain-head and standing-point of her apostolicity, so that every apostle went forth in the name and on the mission of his Divine Master, and they were all able to say, "Christ sent us, and therefore we have come to you." (Applause.)

Thirdly, He made Himself the guardian and guarantee of the Church's strength and immortality; for He said to her: "Behold, I am with you all days, unto the consummation of the world, and the gates of hell shall never prevail against you. I have given you my word, and heaven and earth shall pass away, but my word shall not pass away." Whatever falls against that rock shall be crushed, and whatever it falls against will be crushed to dust. Therefore He declares He is the source of the Church's strength, and she has a strength that no power on earth or hell can resist to the end of time. (Applause.) Now, my next consideration is the love of Christ. He was about to leave this world to ascend into heaven. But before He went He selected one of the apostles and made him the head of the Apostolic College. He made him His own representative; He made him His own vicar; He conferred on him His own powers. Peter was the man thus selected. And when Christ departed from this earth Peter stepped in and took His place—the place of Christ, the Son of God, as His vicar and His visible representative, and he became to the Church, to the end of time, all that Jesus Christ, its divine founder, was. (Applause.) Therefore Peter, as pope, became the centre of the Church's unity, the fountain-head of her apostolicity, and the guardian of her strength and immortality. And the more these three attributes of the Catholic Church shine out in the pontificate of any of the popes, the greater is that pope and the greater is his pontificate. (Applause.) My friends, this great Pontiff is the centre of the unity of the Church. There were a great many popes who went before him; there was a long line of martyr popes, who lived in times when the world was so divided that the pontiffs were compelled to distribute more of their spiritual power to the bishops. There were pontiffs who succeeded these martyred ones—Leo the Great, Gregory I., and another Gregory to whom was given the title of "Magnus." But when do we find the unity of the Church so strongly developed and shown as in the last General Council of the Vatican? (Applause.) Eight hundred bishops from all ends of the earth were there. Never did the Catholic Church behold assembled together so great an array of mitred prelates. Around these eight hundred bishops were hundreds of learned men, philosophers, and theologians, filled with the stores of theological knowledge which the experience of eighteen hundred and seventy years had supplied. There they were, the bishops of the universal Church, no longer confined to this country or to that, but spread out over the whole world, speaking the language of every clime under the sun, arrayed in different costumes, with different habits, thoughts, and prejudices; and there in the midst of them stands the sceptred monarch of the Church of God.

He rises in their midst, and calls on them in the name

of the Father, Son, and Holy Ghost, and in the name of over two hundred millions of Catholics, to make an act of faith in the unity of the Catholic Church. And forth from the recesses of by-gone ages comes a voice crying out that Peter is the rock on which the Church of God is founded. (Applause.) Forth from the martyrs' graves comes the testimony: "The Pope is the successor of Peter." From the depths of mediæval Christianity comes the voice of Thomas Aquinas, saying that the successor of Peter is the Vicar of God. From God's bishops comes a voice proclaiming, "Thou, Pius, art the successor of Peter, the Vicar of Christ (applause), to whose word, speaking *ex cathedrâ*, the Church will bow down as to the voice of Jesus Christ." Will any voice arise in that vast assemblage to deny his claim? No; God's bishops all bow down and say it is true as the Gospel from which it comes. Will any bishop rise up, like Photius of old in Constantinople, to deny it? No. Never was there such unanimity in the Church's proclamation of a dogma as when that dogma comes forth from the lips of Pius IX., "The pope is Christ's Vicar on earth." If this unity, then, this great attribute that so clearly distinguishes her from jarring sects and makes her the image of the one God—one in His personality when He became man, one in His prayer to the Father for His Church— if unity be a characteristic of the true Church, it has never been illustrated so grandly before the world as in the glorious figure of Pius IX. (Applause.) But, more than that, Christ said His Church was an apostolic Church. She is not only a working but an aggressive Church. We Catholics are blamed by our fellow-citizens because, they say, we cannot keep ourselves quiet. "Is it not too bad," they say, "that we can't live in peace and not mind religious questions? These Catholics are constantly pestering us with their Sisters of Mercy, their Little Sisters, and friars, and parish priests, and preaching to us about Catholicity." Well, my friends, we cannot help it. If there be any non-Catholic friends here to-night, I say ' We would let you alone if we could, but if we did you and the world would never become Catholic, and you and the world would run great risk of eternal damnation. *Caritas Christi urget nos.*" Do we not read, "Woe unto me if I do not preach the Gospel of God"? Christ told His disciples to teach all nations. St. Paul repeated the lesson, and preached in season and out of season. We, therefore, cannot let the world alone. The Church must work, must spread the truth, must convert the nations. If there are savage heathens, she must send out her missionaries to them to suffer and, perhaps, to die the martyr's death. Under the burning sun of India or amidst the snowy mountains of the frozen North, the Jesuit or Lazarist will find his way to those who sit in darkness, to teach them the words of Jesus Christ, and receive, perhaps, as his reward the stroke of the lance or the tomahawk, and seal the truth of his mission by the testimony of blood, which may yet convert his savage murderer to the faith of Jesus Christ. (Applause.)

I will ask our Protestant friends where, in the annals of history since Christ founded His Church and the last of the apostles died—where is the nation, where is the province, where is the people that has received Christianity except from the popes of Rome? Who sent St. Patrick to Ireland? The holy Pope Celestine, who said to him, "I consecrate you Bishop of Ireland; go and enkindle the light of divine faith amongst its people." (Applause.) St. Patrick came, and announced to the assembled monarchs and bards of Ireland at Tara, "I am a messenger to you from God, sent by the Pope of Rome." And Ireland took the message of the apostle, because he had the mission of the Pope of Rome. And Patrick ended his mission as he began it, for his last words to his disciples were: "If you have any disputes between you, go to Rome as you would to a mother." (Applause.)

Who sent St. Augustine to England? The blessed and great Pope Gregory. Who sent their apostles through the wild forests of Germany and the north? The popes of Rome.

No man can convert unless he has his mission and diploma from Rome. "No man can preach except he be sent"; and the one to send is the supreme head of the Church of Jesus Christ.

Now, where, on the long roll of sovereign pontiffs, is the pope who has shown more of the power and strength of the apostolical spirit than Pius IX.? It is now nearly thirty years since he began to reign. He has exceeded the years of the pontificate of Peter. His pontificate is an historical miracle, for he is the only pope that has reigned longer than St. Peter. When he began that pontificate the bishops of America were few and far between—scarcely twenty; no, nor anything like twenty. To-day the land is covered with cathedrals; the Catholic faith is the one, united, respectable, and dominant religion of the United States of America, and the episcopate is one of the most glorious branches of the great tree of God's Church. (Applause.) When Pius IX. began his reign there was not a single territorial bishop in England. To-day this great man, in the fulness of his apostolic spirit, has restored once more the glories of England's hierarchy, and has rebuilt the edifice of her stately Church, which seemed to have crumbled to ruins under three hundred years of persecution. (Applause.) His labors extended over the universal Church to the farthest ends of the earth. In the far antipodes, in Australia and Polynesia, on the shores of the Pacific and the shores of Labrador, wherever the sun shines, the Catholic Church flourishes under the apostolic hand of Pius IX. Finally, Christ has endowed His Church with a strength that nothing can resist. We have seen every day, and the testimony of history repeats it, that there is nothing indestructible in this world.

In our own days we have seen the collapse of dynasties that seemed to us invincible. We have seen the proud, courageous soldiers of France dashed to the earth and humbled under the iron heel of their German conquerors. We are compelled to say that everything in this world, no matter how strong it may seem, has in it the elements of weakness, save and except the Catholic Church, because she rests on the strength of the divine promise, that can never fail, and on the principles of justice, mercy, honor, and of knowledge.

These principles are founded on the truthfulness of God. Principles such as these are indestructible. Arms cannot destroy them; cannon cannot pulverize them; armies cannot crush them; brute force cannot break them down; they rest on God, and are a portion of his divine truth asserted amongst men. And such strength and such principles are the strength and the principles of Pius IX. (Applause.) If we compare him with other popes, we will find that the greatest amongst them must take a lower grade than that of our Holy Father. Of all the figures that loom out on the records of history there is none that is greater than that of Gregory, or, as he was called, Hildebrand, who stood up for the Church's rights and liberties, and fought single-handed all the power of the German emperors, and humbled to the dust the greatest and most wicked of them. But if he did, he had Catholic France to back him up and the God of truth and faith to sustain him. He had great and powerful monarchs to sustain him. Pius IX. has stood alone before all the powers of this world. Alone, but that God supported him, he battled with heresy and infidelity. Left alone to the strength of his principles of faith, honor, and justice, the whole world demanded of him the commission of an act of disloyalty to his Divine Master, and in the face of the whole world he flung out his noble defiance and refusal—the words *Non possumus.* That was the occasion when he was asked to surrender a little child to the Jewish religion. A little Jewish child had been baptized. The law of faith says the moment a child is baptized that moment he becomes the property of Jesus Christ and His Church. Such a child was baptized. Pius IX. was called on to give him up and surrender that property of his Divine Master, to play false to the interests of his Divine Lord; and he was summoned to do so at the peril of his liberty and of his temporal dominion. He stood fast to that child, despite the power of England and France and the acts of ambassadors writing their scheming protocols. Everything that was possible was brought to bear on that iron old man, but he stood there and said, "You may tear the heart out of my bosom, but I tell you I will never do it." *Non possumus!* There is the only answer of this grand old man. But, coming from the lips of the Vicar of God, that answer was so powerful that all the powers of a hostile and wicked world were compelled to bow down before it. And I myself have shaken the hands of that very child when he grew up and was filled with all the glory and purity of the priesthood. (Applause.)

It is not only the strength to say *Non possumus* that is characteristic of this great old man. There is one greater attribute that belongs to the Pope of Rome which is well understood by all true Catholics, and that is the attribute of divine sagacity to know and interpret the mind of the Church dogmatically in the proper time and season. And how well every Catholic knows this is the attribute of the Pope!

I once said to a poor old peasant in the West of England: "Do you think the Pope will declare the Immaculate Conception of the Blessed Virgin Mary?" "Whether he does or not," was the answer, "we know it is the truth, and when the time comes he will know better than any one else." In these simple words he showed that he knew this great attribute of the Pope. Pius IX. has risen to the glory of proclaiming, on his own infallible authority, without waiting for a General Council, the Immaculate Conception of the Blessed Virgin Mary. John in Patmos had the glory of seeing Mary crowned in heaven, but to proclaim her Immaculate Conception as a dogma of the Church was a glory reserved for eighteen hundred years for Pius IX. (Applause.) But far more wonderful is the sagacity whose exhibition has followed on the loss of his temporal power. Forecasting the dark ages that were coming on, when with prophetic eye he beheld himself a prisoner and his successors exiles on the face of the earth, he saw the time was come to save the Catholic Church from confusion—to save the unity of the Church in her head. He called his bishops together and crowned the edifice of the Church by the declaration of the infallibility of her head. (Applause.)

The bishops came. He spoke—the wisdom of God spoke in him—and the successor of Peter was dogmatically declared to be what the Church had always believed him to be. The man who is the head of the Church, speaking *ex cathedrâ*, speaking her faith and formulating her dogmas, cannot ask the Church to tell a lie; for the Holy Ghost would come and strike him dead if he dared to tell her a lie. (Applause.) Now, the Pope may lay down his temporal power, to be again given back to him in God's good time. But, be he exile or martyr, there is that in him which the Church declares to be his, and which cannot belong to any other man—the mysterious countersign of his infallibility, and on that infallibility she rests and bids defiance to all the monarchs of the earth. They may hinder her bishops from assembling in council; the Church has her head in the Pope. They may cast her bishops and priests into prison or put them to death; she has the declaration of faith in the same infallible guide, and she owes that to the wonderful energy and sagacity of Pius IX. (Applause) Therefore he, beyond all other popes, has exulted in organizing the Church, in maintaining her unity, increasing her strength; and, therefore, for the temporal crown which he has lost the Church of God sets on his brow the triple crown of this threefold glory. Therefore let us remember that he is our father, and let us honor and praise him. Let us pray that length of days may crown his head, and that, as he has buried so many of his enemies, he may live to triumph over those who remain—(applause)—not, indeed, to seek their destruction, but to take them back into his bosom. Let us remember him as Irishmen, owing our

Catholicity to the Pope, and the preservation of that divine faith to the strong fidelity with which Ireland has always, through good report and evil report, taken her stand by the chair of Peter; and let us all, with one heart and voice, in thankfulness cry out, "God bless Pius IX., Pope of Rome!" (Loud applause.)

"FOLLOW THOU ME."

Discourse at the Funeral Ceremonies of Pius IX. in the Cathedral at Cork, February 21, 1878.

"FOLLOW thou me!" said Jesus to Peter. "Follow thou Christ!" says the Church to her children. How can we follow Christ? In the funeral sermon on Pius IX. Father Burke shows us how the saintly Pope followed the Master. He was an example worthy of imitation. Let us read how he overcame momentous difficulties, how his joy was in the love of Jesus, and how his glorious victories are enjoyed to-day. Then let us beseech our Maker for grace that we may so live as to be worthy to be called "sons of God and joint heirs of Christ."

Father Burke's text is from the 21st chapter of the Gospel of St. John:

This is now the third time that Jesus was manifested to His disciples after He was risen from the dead.

When, therefore, they had dined, Jesus saith to Simon Peter: Simon, son of John, lovest thou me more than these? He saith to Him: Yea, Lord, Thou knowest that I love Thee. He saith to him: Feed my lambs.

He saith to him again: Simon, son of John, lovest thou me? He saith to Him: Yea, Lord, thou knowest that I love Thee. He saith to him: Feed my lambs.

He saith to him the third time: Simon, son of John, lovest thou me? Peter was grieved because He said to him the third time, Lovest thou me? and he said to Him: Lord, Thou knowest all things; Thou knowest that I love Thee. He said to him: Feed my sheep.

Amen, amen, I say to thee, when thou wast younger thou didst gird thyself, and didst walk whither thou wouldst. But when thou shalt be old thou shalt stretch forth thy hands, and another shall gird thee and lead thee whither thou wouldst not.

And this He said, signifying by what death He should glorify God. And when He had said this He saith to him: Follow me.

Peter, turning about, saw that disciple whom Jesus loved following, who also leaned on his breast at supper and said: Lord, who is he that shall betray thee?

"*FOLLOW THOU ME.*" 51

Him, therefore, when Peter had seen, he saith to Jesus: Lord, and what shall this man do?
Jesus saith to him: So I will have him to remain till I come, what is it to thee? Follow thou me.

MAY it please your lordship. Dearly beloved brethren, this was the last apparition mentioned by the Evangelist in which Christ appeared to His apostles. They were all assembled together, James, Andrew, John, Philip, Bartholomew, and others—they were all there, when suddenly their Divine Master flashed into their presence and gave joy to their eyes as they beheld Him, and to their hearts, for they loved Him dearly. He was coming to say His last words, for He in a few hours should disappear amid the glorious clouds of Olivet, so that they should see His face on earth no more. He was now come to say His last words to them—words that were to remain, for they came from the lips of God; words which were to remain as the very charter of the Church which He founded in the shedding of His adorable blood. And He called out of the twelve one man, Simon Peter. He called him forth, and all the others looked wondering; and the Lord spoke—oh! with what awful solemnity. "Simon," He said, "son of John, lovest thou me more than these?" There were all the apostles, and among them one apostle whom Jesus loved —one who was loved so as to be worthy of receiving from his Master on Calvary the grandest inheritance; that was, He gave him the custody of the love of the Virgin Mother of Jesus Christ. Surely there were those who loved Him dearly and well, and yet He says: "Simon Peter, son of John, lovest thou me even more than these love me?" And Peter answered, saying: "Lord, Thou knowest that I love Thee." There was a pause. Again the Son of God spoke, again the same terrible question: "Peter, dost thou love me more than any other man on earth lovest me?" And Peter fearlessly answered: "Thou knowest that I love Thee." The third time He spoke again: "Simon Peter, son of John, for the third time I ask thee, dost thou love me more than other men?" And Peter, appealing to that Omniscience that sees and knows all things, appealing to Christ as his Master, to the God from whom no secret of the human heart can be for a moment concealed, said: "Judge for Thyself. Thou knowest that I love Thee." Next followed the great commission. Having thus tested His apostle's love, He went on, saying to him, "Peter, feed thou my lambs, feed my sheep. Be thou pastor not only of my people, but be thou my pastor of the very pastors of my people, the ruler of rulers of the Church of God—thou only, Peter. To thee I give the keys of the kingdom of heaven; and for thee, O Simon Peter! have I prayed that thy faith may never fail, that thou mayest confirm and strengthen thy brethren. Thou art a rock. Upon this rock I will build my Church, and the gates of hell shall never prevail against it." Peter, then, having declared his love, received his great commission.

One word more remained to be spoken to him, and that was the strange and mysterious precept, "Follow thou me." Peter, turning round to the others, looked at St. John, anxious to know what he was to do, and said to his Master: "What is this man to do?" Christ, turning to him, almost rebukingly says: "Let the others remain; let them take their places. Do thou follow me," he added again. This precept to follow Christ has been already given to all men, unto those who are to bear the Christian name. The Son of God had already said: "If any man wishes to come after me, let him deny himself and take up his cross and follow me." Why, therefore, having given the precept to all men, why does he renew it twice again to Peter personally—why does he make that precept individually to Peter, as distinguished not only from every other man, but even from St. John, the apostle and disciple of love? Because Peter, in virtue of the great commission he received, was called on to follow his Master, even in the highest paths of universal jurisdiction, of unlimited power and government, and, consequently, also into the highest paths of suffering. Having thus spoken, our Divine Lord, having made all things perfect in the organization of his Church, blessed His apostles, and He was taken away from them. They saw Him no more on earth. Turning to them, He said, "See me in Peter," and they did homage to Peter as the vicar and viceroy of Jesus Christ, the true invisible Head of the Church.

Well, dearly beloved, for many a long year he continued in his triple office of love, jurisdiction, and suffering. For many long years he proved his love for his Divine Master. He proved his solicitude for the growing Church that was already spreading on every side under his firm hand, and, dying, he sealed that love, and showed that he had not forgotten the strange precept, "Follow me." For, many years after the ascension of our Divine Lord, there came a morning when the sun rose over the Alban hills and filled the imperial city of Rome with its morning light; and in that morning light an old man was brought forth from out the deep dungeon depths of the Mamertine prison, crippled with deformity, bowed with years, long a prisoner for the sake of Him whom he preached and whom he loved. He is led forth now from the very blackness of the dungeon into the light morning air, and led through the streets of Rome, two men preceding bearing a great cross. With faltering, aged step he climbed the rugged sides of the steep Jerusalem, and there the aged man was stretched out and nailed to the cross. Whilst they were nailing him to the cross he had one prayer to make to them, and it was: "Lift me up, but let my head be towards the earth; for I am not worthy to die like Him whom I saw crucified on the hill outside Jerusalem." Peter, aged, bent, and led a prisoner in Rome, crucified in Rome, thus proved to the Church, to all the world, to heaven and earth, that he had not forgotten the precept of Him who said: "Follow thou me."

And the Church of God mourned for Peter, even as the children of Israel mourned in the plains of Moab for the great lawgiver, whom God had mysteriously buried in the high mountain. But their mourning was soon changed into joy; for as Christ appeared in Peter, so Peter reappeared in Linus, Linus again in Cletus, and Cletus again in Clement; and so the golden chain, unbroken in a single link, is passed down—that chain of which the Church in her conclave held yesterday forged the last link, whilst the first link is in the hand of Jesus Christ, seated at the right hand of Almighty God in heaven. Two hundred and fifty and more are the links of jurisdiction and glory in that golden and apostolic chair, and we, children of the Church, are mourning to-day. Peter has died again; Peter, once again imprisoned, once again held up before the eyes of the world, has yielded his soul upon a hill in Rome. His great and glorious soul has passed away to behold in heaven that triumph of the Church which was denied him on earth, and we, his children, are mourning; we grieve for our father, even though this very morning Peter has risen again, and our sorrow must speedily be changed into joy. We are mourning for Pius IX. That glorious roll of Peter's successors contains the names of the most illustrious names that were born to man on this earth. Martyrs adorned it with their blood, saints with their sanctity, apostles with their zeal. It is emblazoned forth with such names that the world has attached to them even the title "Great." Leo the Great is there, who saved Rome; Hildebrand, the immortal St. Gregory VII., is there, who, dying, having conquered all the world, said to his people: "Because I love justice and hate iniquity, thus I die." Boniface VIII., crowned with sufferings and adversity, is there, and his name is written in letters of gold. There was Pius V., the aged and saintly pontiff who, from his chamber in the Vatican, commanded the elements on that glorious day of Lepanto when the cross was raised up and the enemies of God scattered. Dearly beloved, among these names there is not one, I venture to say, of which history will pronounce a higher eulogium, to which succeeding generations will assign a more glorious place, than the illustrious name of Pope Pius IX., whose loss we are mourning and deploring to-day.

The Church of God, dearly beloved, is divided into

three great portions. There is the Church of God suffering in the expiating punishment of purgatory; there is the Church of God struggling and fighting against all the powers of darkness and the world here on earth; and there is the Church of God triumphant in the halls of the Most High, having gained her crown and reigning in a peace which surpasses the comprehension of men. If the Church here on earth be militant, consequently struggling, consequently open to persecution, fighting day after day for her very existence and for the souls of her children, although the cup of adversity may be brought to her lips, and though she may be commanded to drink to the very dregs, yet the Lord can ever leave His Church on earth with great consolation and great joy. The words are still true of her, "My mouth shall be ever filled with thy praise, O God!" She always gives her argument and motive for gratitude and praise, and among the blessings, consolations, and joys which the Almighty God gave His afflicted and persecuted Church in this age, the greatest of all was the pontificate of Pius IX.—the proudest when we consider the character of the man, greatest when we consider the great deeds with which he characterized it, greatest when we consider the mercy which prolonged that pontificate and lengthened the days even beyond the years of Peter and far beyond the years of any man who ever succeeded Peter in the Church—prolonged that the Church might rejoice under his powerful arm and firm guidance, and that our joy might not be taken away too soon.

The tests by which we can measure the greatness of his character are the three tests to which God submitted Peter. To the test, "Do you love me more than any other man?" Peter answered, "Yes." "Wilt thou feed my lambs and sheep, wilt thou govern my Church?" and Peter answered, "Yes." And to the question, "Wilt thou follow me?" Peter's whole life and death answered emphatically, "Yes." Let us test Pius IX. by the foregoing crucial tests. Did he love Jesus Christ more than any other man? In order to answer this question I will ask you to remember that among the strange and wonderful graces that attended the pontificate of Pius IX., one of the most singular was the rise, the sudden and universal spread, of the devotion to the Sacred Heart of Jesus. The apostle of this devotion, the humble nun, Mary Margaret Alacoque, was beatified by Pius IX., and devotion to the Sacred Heart of our Lord was spread by her. It went forth from his own heart in his encyclicals, in his apostolic briefs, in the number of indulgences which were attached to the devotion. He fostered, cherished, and spread this great devotion, and it is by this I will measure his love for Jesus Christ. Was his heart conformed to the Sacred Heart of his Divine Master? If we look into the Sacred Heart of our Lord and Saviour Jesus Christ, we find in that abyss of divine perfection, in that indescribable furnace of divine love, we find certain loves, certain convictions that stand out pre-eminently, and these were particularly His love for His Eternal Father, His love for Mary His Mother, His love for little children, His love for the poor and the penitent, and His love for His Church. In all these our Divine Lord condescended to give us a bright example in His life and sayings. There was in the Sacred Heart of Jesus an infinite love for the Heavenly Father.

How did He show this? By the spirit of prayer that was upon Him, for wherever there is love there is a natural prompting to have intercourse with the object of our love and to be near him. Intercourse with God is through prayer, and therefore Christ was emphatically a man of prayer. He spent the night on the mountain-side in prayer with God. He prayed at all times and ever communed with His Heavenly Father. It was by prayer He strengthened Himself to meet the horrors of His passion—nay, when that prayer brought with it the agony of Gethsemane, He but prayed the longer, wrestling with the awful sufferings that were coming upon Him. Pius IX. conformed with the heart of Jesus in this—he was pre-eminently a man of prayer. I had the happiness to live some years under the light of his great example, to behold him day after day, but never have I, under any circumstances, beheld the Sovereign Pontiff that he did not seem absorbed in communion with God. But, oh! when he came into any of the churches in Rome and knelt in the presence of our Lord, present in the tabernacle of the Blessed Sacrament, then without a moment's apparent preliminary preparation, then without a moment's hesitation, as if pursuing the natural, habitual course of his thoughts, the whole man seemed to go out from him, and the spirit of prayer which absorbed him seemed to go altogether into the tabernacle wherein was God whom he adored. The very sight seemed to lead his eye as it went forth to behold—in the strong vision of faith—Jesus Christ. His prayers so absorbed him that age, infirmity, everything was forgotten, and the very sight of him at prayer has more than once moved those who do not believe in the presence of the Lord to kneel down from very fear; for they realized that God must be near the man who thus prayed. Second to the love of the Sacred Heart of Jesus was love for Mary, His Mother. Who can doubt it? When He was about working His first miracle at the wedding of Cana, at Galilee, He expressly declared to His Virgin Mother that His time was not come, that the moment had not arrived when He should show His omnipotence by working miracles. But Mary pressed Him, with the calm consciousness that she could almost command, and He told them to fill the vessels with water. Then He, turning, looked, and the water flashed into wine at the sight of God. Why did He do this? Why did He anticipate the time? Why did He work it after expressly declaring that His time was not yet come? Because it was Mary's wish. It was to honor her, it was to give her pleasure, to let the whole world see that He would do great things in and for Mary. When He was dying on the cross, torn from head to foot with scourges, with seventy-three cruel thorns deeply imbedded in His aching head, when the film of death was in His eyes, when the thirst of death was on His lips, and when the agony of death broke and rent his heart, even then He forgot himself and His own sorrows. He looked lovingly to Mary and called the apostle to him He loved best, saying to him: "O my son! behold my Mother; take care of her."

And even as his Divine Master was, so was Pius IX. Tender, pure love of the Mary of purity, the Mother of God, he drew in his devotion of her in his mother's milk. He states in his bull of her Immaculate Conception that he rejoiced in his old age when the holy choir of God and all the bishops called upon him to define the great dogma and declare dogmatically that which the Church always knew, always felt and believed—namely, as St. Augustine said, that when it was a question of sin there should be no mention of the name of Mary. Her name was not to be on the lips of those who discoursed of sin. "In my old age," said he, "let me rejoice, for from my earliest childhood I have loved my Mother Mary." To him was reserved the crowning glory to set upon her head the brightest gem—namely, to proclaim unto heaven that knew it, and to earth that already believed, the eternal truth that Mary was conceived without sin, that the merits of the Saviour were extended to her by anticipation, that she was purified by prevention, and that sin was not atoned for in her soul.

The third love of Jesus Christ was the love of little children. He took them to His breast, clasped them to His bosom, and gave them His love. Even so the heart of Pius IX. loved little children. When he was ordained priest in 1827, and other men engaged in preaching the Gospel either meant to go forth in a mission to foreign lands or devote themselves to an ecclesiastical career likely to lead up to the high places in the Church, the young priest, John Mastai Ferretti, on the day of his ordination went into an orphanage in Rome, took a little room in the place, sat down with the children to teach them, to take care of them, to collect money for their maintenance—in a word, to labor for them and to be their servant. And for seven years he there remained, intending to devote his whole life in the cause of little children, until the hand of God and the voice of the Church came and drew him forth for higher things. When he was consecrated Archbishop of Spoleto, and took possession of the archiepiscopal see, his very first act was to build an orphanage for little children quite near to his own palace, that he might see them and exercise supervision over them daily. Translated again from Spoleto to Imola, his first act was to build two orphanages, one on each side of his palace, for the little children. But he did more: he built asylums for the fallen, refuges where penitents might be sanctified until holiness might return slowly but surely to those who had fallen. Thus was the heart of this man conformed to the very love of his Saviour's heart.

The fourth great love of the heart of Jesus was His Church, my dearly beloved. Oh! how great and wonderful a mystery is this Holy Catholic Church of Jesus Christ. A great and wonderful mystery. For the four thousand years that went before the coming of the Son of God all things prefigured and foreshadowed the Church that was to be in the fulness of time and the perfection of grace. When the time came to found that Church the Eternal God came down from heaven, bringing with Him His own essential and eternal truth, and He left that truth, never to be sullied by the slightest error in her teaching, never to be contradicted by a single principle of her moral law—he left that truth in His Church. "I will send my Spirit upon you to teach you all truth, to keep you in the truth, and I myself am with you all days, even to the consummation of the world."

That He might make that Church all beautiful, all holy, all perfect in her organization, perfect in her doctrine, perfect in her graces, He shed His blood upon the cross. Here are the words of the apostle: "Christ loved His Church and gave Himself for her, that He might present her to Himself not having spot or wrinkle or any such thing, but all perfect, all fair, all beautiful, and worthy to be the spouse of the Eternal Lamb of God." Such was the love that Jesus Christ had for His Church that He died upon the cross for her; such is the abiding love that He has for her that not for one instant has He ever forsaken her, or left her open to the imputation of a single error in her faith or in her morality. And even so did the heart of Pius IX. love the Church. She was his one care. In the day of his ordination as a priest he brought a virgin heart and virgin hands into the sanctuary of his God, and that sanctuary which he entered as a virgin he left as a virgin, to take hold of a virgin's crown in the halls of God Almighty. He loved the Church. The Church, no matter where she was in suffering, found in him her great defender and champion; the Church, wherever she was in difficulty, felt the touch of that firm and steady hand that was at the helm of the bark of Peter, that guided her with persistent wisdom, that brought her through so many storms, and left her perhaps in the most glorious unity, fidelity, and discipline to which ever this Church of God has attained on earth since the days of its foundation. Dying in the halls of the Vatican, with the rattle of death in his throat, when the hand of death had seized upon him, among the last words spoken to the cardinals and prelates around him were, "Guard the Church that I loved so well!" It was his love for the Church that sustained him, it was his love for the Church that enabled him to outlive the years of Peter, it was his love for the Church that enabled him, even in his old age, to endure imprisonment and misery and heart-breaking persecution; it was the same love that upheld him and that sustained him that upheld the Virgin Mother at the foot of the cross, when any other mother would have died long before at witnessing the sufferings of her Son and her God. Therefore I hold that this great man's heart was conformed to the heart of Jesus Christ; and that in the day when the Lord raised him, an humble and almost unknown cardinal as he was, to the supreme dignity of the Papacy, in that day God surely said: "I have found David my servant a man after my own heart, and with my holy oil I have anointed him."

But, dearly beloved, beautiful as was this character, the

personal character of Pius IX., beautiful in his love for God, his love for the Mother of God, his love for the little ones, his love for the penitent and the afflicted, and the large attribute of mercy that was upon him—for he began his pontificate by opening prisons on earth, and he closed his pontificate by using the key that he alone could wield, and, let us hope, opening the gates of heaven at the last cry of his persecutor, to the man who had taken from him house and home, and who turned from his death-bed in the Quirinal to the death-bed in the Vatican and cried, "O my Lord! remember me"—beautiful as all this is, there is another great question which we must ask ourselves, and by which we must test the character of Pius IX.—namely, did he administer in the mighty office that God had given him as Christ demanded that Peter should administer the Church of God? "Feed my lambs, feed my sheep," He said. The food is doctrine. "Thou art the rock upon which I will build my Church." The rock means firmness that never would yield to any persecution, never be shaken by any storm, never compromise that faith in any shape or form whatsoever. Did Pius IX. do this? O my beloved brethren! when we come to consider him no longer merely as a man but as a Pope, we are simply astounded and crushed. Our very minds within us labor, and labor ineffectually, to conceive how great and terrible is that office to which a man is exalted when he is made the head of the Catholic Church! How terrible it is! What an awful thing it is to think that a man is made the viceroy, the vicar, the representative of the Lord Jesus Christ; that he receives all power, because the Son of God said, "All power in heaven and on earth is given to me, and even as the Father sent me I send you"; that there is no limit to his jurisdiction; that he can touch the Church, not only here on earth in every one of its members—that every bishop that grasps his crosier, every priest that lifts his hands, must do so under the sanction and with the knowledge of the pope, or else his acts are sinful, if not null and void—but that also his power passes into the kingdom of glory by the act of canonization, and into purgatory by the power of indulgences! When we consider that all this is involved in the idea of the Papacy, is it not a terrible responsibility?

Every other office ever conferred upon man shrinks into utter smallness, shrinks away into almost nothingness, compared with the awful dignity and jurisdiction of the office of the Papacy. Moses was raised by the Almighty God to be a lawgiver to the people, and the Scripture says of him that the Lord God made him like the saints in glory, magnified him in the fear of his enemies, sanctified him in faith and meekness, crowned him with honor and glory; and yet what was Moses's office compared with that of the pope? He was the legislator for a particular people, the Jews; the pope is the legislator for the whole world. Moses administered the law of which the apostle speaks as "Poor miserable elements, that never brought anything to perfection"; the pope administers with supreme power the perfect law of Jesus Christ. Aaron, again, was raised up to the priesthood of the nation, and, says Ecclesiasticus, "the Lord God crowned him with honor, and gave him a golden cincture, and made with him an everlasting covenant for the priesthood." But what was that priesthood compared with the pope's? It was but a shadow, an umbra, a promise which was to be fulfilled in the new law according to the order of Melchisedech. He was consecrated, but he only offered in sacrifice the blood of the fatlings of the flock; the Pope of Rome offers in sacrifice and sheds mystically the divine blood of Jesus Christ at Mass. And great was his office—great in its authority, great in its unlimited jurisdiction, great in its extent over all men. Pius IX. was a living instance of the truth of the theological principle that when Almighty God destines a man for any office or any function, no matter how high, He gives him graces necessary to fit him for it. Thus Mary, the Mother of God, according to St. Thomas, received such grace that she was fit to be the Mother of God.

He was called to his mighty task. He is gone; he has

left behind him an imperishable name and a perishable body; but his soul, with all its responsibilities, is gone before the judgment-seat of the Lord to give an account of the longest pontificate that God ever gave to His Church. He is gone to render that account, and I say that when we look back upon his administration of the Church of God we cannot but conclude that that account was favorable, and has been received by the invisible Head of the Church as worthy of the pontificate of the Church and of heaven.

Never, dearly beloved, and it is a remarkable fact, never in the history of the Church was she so persecuted as during the pontificate of Pius IX. Secondly, never was she so united as during the pontificate of Pius IX.; never was she so extended over the earth as during his pontificate; never was she so persecuted. There are many forms of persecution. There is the persecution of the sword; and God, when He allows the sword to fall on His Church, pours out a pentecost of graces; priests and people sanctify their faith by becoming martyrs. Such was the case with Ireland. Three hundred years ago hell and earth demanded the blood of the Irish people, and the Irish people willingly lost their blood and became martyrs for God and His Church. But among other forms of persecution there is the persecution which, by legislation, tries to limit the legitimate action of the Church, tries to take away from her her just and necessary influence over the education of her children, tries to interfere with the jurisdiction of her bishops, makes war upon the necessary immunities and privileges of her sanctuaries; even of persecution that tells a lie, and then tells the Church that she must not answer it by telling the truth. Even such is the persecution of our day. It is the persecution of law, laws made here and there, one law declaring that the clergy are no longer exempt from service in the army, dragging the priest from the altar and the monk from his convent, and putting them into the ranks of the soldiery to shed blood—which is so abhorrent to anointed hands—and the law telling bishops that they must have no intercourse with the Pope of Rome, that they must not write to him, that they must not instruct their people, or publish a pastoral without first submitting it to the inspection of an official who, perhaps, is an infidel; laws secularizing the education of children and handing it over to men who avowedly profess that they do not believe in the existence of God. Such persecution has been by every agency of the world's power directed in an especial manner against the Catholic Church.

Never was she so united, never were the episcopate and clergy so obedient to their head, never was order so perfectly established within her, never was the spirit of religious discipline so largely extended among all orders in the Church of God; it has been a revival; it has been as if another pentecost of grace, as if union, piety, and order, had been flung forth from the hands of Pius IX.

Never was the Church so extended. To-day hierarchies have been established in several parts of the world of the existence of which former popes were unaware—in North America, in distant Oceanica, in persecuting England, in Scotland, everywhere through the length and breadth of the earth. This is owing to the labors of Pius IX., who transfused his energetic spirit to bishops, priests, and people alike, and who has gone down to his grave, forth to his crown, leaving the Church of God, even if most persecuted, in a more perfect form of discipline and union than she ever attained to before.

What shall we say of his feeding the lambs and the sheep? One thing, my dearly beloved, as Catholics know, he has done. And if there be one to-day here who does not know it, even to him I say that he must recognize the fact that if God has spoken, if God has revealed any truth to men, that truth must come by the voice of authority; that truth must be made known by a living voice; that truth must be guaranteed from all error; that truth must be taught clearly, emphatically, in every language, if the belief in that truth be necessary to faith, and if it be true that without faith it is impossible to please God or save our souls. What is called dogma, therefore—that is to say, the solemn attestation of the infallible voice to the message of God—this telling of the truth and preaching it, is absolutely necessary for mankind, and it is the greatest blessing that we have. Now, twice during his long pontificate did Pius IX. proclaim the revealed truth as the guided witness of that truth. The first proclamation was in 1854, when he defined the Immaculate Conception of the Blessed Virgin Mary; the second in 1870, when he defined and declared that the Pope of Rome, the visible head of the Catholic Church, when he speaks as pope, solemnly and to the universal Church, is infallible under the guiding hand of the Holy Spirit of God. These two dogmatic utterances mark the pontificate of Pius IX. I ask you to consider them both, for out of these two utterances we gather the great mind, the far-seeing thought, the anticipative wisdom of this mighty man to whom God confided for so many years the government of His Church.

Dearly beloved, the Church of God, from the day of the Council of Jerusalem down to the Council of the Vatican, has spoken from time to time, always with unerring voice, always in clear language, bearing testimony to the faith; but her definitions, although most important, only touched certain principles and certain facts. Thus, for instance, the Council of Nice declared the divinity of Jesus Christ, which the Arians contested; the Council of Ephesus declared that the Blessed Virgin was truly the Mother of God, which the Nestorians denied; the Council of Trent declared the presence and the manner of the presence of our Divine Lord in the Holy Eucharist, which the heresies of that day denied. But all those definitions of truth, all those dogmatic utterances, presuppose one truth, they all take for granted one great truth which was in the mind and heart of all, yet which had never been dogmatically defined—namely, that there was a living, teaching, infallible voice in the Church of God, and that was the voice of Peter and Peter's successors. How do I prove this? Every council of bishops that ever gathered together in the Catholic Church, first of all before they dared venture to say a single word on faith, the first thing asked was: "Where is Peter?" Where is the pope? And until the pope appeared personally or by accredited legates no man ever dared to touch upon faith; and when definitions or dogmas were agreed upon no bishop ever dreamed of publishing them to his people or his diocese until the hand of the pope had first rested upon them and the voice of the pope had declared: "This is the truth." So we see that the Church by her councils, definitions, and dogmatic utterances always took for granted this great truth, and this is the fundamental truth which explains all the rest. For unless we admit this we cannot see what right the Church, at Nice, had to define the divinity of the Son of God, or, at Trent, to define transubstantiation. Now, to Pius IX. was reserved the mighty glory of bringing forth this fundamental truth, of placing it upon the imperishable, eternal basis of dogma, of defining and declaring it clearly to all men. That one dogmatic definition clears away all difficulties and all the mist that might hang over other previous definitions of the Catholic Church. Behold the mind of the man! It is not merely an individual fact, it is a dogma affecting all other dogmas, sustaining all other dogmas; it is an explanation of everything mysterious in the Church of God, that in a fleeting, a fading, and a changing world shall remain indefectible, incorruptible, unchangeable, the Word on her lips ever the same, and that most assuredly the Divine Word and the truth of Jesus Christ.

The other definition, that of the Immaculate Conception, is also a revelation of the great mind of that Pontiff, dearly beloved. If the Church of God is a great mystery, she alone is truthful where all others are liable to error, she alone is unchanged where all around her is changing, she alone is indestructible and eternal where all around her is dying or dead. If, I say, the Church of God is a great mystery, so in all those things is Mary, the Mother of Jesus Christ, a great mystery, the centre around which revolve strange, mysterious things. O my dearly beloved!

what a mysterious thing it is to think that a woman should be a mother and yet remain the purest of virgins, fit to be the virgins' queen and the angels' queen in heaven. To think that she should remain a virgin and be yet as truly mother as ever suckled babe on her breast! What a strange, mysterious thing it is that a child of earth, a child of Adam, should be Mother of God, the Mother of the eternal God, who came down from heaven, and, entering into her immaculate bosom, took upon Himself her virgin blood and flesh, receiving in Mary and from Mary a human body and a human soul; for Jesus Christ, though in nature human and divine, is still but one in person, and the very flesh and blood that He took from Mary is adored by all the angels in heaven, and shall be for eternity. Was it not a strange thing, also, that Mary's body should have been taken up into heaven without undergoing the corruption consequent upon death, that in her the glorious resurrection which we all hope for should be anticipated? This for a time was an unexplained mystery, until Pius IX. declared her immaculate, and this explains all. Her virginal soul was never tainted or sullied by sin, and why, therefore, should she suffer corruption when it is written, "O Lord! thou wilt not have given thy holy one to see corruption"? In the same way is it that the dogma of infallibility explains all the mysteries which surround the Church of God.

How great, then, was the man! how great was the wisdom that to remedy the evils of an incredulous age placed the sacred interests of the Church of Christ on the magnificent dogmatic basis of the infallibility of His vicar and the Immaculate Conception of His blessed Mother! This work of the great Pontiff Pius IX. was the rock that upheld the Church of God. Where was the hand of the persecutor raised to strike a blow at the Church that did not fall on the sacred person of Pius IX.? Where was there ever a voice raised against her that the aged man in Rome did not answer the challenge, speak out the truth, and destroy error with that terrible courage which was for us the grandest feature of his character? When the whole world would fain draw him into some error, back from the rock of Peter came the word, *Non possumus*. "I defy the whole world," he said. "If I had a thousand lives I could lose them; but one thing I cannot do, and that is to sacrifice the true interests of the Church of God." Such was the heart and the soul that had to be tried by the three tests to which Christ submitted Peter. It was no flowery path that Christ pointed to when He commanded Peter "to follow me." It was a path, indeed, of the highest jurisdiction, the highest glory, but it was also a path of suffering, a mountain path, strewn with thorns. The heart of Pius IX. was as tender for the poor as the heart of a mother for her child. I have often seen him when the poor and the afflicted crossed his path descend from his carriage and listen to the tale of some miserable creature, and as his purse gave bounty his eyes gave tears of pain. Yet that tender heart suffered the most acute pain— namely, that of ingratitude. The first of his acts was to open the prisons and recall the exiles, but their first act was to raise the hands he had emancipated against him, and to drive him forth into exile with curses and maledictions.

Even as Mary at the foot of the cross felt the tortures of her Divine Son more acutely than if she herself suffered them, so Pius IX. felt the indignities heaped upon his Church more than any personal wrong. In every cardinal deprived of his dignity he felt humiliated; in every oppressed priest he felt oppressed. Like Peter in the Mamertine prison, he languished in the Vatican, seeing the series of persecutions to which his Church was subjected. But at last he was taken away, after many years of sufferings, to his Father in heaven. For this the Mother of God knelt before the throne of her Son, the blessed Margaret Mary Alacoque knelt before the Sacred Heart, and prayed that the aged Pontiff might be released from his sufferings; and so while we hoped that he was to see the redemption of Israel, to see the darkness turned into light, the angel of death received his high command and took away Pius IX. Well may we say we shall not look upon his like again! One of the greatest, if not the greatest, of the popes is gone, but he has left an imperishable name. But though we mourn to-day, we yet have cause for joy, for out of the grave rises the figure of his successor. God has already spoken; the question was asked in the solemn Conclave, "Is the Lord's anointed before me?" and to-day Leo XIII. wields the sceptre of Pius IX. The pope does not die, the Church does not die, though Pius IX. may die.

And who is this man chosen to fill the place of power and jurisdiction? He is strong still, not too much advanced in years, for he is only sixty-eight years old, a man of prayer and of most genial courtesy, kind and tender, but at the same time firm as a rock in the assertion of justice, a man whose glorious qualities have already proved themselves to the Church of God. And do not think, my brethren, that I am speaking from imagination, for I have had the great honor of knowing this successor of Pius IX.; he was the bishop from whom I received orders many years ago. I speak from my personal recollection of him, and I believe that the Spirit of God has rested upon the most worthy and the fittest man to take the great vacant throne of the Vatican. I hope and trust that the motto here to-day—*Hiberniæ pate, amantissimi*—will be realized in him, and that the tender, true love of the people of this land will be amply deserved by Leo XIII. Therefore, though we mourn, we must be joyful. The Pope is dead, but the Pope lives; Peter has come to life again, and our sorrow must give way to joy. Let us therefore mingle our prayers of hope for the living with our prayer of tender recollection for the dead.

The Pontificate of Pius IX.

This lecture was delivered some years ago. It will be justly prized as a faithful delineation of the most remarkable pontificate since the days of Peter.

MY FRIENDS: The subject of our consideration this evening is the grandest that could occupy the mind or employ the tongue of man in this sad age of ours; it is the pontificate of Pius IX. This nineteenth century, of which we boast so much, is an age of great material progress, an age of railways, of electric telegraphs, of ocean steamers, and of discoveries of every kind. But side by side with all these material improvements, this age of ours, considered morally, intellectually, and spiritually, falls short of many of the centuries that went before. In former ages, although material civilization was less, still there was great improvement from time to time amongst the people in some great, noble cause; as, for instance, when Catholic and Christian Europe sent forth its chivalry, and men exposed their lives and shed their blood—for what? To vindicate the sanctity of the Lord's sepulchre, and to keep floating over the tomb of Jesus Christ the standard of the cross. In subsequent ages we see how kings went forth from their thrones, from their palaces, and from all the luxuries that surrounded them, and exposed themselves to a thousand dangers in some high, noble, and chivalrous cause; as when a prince of the house of Austria led all the intelligence, the energies, and the bravery of Christian Europe into battle with the Turks on the waters of Lepanto Bay. But in truth, if we examine public events in this nineteenth century, we find nothing great, nothing noble, no magnificent idea animating the nations. The freedom of America was accomplished before the eighteenth century closed. The great events in your war go along with the glories of the century before our own; and, with the exception of Catholic emancipation, there has been no great and noble act of any nation in this nineteenth century. Catholic emancipation is not the glory and not the volition of the government from whom it was forced, but of the Irish people, who, by their constancy and their religious fidelity, triumphed over their old enemy. This century was ushered in by the terrible French Revolution, which flooded noble France with the blood of its best and most loving sons. The nineteenth century has witnessed the coalition of all the states of Europe, all banding themselves together to bring down by brute force the greatest military genius of this or any other age, the first Napoleon. The nineteenth century has witnessed the uprising of a people in a senseless, brainless rebellion, and it has witnessed the terrible retort of kingly brute force and the extinguishment of the principles of a nation. The nineteenth century has witnessed one nation invading others, its neighbors, without any pretence or cause of justice whatsoever. There have been wars in this century, my friends, but from the first day of the nineteenth century down to this I will venture to assert that not a single religious war has been waged, not a single war has been carried on that has not been founded on injustice— not even the Crimean, in which France and England united to crush the power of Russia. There did we see the eldest son of the Church allied with a Protestant and a most infidel power to wage war on the side of Mohammed against Christ. This nineteenth century has witnessed what Europe never saw before: robbers crowned with kingly crowns and seated on royal thrones. Such a robber was the late ruler of France.

What right had he to invade the dominions of Austria? What right had he to claim the title to the northern portion of Italy, the ancient cradle of the house of Savoy?

What right had William of Prussia and Napoleon of France to wage war, during the progress of which, though it cost oceans of blood, it came out that the motive was one of mere policy. Also the robbery caused by these two thieves—I can call them nothing else—who were plotting through their ministers to divide Belgium, an independent state, between them. Bismarck was the thief who first proposed the robbery to Napoleon. Good God! has it come to this, that the rulers of Europe, the kings and emperors of the nations and people, have their blades ready in their hands to shed blood because one outwitted the other in robbery? This came out plainly and squarely in the mutual accusations of the prime ministers of France and Prussia.

The nineteenth century is coming to a close; and a fitting close of this age of ours is the highway robbery of a king invading the dominions of a poor, weak, unarmed old man, and taking from the Pope Rome and his papal dominions. They have no title under heaven for it; they have not the plea of justice or even exigency for it; they do it simply because they are able. Just as a housebreaker or a burglar might go into your house to-night or to-morrow and rob you of all you had in the world, and if you asked him: "Do you know what you are doing? do you know that you are a scoundrel and a robber?" and he should say: "No. I am able to do it. I am a stronger man than you. I am only doing what Victor Emmanuel did to the Pope."

But amidst all the meanness and all the commonplaces of this age there is one magnificent spectacle, one thing that marks the nineteenth century with the greatest glory, and one peculiarly its own, and that is the pontificate of Pius IX. (Applause.) Whatever else this century, our age, has failed to produce, it has produced the noblest Pope and the grandest man that ever sat upon the chair of Peter. Whatever else may be written on the face of the history of the nineteenth century, in letters of blood or in letters of black ink, there is one thing that must be written in letters of burnished gold, and it is the pontificate, glorious and magnificent, of this saintly old man who sits in Rome in all his afflictions, still crowned with the honor and the glory of which no man can deprive him, Pius IX., the head of the Catholic Church. (Applause.)

But, my friends, assertion is not proof, and the man who makes an assertion so bold as mine must be prepared to prove what he says, or else it would be far better for him not to speak at all. The grandest thing in the world, save the conception of the sacred humanity of the Son of God Incarnate, the grandest thing that the world has ever seen is the Catholic Church, founded by our Divine Lord and Saviour Jesus Christ, representing upon this earth the unity, the sanctity, and the eternity of the Almighty God who made it—a unity all the more wonderful in a world so divided as ours, a sanctity all the more wonderful in a world so unholy and defiled as ours, an eternity all the more wonderful in a world so evanescent, so changeable, so transitory as ours. And this is the meaning of the word of Scripture when the Psalmist says: "God is wonderful in all His works." Every work of God is wonderful, because everything that exists participates in some form or other in the attributes of God; and the more largely anything participates in the divine attributes the more wonderful that thing becomes, because it is the more like to God. Now, among all the things of this earth there is nothing that shows so highly and so flatteringly the attributes of God as His holy Catholic Church, for she represents the unity of God in the unity of her doctrine of conscious obedience. We have unity of doctrine. We are two hundred millions, my friends, scattered all the world over. We find ourselves sometimes in communities; as, for instance, in the great cities of New York and Brooklyn, where Catholics are numbered by hundreds of thousands. Sometimes we find ourselves in communities of nations, as in the green old mother-land that bore me, where that whole nation, blessed be God! is Catholic.

Sometimes, again, we find ourselves broken up into

small communities in the midst of our Protestant brethren and fellow-citizens, the Catholics only representing a unit in the community. You sometimes find a Catholic family in the far West, out on the bosom of the vast prairies, settled down in a little shanty on the banks of a little Western river. But wherever you find it, whether in nations, in cities or small communities, in individuals, if you find one Catholic you find personified in him the certain faith of two hundred millions of men. (Applause.) Question one of them, and if he knows his catechism you have the response of all. Ask him, and he will tell you what the 200,000,000 will tell you, if you have only time and patience to go and ask every man amongst them; there is no difference of opinion or belief in their doctrines. God, in His true Church, has wedded together two hundred millions of intelligences varying and dissenting on every other point, and He has made them united in faith. In their obedience, in like manner, Catholics are one. Ask any Catholic in the world—and you have asked them all—who is the head of the Church, and the answer will be, "The Pope of Rome." "Do you acknowledge him as the head of the bishops and people?" Yes; in every single point he is the highest of all. Even as the proud Egyptian pyramids, taking hold of the earth, covering acres of soil, sweeping aside and resisting the power and might of successive ages, yet still, tapering up to the summit, end in one single block of stone pointing to heaven; so the Catholic Church, spreading herself out and covering the whole world in such strength that neither time, nor the world, nor hell can destroy it, she yet tapers up toward God through the succession of the clergy, the clergy bearing their episcopacy, and the whole hierarchy of the Church terminating in one man who is the head of all, the commander whose voice all obey, because that man represents Peter, and Peter represents Jesus Christ, the Head of the Catholic Church. (Applause.)

The Church represents the sanctity of God. For two thousand years she has stood before the world, and every philosopher, every learned man, has looked upon her with a keen, searching, hostile eye. Every fault has been placed upon her, every sharp cunning conceivable has been flung at her. Yet she stands before them all, with the simple word upon her lips : "Tell me, O ye learned men, ye philosophers! at what time, in what day, in what hour, at what moment of my existence of two thousand years can you prove that I have sanctioned, encouraged, or even tolerated the slightest sin? Where is the child of mine that will be able to rise up in the valley of Josaphat and say, 'O mother! I believed in you and you told me I might tell a lie'?" "I never said it," the Church answers. "O mother! I believed in you, and you told me I might nourish a passing impure thought." The Church comes forth and says, "In the name of God, thou liest. Thy perdition is on thine own head." Not the slightest sin, or approach to sin, is tolerated in the intelligent and magnificent morality of the Catholic Church. She reflects the sanctity of God in the prayer that never dies from her virgin lips for the outpouring of those graces in the sacraments that, when partaken of, make holy, even as the angels of God, the greatest sinner on earth. If they submit to the Church's influences, she, like God, is not only holy in herself, but she is able to make them holy. She represents the eternity of God, for Christ our Lord founded her upon a rock. But is that rock Peter? Says the apostle, "The rock was Christ"; and the rock was Christ, the broad, eternal, God-like foundation of the Catholic Church ; and upon His divine bosom He planted the visible rock, who was Peter, saying, "Thou art Peter, and upon this rock I will build my Church." Peter was the rock set upon Christ, for, says St. Paul, "the Church is founded on the foundation of the apostles and the prophets, the great corner-stone himself being Christ Jesus our Lord." The Church cannot fail until Peter fails—until Peter fails in his successors. Peter cannot fail until Christ fails ; Christ is God and cannot fail ; therefore the Church of God shall live for ever, and the gates of hell and our enemies shall never prevail against her.

Kingdoms and empires may pass away; human greatness is but the dream of him who dreameth in the morning; man may come and man may go; but the Church stands for ever. Human weakness may reveal itself, as it does every day, in the old forms of detestable sin and crime. Society may groan under its own miseries and its murders, its impurities, its abortions, its dishonesties, and men may cry out in their despair, as they cry in the daily press: "When shall this end? When shall we have justice, purity, and honesty?" They do not recognize the fact that no blood, no impurity, no dishonesty, no sin can ever be tolerated by the Church of God, or approach the Catholic Church. And she alone is the saviour of society, because she alone, in her dogmas, can create what the world is crying out for in this our day. The world may divide itself, as it does, into a thousand schools of philosophy, a thousand schemes and systems of varying opinion or religion. Every religious teacher may come out with his own scheme, as you will find by reading the daily papers. You will read there a mumble-jumble of doctrines; that such a man teaches one thing, another man teaches the very opposite, and that Mr. So-and-so is considered a very pious sort of a religious man, for he condescends to acknowledge the existence of God and the divinity of Jesus Christ. There is no unity in the conflicting opinions of the world; and yet men are blind enough, wilfully blind enough, not to perceive the magnificent unity, second only to the essential unity of God, which guides the councils, animates the words, and personifies the obedience of the Catholic Church. Well, my friends, if you consider these things you will be obliged to conclude, even if you are not Catholics, that there must be something divine in the religion which captivates the intelligence of two hundred millions of men, and which makes that intelligence as one mind and as one man in its expression of religious belief. It touches with a sanctifying hand every form of sin, and by destroying sin changes the sinner into the child of God. Beginning with the Sacrament of Baptism, it goes on to the Sacrament of Penance, and from that to the Holy Communion, until it finally wipes away the very latest miseries and fears which will attach themselves to the simplest and holiest by the consoling and sanctifying Sacrament of Extreme Unction. There must be something divine in a Church that has been able to stand for two thousand years; that has never allowed any political or philosophical question to pass by without examining it and judging of it; that has never feared to take up any enquiry of science; ready to meet every enquirer, give him his answer, and prove it to him. This Catholic Church never dies; never knows how to die; never grows old; will never know the day of dissolution. And the Church alone, like unfallen man, will pass from its militant state to the triumphant, and will reign as the Church of God, for ever and ever, in heaven.

If such be the condition and attributes of the Catholic Church, if history proves that these are her attributes, it is natural, my friends, to expect something great, something far more than ordinary, something grand and heroic in the man whom Almighty God selects to make the head of that Church. Consider for a moment the two official attributes of this man; then we shall gather what we may expect from his personal attributes. Officially, the greatest attribute of the pope is infallibility as head of the Catholic Church. The pope may tell a thousand lies, but there is one thing that he cannot do: he cannot tolerate a lie or command the Catholic Church to believe a lie. Understand me well. This is a question not understood in our day. Some Protestants, especially, imagine that when we talk of Papal Infallibility we mean that the pope can do no wrong. The pope can do as much wrong as you or I. The pope goes to confession every week like every other priest. If he does not go there sorry for his sins, making up his mind to renounce them, and does not perform his penance, he may be lost like any other man.

But remember we are not talking of him now as an individual, as a person, a mere man, but as the head of the Catholic Church. As the supreme pastor, the supreme ruler of the Church, the first attribute that belongs to him is that he cannot command the Catholic Church to believe a lie; therefore he cannot tell a lie to the Church in his capacity, speaking *ex cathedrâ*—that is, from the throne of Peter as the head of the Church. And this stands to reason, my friends, for the Catholic Church is bound to accept the pope's words when he speaks as head of the Church; she is bound to bear allegiance to him and to take the law from his lips. There is no appeal from him when the Pope speaks the doctrine of the Catholic Church on such and such a point.

The Scripture speaks of that Church: "Wisdom, Divine Wisdom, hath built unto herself a house, and she carved out seven pillars of stone." What are these seven pillars? "That of old, a Temple of Divine Wisdom," says St. Bernard, "they are the virtues of *Faith, Hope, and Charity*, theologically, and the virtues of Temperance, Prudence, Justice, and Fortitude, morally." Upon these seven pillars the Church of God rests; the Church was founded in faith; the Church lives in hope and has divine grace and charity. The Church has prudence beyond the most prudent of men; justice that has never compromised itself by the slightest concession; fortitude that has been able to fill the world with martyrs; and a temperance that reveals itself in the highest form of holy asceticism, in those who are consecrated to the cloister. And as it is in the Church of God, so is it with the interior character of the glorious man who stands at the helm and guides the ship of the Church. Pius IX. is a man of faith. He has been ruined by showing his faith in his own people—in the faith of the heart of Italy, in the faith and integrity of the Italian people. That was human faith, and it was destroyed and crumbled away before him by the ingratitude of his own Roman people. But he had a higher faith; he leaned upon God with the most implicit faith. From the day of his coronation to this hour he has lived in faith; the Church has always rested on faith. I have seen him in the most of his difficulties; I have seen him when Rome was threatened; when the bishops, prelates, and cardinals came to him, saying, with pallid lips: "Holy Father, you must fly; your life is in danger." And then unmoved, with a smile of supreme confidence in his voice, I have heard the grand old pontiff say: "Where is your faith? Remember the words of Christ: 'Have faith in God, and if you have that you can say, Move this mountain, and it will be moved.'" Never for an instant did his divine faith falter. (Applause.)

He remained firm and as immovable as the rock upon which the Church of God is founded, while the most learned men in Europe rose up and departed from him and from the Church, and he, like the Divine, unerring Master, said: "Will you also leave me? If the whole world leave me, my faith shall never move." Firm as a rock, when England and her clergy approached him in a spirit of compromise, and only asked certain conditions, when they would yield and return to the communion of the Catholic Church, the answer of the pontiff was: "No conditions, no compact can I make that would compromise the deposit of the Church's faith. If you do not believe, I can never receive you into her bosom."

A man of hope! O my friends! how magnificently strong is the hope that sustained the old man in the extreme old age that crowned his poor, venerable head. In the midst of the afflictions that would have broken a strong heart, when the temporal crown fell from his brows, and the hands of Catholic men placed upon him a crown of thorns, he was still sustained with a mighty hope within him.

Well did he say with the apostles: "We are saved by hope." Still did he remain at his post, cheering the disconsolate, animating the faltering, sending out his word from year to year to the earth, proclaiming: "I am here a prisoner amongst my people; but I know what I hope for,

and the victory and the triumph shall be mine at last."
(Applause.)

A man of love! Where was there ever a man with charity such as his? O my friends! if you had only beheld him, as I have often seen him, descending from his carriage in some by-way of Rome, going in there amongst the poor people; the women coming out from their houses, bringing their children to him to receive his blessing; distributing his liberal alms, himself so poor—their gratitude finding vent in a stream of tears, as they bowed to receive his graceful benediction. He passed amongst them as the very personification of Him who walked amidst the pathways of the poor in the fields of Judea and of Galilee. A man of love! As well have I often watched him in some quiet nook of the church, surrounded by the nobles and by the brilliant dignitaries of the Church—himself the idol of the Romans. The moment he came before the presence of the Blessed Sacrament, amidst the smoke of incense the old man prostrated himself, and there you almost saw with the eyes of the body the heart of that old man going out from him on the wings of love. You see him enter the tabernacle and hold communion—the communion of charity—with Jesus Christ; you see the tears after a time stream from his eyes, and you see the aged head bowed down, scarcely able to conceal from the vulgar gaze the enraptured expression of love that overspread his countenance.

This is the man which the Church of God, in the midst of her afflictions and joys, upholds and obeys in this our day. Prudence is his. If ever there was an exhibition of prudence in man, it was in the last action of Pius IX. before he was dethroned. Prudence means a virtue, my friends, that is capable of foreseeing what was to come. *Prudentia* is the Latin word for it. It means prevision of what is to come. We say that is prudence when a man makes a good investment in land. He buys a landed estate that is out of the way, because he foresees that in a few years it may be of immense value. It becomes built upon, and streets opened to it. Then people say, "What a prudent man he was"! and men say more than this: "What a foreseeing man he was!"

Prudence means foresight. Very few men have this virtue in its highest degree. There is a prudence that keeps a man from the ordinary, little battling worries of life; but the prudence that is the highest of all, that rises up on the wings of intelligence, soaring like the eagle beyond and over the ordinary interests of mankind, is able to take a glance of the things going on and prepare for them. This magnificent prudence is the inheritance of the popes. The learned, perhaps the most learned man on the earth— Dr. Newman—speaking of the popes and their action on society, says, "Their leading virtue was prudence." It was their prevision that met and disarmed the mighty barbaric hordes that broke up the Roman Empire. It was their prevision that enabled the state to defend itself against the Turks and saved Christendom from the degrading yoke of the Mohammedan religion. It was by their prudence that they were enabled to save the rock of Catholicity from out the confusion of the French Revolution; but never in the history of the pontiffs of the Church of God is there an act of such supreme prevision as the act of the last Council of Rome, when the whole Church of God assembled, and, represented by its eight hundred bishops, declared as a dogma of the Catholic faith that the Pope possessed personal infallibility as the head of the Church.

Let me prove this. When that definition was pronounced, and after the old, original acknowledged faith of the Catholics was put in the form of a dogma—an article of faith—how few thought of what has come to pass since the day when that definition was defined; when your bishops and all the bishops of the world were assembled. I was there at the time. I witnessed everything. I never thought that the Pope was so near the loss of his temporal dominions. No bishop or cardinal thought it; we could not understand the whole thing; we could not understand why that council was called and pressed on so by the Pope himself; we did not foresee that a Bismarck would arise, like another Antichrist, to persecute the Church of God; we did not foresee the downfall of France and the triumphant revolution of Italy, with the deeper ruin of the temporal power to the Pope and the possible expulsion of the person of his successor from Rome. These things no man foresaw except one. No man saw what was coming; but a prudence more than human prepared the Church for the emergency.

For two thousand years the pope has been in Rome. Surrounded by the prestige of his temporal power, he represented, as Pontiff of Rome, palpably and visibly, the Church of God. He was recognized by the whole Church. It was easy to know him, easy to find him. He was like a burning light in a candlestick, lighting up everything. The kings of Europe recognized him; but they take him out of Rome and send him an exile amongst men—send him a stricken wanderer on the earth, without the prestige of his temporal power, perhaps hunted by those diabolical persecutors, those crowned tyrants, those kings' prime ministers who warred against him that ruin and confusion might come to the Church. The bishops might be tempted to rebel. The Church is full of examples of bishops who have from time to time rebelled against the pope. Now, when the storm was coming, the spiritual authority of the pope was put in form and recognized directly as from God.

This infallible authority from God is required to be the very central bond of the Church in the days of her weakness that have come upon her. Almighty God inspired this man with the thought that the moment had come for the Church to commit herself to set that sign upon her Pontiff which, wherever he be, in exile or in misery, no other man can tear it away—the sign of his personal infallibility dogmatically recognized in the head of the Catholic Church. (Applause.)

He now can enforce his decrees—they are the *Curia Romana*. He cannot now, as in the middle ages, call a secular army to enforce his decrees. He cannot now lean on the loyalty of king or kaiser; they have all turned against him. All are his enemies; yet the moment when every human aid, when every human faculty, every human prestige was withdrawn from him, the heavens were opened and the dogma of Infallibility was let down upon his head from the bosom of Jesus Christ, the God of Truth. It shines out upon the uncrowned head of the Church's monarch. Pius IX., the grandest Pope that ever lived, received the recognition of the Holy Church of God as dogmatically infallible. (Applause.)

Now he may go from Rome to-morrow and he may hide himself in any corner of the earth ; now he may go pursued by the bloodhounds of tyranny and revolution ; but now at least we know that when he speaks to the Church no prince, no nation, no bishop can for an instant cavil at his decision without inheriting the wrath of God and the curse of heresy and separation from the Catholic Church.

His justice ! One of the greatest charges that history makes against some of the popes of the middle ages was that they had great power and great wealth, and were fond of their relatives, as every man is. (Laughter.) They allowed the ties of nature to become so strong that they enriched some of their relatives. It was called nepotism. Injustice is charged, and the Church is looked down upon ; and some people imagine that the Pope is impeccable—the Pope cannot make a mistake.

Pius IX. may take some priest, and make a bishop of him, who is, perhaps, unworthy; but the Church would not approve of it. Nor is he infallible in his actions, but only when he teaches the Church the word of God.

Mark the grand character, the rigid, exact justice of this aged man, which I will describe to you. He was made Pope six-and-twenty years ago. He had several brothers with large families, and their friends came to them felicitating and congratulating them, and said to them : " Now that your uncle is made Pope, of course you will get an estate." You know this business of nepotism came up again amongst them. Well, the nephews and cousins thought they had nothing to do but go to Rome and see if the uncle would do anything for them. The very first thing that Pius IX. did as soon as he was made Pope was to make a law that no relatives of his were to enter the gates of Rome. He stands before his enemies to-day, and not one of them has accused him of nepotism and injustice.

His temperance. He don't know the meaning of what you call temperance, that keeps you from getting drunk. Pius IX. has been six-and-twenty years Pope. For the six-and-twenty years he has eaten and drunk so moderately that his personal expenses for eating, drinking, and clothing cost but one hundred and twenty pounds sterling a year—that is, six hundred dollars a year to keep him in food, drink, clothing, and personal expenses. The Queen of England has a thousand pounds a year for every pound Pius had when Pope of Rome, and, whether she spends it or not, she takes it all. (Laughter.)

His fortitude. We have already seen by the "*Non possumus*" that he is the strongest, bravest, most heroic man that ever sat peaceably upon the throne of Peter, and that he fills his office with a fortitude which no power on earth nor hell could overcome. He is dear to the Catholic world—to the Irish world. To the Catholic world he is especially dear, inasmuch as a grace was given to him that was preserved for him for two thousand years—the grace that was never vouchsafed to any other pope—the grace which, like every grace which is divine, makes him singular among all the other pontiffs.

A grace that was preserved for him in the mind and councils of God from all eternity—namely, that the woman whom the evangelist saw crowned in heaven with a crown of twelve stars, that the woman whom Almighty God spoke of as the crowned woman who was to crush the serpent's head, that the woman who was crowned with the blood of her Divine Son that fell upon her head from the bleeding hands which were stretched out over her on Calvary, should receive from the hands of Pius IX., in his dogmatic definition, the last crown that the Church of God could put upon her head in the proclamation of the Immaculate Conception of the Blessed Virgin Mary.

Twelve hundred years ago a heretic denied that Mary was the Mother of God. The moment that this word passed the lips of Nestorius the whole Catholic world was moved as one. Every man and every woman felt it as a personal insult. They called for a council, and a council was held in the city of Ephesus. The bishops came from all parts of the world ; the people came from all the nations, and the great city was filled with an excited, alarmed, and indignant throng, waiting by thousands outside the council chamber. In the moment that they declared by a dogmatic decree the doctrine that the Virgin Mary was the Mother of God, such was the impatience of the mob that a bishop came out to tell them: "It is decreed, and it is Catholic faith, that the Virgin Mary is the Mother of God." The people received it with a shout and clamor ; the Catholic heart expanded ; like an electric flash it went from land to land, and the churches proclaimed Mary's divine maternity, and the whole Catholic Church was filled with joy. Why ? Because one of the marks of the true Catholic Church is love and veneration —quick, ardent, personal love for the Blessed Virgin Mary. Most singular is it. The Gospel says that Mary, inspired by God, said : "Henceforth all generations shall call me blessed." Remember that is in the Gospel, that all believe. Every Christian that believes the Gospel believes that all generations should call Mary blessed. Yet, strange to say, outside the Catholic Church she has not received any title. She is called the Virgin, any name you like. And sometimes we are called blasphemers ; I will not say by foolish men or by irreverent men, but the drift of the Gospel shows that the Catholic Church must be the Church of the Gospel, for the Catholic Church alone calls Mary "blessed." My friends, the spirit that was awakened by Nestorius one thousand two hundred years ago broke out again in this century, and the whole Catholic world with one voice cried out in acclamation with the word of Pius IX. that Mary had never sinned. By divine preventing grace and the anticipated application of the merits and the blood of her Divine Son she was preserved from sin, and even Adam himself did not sin in Mary. You will ask me, Why was this defined? Ah! behold the importance and wisdom of the Pontiff.

In this age of ours there is a spirit of insubordination to authority, to prevent which came this dogma of infallibility. Outside of us—the Catholic Church—the world is drifting very rapidly to the denial of the divinity of Jesus Christ. Protestantism to-day, in every land, is assuming the form which is called "Unitarian"; and it is the boast of the Unitarians that they are disturbing all the views, all that is intellectual, and all that is spiritual in Protestantism. Every Protestant writer nowadays is speculating about the divinity of Christ. Read the lectures and sermons in the New York papers and you will see freely discussed the divinity of Jesus Christ. It is an open question, and some believe that time will change the divinity of Jesus Christ—the very corner-stone on which the Christian religion is founded. I may call myself a Christian; so may the Sultan of Turkey; so may the Emperor of China call himself a Christian—as good and just as much a Christian as any other. The Protestant who denies the divinity of Jesus Christ is no more entitled to call himself a Christian than the Emperor of China, who is a pagan. Now, the Church surrounded that mystery of the Incarnation with every form of dogmatic defence that could be devised, and threw a rampart of eternal truth about Him who is the Divine Author of all truth. One thing alone remained. One of the arguments used to deny the divinity, and shake the faith of those who believed in the divinity, of the Lord Jesus Christ was that He was the Son of Mary. Men said: "How can you say He is God? He is the Son of Mary. Mary was the daughter of Adam. Adam was a sinner. Consequently how could God be born of a sinner?" There was the argument. How was the Church of God to meet it? She had to assert dogmatically that Mary was the Mother of God, to cement her infallible love and express that deep burning faith, that divine instinct in the mind of God about Mary. Pius came forth at the head of the episcopacy and proclaimed to the world: "Let no man say that Jesus Christ is not God because Mary was His Mother. I declare, in the name of God and of our Church, that that woman, though a child of earth, had never sinned. Even in her conception she was freed from sin in order to be the Mother of God." And thus did the Church place the last crowning stone of that edifice of defence of the divinity of our Lord by proclaiming the Immaculate Conception of Mary.

Catholics are thus assured that the most exalted person on earth in spirituals is the Pope of Rome.

God governs the Church through the pope, therefore there is no appeal from the Church, and it has been the recognized doctrine of the Catholic Church, from the day she was founded to this hour, that there is no appeal from the pope; therefore he is the ultimate tribunal of the body that is passing sentence by the grace of Almighty God, to all men, of the truth for ever. Mark this: the Catholic Church has always taught of necessity that she cannot teach a lie; the Catholic Church has always taught she is bound to obey the word of her head, her pontiff; therefore the pontiff, when he is teaching that Church, cannot teach her a lie; for if he did the Catholic Church would be bound to accept the lie and bound to obey. She cannot accept a lie, for Christ, her Lord, has said, "I am God, and the gates of hell shall never prevail against her"; therefore, though a traitor be the head of the Church, he cannot teach the Church of God or command her to believe a lie.

Every state, my friends, every nation, has its ultimate tribunal from which there is no appeal. For instance, if you go to law with a man in England or in Ireland, and the judges decide against you, you can appeal to a higher court; and if a higher court give it against you, you can appeal to the House of Lords; and if the House of Lords are against you, you are bound to submit—there is no other appeal. And so here in the United States. But if the Almighty God establishes upon earth an arbiter that never could act unjustly, then you would be obliged to say, "The decision must be just, I have no appeal from it." Now, God says that the Catholic Church can never believe a lie or teach a lie, and the Catholic Church is bound by the decision of the pope, and there is no appeal from it, and, therefore, she believes she cannot tell a lie. This is the first attribute of the pope. Now, consider this, my friends: infallibility, impossibility of teaching a lie, impossibility of making a mistake in the matter of doctrine, is the grandest prerogative of the pope in the Universal Church, and thus it is, you see, why it happens that this brings him so near to the Almighty God that, before him, as he stands there—as the head of the Church—all the rest of mankind dwindle into nothing. He stands there and he speaks; he says to the Church: "Hear me, O Church of Jesus Christ, hear me!" and the whole of the Church says: "I will hear what my ruler speaks to me." The Infallible Church bows down before him and says: "Speak thou, for the Church, thy servant, hears." He speaks, and the moment he opens his lips with dogmatic utterance I no longer see in him a man, but I see reflected the infallible light of God, and hear the word of Jesus Christ on his lips, in the word of which it is written: "Heaven and earth shall pass away, but my words shall never pass away." It is really awful to consider a man invested with so much of the attributes of God.

The second great official attribute of the pope is supreme authority over cardinals, archbishops, bishops, priests, laymen, and every other man that professes the Catholic doctrines.

The pope exercises unlimited authority in religious matters—remember, I say in religious matters—in spiritual matters we are all bound to obey him, the highest dignitary of the Church. The moment a man contradicts a word of the pope, or rebels against it, be he bishop or priest, not of course in the essence of his ordination, but in the legitimacy of its exercise, he is an absolute heretic, and goes out from the Church. He may be the most learned man in the world, the greatest professor, a man of the greatest popularity, wielding a whole people, and shaping their destinies; at that moment there is an end to him. Not a man amongst us—the humblest Catholic in the world—will touch him or have any more to say to him.

Now, in order to have these official attributes, you can easily imagine that the Almighty God, who guides that election of the head of the Church, will select a great man, a man whose sanctity of life, whose purity of heart, whose devotion to the altar and the Church will in some degree fit him for that magnificent dignity. And, in truth, the proof of this lies in the fact that although we have had a succession of hundreds of popes, going through the ages of history side by side with their contemporaries, though many of them had their faults, and though many of them committed sins, yet taken in the whole they are as far beyond the kings and emperors in sanctity and purity of life, in education and grandeur of character, as they, the kings, were beyond other men in imperial power. In that long roll of saints and martyrs I claim that since the day Peter received the keys from Christ never have those keys been held by a nobler character, by a grander man than the aged Pius IX. (Great applause.)

For proof of this only look over the pontificate with me in some of the salient points. You know, my friends, that it is now six-and-twenty years since Pius IX. was elected to be the Pope and head of the Catholic Church. He is the only man of all those that succeeded St. Peter who has outlived the years of Peter upon the pontifical throne of Rome. It was considered a kind of proverb in the Church that no pope should live as many years in this Papacy as St. Peter, who lived twenty-five years. Pius IX. was the first pope who has outlived the years of

Peter. I was in Rome as a youth in the first year of the pontificate of this man; I am speaking to you this evening, not of things I have read in books, or that I have heard from other men. I am speaking of a country in which I have lived the best years of my life, of Italy, and the city of Rome. I am speaking of the things I have seen and judged of with my own eyes and with my own mind. I saw in 1847 in Rome a young man whose hair was black as the raven's wing; his eye was bright with the commingled beauty of the pure soul that shone through it, in the manly vigor of his youth, erect in form—for this man was educated in his youth for a soldier—stately, kingly—more than kingly even in his material appearance; he seemed a man every inch fit to be a ruler of his fellow-men, with a conformation and a form indeed where the very God had seemed to set the seal and give the world assurance of a man. And in that day, when my young eye, fresh from the green isle of Erin, full of Irish faith, of Irish love, as I looked with a timid glance on the Vicar of Christ in that day, he was surrounded by the plaudits of the Roman Italian people. The whole world echoed in praises of Pius IX. The king of Italy, the archdukes of Italy, the kings of the various nations of Europe were loud in their praises of the new Pope. Even in America the echoes of his praise were caught up—(applause)—and proclaimed by the most eloquent tongue of America's last though not least of statesmen—by the tongue of him over whose grave the nation is weeping to-day. (Renewed applause.) Why did they praise him? Ah! my friends, they praised him for the act by which he began his pontificate, which showed the genius and character of this noble mind.

When he came to the throne there had been trouble for years in Italy, and he found many of the Italian people, his own subjects, languishing in prison for their rebellion or attempts at revolution, and for their unquiet dispositions. He found that many of them were in exile, some living in Paris, some in London, and some here in America. What was the first act of the new Pontiff? The moment the tiara was on his head and the sceptre of his apostolic reign was in his hand, the moment he spoke as a monarch the first words were: "Open these gates and let them out. Come back, you exiles in every foreign land. Come back to your own blue sky and sunny soil. Come back to the bosom of Italy. I am not so much your king as your father. I will trust myself to the love, to the gratitude, and to the affection of the people." (Applause.) This act I witnessed. I saw the exiles return and bathe the hand of their liberator with their grateful tears. I saw the eyes of the little children whose fathers came back to them from out the dungeons and the prisons, rejoicing under the smile of the man whose hand had unbarred those prison-gates.

The whole world rejoiced, but Pius IX. was destined to know the vanity and the folly of human popularity. Oh! thrice foolish is the man who would build a house, or his life, or his soul, on such frail, sandy foundations as the applause and plaudits of men. Thrice befooled is he that grasps for such glory, for God will permit him, even in this world, to outlive the breath of his passing fame. And unless he has built his hopes, his reputation, his character, his soul, on some more solid and unshaken foundation, then all will crumble to ruin, and the aged man will live to weep over the words of praise that resounded in his ear in thunder-tones from the plaudits of men. That word is like the morning summer wind, that moves the foliage of the acacia-tree, then passes away to salute some other hillside and refresh some other field.

Pius knew it. I saw him silent and unmoved. He saw and recognized it, even as my young eye did the grandeur of that character, because of the depth of his humility, for men were disposed to raise him higher and higher in popular estimation, and cried out: "He was the saviour of men! There never was such a pontiff on that throne." I saw, as the shouts of their applause grew louder, that the object of that applause went down deeper, visibly deeper, in the depths of his own personal nothingness and humility, humbling himself before God; then was I reminded, looking upon him, of the word of the royal prophet of Israel. "I swear," he said, "that the more the Lord, my God, shall lift me up before His people the more will I humble myself, and will cast myself down before Him." That humility came in order to preserve him, for if the man had built on the foundations of his splendid character and the passing praise of the hour, he would have crumbled to ruin, and his heart would have broken under the reverses that God sent to him. In a few years the same people that cried his name with acclamation on that occasion turned against him, and demanded entrance with their cannons at his palace-gate, that he should meet a revolutionary principle, inconsistent with his position and inconsistent with their own salvation and happiness, and the ungrateful children whom the Holy Father had brought forth from their prison-houses, whom he had recalled from the land of their exile, made use of the liberty he gave them to drive him into exile.

Then came the second great trial in his life. A few years ago a Catholic servant-girl in a Jewish family, in Bologna, took a little child, newly born, and baptized him secretly, without telling the parents. Now, my friends, you must know that the Catholic Church does not allow this. The Catholic Church teaches two things: first of all, it teaches as to divine faith that by baptism the child thus baptized becomes the brother or sister of Jesus Christ, incorporated in him by divine grace, appropriated to God, is a child of God. That little child that was born was the child of Adam, the child of sin. "We are all born children of wrath," says St. Paul. It is an article of Catholic faith. The water of baptism touches the child's head, and the affiliation passes away, and that little child becomes a child of God. The Catholic Church teaches the moment that child is baptized it becomes a member of the Church of God; consequently He grasps that little one and asserts His claim upon it.

The Catholic Church teaches, on the other hand, that

the parents have a right over the child, and if the parents are infidels or Jews, and if they refuse to have their child baptized, the Church does not coerce ; the Church respects the parents' right, and says, "Although I come into this world to spread the kingdom of God, still, if the father and mother refuse it for their child, I must respect their rights." That is the Catholic doctrine. Therefore the Church says, "If any one baptizes the child of a Jew or an infidel without the parents' consent, that person is guilty of a grievous sin" ; nay, more, the Church threatens such a person with her censure of excommunication.

The servant-girl in question committed a grievous sin, and fell under the censure of the Catholic Church, but the Catholic Church had to acknowledge the fact that the child was baptized. What followed from this? It followed that the Catholic Church was obliged to ask the parents of the child to bring it up a Christian, because he was baptized a Christian. The parents refused, and Pius IX. was the temporal sovereign, and these Jews were his subjects ; and also as the head of the Church Pius IX. was obliged, by the doctrines of the Catholic Church and by her discipline, to secure to that child a Christian education until he was seven years old, and could decide for himself whether he would continue to be a Christian or go back to the religion of his parents. The parents refused, and Pius IX. was obliged, of necessity, to place the child under the care of a Christian teacher until the hour arrived to tell him, "You were baptized a Christian secretly. The person who did it interfered with your parents' right for a time, but does not interfere with their rights for the time to come. Will you be a Christian?"

The child said, "I wish to be a Christian and a priest" ; and a priest he is to-day ; I knew him in Rome. (Applause.) The Jewish father and mother appealed to the different nations in Europe, and England among them sent word to Pius that that child should be brought up a Jew. He said, "I cannot bring up the child a Jew. The child is a Christian ; how can a Christian become a Jew?"

"Then give back the child," they said, "to his parents." "I cannot do it," he answered; "they will bring him up a Jew. But when that child comes to the hour of reason he may go back to them, if he likes; they may see him, and love him, and nourish him. I will leave him with them, provided they give him his choice, and let him be a Christian, if the grace of baptism educate him in that direction." They would not do it; they said, "We want to make him a Jew"—a personal enemy of God, in whom he was baptized. France and England threatened to send their fleets to bombard our cities—"We will drive you out of Rome." The old Father says, "You may do it; I cannot help that. You may do more than that—you may pluck this heart out of my body, cut off this head, shed every drop of blood in my veins, but there is one thing you cannot do, and I cannot do, and that is, betray Jesus Christ by giving up that child. *Non possumus*," he answered, "I cannot do it." He did not say, "I do not wish to do it. I must not do it." He says, "I cannot do it." I assert that the *Non possumus* of Pius IX. are the grandest words that ever came from the lips of man.

Those who were not Catholics did not understand the nature of baptism. By baptism we become one with Christ; by baptism we become members of the Church of Christ. All those non-Catholics did not understand it. He said to them, "You make the case your own"; and if there are any here who are not Catholics let them just realize the doctrine of baptism, and they will see at once that the Pope could not do anything else, and that *Non possumus* resounding from the lips of Pius IX. are the grandest words that can be engraven on his tomb. "Here lies a man whom the world in its wisdom endeavored to coerce into sacrificing the interests of Jesus Christ and His Church, and here lies a man who answered: NON POSSUMUS—I cannot do it."

I believe, my friends, that the case of that child was the beginning of the troubles that I have spoken of to-day: the loss of the temporal dominions of the Pope and a bloody revolution. There is a society in Europe which has permeated through all ranks, in all the nations, and has found its way into every grade of society—in fact, has honeycombed and burrowed completely the very foundations of society—everywhere except in glorious Catholic Ireland, and that society is called the Society of Freemasons. A great many worthy men are entrapped into that society, because they do not know its real meaning. But one of the fundamental principles of European Masonry is war against the throne and war against the altar of God. Against the throne that war was waged in the many revolutions that have marked the end of the last century and the middle of this one. The war against the altar has been going on in every nation of Europe, furious, persistent, terrible, and uncompromising—war since the days that Voltaire wrote "that the last of the kings should be strangled with the last of the priests."

Pius IX. represented the throne as temporal ruler of Rome and represented the altar as head of the Catholic Church, and the consequence is that in the last three-and-twenty years the combined, united efforts of this society of Masonry have been concentrated upon the one power of Pius IX., the representative of Jesus Christ. Against him even a Scribe and Pharisee forgot their hatreds and their differences, that they might combine against him. Against him, even as Pilate and Herod made up their private little differences and became friends in order that they might combine against the Lord Jesus Christ to put Him to death, so every other interest of Masonry was considered secondary, and the power of every element of this wide-spread society was all concentrated in destroying the power, and, if possible, in shedding the blood, of the Sovereign Pontiff. For twenty-three years he has stood serenely before them ; for twenty-three years he has met all their scoffing. They succeeded in getting up an unjust war against him ; they succeeded in shedding the blood of the gallant, true-hearted, and the brave men that, shoulder to shoulder, stood round the old man's throne, though they were but one to a thousand. Yet still they fought like men, and, blessed be God! Ireland's arm and the most faithful of her sons were around him. (Applause.) They succeeded in robbing and in plundering the defenceless man of the last square rood of his inheritance, and endeavored to bring down his white hairs in sorrow, anguish, and despair to the grave.

Worst of all, against him to-day—a sad prisoner in the abandoned hall of the Vatican—they are making malicious charges—ay, false as hell. They published in Italy, and reproduced in other lands, their books and other pamphlets—against what, do you think? Against the moral character of Pius IX.—a man whose reputation is as stainless as the untrodden snow, a man whose life has been before the world from his earliest youth to his extreme old age—the man who has lived in the face of the whole world, the man against whom his bitterest enemy cannot breathe the word of slander. This is the man whose character they are trying to destroy, after they have destroyed his temporal power. But what wonder? When the Son of God was nailed to the cross was He not there expressly charged as being a seducer of the people and a malefactor and blasphemer against God? Surely the servant cannot expect better treatment than the Master. And yet, my friends, if we go a little deeper, passing from these external agencies that act upon him, passing from his exterior character as the head of the Church—what a magnificent man he is! As I once heard an old woman in Ireland say, and she expressed the very mind of the Church: "Father, dear, I always believed in the Pope, but I never loved him so dearly as I do now, because he has declared that the Mother of God was conceived without sin." This is the mind of the Church; for the great heart of the Catholic Spouse of Jesus Christ enlarges itself in love to him whom God gave the grace and the fair privilege of declaring Mary's immaculate conception. Upon that love, almost miraculously singular, Pius IX. has sustained himself up to this day, and will sustain himself until his loving heart has passed from us to an honored sepulchre.

I love him not only as a Catholic, because he has proclaimed the immaculate conception of Mary, my Mother; I love him not only as a priest, because by his latest defence of the dogmatic decision of the Church of God he has secured to me for ever and for ever the lights that never can pale, for the guiding voice that no man can contradict, for the security and certainty of our faith ; but I love him as an Irishman, because, in the midst of his sorrows and of his troubles, he had time to think of the fidelity and the love of the Irish people for their holy religion ; and he was the first pontiff that ever rewarded an Irishman in a grand and royal manner. (Applause.)

Other popes have been accused of caring little about Ireland. One of them has been accused of caring so little about Ireland as to throw it into the hands of Henry II. of England, saying to him, "Take it, if you like it." But, thanks be to God! I have lived to see that proved to be a lie. (Applause.) Mr. Froude, whatever he takes home from America, will take home one thing with him, and that is a document from an Irish bishop—the Bishop of Ossory—that I think he will not be able to get over. And that document proves to demonstration that no Pope of Rome ever gave Ireland to England. (Renewed applause.) That the domination that has been carried out through blood and injustice was begun in perjury and in lying has now become a matter of history. And I thank God for it, because it has wiped out of the mind of many an Irishman the uncomfortable feeling that a pope thought so little of our native land. Thanks be to God, that day never dawned, and never will. (Applause.)

Pius IX. gave to the Irish Church her first cardinal— that is to say, he gave to the Irish a voice in all councils of the Church. When the question comes to selecting a pope as the head of the Catholic Church—when the question comes of bringing out three or four men, without any prior selection, asking the Holy Spirit of God, "Is this the anointed that is before Thee, O Spirit of Truth?" that is the highest council that can be upon this earth, and for fifteen hundred years every nation has been asked to join in that important question. Yet Ireland, faithful, suffering, never had been, until Pius IX. said to an Irishman, "Take thy place, O child of a martyred race ! among the princes of the Church of God, and thou shalt be amongst those that shall ask the question of the Holy Spirit, Who shall guide this Church?" And if the answer should ever come, ".The son of Erin !" then the son of Erin has the right to wear the Roman tiara. (Applause.)

And in making the selection he chose a man whom I have the honor and the privilege of knowing intimately and well. I have lived under his jurisdiction for many a year. I have studied his spirit, and I will say this—I say it from the conviction of my heart—that in raising Paul Cullen, the archbishop, to the dignity and the grandeur of a cardinalship Pius IX. laid his hand upon the head of as true and as loving a son of Ireland as ever lived. (Prolonged applause.) Some deny this among us, a privilege that we claim to ourselves; but I do say this again—that if love for one's native land ever burned pure and bright in the heart of man it burns in the heart of Cardinal Cullen. (Renewed and prolonged applause.)

He selected a man whom he knew would do honor to the land of his birth, and would fitly represent amongst the cardinals of Rome and the representative princes of the Church the land which once bore the title of the "island of scholars as well as of saints." I have studied the character of the eminent personage of whom I speak, and I have failed to decide in my own mind, from a minute, familiar examination of him—I have never been able to decide which was the greater, the vastness of his ecclesiastical knowledge or the humility of his pure heart and spirit.

Honors have been worthily showered upon him; he has borne them with a humility corresponding with the greatness to which God has lifted him up. In the last Council of Rome it was the honor and glory of Ireland that our cardinal stood forth acknowledged one of the greatest theologians, one of the first and wisest men, one of the deepest thinkers, and one of the coolest and best heads of the age. (Applause.)

For all this I thank Pope Pius IX. I honor the aged man who so worthily fills the highest throne of earth; I honor him more than if I saw him crowned with the thrice resplendent tiara of human praise, human glory, and human power. Oh! I honor him in his old age. For even as Peter was imprisoned in Rome, so Pius is imprisoned to-day in Rome, and the crown of empire has fallen from his head; but the crown of thorns is surmounted by the higher crown of spiritual dominion which God put on the head of Peter, and which no man shall ever pluck from the brows of Peter's successors. I hallow him. I go back with joy to the past, when the occasion was given to me of beholding him and receiving his benediction, when his fatherly smile was bestowed on the Irish friar. I hallow him in the hall of my memory. I have seen him in glory; I have seen him in sorrow; but I hallow him with a louder voice as I behold him in the light of that future which my faith reveals to me, coming forth from out his prison-house to ascend his throne once more crowned with the honor and glory of which the world cannot longer deprive him, coming forth the representative of Eternal Power as well as of Eternal Justice, to wield once more in undisputed sway the peaceful sceptre of God's designs in nations, and with an acknowledged royal hand to point out to all the people of the united world the path to freedom here and glory in the world to come. (Prolonged applause.)

Eulogy of the Late Cardinal Barnabo.

In this sermon, preached in the cathedral of Dublin, Father Burke has portrayed the very remarkable life of a wonderful and holy man. The lesson we may learn from his life is that, no matter what trials fall to our lot, if we really desire in our hearts to do so, we may "fight the good fight, and keep the faith."

"I have fought the good fight; I have finished my course; I have kept the faith, and I know there is reserved for me a crown of justice which my Lord will give me, for He is a just God."—St. Paul, II. Epistle to Timothy, iii. 7-8.

CONSIDER, dearly beloved, who he was who spoke these words. He was one of the highest of the apostles, though not the chief—the apostle familiarly styled the Apostle of the Gentiles. He carried the announcement of the Word of God amongst nations who never heard the name of God in the blindness of their idolatry; he converted idolaters to God, whom they confessed they knew not, and in every tongue proclaimed the cross of the risen Saviour. A remarkable man truly was this great apostle and teacher of the Gentiles. He was not the head of the Church; he was under the obedience and under the supremacy of Peter, the Great Pontiff, but to Peter he was bound by ties of sublime love and endearment. Although he was not the head of the Church, yet he speaks of himself as being burdened with the care of all the Church. And now, drawing nigh the close of life, he says: "I have fought the good fight; I have finished my course; I have kept the faith." Well might he in all humility boast that he had fought the good fight, for he had conquered all his adversaries during that long-continued struggle from the day when his eyes first opened to behold the vision of his Lord, and which only ended when he yielded up his life. His life was one continued trial of perils, which he himself tells us. He was in perils on sea and in perils on land from open enemies and from false brethren. Yet his brave heart never knew one moment's fear of duty.

"I have finished my course," he said, and assuredly a noble course was that drawing to a close. The nations of the Gentiles had heard his voice. He sent his disciples into far-distant lands, and every one who heard him bowed down to the name and glory of Jesus Christ. "I have kept the faith," well might he exclaim. Not only have I kept it but I have spread it abroad. The faith not only remained to him in all its integrity, strength, and purity, but remained in him a light burning to the illumination of the Gentiles, that went forth from him unto peoples who from the first days of their history had walked in darkness and the shadow of death, called to the admirable light of God. Consequently he looked forward to his crown with all the confidence of Christian hope when he said: "I know there is reserved for me a crown of justice which my Lord will give me on that day, for He is a just Judge"—one who will not forget the labors of His faithful servant, who will repay fidelity with generosity, who will reward those who will give their mind, heart, life, and strength to His service—to the service of the Church, His great messenger upon earth. The words of the apostle strongly and forcibly apply to the great prince of the Church who has been taken away in the hour of her deepest sorrow and of her direst necessity—a man who, though not head of the Church, yet, like the apostle, was burdened—the man who, after the Supreme Pontiff, filled the highest and the great position in the Christian world—who, after the Supreme Pontiff, was the guide, the father, and the protector of the holy Church, lifted up into the highest councils, not by any craving or prompting of ambition, but by the mere force and necessity of a holy life, a great mind, and a devotedness such as the Catholic

Church alone can create in every rank of her hierarchy, from the most exalted to the humblest.

"I have fought the good fight," says the apostle. Now, blessed are they who, called by the Almighty God to serve Him in His sanctuary, find no let or hindrance to their entering into the holy place of God, whose youthful steps are surrounded by the blessing of sweetness, who live in tranquil times, and in the midst of undisturbed traditions of holiness; but more blessed is the man who, gifted by divine wisdom and divine fortitude, in the days of his early youth is able to fight his way into the sanctuary of God, so that, when he enters as a young Levite, it is not merely in the promise and the hope of what is to come, but a victor crowned, and with the maturity of the cross already on him. Such was the entry into the sanctuary of God of this great priest for whom the holy Catholic Church is putting up its prayers in sorrow and tears to-day.

A traveller landing from a strange country on the shores of the Adriatic, wending his way to the Eternal City, descends the slopes of the Apennines into one of the loveliest valleys that bloom on earth—the Vale of Umbria—enriched by all the beauty of nature, and with everything that gladdens and strengthens the heart of man, and rich also in the traditions of the greatest artist and the greatest saint of the Church of God—St. Francis of Assisium. Its olive groves are familiar with his prayers, its city with his miracles and holiness, and there in this city—the ancient city of Foligno—Alexander Barnabo was born of noble Italian parents. Reared up during the earliest days of his childhood in all the traditions of Catholic faith and in all the traditions of sanctity, he seemed from the beginning a child of benediction and promise. At this time a mighty revolution raised its head—a mighty despotism had raised its head, overshadowing all Europe—a revolution the most terrible that the earth ever witnessed. And a dictator arose—a mighty universal conqueror, who crushed not only all the nations, but laid impious hands within the sanctuary on the sacred person of the vicar of Jesus Christ. These were days when it was not easy for the youth and Christianity of France and Italy to enter the sanctuary, and the more distinguished and the more noble the greater the difficulty. For, besides the ordinary obstacles—the world, always tempting for those of more distinguished birth; the young blood, with passions to be subdued and frozen into the icicle of Christian purity by the touch of divine grace; the devil, always in wait, and trying to turn aside every noble and generous soul from the service of the sanctuary—besides these there stood at that gate the mighty conqueror, the sword in his hand, dripping with the blood of nations, and seized on the youth of France and Italy, to immolate them before the altar of his ambition rather than to permit them serve the altar of the true God.

The young nobleman of Foligno was taken away in his thirteenth year from the mother who loved him, forced to go from Italy to France, compelled for the time being to devote himself to study preparatory to a military life, whilst his young ambition sought to be inflamed by promise of military glory. How sad to think that one whose ambition was like the Curé of Ars, who desired to be permitted to live within the sanctuary, to be an object even the least in the house of his God, should be denied that privilege! How sad to think of him dragged from the holy tabernacle of God! How sad to see the young Italian nobleman, whose thoughts from early childhood were directed to the sanctuary, taken away and carried under the mighty shadow of the great military dictator! Like the holy youth of Israel carried captive to Babylon, who forgot not the God of Juda, so he in the midst of his young companions, witnessing their worldliness and all the evil examples surrounding him, closed his ears to every evil maxim, and preserved for his God the immaculate purity of his heart and hands unstained by the defilement of sin and the shedding of blood. And when the inevitable peace that follows every war against the Church of God and leaves her triumphant came, and when inevitable ruin, sent by the Almighty, as He will send on every hand that dares to lift itself against the Church—when that ruin came like a thunderbolt of heaven, and he who in those days had done outrage and insult to Christ's Vicar was sent to wear away his lonely heart on the ocean rock, the young emancipated soul again, with all the natural ardor, with all the natural love which the God of divine grace had put into his soul, sought his home in the sanctuary and received the priesthood. To that priesthood he fought his way against every power; to that sanctuary and priesthood he brought a holy, pure heart, and hands unstained by sin; but he brought also a mind pre-eminently and singularly gifted by God, and a strong, manly energy which remained to the last days of his life, and which appeared in his every action, as if all the energy of his nature was concentrated in every act. Dearly beloved, it has been said of old, not only by her children but by her enemies, that never was there a power on this earth that is so quick to discover promise of ability, endowments of soul and mind, energy of her divine purpose—there never was a power that so loved to bring forth from its hidden recesses the true gold of genius and sanctity as the Roman Catholic Church. And it is little wonder, therefore, that the young priest was soon a marked man in the eyes of his ecclesiastical superiors, as one who could do, and was willing to do, great things for the Church of God. To this was he called, laboring for his Creator. He sustained the work to the last, laboring every day of his life. He died, and he fought the good fight in his youth; he had finished his glorious course; he had kept the faith, and had given the faith to the nations, and well might he have said: "There is reserved unto me, I know, a crown of justice which my Lord will give me, for He is a just God."

Now, consider to what this man was called in the Church of God. We have seen, dearly beloved, that from the beginning some of the apostles were devoted to a mere domestic line of apostolicity, preaching the faith among the children of Israel and the households of Juda; to their own kith and kin they proclaimed the Gospel, bringing forth, as examples, the miracles they had witnessed of our Divine Lord; whilst, on the other hand, the great apostle of the Gentiles went out to preach for all—out to the nations, to those who were in utter darkness, did he go forth to proclaim in every tongue the name of Jesus Christ. Down to our own time Rome, the centre, the head, the heart, the soul of Christendom and Christianity, on which Christ our Lord lavished His particular graces—Rome has had marked out from the beginning this two-fold character: a domestic legislation with its local tribunal for the nations who kept the faith; but for the nations who fell away from the faith, or who never had faith, but received it for the first time, or for nations newly discovered—these Gentiles, these nations in which the Church is struggling with primeval idolatry or acquired heresy—in those countries where the Church is not acknowledged at all, where she has to fight her way without the slightest recognition save the recognition of persecution—for these Rome has a special organization. It is called the Propaganda, or the great College for the Propagation of the Faith. Armed with pontifical power, this tribunal has to direct the action of the Church militant in her natural mission—the great contest with infidelity and heresy. This great tribunal, with pontifical power, was intended to push the work of conversion and send the light of the Gospel into every land throughout the earth. Its first mission begins where the Esquimaux, in the icy plains that surround the North Pole, hunt the wild fox and polar bear, and there it proclaims the name of God amongst men speaking a language no man understands save the Catholic missionary; it proclaims His holy name to southern latitudes where the shadow of man is not passed, where the vertical sun makes the land a desert, where the rivers are dried up; it proclaims God to the perpetual snows of Northern Russia, and to the country around the Euphrates, that sent from out the rising sun the Magi, in strange costume, speaking strange words, to look for Israel's God.

It proclaims God to the far away West, beyond the "Father of Waters," beyond the plains that stretch on the shore of the Pacific; further still, launching forth into that silent ocean, amongst islands yet inhabited by barbaric tribes, it proclaims His holy name, till you come to the new continent—Australia. All these vast territories lie under the eye of the Propaganda, and their inhabitants look to that great centre for the light of truth, for government, guidance, and for that animated energy that will send forth missionaries to speak in every language and in every clime the name of Jesus Christ. The man who is called to preside over this vast and mighty tribunal is, next to the supreme head of the Church, the most important personage in the world. He must be full of wisdom; he must have the most varied knowledge for the conditions of all these various countries; he must have an energy superhuman. He has four thousand bishops and as many dioceses under him. They come to him with all their difficulties, doubts, and dangers. He is the centre of that mighty organization by which the Church goes on, as said of her, destined until the end of time, conquering and to conquer. And to this position of unexampled labor and responsibility was the great and holy man for whom we have been praying to-day called, and, whether as secretary or cardinal of the Propaganda, he has been for a quarter of a century the very centre of that mighty system, and forth from his mind, from the seal of his heart, from the superhuman natural energy of his character, intensified by his devotion, came that strange and wonderful power which has made the Propaganda the real consolation of the Church for the last twenty years. A strange sight it was indeed, that it has been my privilege more than once to witness, to stand there in the cardinal's office chamber, where he receives the various missionaries, to see them— the grave Oriental bishop in his gorgeous robes, grand-looking and kingly, speaking of the sorrows and cares of

people who had never been heard of in this western world;
to see this man, who had journeyed for months from the
cradle-land of the world. Outside the door is a Jesuit,
waiting to be heard, who has come from the northern portion of North America, whose eyes have for many years
scarcely seen anything but snow and frozen rivers. Perhaps standing side by side with him is the bronzed and
embrowned foreign missionary from the Cape of Good
Hope, or the strange-looking Chinese missionary, who,
perhaps, only escaped from prison to recount his trials,
and on his return bear the pain and tortures of those who
were languishing in the cells.

In a word, a motley group representing the universal
apostolicity were there, and he, with a patience that nothing could overcome and with an energy that nothing
could break down, was answering all. For God had
prepared him by his exile and contact with the outer world
for this mighty work. He acquired the widest knowledge
and experience of the locality of each diocese and the
wants of each people. And so he labored from the morning watch even until night, working, toiling as a common
slave in the holy Church of God. For him there was no
rest. His work was holy. And what was his recreation ?
The moment that he could snatch an hour from the labors
of the day that hour was spent with Jesus Christ in the
Blessed Sacrament ; or he went with hurried steps to some
convent or place where a mission was going on to instruct
little children ; or he went into the confessional, to become
the victim of his zeal. Every one cared for his mind and
heart except one, and that one was his own great self.
Well might he say with his daily breath : "I have finished
my course!" What was that course ? The restoration of
the ancient hierarchy to England. Well might Augustine
and the ancient saints of England bow down from their
thrones in heaven to welcome him who restored in his
latter days that magnificent work which heresy shattered
to pieces. He restored the hierarchy to her.

His great mind went out to the ends of the earth. The

American Church, from being small, has become, under his fostering care, one of the grandest vineyards in the garden of Jesus Christ. His name was known and venerated by the solitary missionary out in the Western plains. His name was known to the savage tribes of Indians, receding further and further into the wilds of Texas before the advancing but, I regret to say, demoralizing civilization of the present day. The sad announcement of his death was heard with grief on the banks of the silent rivers by Christians to whom the guidance and government of the great Barnabo was love and consolation. He established the hierarchy in Australia, far away in the antipodes, and in the ends of the earth his name was known. "I have kept the faith," well might he say with his dying lips. He was the centre of the faith at that sacred place, Rome— Rome, the Jerusalem of the new land ; Rome, sanctified above all other places on the earth ; Rome, to us all that Jerusalem was to him of old who said : "If I forget thee, O Jerusalem! let my right hand be forgotten." His death was a calamity to the present sad situation of the Church. He was gifted with a disposition which no adversity could sour, which no persecution or difficulty could cast down. There was in his heart a fund of manly courage united with the highest form of resignation to God's will which made him trebly dear to the great Pontiff and all the prefects of the Propaganda, who regarded him with the tenderest and most lasting friendship.

Oh! think of it: during the last two years of his life his immense labors night and day had reduced him to utter blindness. Yet when the sight was gone the eternal light of faith illuminated his soul, and every day during that blindness, still laboring, he was conveyed to the Vatican, and there, sitting at the feet of the sorrowful and almost heart-broken Vicar of Jesus Christ, chased every depressing thought from the Pontiff's heart, filling him with joy in the midst of his persecutions to see that there was one great heart that bore the pains of the Church's sorrow so lightly, not, indeed, that he did not feel them keenly, but because his great soul never lost sight of that divine light before him, just as the pillar of fire before the children of Israel. No matter how dark the night or how dreadful the thunder, the pillar of fire, the assurance of their God that they should conquer, was before them.

Brightly did the lamp of faith burn before the eyes of the great servant until, in the brightness of that light, he could afford to rejoice even in the darkest hour of the Church's tribulation. He has gone. We also have our great prelate, and we were under his grand government. We also, who for three hundred years have been daily battling with every spirit of persecution for that faith which is our true light—we who are in this our day once more adorning the temples of our God with more than their first splendor—we were under the care of this great man. He loved us and our people. He was as familiar with the name and history of Ireland as if he were one of our own blood. He had attested his love by the earnest care with which he watched our interest. On the death of this great man, who loved our people, the Irish heart felt a pang of grief, for they knew how he had labored to obtain for Ireland the crowning dignity and blessing of her first cardinal, who, not only as prelate and cardinal in Rome, but as friend speaking to friend, conquered every difficulty and subdued the repugnance which humility dictated in the person of our own great prelate. This great cardinal rejoiced with a mighty joy when he saw one of the nations of his Propaganda crowned with the highest honor of the Church. To-day prayers are offered up for him all over the earth. Although his mind was great, his heart greater, and his works greatest of all, we can only say, as the apostle said, with the firmest hope and with the firmest confidence, that there is reserved for him a crown of justice and glory which the Lord, whom he had served so faithfully, will not deny him. That crown perhaps already rests on his head, already shines on his faithful brow, and probably at this moment he is laying before the invisible Head of the Church the prayers and tears of the faithful. But it is still our duty—a duty dictated by faith, dictated most of all by gratitude to him who was the lover of our race, the great ecclesiastical prefect of the Propaganda—to send up our prayers to heaven for the illustrious Barnabo, that if perchance he may be suffering now for some trivial sin which might fall on the soul of the most just, the Lord may hasten the time of his deliverance, for surely when that time has arrived great is the voice and true the heart that will plead in heaven for the Church of God.

THE LIFE AND CHARACTER OF ST. DOMINIC.

The Calendar of the Saints contains no name which shines brighter, or which should be held dearer, than that of St. Dominic. In this discourse, preached in the Dominican Church of St. Saviour, Dublin, on the Feast of St. Dominic, 1877, Father Burke has given us an interesting and faithful sketch of the great saint in which there is much food for meditation.

JUDGING the heart of the Divine Saviour by His words and actions, we would find that His heart was absorbed and inflamed with four great loves. The first passion of His heart was His love for His heavenly Father, for the atonement to whose justice and the consummation of whose glory He came down to die upon the earth. The second love of His heart was His love for His Virgin Mother. With what confidence He trusted to her tender arms and with what affection He clung to her virgin bosom! He loved her and He honored her; for it is written in law, Honor thy father, thy mother, and by God, the Maker of the law, was its precepts pre-eminently fulfilled. The third great love of Jesus' heart was the love He bore the pure and holy Church which He had established. His zeal was for her honor and glory, for the truth of her doctrine, the purity of her moral law, the faithfulness of her children, the stateliness of her temples, the zeal and holiness of her consecrated ministers, that she should be beautified and recognized amongst men as the spouse of God and the most glorious institution that ever existed on this earth. After His love for His Eternal Father, for His Mother, and for His Church comes His love for human souls. He loved human souls, and He sacrificed Himself for human souls, ay, even to the last drop of blood in the sacred chalice of His loving heart. He knew their value, the eternity of their existence, the glory of their mission—to bless and praise the Father through all time—and He came down from heaven and died upon a cross to save them. This sacred heart of Jesus, with its four great passions of love, was the model of all sanctity for all time. Now, consider the character of St. Dominic, and if it be found that his heart was modelled on the heart of Jesus, join in the praise of Dominic with the angels and saints who that day praised and honored him even before the throne of God, and thus offer a tribute of love to the heart of Jesus. It is an old story, this life of Dominic, fully seven hundred years old. In 1170 Dominic was born. One might tell of the nobility of his blood, and might trace his descent from a line of kings and emperors; but the armorial bearing of sanctity that was emblazoned on the shield of Dominic is higher than any human heraldry can reach, and zeal and sanctity were the devices upon the glorious escutcheon that he bore. He was born of holy Catholic parents. His mother, herself a sainted woman, watched over his infancy to preserve and guide the first dawning of reason in his soul, that he should learn the things of God before he was made acquainted with the iniquities of the world. But the holy woman had an easy task to perform, for the mind of the infant Dominic turned instinctively to heaven. Scarcely was he able to walk when he would start out of his cot on Friday nights and lie down on the cold, hard floor till morning, resigning all the comfort of his infant bed. He knew not why, but his mother had told him of a certain Baby that was born in the manger of a stable, and holy instinct impelled him to make his infancy like the infancy of Jesus.

When he was seven years old he was placed in the charge of his uncle, a holy priest, and for eight years afterwards he lived, like Samuel, in the sanctuary. He learned to bow his head in prostrate adoration at the august sacrifice of the daily Mass. He lived in an atmosphere of prayer; already he fasted and mortified his infant flesh; no stain of sin was upon him, no impulse of temptation was seen to move him. His purity was angelic; no thought that might shame an angel crossed his mind, no word that might scandalize an angel was heard from his lips. In his fifteenth year he was as pure of soul as when he was carried from the marble baptismal font with the water of regeneration still glistening upon his infant brow. At fifteen he was sent to the University of Valencia, in Spain, there to remain till he had completed his five-and-twentieth year. There he should live amidst sights and scenes and words of iniquity and sin, there amid all the hot passions, the unbridled recklessness, and the wild license of youth. In the midst of this whirlpool of temptation the holy youth Dominic spent ten trying, ten terrible years of his life. He spent them after the fashion of the youth of Jesus, for the Babe whom in his infancy he had imitated was still dwelling in his heart and protecting him from all peril. Thus, saith the Lord, he hath moved with me in peace and in justice; truth and holiness were upon his lips, and no iniquity could be found in him. With the sensitive instinct of sanctity he shrank from the sin around him. He sat in his room, with the crucifix before him, intent upon knowledge, human and divine, or he knelt in some lone corner of the cathedral pouring forth his soul to God. Four years he devoted to the study of earthly science and earthly accomplishments, so highly prized by the world; but when he had reached his twentieth year he put away those things from him for ever. He turned, the ancient chronicle of his life relates, with all the love of his virgin heart, with all the force of his powerful and enlightened intellect, to the study of the Scriptures and the things of God. His future life was devoted to divine knowledge and to prayer. His life was retired and solemn beyond his years; he was never found in any place of public resort or amusement. Like his Divine Master and Model, he was frequently seen to weep, but never to indulge in frivolous laughter. About this period St. Dominic made the great sacrifice of his early life. A great famine came upon the country, like the terrible famine that overwhelmed our own country some thirty years ago. St. Dominic's resources were ample, and he devoted them all to the relief of the poor. But these resources were exhausted, and the famine was unabated. Then his heart was still more moved, and he sold his books to buy bread for those that starved—those books of philosophy and theology which he so much loved. It was a time when books were scarce and difficult to be obtained; printing was not then invented, and in those days an estate was often given for a book. But Dominic surrendered this without regret in the cause of charity, and, turning to the crucifix, he exclaimed: "O Divine and Eternal Wisdom! thou art to me the sole fountain of knowledge henceforth and for ever more!"

Another instance of his marvellous charity is recorded. A widow, like to the widow in the Scripture, was deprived of her son, her sole support. Her son was sold to slavery. Dominic heard of this, and his heart was touched with pity, and he said to the woman, "Weep no more, O woman! but tell me the cause of thy grief"; and she told him that her son was taken away a slave, and that she should never look upon his face again. And he discovered the place of the captivity, and resolved to restore the son to the mother, and to take upon himself the condition of a slave. And God, as with Abraham of old, was pleased with his servant, but did not exact the sacrifice he would make, and He found other means to deliver the slave from his captivity. But on that day Dominic obtained the noblest crown of the martyrdom of exalted love, and God did not refuse him the assistance he had prayed for in his studies. He was learned beyond his fellows; the most learned men in the university, the most distinguished scholars in the schools held their peace when the young Dominic spoke of theology. His word on this subject was law, and no one dared to dispute when he had spoken. He was, indeed, a man after God's own heart—no stain or shadow of sin was upon him. Upon the grace which he had received in baptism he built a magnificent superstructure of grace. His heart was filled with the first great love of the heart of Jesus, the love for his Heavenly Father, and he enrolled himself among the servants of God. The holy oil of the priesthood was poured upon his head, and with the sacred unction his hands were anointed, and head and hand were henceforth dedicated to the sole service of his Saviour—that head endowed with intellect and enriched with knowledge, that hand clean of all guilt before God. At twenty-five years of age he renounced all the brilliant and alluring worldly prospects that lay extended before him, and returned to his home to receive the grace of ordination. The young prince, even as a priest, might have aimed at power and distinction. Emperors claimed him as a beloved relation, kings called him familiarly by his name as one among themselves. The Church always desired to select the most worthy ministers in her service, and was always anxious to compensate for great sacrifices made in her cause by such distinctions as it was in her power to bestow. But Dominic turned away from all those distinctions, and he buried himself for nine years in the monastery at Osma. The canons of the Osma cathedral had formed themselves into a regular community, formed upon the rule of St. Augustine. Thus they lived, giving their lives to poverty, obedience, and devotion, to prayer and the contemplation of God. This order St. Dominic entered, and the moment he entered the chapter all felt that a new light of purity had shone out among them. The oldest and most experienced among them received new grace, new fervor, a consciousness of what God could effect in the spirits of his chosen ones.

Their rules were strict and austere. At twelve o'clock they rose to pray; their matins said, they were permitted to retire, and returned to their cells in profound silence and holy contemplation. Dominic alone remained. He came out from his place in the choir behind the altar and took his station in front of the sanctuary, and there through the long, silent hours of the night, alone with God and with the angels of God, he poured forth his whole soul in prayer. Then God heard from the lips of this man such words as He hears in heaven from the highest and holiest of His angels—such burning protestations of love, such ardent aspirations to be permitted to suffer and to die for the love of God. And when the gray dawn broke through the cathedral windows, and the canons returned, they found him changed, and pale, and exhausted, like one worn out by terrible physical exertion—prostrated by the violence of his emotion. And there were traces of tears on the pavement where he knelt before the sanctuary, and another stain there was, too, upon the stones—the stain of blood. For this faithful man, as he knelt alone, would beat his shoulders and scourge himself with a scourge of iron till the blood streamed down, as it streamed from the body of Christ when He knelt in His agony in the garden of Gethsemane. Thus for nine years of his priesthood his life was spent in the sanctuary, and his heart was consumed by the love of God ; but, save his glorious example of purity and sanctity, he had as yet done nothing for his fellow-men. He had as yet only attained to the first of the great loves of the heart of Jesus Christ—the love for his heavenly Father. At length came the period when the holy father went forth from the cloister, from the house of his predilection and devotion, and his name now rises clear and bright in the horizon of history.

He set forth with regret, hoping for the day of his return, that he might there end his days in the holy contemplation of God. He went forth with his bishop to travel in the more northern portions of Europe ; but even on his journey he preserved in all their strictness the austerities of his order. But the moment he entered into the district of Provence his heart refused to beat, his brain to think ; the whole sanctity and purity of his life revolted from the terrible scenes he there beheld. Those fair provinces, the fairest in Europe, were invested by the terrible and pernicious heresy of the Albigenses, in reality but another form of the old Manichean heresy, that had crawled like a venomous snake through the ranks of the faithful even while the Church lay hid in the tombs of the catacombs.

They held the blasphemous doctrine that Almighty God was the author of evil, and was responsible for every sin that was committed by man; that no man was free to avoid sin if it lay in his path; that man had no power to avoid evil; that all manner of crimes, lying, adultery, drunkenness, and debauchery, might be freely committed. They denied the free will of man; they denied the existence of a place of future punishment or reward; they degraded God to the condition of being the author of evil, and man to the slave of it. Those worse than atheists made their God a demon by denying His greatest attribute, His infinite holiness. This licentious doctrine had everywhere spread throughout the country. The great barons patronized it; the common people liked it. The Catholic churches were pulled down, the priests were driven from their flocks, the nuns from their convents, bishops from their sees. The voice of prayer was no longer heard, and the abomination of desolation brooded over the land.

All at once the mystery of his future life dawned before the eye of this great servant of God. He understood that his life henceforth was not one of peace but of war. He understood that he should return no more to the quiet and holy cloisters which he loved, that he must draw the sword of truth, that he must arm himself with the helmet and breastplate of faith and justice, that he must arise, like another David, for the people of God, and strike down the Goliah of heresy that assailed them. He thought he heard ringing in his ears the words of God: "Thou shalt smite them, and thou shalt be as a wall of brass and iron to resist their power." He felt it his mission to restore peace and happiness, truth and religion to those fair but tempted provinces. Then, indeed, the third great love of the heart of Jesus welled forth in the heart of Dominic, and he resolved to abandon for ever his beloved cloister and to devote every energy of his soul and brain to stamp out this pernicious heresy and restore unity and peace to the

Church of God. All Europe was then Catholic, and the nations around, in the interests of religion, and fearing that those pernicious doctrines might creep into their own lands, had armed themselves to make war upon the promoters of this pestilent heresy. And Dominic watched the war, and never was greater human wisdom displayed than by the combatants on either side. And the passions of men were excited, and oceans of blood were shed; but the great end appeared as far from attainment as ever. And Dominic waited and prayed, and now his heart was inflamed with the second great love of the heart of Jesus— the love for His Virgin Mother. Greater, far greater than the love he bore for his own sainted mother, who had borne him into the world, was the love he bore the pure Mother of God, who had conceived him into spiritual life in that hour of her sore agony when she watched the form of her expiring Son upon the cross.

Heart-broken at the desolation of the holy Church, the spouse of Christ, Dominic wearied Heaven with prayer, and night after night he implored the assistance of God through the intercession of his Mother. And lo! in a vision that assistance was vouchsafed him. As he knelt one night in the silent church, while in the country all around him the clang of battle and the cries of rage and agony were heard, while prostrate in prayer, suddenly a sound of ineffably sweet music filled the church; the carved saints and angels around seemed to grow resonant with celestial harmony. He saw in the air above him the holy Virgin clothed in white raiment, the snow dull by comparison beneath her feet, and on her head a crown of twelve lustrous and shining stars, and in her arms a Child of surpassing beauty, whose features resembled those of the Virgin even as the features of an earthly child resemble those of its mother. Then Dominic's soul was lifted up, and he broke forth into a grand *Te Deum* of praise and adoration. He rejoiced exceedingly to see the Virgin, and the Child in the arms of the Virgin Mother. And the Lady bent down to her servant, and, giving him the holy beads she held in her hands, she said: "Take this and preach my rosary. Teach them to pray, teach them the great mysteries of the life of my Eternal Son. Teach the people to love my Child and worship Him in contemplation and in prayer."

Mary returned to heaven, and next morning Dominic went forth on the mission she had given him. He stood erect between the two contending armies. "A truce," he cried, "to your wars; Christians, unite with me in prayer." And he preached his first sermon on the rosary, and he knelt upon the ground and prayed. And the Christian soldier bent his mailed knee to the earth, and the heart of the heretic was softened as he listened to the mysteries of man's redemption, and soon both armies, that had been engaged in bloody battle, joined together in peaceful prayer. And soon, too, the rosary of Mary, preached by St. Dominic, brought back one hundred thousand erring souls to the fold of Christ. That prayer, the most beautiful that ever issued from the lips of a Christian, the "Our Father," is taught us by God Himself; the "Hail Mary" learned at the lips of an angel; the "Holy Mary" given us by the Church; the "Glory be to the Father" an act of faith in the Blessed Trinity and profound adoration for the Three Divine Persons. The rosary was one of the brightest weapons in the armory of God for the defence of the Church and the overthrow of heresy.

The fourth love of the Sacred Heart was strong in the heart of St. Dominic when he labored thus long and earnestly for the salvation of souls. To the end of his life he labored, and before he died he had a great and strong reward, which has been accorded only to two of the saints of God in the history of the Church. St. Patrick was one of these; he was the only saint that converted a whole nation, that found it pagan and made it Catholic, and so Catholic to the end of time. St. Dominic was the only one that so stamped out and destroyed a heresy that no trace of it remained, and even its name has passed away. The fruit of his life, as God promised His disciples, has remained. It is now more than six hundred years since St. Dominic was borne high up into heaven amidst the choir of rejoicing angels. Nations have risen and perished since. Great men have had time to grow great and to be forgotten. Cities have been built and fallen to decay; the very appearance of the material earth has altered; and all through that period to the present day his children have followed in his footsteps, have been animated by the four great loves that filled his heart, have lived and died for the faith of Christ. To contemplate the sufferings and persecutions they endured we need not look to the fury and intolerance of the Turk, the relentless and despotic bigotry of the czar, or the subtle cruelty of the emperor of China. We may turn our eyes towards home. As the English historian tells us, six hundred Dominican friars perished for the faith of Ireland during the persecutions in the reign of the gentle English queen. But we have survived the storm; and I pray God that while the shamrock springs from Irish soil Ireland will have Dominicans to follow the example of their great founder, and to preach from Irish lips and Irish hearts the faith of Christ.

St. Thomas Aquinas.

In this sermon Father Burke graphically delineates the life of one of the greatest of the saints. For centuries the Church has held in high esteem the writings of St. Thomas, and the people of many generations have been taught to regard him as the model of purity and virtue. In this sermon, as in others, Father Burke conveys a lasting impression to the minds of his readers.

For the text of his discourse Father Burke used these words: "That man is approved whom God Himself hath commended."

WE have heard already these words of the apostle, in relation to the great saint for whose festival we are preparing, in the testimony which God the Father hath rendered him by the ministry of His angels, covering him with the cincture of purity. We have considered the testimony which God the Son rendered to His great servant, saying to him in that miraculous manifestation: "Thou hast written well concerning me, O Thomas!" This evening it remains for us to consider the testimony rendered to this great saint by the Holy Ghost, the Third Person of the Blessed Trinity, in order that the word of the apostle may be fulfilled in all its fulness. "That man is approved whom God Himself hath commended." We know, as I told you, that God, the First Person of the Blessed Trinity, revealed Himself and acted towards His creatures, as St. Paul tells us, by the ministry of the angels in the old law. We know that God the Son, the Second Person of the Blessed Trinity, revealed Himself and acted towards His creatures through the sacred humanity which He assumed.

Now, as God the Father acted through the ministry of His angels, as God the Son acted through the ministry of

His sacred humanity, so God the Third Person acted and acts in this world through the ministry of the holy Roman Catholic Church. She is to God the Holy Ghost what the angels were to God the Father of old, what the sacred humanity was to God the Son in His Incarnation. Such is the Church to God the Holy Ghost—His messenger, His leading instrument, the chosen means adopted by Him by which He is to reveal Himself unto the children of men. She is more, this Church of God is far more, to God the Holy Ghost than were the angels to God the Father, for the Eternal Father used them merely for the purpose of messengers unto men, but He by no means dwelt or took up His dwelling amongst them. But, even as God the Son, the Second Person, abided and abides in the sacred humanity which he took from the Blessed Virgin Mary, so God the Holy Ghost took up His dwelling in the Catholic Church and abides in her. Oh ! great and mighty glory of God on this earth, that the Lord should dwell in the midst of her, pouring forth His rays in unerring truth, director of this great Church, the teacher of the world, pouring forth sanctity in that moral doctrine, untainted and untaintable, which is poured forth amongst men from the lips and illustrated in the holy action of the Church of God. For remember that as her word is the word of eternal truth, which cannot err, so her action is the action of unerring sanctity, which cannot be defiled, although there are in the Church, and have been found from the beginning, those who profess themselves her children, weak in faith and faithless. The infidelity of this individual or that, this nation or that, has no place in the unerring faith and infallible teaching of God's Church. There are to-day, as there were of old, children of the Church of God, perhaps in the sanctuary as well as out of it, whose lives and acts may not bear the test of Gospel criticism.

Just as the infidelity of a man or of a nation is no real reproach to the Church's truth, so the wickedness of a man or the faithless morals of a people are no real reproach to the Church's sanctity. She is essential truth, because of the Spirit that is within her. "I will send you," says He, "my Spirit, the Spirit of Truth, which will abide with you unto the end of the world," without intermission or interruption. The Spirit of Truth is in the mind and on the lips of the holy Church of God: in her mind, because, says the apostle, "she has the word of Christ"; on her lips, for the apostle said: "Even if an angel of God descended from heaven to preach any other gospel than that which you have heard from our lips, believe him not"; he must be false, because we have really spoken the word of eternal truth. But the same Spirit of divine truth is also the Spirit of sanctity. He is called, as the Holy Ghost, *Spiritus Sanctus*, the Holy Spirit—holy Himself, for He is God, and able to produce holiness in all those in whom He rests. Whenever our Lord, the Saviour of the world, would confer on His apostles the gift of infallibility, inspiration, and sanctity, He transmitted that gift by breathing on them, saying to them: "Receive ye the Holy Ghost." Now, from all this we gather two great truths: that the Holy Spirit of God abides in the Catholic Church by the gift of her Divine Lord, remaining unto the end of time as at once the guardian of the Church's truth and the guardian of the Church's sanctity or holiness. Whenever she speaks, it is the Holy Ghost that speaks. Whenever she bears testimony to doctrine or to man, it is the Holy Ghost that bears that testimony. Whenever she exalts the man, it is God Himself who exalts him. And therefore it is that the truth of the Catholic Church can never fail, because of the abiding Spirit of the Holy Ghost; so also the Catholic Church alone is able to confer the title of immortal and imperishable fame, because her title comes from God. Why do I say all this? Is it that I doubt your faith in the Church? No, no; but I wish to recall to your minds the purpose for which the Holy Ghost remains in the Church. The office which the Holy Spirit fulfils in the Church, the purpose for which He remains, is to preserve her faith, to create, foster, and increase her sanctity and grace; the office which the Holy Ghost fulfils in the Church of God is to bear testimony to the truth, to mark her saints, to bear testimony to them, to exalt them and confer on them the crown of unfading glory, to give what He alone can give, an immortal glory, celebrated on earth and in heaven, destined to be imperishable on earth as long as it remains, and, when earth rolls away, to gain for ever an immortal and imperishable crown in the kingdom of God's glory. Once more, therefore, in order that we may understand the subject to which we approach, when the Catholic Church speaks the Holy Ghost speaks.

Do you remember, dearly beloved, that when Moses spoke to the Jewish people of old he always expected them to receive his word as the Word of God? He told them distinctly that although he was only a man they should remember it was their God that spoke, because he was the chosen mouth-piece of God. Whenever they received him he always spoke to them as of receiving God. Whenever they disobeyed him the first thing he did was to retire to some silent place, kneel down, and say: "O Lord! the people have disobeyed me, be not angry with them." Whenever they quarrelled with Moses God took up the quarrel. Whenever we read that the people rebelled Almighty God said: "Let me wreak my vengeance on these people." When Core, Dathan, and Abiron rebelled, and refused to be subject, Almighty God said: "Bring out these men before the tents of the children of Israel. They have rebelled against you. Be silent, pray not for them; for I will cause the earth to open and hell to swallow them up." Those that had rebelled were placed together, and the earth devoured them. Why? Because it was not the man but God Himself against whom they rebelled. That which was conferred on the Jewish lawgiver Jesus Christ has conferred on the Catholic Church. Never were more awful words spoken than these: "As the Father hath sent me, so do I send you. Amen, I say to you, he that heareth you heareth me, and he that despiseth you despiseth me." They took the men to whom Christ spoke these words, subjected them to every kind of persecution, put them into prison, to torture, to cruel and ignominious deaths. How little they knew that whilst they were despising and persecuting Peter, James, Andrew, Philip, and all the apostles, it was in reality Jesus Christ whom they were persecuting!

So, in like manner, when the Church of God bears her testimony to any doctrine or to any man, that testimony is the testimony of God. If you accept the testimony of man, the testimony of God is greater. Every one of those apostles spoke as if God were speaking. Now, dearly beloved, what follows from all this? It follows that when the holy Catholic Church looks on any one of her children, examines his life, examines his writings, examines his own personal character, and then proclaims to the world what manner of man he was, what manner of mind and heart was his, then it is the testimony of the Holy Ghost, the Third Person, speaking through the lips of the holy Church. We have seen further testimony to Thomas, the great Dominican doctor, given by the ministry of angels. We have heard the testimony of God the Son, saying in that miraculous manifestation, "Thou hast written well of me, Thomas." Now nothing remains but to listen to the voice of the Church. What weight does she bear for those who, having the conclusive testimony of the holy Church, have the testimony of God the Holy Ghost the Third Person of the Blessed Trinity? We have the very loving voice, the testimony of the Holy Spirit to the mind, the heart, the personal sanctity of this wonderful teacher of the Church's doctrines. Dearly beloved, how are we to gather what the Church says, what the Church did, how the Church feels, of any man?

There are many sources of information; there are many witnesses in the Church of God. The Church is a living thing of principles and motives. She is capable of joy; she can be oppressed, persecuted, harassed, and dishonored. At this very moment the Church is steeped in sorrow. The world is heaping persecution and distress upon her. She is a vast, mighty body, spreading all over the world, from end to end of the earth. Her voice is heard in every clime, in every language, and among every people. Whilst her action is spreading all over the earth, her word is the same in every tongue, her Gospel the same in every clime, for it is the one truth, reflection, and action of the Spirit of God. Therefore, one scarcely knows which to admire most—the extent and diversity of her authority, or the wonderful union of thought, word, doctrine, and morality which is the reflection of the infinite unity of God. In this mighty body there are many sources of information: her great religious orders, numbering their thousands of priests, founded everywhere, established and illustrated by saints—the ancient Order of St. Benedict, the Dominicans, the Franciscans, the Augustinians, the mighty and ancient Carmelites, and coming down on the stream of history to the more modern, mighty institution of the Jesuits, and the great order instituted by St. Vincent de Paul, the Passionists founded by St. Paul of the Cross, and so on in one great series, through which some of her greatest saints reveal and reflect the mind of the Church; then, again, learned men, individual saints, bishops, cardinals, learned men who were not saints—not canonized by the Church, and yet reflecting the Church's mind in those great seats of learning—universities founded by the Church, which is at all times the light and the civilizer of the world, which brought society to what it is to-day in true civilization from out the chaos of its elements in the beginning of the Christian era—in the fourth and fifth centuries—which founded those great universities to be the guardians of faith and morals, and which were destined to bring the world on in the march of true civilization; others not in the Church, outside of the Church's doctrine, shed the light of learning on her, even whilst they hate her; the sanctity of all the Church assembled in council, from time to time and from age to age, resolving, under the guidance of the Holy Ghost, the greatest questions, interpreting the obscure points of Scripture—are sources of information and testimony. All united bear their common praise and admiration to this great man, until they place him on the highest pinnacle of intellectual and saintly glory.

Now, what testimony has the Church rendered to this great saint ? Surely when we reflect that at a time when the intelligence of man was trying to emancipate itself from the dominion of God; when most learned philosophers, searching the depth of human knowledge, pushing their studies through all the mysteries of man's nature, began to doubt whether the things God revealed were compatible with reason and the intelligence of man; when every form of heresy arose, deism and pantheism, and the errors that grew out of them in the latter ages were all tormenting and persecuting the Church, God gave in that very age a man who was able to see into every source of knowledge, to master every known science, to learn all the Scriptures, to take them into his mind, not as they lay on the dead page, not as they were interpreted by this one or that, but as they came from the mind of God, who revealed them; to take up every objection and argument by pagan, infidel, or heretic, no matter where; who was able to anticipate in his mighty intellect every objection that was made during the six hundred years that elapsed since his death; to annihilate and confound them, and to furnish an answer to every objection to Catholic truth and morality ; to reveal the nature of God, the unity, trinity, and every attribute ; to describe in wonderful language the mysterious union of God and man ; to enter into the whole question of Christ's descent to take a human heart, intelligence, spirit, strength, and weakness ; to analyze them all with the keenest and closest attention. Every difficulty was removed by this one master mind. Surely it must be interesting for Catholics to know what testimony the Holy Ghost bears to this superhuman intelligence, from the sources whence testimony can be derived.

First, the testimony of the great religious orders. It is now six hundred years since Thomas Aquinas passed away, leaving behind him a body that had never been touched or tainted by anything like sin. It is six hundred years since death sent to God that mighty intellect that seemed already to have seen and contemplated Him on earth. Every religious order in the Church of God has spoken these six hundred years in honoring, exalting, and bearing testimony to this great saint. Of his own order I will not speak. It would not become me, a member—though the least and most unworthy of members of that order—one wearing the self-same habit in which Aquinas was clad—it would not become me to speak of honors and glory which his own order conferred on him. In every age for these six hundred years that Dominican Order has produced some of the highest and most eloquent philosophers in the Church of God. Their works fill every ecclesiastical library; their guide and master for six hundred years has been "Aquinas." The great Order of St. Francis, formed about the same time, was a rival in the generous race of apostleship and martyrdom. St. Bonaventure was the first to proclaim the glories of St. Thomas. The more ancient Order of St. Benedict proclaims that when it is a question of exact science, of dogma, or morals, St. Thomas Aquinas is the great authority. The regular canons of St. Genevieve had a rule which obliged them to study him.

The great Society of Jesus, St. Philip Neri, and St. Vincent de Paul have adopted St. Thomas of Aquinas as their guide in all matters of belief. St. Ignatius left it as a rule for the Jesuits to study him. Their two greatest generals, Claude Acquaviva and Muzio Vitelleschi, renewed the saint's injunction. Bellarmine, the great controversialist, whose name is familiar in every Catholic land, lays down the principle that Thomas Aquinas is the saviour of his belief. Passing from religious orders, we come to the saints. Here we find such great saints as St. Philip Neri, Charles Borromeo, Francis de Sales, Vincent Ferrer, who thought it a glory to be imitators of his intellectual and saintly glory. Learned men such as Pico della Mirandola, Cardinal Bessarion, and Bossuet, the great and mighty orator, the more than Cicero and Demosthenes of the glorious Church of France, displayed some of their richest thoughts and grandest eloquence when they came to speak of St. Thomas of Aquin. You will be surprised that one, not the least, of his followers was that gifted man Henry VIII., who made a noble beginning. When he read Luther's first book he turned to St. Thomas of Aquin, and without much difficulty or labor compiled a book from his reading in which he shattered to pieces Luther's arguments against the seven sacraments, for which he received the title of the Defender of the Faith—the faith which he afterwards betrayed. Erasmus, that mild cynic, suspected though not convicted of Protestantism—that keen intellect, which seemed to have no respect for man and very little for God—speaks of St. Thomas, saying: "When I come to contemplate and speak of him I am like a man looking at the sun in mid-day, blinded by its brightness."

We find the universities of Salamanca, Alcala, Louvain, Douay, Bologna, Naples, Padua, and Turin all admitting and incorporating the fundamental rules of St. Thomas as the test of true belief. Oxford and Cambridge, silent to-day, who have much to say of this world but nothing of God, because the blight and cloud of heresy is on them, were once eloquent in praise of this master man, and were able to produce such men as Roger Bacon and Wolsey. They are now silent as the grave, because the curse of heresy is on them, outside the Church. Grotius, the greatest man that the revolution produced, who had intellect enough to make another Aquinas and heart enough to make a saint, but who prostituted them by beginning as a Catholic and ending as a Jew, through all the wanderings of his mighty genius had the one vision ever before him, answering all his doubts and shattering all his arguments—the mighty genius of Thomas, whom he loved to study in his youth—and who said: "Take away Thomas, and I will shatter the Catholic Church."

He was wrong. If Thomas were never created the Catholic Church would remain. No saint or doctor was necessary to her to whom the promise of God had been given. Yet still he admitted that every heresy that hell could inspire was shattered by St. Thomas. Let us leave behind human testimony, even if of enemies of the Church yet all the stronger, because it was wrung from them by agencies and intelligences before which even devils were forced to bow down. Let us come to the testimony of the vicars of Christ, the popes of Rome, who for six hundred years in successive diplomas, briefs, and bulls gloried in honoring St. Thomas, from Urban IV., who wished to make him cardinal, down to Pius IX., who sent his blessing and a plenary indulgence only two days ago to every child who would worthily celebrate the festival of this great saint. Gregory X. called him to the Council of Lyons; Innocent V. called him another St. Paul; Benedict XI. says: "Thomas is my master and my guide"; John XXII. says: "*Quot scripsit articulos, tot fecit miraculos.*" Urban V., Nicholas V., Pius IV., Sixtus V., Clement V., Alexander VII., and Benedict XIV. are loud in his praise. The Councils of Lyons, Florence, and Trent all honor him. Let us pray that in contemplating and loving so great a saint we may come to behold him in the kingdom of God's glory.

St. Patrick.

Of the many discourses delivered by Father Burke on St. Patrick none is better than the following, which was preached in St. Saviour's Church, Dominic Street, Dublin, after the twelve o'clock Mass on St. Patrick's day, 1877. It is a tribute worthy of the great saint of whom it speaks.

"And Jesus, answering, said: Behold the kingdom of God is within you."

THESE words, dearly beloved, are taken from the seventeenth chapter of the Gospel according to St. Luke, and they were spoken by the Son of God to the Jews, even unto the Pharisees, but in their fullest and highest meaning they apply especially to the apostles. "The kingdom of God," He says, "is in you." If men are to see that kingdom, it *must* be in you; if men are to enter into that kingdom, it must be through you; whatever "the kingdom of God," "my kingdom," means must be published, taught, and exemplified by you. And therefore, dearly beloved, amongst all her saints in their various orders the holy Church of God gives the first, the highest, and the most important place to her apostles. Before her martyrs, before her confessors, before her holy consecrated virgins, although they are the crown of peculiar glory, come the apostles first of all. And now consider briefly what this apostleship means. It is clear from the Scriptures that when our Divine Lord spoke, as He frequently did, of His own kingdom, calling it at one time "my kingdom," and another time calling it "the kingdom of God," He meant precisely and definitely the holy Church which He was about to found upon earth. For the kingdom of heaven, as He calls it, cannot mean the heaven of the blessed, where they see God face to face; and why? Because Christ our Lord, when He speaks of the kingdom of heaven which He was about to found—namely, His holy Church—attributes to it certain qualities, certain facts that are not found in the heaven of His glory. For instance, in one place He says: "The kingdom of heaven is like unto the net which a man casts into the sea, and in which he takes up everything, good and bad." Now, it is clear that this kingdom of heaven cannot be the kingdom of the glorious heaven above, for there is nothing bad there, but only the good; whereas in the Church upon earth we have her children good and bad, those whom she encourages, those whom she sanctifies, and those over whom she weeps, seeking their conversion and their turning to God. The kingdom of heaven, therefore, of which the Saviour speaks means the Church. And, turning to His apostles, He said: "Amen, I say unto you, the kingdom of heaven is in you—you are its heralds, you are to go forth the light of the world"; as He calls them elsewhere, "Vos estis luces mundi"—"You are to illumine all men, that they may see your light, and not only your light, flashing upon their intellects and flooding their souls with light, but that they may see also your works and your saintly deeds, and in them give glory to your Father who is in heaven." Now, dearly beloved, why does the Church put the apostles at the head of her saints? For the simple reason that everything of good and sanctity that there is in man or in the world must come to man through divine faith. Whoever creates faith in the soul of man is the true father of that soul; whoever gives the light to a nation is the real father of that nation. It is not only in that light that the life of a man's soul begins but the life of a nation begins, and therefore of our Divine Lord it is written: "In Him was light, but the light was the light of heaven."

Her divine life, her supernatural life, is no other than the light of divine faith, and all her gifts flow from this. "Whatever," says the apostle, "is not of faith is a sin"—that is to say, wherever there is virtue available for eternal life, wherever there is virtue to be crowned in the kingdom of God and acknowledged by Him as genuine, that virtue must spring from faith, that virtue, no matter what form it takes, must be enlivened by divine faith. Therefore, elsewhere it is written that "without faith it is impossible to please God." Impossible! I care not how grand be the natural faculties of the intelligence or of the soul of man, if he has not faith, and that faith the one genuine, divine faith, he cannot please God. And hence the apostles are the fathers of the faith, because they were chosen by Christ our Lord to spread the faith. Therefore they are the highest of the saints; and, speaking of the kingdom of God, the apostle tells us that it is founded upon the foundation of the apostles. They are the foundation-stones of the Church of God, upon which all the superedifice of purity, of holiness, of godliness in every form is built up and erected. And, dearly beloved, why does He call His Church the kingdom of heaven? For the simplest of all reasons. There are two heavens mentioned in the Scripture, the heaven upon the earth and the heaven around the throne of God, and both here and there the very essence of heaven consists in the knowledge of God. Whoever knows God, whoever has a clear, accurate, supernatural knowledge of God, that man is in heaven, whether on earth or in the kingdom of glory, by the very fact of the knowledge. Any of us leading a good and holy life, and dying in the grace of God, and passing from earth to heaven, beholds before the throne of the Most High only the things that he knew well on earth by divine faith. The manner of knowledge is changed, the condition of that knowledge is changed. Here, indeed, we know it, but we see it only darkly as in a glass; the cloud of faith is between us and God, and still we know. In heaven that cloud is broken, the veil is rent, and we see even as we are seen; and therefore, although the knowledge does not change in a single iota, the condition of that knowledge and its manner *are* changed, but the heaven remains the same.

When, therefore, our Lord said to His apostles, "The kingdom of heaven is in you," He meant, "The light of God is in you, and from you it must go forth unto the illumination of the Gentiles and the resurrection of the whole world." The first of the apostles to whom Christ our Lord gave this word received it by direct and divine inspiration, and they went forth, and in every land their voices were heard, and the principal nations of the world were converted by them. They sowed the seed everywhere, but they were only twelve in number and the world was wide; vast portions of it were not yet discovered or civilized, and the work of the apostleship passed from the twelve who received it from Christ to the holy Church of God in her one, visible head, and she continued the work and became the apostle of nations. Three hundred years and more rolled away. The light was spreading rapidly; but certain regions far, far away, isolated islands in the ocean, great territories separated from the rest of the world by vast and impassable mountain-ranges, remained still in barbarism and obscurity. And amongst these was an island far, far away in the western ocean; so far away that no foot of Roman legionary or tribune ever desecrated its soil; so far away that it was called amongst the ancients the *Ultima Thule,* or the last stretch, and the outlying district of creation itself, known only to the ancient civilized nations of Greece and the East, known only by a vague tradition of extraordinary intellectuality, of desperate valor, and of an unearthly and unnatural barbarism and savagery of conduct among themselves. They were spoken of as men who united the greatest and most opposite qualities, at one time generous beyond all other men, at another time cruel, savage, and vindictive; their poetry was known to be, although barbaric, of the very highest kind; the land was famous for its richness, for the valor of its chieftains and people; but beyond these vague traditions of this far-distant island, called by the Grecians "the most ancient land," called by others in the Celtic tongue "Ierne," or Ireland, nothing else was known.

ST. PATRICK.

The fourth century was drawing to its close; the year 400 had almost come upon us. It was about the year 386 or 390 when a king from this island of Ireland went forth with his war-ships out upon the face of the ocean and scoured the northern shores of France, destroying the towns and villages, capturing the inhabitants and carrying them off into slavery. Now, this northern part of France, which was ravaged by Niall of the Nine Hostages, the fierce though heroic Irish king—this northern coast of France was a most favored country both in nature and grace. It was fruitful and beautiful, and it was also Christian, and already Christianity had flowered into all its holiness there. And a young man, the son of a great noble in one of those northern cities on the coast of Brittany, was taken prisoner and carried into Ireland. He was sixteen years of age—he had been born in the year 372. Sixteen years of age, born of Christian, Catholic parents, most carefully and luxuriously reared, and he tells us in his own confessions that up to that time he had scarcely learned to love God.

Now he is taken suddenly from the bosom of his family, thrown into the hold of one of those war-ships of the Irish king, borne roughly across the boisterous ocean, and then flung on the northern coast of Ireland and sold as a slave, turned out in hunger and in nakedness to feed the cattle upon the cold, bleak mountains of the northern province of the land. There he remained month after month, year after year, and in that bitter exile, not knowing the language of those who were his masters, severely tasked, scourged and beaten, neglected and despised, there this young Christian, Patrick, first turned his heart to God, for there was no hope or comfort left to him upon the earth. His young heart yearned for joy, but here and all around him was desolation and bitterness; and, finding no joy upon the earth, a happy necessity compelled him to turn his heart to God—to that God whom he himself confesses he had hitherto neglected, though he had never violently offended Him by mortal sin. And so he began to pray, and the light of God streamed in upon his soul. He prayed day and night; to the enforced fasting he added an additional fasting of love; to the stripes that were inflicted upon him by the cruel, relentless hand of his pagan master he added the voluntary discipline of penance, and he wept bitter tears for the slight sins and youthful follies of his age. And thus he prepared his soul; and after a few years, when he escaped from his exile and his slavery, he was already a saint, matured for God and for the great purposes for which God had destined him. Returning to his native land, he thought at first that he would forget the land of his captivity, which had nothing but bitter memories for him; but, strange to say, like every stranger that ever yet was known to have set foot in Ireland, there was something in the air that he breathed, although it was chilled with the northern winter, there was something in the soil on which he trod, there was something in the rude but generous, romantic character of those who had been so cruel to him, that drew his heart and his memory back to the land. He was already more than half Irish; the natural heart of the man yearned for the land in which he had known nothing but tears, and presently the Almighty God adds the supernatural longing of grace. "I was musing," he says, "after my return to my own people and to my own land, and even amid the joys of my restoration to them, I was musing and thinking with a sorrowful heart upon Ireland." How strange, how strange, that his heart and his memory should go back to the land of his slavery and bitterness! "And in the night-time," he adds, "I heard a wailing sound as of voices carried across the salt sea of the western ocean, and it fell upon my ears and said: 'O youth! O young man of God! return to us once more and remain with us.' It was the voice of the Irish people," says Patrick, "and my heart failed within me."

Then he determined that to this land and this people he would return. Then, even as Ruth clove to Naomi of old when she left the fair and luxurious land of Moab to return to her own country of Palestine, and Ruth said: "I will go with thee and remain with thee, and thy people shall be my people, and thy God shall be my God," so Patrick turned his longing eyes to Ireland. He stretched out his hands over the sea and said: "I will return to thee, O strange and attractive land! I will go to thee and cast my lot in thee, and thy people shall be my people, but thy god shall not be my God, for I will teach thee of the true God, and thou shalt be the glory of the nations and the delight of God's holy Church and its brightest gem." Then, dearly beloved, having attained to the age of manhood, he began another phase of preparation for his apostleship—namely, the preparation of study; and you will be surprised, perhaps, to hear that St. Patrick spent at least thirty years studying and preparing himself, and that, as far as we can ascertain, he was a man sixty years of age when he returned to Ireland as her apostle. Thirty years of study; what is the meaning of this? In order to understand and consider what the apostle must be, the apostle who goes forth in the name and with the authority of Jesus Christ from His Church to evangelize any people and to bring them forth from the darkness of their idolatry into the admirable light of God, that man must be furnished with at least two things—namely, he must, first of all, be possessed of all divine knowledge, he must know the message which he has come to deliver, he must know it in all its exactness, in all its integrity, and in all its extent, in all the length and breadth, the height and depth, of its meaning. Consequently he must know all divine things. Therefore of such a one is it written: "The lips of the priest," says the prophet of old, "shall keep knowledge, and the people shall demand the law at his mouth." He must know everything that is necessary in order to form a pagan people into perfect Christianity; therefore he must have the whole and entire deposit of Christian knowledge lodged in his heart and ready at his mouth.

This is not enough; no nation was ever yet converted by the mere preaching of the Word of God. Although the

Word of God is declared to be penetrating as a two-edged sword, reaching the very spirit; although it is declared to be strong as the warrior's shield in the hour of danger with which to turn aside death in a thousand forms, yet the Word alone never converted a people unless the man who preached that Word, who preached it with authority, who preached it as one sent, who was able to produce his credentials and prove his mission—unless that man were in his own person, in his own conduct, in his own life a living model and example of the Gospel which he preached. In vain will he preach any virtue if those who hear the praise of the virtue, turning their eyes upon the preacher, behold its absence in him. In vain will he call upon them to tread the pathways of Christian purity and charity if he is not himself transparent in his purity, even as an angel of God. In vain will he call upon them to despise the things of earth, and to lay hold of the invisible things of heaven, unless he gives them in his own person an example of one who knows how to trample upon the good things of this world in order to secure the things of heaven. And therefore, dearly beloved, no nation is converted except by a celibate. No nation is ever converted by the mere hearing of the Word; they have eyes to see, hands to feel, minds to reflect and reason, and the man who preaches the Gospel of Christ to a pagan nation must be the living impersonation of those virtues. St. Patrick, as I have already observed, had the first—namely, the sanctity burning with the love of God, anxious to devote himself to the service of God, breathing only one ardent desire to shed his blood and give his life a thousand times for the love that burned in him for Jesus Christ. He must, however, learn the whole length and breadth of the Christian law, he must become the most learned as well as the holiest of men, before he can expound the law to the people who, although pagans, were already far advanced in civilization and all pagan philosophy. It was to no ordinary race that God sent this apostle, it was to no brutish, savage people sunk in intellectual apathy. When he came to preach this Gospel history tells us that this apostle was obliged to face the most learned philosophers of the pagan era, that he was obliged to preach words which would charm the ears of poets attuned to sweetest measure, and who were accustomed to lead the councils of the nations to the high-sounding harp. It was to such men he came, who were able to attest and analyze every assertion of his. Therefore, knowing them so well, he prepared himself by thirty years of study, and now, when he is sixty years of age, he kneels down in Rome at the feet of St. Sylvester, and receives his blessing and apostolic ordination and the command to teach the Irish people the Gospel of Jesus Christ.

He came, and the winds of heaven favored in every breeze his coming, wafting him along out into the western ocean, until, like the earliest fathers of whom we read, he saw the streak of island green, and cried out: "There is my Innisfail, the island of destiny." He came, he landed in Ireland, the mitred man with saintliness and grace upon his lips, with learning in his mind, with jurisdiction in his hand. Oh! blessed amongst the hours, most blessed amongst the ages of our national existence, the hour when the sands of Ireland lovingly clasped his feet. For it is written: "Oh! how beautiful are the feet of those who evangelize peace and all good things." He came, and he raised up his voice, raised up the sign of the cross, unfurled the standard of Jesus Christ, preached the Gospel, and taught the people of Ireland, from the king upon his throne, from the Druid in his sacerdotal robes at the altar, the minstrel sitting in the council-chamber, the young princes returning from the battle-field or from the chase, down to the humblest peasant in the land—for there were no serfs; never, never in Ireland was there slavery, never, in its worst day, was there the servitude known to all other nations. They rose at his word, they listened to his accents, which fell like music upon their ears; they heard their own grand Celtic tongue, learned on the mountains of Donegal amongst so many miseries and tears, and now resounding and thundering through the land the holy names of Jesus and Mary. They learned the Gospel of God's love for man and their own vileness, and like one man the whole nation rose and welcomed the apostle, took the message from his mouth, engraved it in their hearts, and illustrated it at once by a life almost magical in its suddenness and perfection. Such is the brief history of Patrick's apostolic career. Unlike every other apostle ever sent to a people, no difficulty lay in his way. We read of no persecution, no contradictions of the deep, acute, philosophic mind disputing only that it may learn, but the moment that it has learned docile and humble as the mind of a little child to receive the truth of Jesus Christ. No martyr's blood was necessary to fertilize the soil, no tear of sorrow did she ever demand from her great apostle's eye, no agonizing hour of uncertainty ever troubled him in the full peacefulness of his career; the word of promise spoken to Moses of old was fulfilled and realized in St. Patrick. "Go," saith the Lord, "and I will give thee every land upon which thy foot shall tread." He came conquering and to conquer, and the brightest, the strangest page in the history of the Church of God is the page that records the instantaneous conversion of the Irish people. He is the only apostle on record that found a nation entirely pagan, and before his death there was not a single pagan of note left in the land. According to the most ancient record, St. Patrick at one hundred and twenty years of age raised his dying hand to bless the island of his destiny. Ireland at that hour was not only the most Catholic but she was already one of the most holy nations that God had gathered into the bosom of his Church.

But, ah! dearly beloved, whilst our fathers were charmed with the harmony of his doctrines, whilst they received with the assent of eager yet acute minds the splendid truths that their apostle taught them, whilst the mystery of holiness was upon his lips, and from his lips passed into their souls, there was another lesson which Patrick taught the Irish people—a lesson which he taught them forcibly and powerfully, and which they learned quickly and well—and that was the lesson that sanctity of life must accompany and crown Catholic faith in the heart of every man and every people ; that faith without works is like the body without the soul ; that faith without sanctity is only a greater judgment, for it is a greater sin to sin against the light when one has received it than to sin in darkness when one has never known that light. And having taught them the Catholic faith, Ireland's great apostle next taught them the secret of Catholic holiness, and here his work was easy ; it involved no labor of preaching, it involved no great exercise of any faculty of his ; he had only to live, to live before the people. He let them see him, and then the action of this man's life seemed to cry out eloquently with the apostle: "I have taught you the love, the love of Jesus Christ ; now be you imitators, as I also am, of my Lord and my God." And, in fact, every virtue most beautiful in the Christian shows out in him. He was a sinless man, in whose transparent, holy life the bitterest or most observant enemy could find no flaw or fault ; yet he was a most penitential man, fasting every day of his life, scourging himself, rising in the night and spending the time in prayer, at one time going into the lonely island in Lough Derg, still called Patrick's Purgatory, for there he anticipated by a voluntary penance all the pains and penances with which a merciful God cleanses the souls on earth. At another time, in the beginning of Lent, he climbed up the steep sides of that barren mountain that rises up in the western wilds, still called Croagh Patrick, rising up mysteriously, the Soracte of Ireland, in the midst of a barren solitude, rearing its head into the clouds. He climbed its rugged sides, and when, like Moses of old, he had attained the summit of the mountain he knelt down and spent the forty days of Lent. Tears were his only food, he wept night and day, and it was only when the light of Easter was about to break on the land that his children who waited for him saw him coming down as Moses descended from the sides of Sinai—the light of God beaming on his face, the sanctity of God, like a halo, round about him, and the word which was spread before became irresistible, and his victory was all the greater in the land. And with all this prayer, this poverty of life—for he went through the land lonely and on foot, and it was only in his extreme old age that he would permit the love of the Irish people to furnish him even with a chariot in which to be carried from place to place—he labored all day long in poverty, content with the merest necessaries of life, in unfailing prayer, and in fasting and in humiliations · for in his confessions he begins the book : "I, Patrick, a sinner, and one of the most unworthy of men," yet he was at the time one of the most distinguished saints of the Church.

Thus the Irish people beheld in him an illustration of his doctrine, and what was the consequence ? The most natural in the world for a lively, generous, impulsive, and earnest people ; they saw that Patrick was in earnest, they became earnest like him ; and the moment they received his doctrine their first conclusion was : As we believe what he tells us, so we must live as he lives. The consequence was the most extraordinary recorded in the history of the world : the whole nation became a nation of saints. Monasteries sprang up in every quarter of the land, convents and great houses for recluses covered the hills, and the valleys were crowded with hermits. The Church and Pope of Rome, who expected to hear of the grain of mustard sowed in the soil sprouting up here and there and crying loudly for martyrs' blood, the pope and the Church were almost instantly amazed, for Patrick's first message was : "They are all Christians, they are all Catholics, and they are all almost saints." But how grand, how magnificent is the prospect which the genius of history points out to us ! It is true we have to go back far, fourteen hundred years, we have to go back through many ages, and then to behold Ireland in the first light of her sanctity, of her purity—Bridget in Kildare, one of the most glorious and brightest of the Church's saints, leading the maidenhood of Ireland, consecrated to holy purity; to behold Benignus, the bishop, spreading the sanctity of the Church in his own example, and the father of monks; to hear the sweet legend of Nelius of the Clean Hand, because when he was brought a little child to St. Bridget she laid her hand upon him and blessed him, and said: "This child will grow and become a priest, and attend me when dying, and give me the Blessed Sacrament for the last time." And when the child heard this he wrapped his hand up in a clean cloth and touched nothing with it until he opened it to receive the chrism of his consecration, that it might be worthy to take the Body of our Lord and lay it on the virgin's lips. Patrick received, even upon this earth, the reward of the apostleship which the other apostles only received in heaven, for he saw his labors crowned with sanctity on earth.

And now, dearly beloved, we may perhaps think that which grew up so suddenly would fade equally suddenly, for we know that if the gourd of the prophet sprang up in one night and formed a shade under which he took his rest, that it withered as speedily away when a little worm gnawed at the root. Was it to be so with the Church of Ireland's faith and Ireland's sanctity; was it to wither as quickly as it sprang up? Answer it, O ye ages! answer it, O ye nations who have tried the strength of this root! Every worm that could assail it has fixed his venomous teeth in it, but in vain; in vain the fire of the Dane consumed the land; it could waste everything, but left Ireland's Catholicity untouched as of old; in vain came the storm of successive persecutions; in vain was the land wasted over and over again, flooded in blood, steeped in tears; in vain was the whole aboriginal race stripped of everything they had in the world and driven out to die in the wasted places of the land—in vain all; everything that earth could try, that hell could essay, has been tried in vain.

Ireland's Catholicity, like the mountain oak, like the cedar of Lebanon, defied every storm for fourteen hundred years, and, blessed be God! we her children who are in her arms to-day behold that ancient truth as fresh, its leaves as green, its flowers as fragrant, its fruits as rich as on the day that the saint lay down in the northern land and blessed the country which God had given him, and, dying, said these last words in the Irish language: "O Ireland! this is my prayer and this is my prophecy: Other nations may lose all that God gave them; Ireland, my land, will never lose the pure, true faith which she has received!" She has not lost it; she can scarcely go through greater trials than she has already. The past is the clearest guarantee for the future. Beloved brethren, I have no fear for the faith of my land, but I call upon you to-day to do what our fathers did of old whilst you cling to the faith—to remember, like the Irish fourteen hundred years ago, that you must illustrate that faith by sanctity of life. If you believe what Patrick taught, you must endeavor to live, as Patrick lived, sacramental lives, lives of purity, of heroic devotion to God and to His holy Church, to His vicar on earth, with whom Patrick bound us, so that when we come to heaven's gate and claim entrance there, on the strength of the faith that Patrick taught us, our father in heaven, who is praying for us to-day, may acknowledge us for his true children and say: "They are mine, my likeness is upon them; they are like their fathers to whom I preached; they are like their martyrs from whom I sprang; they have to-day the faith, they have finished the good work. Crown them, O Lord! as Thou hast crowned them with faith."

St. Ignatius.

THE following is an abstract of a sermon preached by Father Burke in the Church of St. Francis Xavier, Dublin, on the Feast of St. Ignatius of Loyola, the founder of the Society of Jesus. He took for his text:

"And the Lord said: This man is to me a vessel of election to carry my name before the Gentiles and kings, and children of Israel, for I will show him what great things he must suffer in my name."

THESE words came from the lips of our Lord and Saviour Jesus Christ when He was describing the character of St. Paul, who was to go forth in His name to convert the nations of the earth. "This man is to me a vessel of election, followed with my grace, and Spirit, and Word. He shall go forth, and there shall be this sign on him—that the burden of his message shall be the glory of His name. That name shall be pinned to his brow as a crown of glory." The Lord said that the people of the earth should hear the Word from his lips, and a vision of grace should spring up before him. He should suffer for His name's sake—for the sake of that name which is the glory, the love, and the message unto all nations. St. Paul was the greatest apostle, the greatest of founders of the Church, described by our Lord and Saviour Jesus Christ. The holy Church which was founded by the Son of God was founded not only in the faith, that she should teach the nations of the earth; but she was also founded in holiness, that she should be the prolific mother of saints. As she was founded in faith, so through the grace of holiness the Church was ever able to produce saints as great as St. Paul, and as powerful before nations, and who gloried as much as he did in the name of Jesus. Fifteen hundred years had passed away since St. Paul died outside the walls of Rome, with the word of Jesus uttered by his lips, still struggling in the agonies of death. Fifteen hundred years after his death a saint great as he—great in the name that was engraved on his heart, and great in the suffering endured for the name of Jesus—a second St. Paul, was given to the world in the person of St. Ignatius Loyola, whose name filled the Church with hope and resounds to-day in heaven. We have come together for two purposes: first, to honor the Lord in that great saint. "Praise ye the Lord in His saints in the firmament of his power" was a divine command. The second purpose is to consider the character, the work, and the life of that great servant of God, and to apply the example of his glorious life to our own actions and souls. We will consider the personal character of that great saint, of whose life we will listen to a brief sketch ; as also of his work in the Church of God, which affords an illustration of how wonderfully the character of the Father is ever reflected in the sanctity and graces of His children. We should dwell upon the life of St. Ignatius that from his sanctity we might learn the secret of sanctity, and, imitating him, we might find out the way to our Lord Jesus Christ.

In the kingdom of Spain—the great, grand, magnificent mother of saints, the privileged nation, which, beyond all others, has produced founders of great religious orders—in 1591—nearly three hundred years ago—St. Ignatius was born, and at that time Martin Luther was nine years old. These two grew together under the eye of God, who sees all things. One grew into infernal proportions to his last awful heresy ; he grew and strengthened for the purpose of destroying, if possible, the indestructible Church of God and ruin the nations. The other grew in strength, in magnificent proportions, splendid in body, noble in mind and soul, and ardent in devotion. He grew in greatness, and in that chivalrous nature which God made the basis of his superhuman work. He grew to combat the destruction which the arch-heretic Luther endeavored to bring on the Church of God. He was of noble birth, and came into the world surrounded with everything which that world could yield him, and for a time the youth seemed to lend himself to the practices of the world and the "virtues" of the court. He was brought up at court, trained in courtly manners and courtly etiquette. He was educated befittingly for a man in his exalted station of life. He was given to reading stories of great deeds of valor performed by the nobles. He was generous to a fault, and brave even to rashness, and it was but natural that, when a young man, he selected the profession of arms. Then he enured himself for some years to all the hardships of a soldier's life. He was admired by his fellow-officers for his great daring. No forlorn hope or beleaguered city had terrors for him; he gloried to stand in the breach, and for his great bravery his fellow-soldiers loved and admired him. There was in him a singular combination of mind and body. He had all virtues and no vices, yet he was not a holy or a devout man. All his virtues seemed the natural growth of his magnificent person. He was generous to a fault, and always gave to the poor what he had. His purity was more. No word of obscenity ever escaped his lips, and on that account the reserve observed in his presence could not have been greater had a consecrated priest or holy man been present. He loved, and his love was a pure one. His ideal beauty was of that chaste, venerable form that would arise before the romantic imagination of a mediæval knight; it was a fair and splendid ideal, and his love had no grosser element. At thirty years of age he stood on the ramparts of a severely beleaguered city. He had only a handful of soldiers around him. His enemy was a large host, but there he stood, brave and resolute, encouraging those who surrounded him. In his left hand he held the banner of Spanish liberty, while hailstones of shot and shell rained round him, and the besieged held out until he was knocked down and seriously wounded, and the enemy entered the city over his prostrate body. His defeat under the circumstances was grander than a victory. The whole world rang with his name while he lay stricken in body and tortured with sickness. He was spared from death, and his mind turned to the God of heaven and to prayer. He had a vision of St. Peter, who said to him: "Thou shalt live, and regain thy strength."

He was not told why he was to live, but while he was lying on his bed of sickness he sent for some works of chivalry and romance, and they could not be supplied to him. The only book in the place was the "Lives of the Saints." At first it seemed rather dry, as he was not given to spiritual reading, and was no lover of holy books. He could not help reading the book, he had no other; and as he read of the brave, heroic power and mighty intellect he asked himself if men had really lived such lives as those, and if they had fought their way and carved their entrance into heaven by such holy work as theirs. He asked himself why he should waste time in endeavoring to spread dominion for earthly kings, who must perish as well as himself, when he might do battle for the kingdom of Jesus Christ, and earn for himself a place in the kingdom of heaven. A voice said to him: "Thou shalt find work for which the Lord hath created thee." God had not given to the man strength and courage to build up for himself a passing name, but he was created for God's own purpose. He shut the book, and, lifting up his arms to God, resolved to be a saint. His courage remained with him; he was a soldier in the beginning; he was destined to be a soldier unto the end. His feeling of love remained, but not love for the same ideal; for a vision of Mary, the Mother of God, the Virgin of virgins, appeared to him clothed in the sun, with the moon beneath her feet, and a crown of twelve stars on her head. It was then that he pledged himself to stand in the bastions of the Church and do battle for God. That took place in 1521. He rose from his sick-bed, his arm as strong as of old, his courage as high, his resolution as grand; all that was good in the man had returned, all that was not was cast out. He scourged his flesh, so that it might be obedient, and after three years, partly spent in Spain, partly in Italy, and partly in the Holy Land, he studied for the priesthood in the University of Paris. It was there his saintly nature became matured and developed. It was there, too, that a vision of his mission came to him; the vision began to look out into the distance, and, hearing of the heresy of the nations, St. Ignatius comprehended. It seemed as if he heard a voice saying: "Arise, O man! whose heart never failed, and who is a lover of Jesus Christ; seize on a few of those youths around you, and lay hold of all this reviving of pagan literature and this heresy; go forth into every clime, carrying my name with thee."

The young Spanish professor whose eloquence and learning dazzled his fellows—Francis Xavier—was in the same college, and Ignatius prevailed upon him and eight others to consecrate themselves to the Lord. When asked what name their new religious society should have Ignatius, with the dearest name still uppermost, said, "Jesus," and thus it took the name of the Society of Jesus. The consecration of the order took place in 1535, on the Feast of the Assumption. St. Ignatius was made general superior of the order. For fifteen years he was increasing every day in sanctity. He died in 1556, having wisely governed the order, founded hundreds of colleges, and sent missionaries to all parts of the world, whom he directed from his central station in Rome. His body was buried under the great altar of the Jesuit chapel in Rome. His literary works, "Spiritual Exercises" and "The Constitution of the Society of Jesus," were models of purity and literary ability, and were most valuable to the Church. They were remarkable for deep, clear, profound knowledge, and even Lord Bacon, a Protestant, has, in one of his works, paid the highest tribute of praise to the system of training practised in the colleges of the order founded by St. Ignatius, which order was feared and persecuted throughout the world as the soldiers of Christ, ever to the front to stand in the breach, guarding the faith and receiving in their own persons insult and persecution. Yet when they were persecuted and banished from their homes Ireland was ever ready to afford them a refuge and to welcome them to her Catholic bosom, there to rest awhile their weary heads. (The very reverend preacher concluded with a sublime peroration.)

St. Francis Xavier.

THE Feast of St. Francis Xavier, the Apostle of the Indies, was celebrated in the Church of St. Xavier, Dublin, December 3, 1877. The sermon was delivered by Father Burke, who took for his text: "God is wonderful in His saints."

THE triumphs of Almighty God are made manifest in all His creations. The very heavens speak the glory of God, and the silent stars proclaim His power. The office of nature is eloquent in having its beauties revealed in every new form of creation. How much more are His distinct attributes rendered conspicuous and wonderful when we contemplate His saints, when we contemplate these mighty living officers who proclaim His name and glory, when we contemplate those who at the highest were so united to God as to be lost in good deeds to themselves, and to live only for God—devoted, with all the energy of a great nature, not to any personal or worldly thing, but only faithful to the Word of God, and so devoted to Him as to be able to command the elements and to exalt themselves for Him! God manifested Himself by instructing and by the wonderful revelations in His saints. It was through His saints that He provided for all the wants of man. Three hundred years ago, in the sixteenth century, when there were disloyalty to authority, imperial changes, despotism, the pulling down of laws, the sweeping away of ancient universities, and disruption in all those elements that constitute civil, social, and religious society, this great order of Jesus Christ was established. Often in that century the voice was demure of those who spoke in the language of faith. In that century it was to be despised by man. Up to this period all religious belief was founded upon one and upon the only principle upon which it can rest—namely, the essential truthfulness of God, the essential truthfulness of the utterances of God, and the invariable truthfulness of the living consciousness of God —namely, the Catholic Church. Every man who believed in the Catholic Church acknowledged the authority of the Church, his mother; but at this time her authority was to be broken up, the very basis of her foundation was to be shifted from the rock upon which Jesus Christ, their Lord, built it, and there was to be set up in her place mere human opinions and private judgments. Under the spreading rays of the universal increase there was a thirst for knowledge of every kind. Notwithstanding that at the time the Greek Empire had just fallen, the libraries of Constantinople had been all carried away and found refuge in Western Europe, the Greek and Latin schools were discovered disseminating knowledge on every side, and those who never read before began to read. Wonderful were the things realized in foreign lands. New countries were discovered in the West, and at this time the Catholic Church seemed to be in danger, if ever in danger she could be supposed to be. The great centre of knowledge was removed, and insidiously turned into schools and universities of Europe. The new spirit was awake, and now it was for the Lord God in His supreme wisdom to investigate the things that were to come, and make preparations in the Church—to furnish her with new weapons to fight the new wars, and with her champions to come forth and wait for the signs by which men were to know. In these days the University of Paris was the greatest seat of learning in the world. The youth of Christian Europe, by the discoveries of new arts and sciences, were attracted there. In the midst of all these there came from Germany a youth of Christian principles and allegiance to the Church to be a lecturer in the university—a youth of much ability, though yet a student and heir to an illustrious name. Men told of him how he had already distinguished himself in the battle-field.

The great name went before him. The student of Paris, Ignatius Loyola, who had asserted bravery and honor in the face of the world, was among them; but how did they find him? They found him broken with fasting and mortification. He seemed to have forgotten himself, forgotten his history, forgotten the ancient passions that made him the honored foreigner, the great prize the world had made —this man, who seemed to know nothing, to think of nothing, to live for nothing, to speak of nothing but love for the Church of God. He moved among those students, and at once a feeling spread that the Church of their God had attached itself to the university, and that the man of God was in it. There was also in the university a young Spaniard, equally noble, far more distinguished than Ignatius in all the competitions of the sciences of man, and who had been for nine years previously in the university —who had made his mark, and who was spoken of as the greatest and most industrious of young doctors—a man who was chief of all in learning and philosophy. He retained a great name. This was Francis Xavier, who came from Pampeluna, at the foot of the Pyrennees Mountains; young—for he was only twenty-one years of age—already known, strong of body, vigorous of intellect, and beautiful to behold; in manner generous, soft in his affections and heart, and with a capacity to compete with the world in science. But in the midst of all this worldliness there was one in this university that recognized that the vassal of nations was Xavier's joy. Thus at this period this learned foreigner was teaching, to the great admiration of those who heard him, in the university. He descended one day from his chair, having charmed the professors and students around, amongst whom was Xavier, who went to his room filled with thoughts of his ambition, when Ignatius crosses his path, looks at him with sad, reproachful eyes, nears him, and drops into his ears, in the voice of the Gospel: "Suffer what you will, it benefits man nothing to gain the whole world if he lose his own soul." A wonder from God was revealed; the man who spoke was gone. Was Xavier going to yield himself to the world and take the attractions and pleasures which swept to him? Again and again Ignatius crossed the path of Xavier, and day after day did he repeat to him: "What shall it benefit thee to gain the whole world if thou lose thy soul?" Xavier took thought and consulted. There were five other students in the university, all of them men most distinguished in every walk of science, men who have left behind them in the annals of the Church sacred and glorious names. Ignatius gathered them all. And now to place the freedom of confidence which was needed in the foundation of the Society of Jesus, and then to plan the great, wonderful work which God had pleased him to do—in His wisdom He is equal to all the wants of His Church—this silent patriarch, soldier, and prince now turned to God with all his youth, and began to brood on the mysteries of the time. He saw the world was changing, and he saw a new spirit was coming up. He considered three laws—self-denial, devotedness to some purpose, and organization. Around him he saw his own countrymen going forth to unknown seas, sacrificing their lives in the paths of discovery of every kind. He observed men ready to give their lives in the great cause of scientific power. He saw these men denying every pleasure of the living; he saw them day after day investigating until they came to some work of discovery. Finally, he saw the world organizing itself—the whole world forming itself into societies—and said: "What these men do for the world for self, I will do for God and His Church."

This was the grand idea of the young patriarch, and afterwards his doing. He asked the six young men if they were willing to die for God; secondly, if they were willing to devote themselves to the purpose of God and His Church; and thirdly, if they would form themselves into an organization, founded pre-eminently on this one great principle—namely, the one mind carefully formed with integrity and wisdom, whose greatness and honesty should command the united action of them all, and whose intellectual light they were to carry out in obedience to the principles of this one mind. Francis Xavier was the first to understand the decided mind and explain that which Ignatius and the others followed. And so in the year 1534 these seven men went up to an oratory on the hill of Montmartre, near Paris, and there they bowed themselves to God, and swore their lives away to the Church of God. Now, from that hour began the history of the Society of Jesus Christ—fifteen hundred and thirty-four, nearly three centuries and a half ago. Through all these years it has lived in the face of the whole world and before the Church of God, and has carried out the grand purpose for which it was founded. It has spread self-denial, devotedness, and organization, and is able to cope with the strictest form of political organization. During that period this society has been the object of continued, constant, and oppressive persecution outside the Church. With what result? That the society and the Catholic Church are feared throughout the world as much as ever they were. For eight years after his surrender to the Church, Ignatius, Francis Xavier, and their colleagues spread the light of the Gospel under their spiritual father and patriarch, and under the influence of his mighty mind. During these years he was engaged in labors for the Church. He partly labored in Venice, visiting the poor and tending the sick; no sacrifice was too great; no mortification or patience too terrible; no revolting case of leprosy too disgusting for him to attend or relieve. And thus did he live until 1541, by which time, after years under Ignatius's guidance, he found that the affections of that large and generous heart all belonged to the Church of God. When Ignatius discovered this he determined that his apostolic son should go forth to preach, and here was a work put up before him. King John III. of Portugal, a most religious prince, found himself the possessor of enormous territories along the shores of the Indian Ocean and towards the Northern

Pacific, inhabited with millions of uncivilized people, all in the darkness of idolatry or of the equally dark idolatry of Mohammedanism, and the consciousness of this smote the king; but the awful feeling came upon him that the work of their conversion demanded a saint, and in the sixteenth century it was hard to find saints. Saint Teresa was in a cloister, and Saint John of the Cross was engaged in his work of reform. But a saint to go out and captivate the mind, to charm all the race of men—where was such to be found?

A young student of Paris told his majesty that Ignatius in the university had with him some others that were all that the king needed. Accordingly a mandate was received from the Sovereign Pontiff, and Ignatius was called upon to send two of his companions to spread the doctrine of the Catholic Church amongst millions and millions. Ignatius gathered to his list his apostolic son, Francis Xavier; and even as the heart of the brave soldier bounded with joy when the hour of battle came to send him to death, but still to glory, so did the heart exult in him when he was doomed to go and preach the Gospel. We find him, therefore, in 1541 sailing for the Indies, and after thirteen months' voyage he arrived at Goa. Then he began his labors. It was not merely preaching the Gospel to the citizens; Xavier undertook to preach it to whole nations. For ten years and a half he labored in India proper, partly in the land adjoining the Indian coast, partly in the quarters of the Japanese Empire, going from nation to nation, receiving insults, speaking to the assembled high-priesthood, scattering the Gospel from land to land, until his converts were reckoned not by thousands but by hundreds of thousands. He preached the Gospel from morning until night, and with the touch of his hand or with the sign of the cross the lepers were cured and the paralyzed rose up and renewed their stand. A pagan father came to him and said: "O thou creature from a foreign land, and Christian of a stranger dark! thou sayest that thy Church is the true Church. If thy God be the true God, give me back my child that I have left dead at home"; and Xavier answered: "Go back and thou shalt find her living." The pagan father went back and found the young maiden well, and putting her arms around him she said: "My soul had gone forward and a demon was about to catch me, when a man of strange appearance came and brought me away." The pagan father brought his child to Francis Xavier, and she exclaimed: "Oh! it is he. This is the saint that saved me from the demon." On another occasion, while in the neighborhood of Malacca, a mother flung herself down at his feet in great grief, saying: "O father! man of God, my daughter is dead and is three days buried." The glory of the living God flashes from his eyes, and in the power of the Spirit he prays, and, turning to the woman, says, "Good woman, open the grave and thou wilt find thy daughter living there." Brought back from the very corruption of death by the saint of God! Yet all this time, night and day, he continued in the course of the conversion of nations. They found him writing home to Ignatius; he never took a pen in his hand to write to him but in a kneeling position. He moved not without his counsel. Xavier's was the voice that spoke, Xavier's was the hand that was uplifted, but the soul that guided Xavier was that of Ignatius. The society was growing at home; the troubled spirits of heresy and infidelity were starting up, and, starting as they were, Ignatius was increasing the number of laborers in his field. No thought broke upon the grand mind of the apostle, no thought communicated with him. Xavier was aspiring to be the evangelistic apostle in the great country of Asia. From Japan he was to pass to China, astonish that country, and pass from China to Siberia, still spreading the light of the Gospel.

This was a vast design, and filled the mighty mind of the saint, and he gathered himself up to fulfil it. He sailed for China and landed at Cochin, just opposite to the quarter he was about to invade for God. He lost half the sailors he had employed through sickness, and he knew that death awaited him; he almost told the time. He had two great saints with him who came of a soldier race. He smiled in the face of death; three times was he shipwrecked. Death was shuddering around him, and yet he had his work to do; but he was abandoned by the sailors. He was then only forty-six years of age. In one of his letters to his brethren at home he expressed himself thus: "If God be to me what He has hitherto been, and if He give to me ten years of life, I will go through Asia, Turkey, and the northern parts." The apostle was in the bloom of his life, in the strength of his great learning, but God called him, in the ecstasy of his longing, to crown him for his love. Abandoned by his comrades, stricken down with fatal fever—the very blood in his veins nearly burning—he lay down on the shores of Sancian, and turned his weary eyes towards his land. After a time the pains of death came upon him, and now another land opened before him; now, with the pallor of death on the face of neglect, he threw out his dying arms in the ecstasy of joy, cried out His name, and exclaimed: "*In te Domine speravi, non confundar in æternum,*" and died. Glorious soul, which, proudly crowned, escaping from a body broken and bruised by self-mortification, emaciated by fasting, growing old before his time, passed to the heavens! Without a friend or a hand to moisten his lips that soul passed away to its Judge. In less than one hundred years after, in 1628, his Holiness Paul V. canonized this saint, and well he might.

That poor, broken, emaciated saint was found three days after in the tabernacle where he died, uncorrupted, fresh as ever, so much so that when they came upon him they all cried out: "He is not dead! He is alive!" Entering the city of Malacca, to which the saint was brought, the bishops and priests and the principal citizens of the town came in procession. There was a pestilence raging in the city, and at the moment the body of St. Xavier crossed the city, that moment the dying recovered health and the very signs of pestilence ceased. The blind were led to him, and the moment the uncorrupted hand would move towards the blind eyes they were open. The most astounding miracles occurred every day during his life, until the pagans were obliged to invoke his instructions and proclaim Christianity in the Indies. The example of his life taught them many things. He consented, on the day of his vow to do good in the hands of Ignatius, to surrender his life, with all hopes and pleasures, to God. He died for the Sacred Heart of Christ, and sprang up again into another life. If there be any one willing to adopt a like course, let him surrender himself and cast his life into that sacred cause, and then will he live. The army that the apostle of the Indies left behind him stands to-day as it did of old—first in the army of God. It has mustered together from every land, and carried the name of Jesus, aided and assisted by the hand of Jesus Christ.

St. Vincent de Paul.

The following is an abridged report of a sermon delivered by Father Burke on the feast of St. Vincent de Paul, July 19, 1877, in the beautiful church of the Vincentian Order, Sunday's Well, Cork. The charity of the great saint is strikingly portrayed. After the first Gospel Father Burke ascended the pulpit and gave the following text :

"I found David a man according to my own heart. With my holy oil I anointed him."

THESE words are found in the Book of Psalms. Among the many wonderful works of God, the greatest and most wonderful of all is His saints; therefore the Scripture tells us that God was wonderful in His saints. We are told to look on them, to contemplate them, to admire them, and in them and through them to give the praise most acceptable to Almighty God. But why is God so wonderful in His saints? Because the highest effects of God's omnipotence came forth both in the order of His nature and the order of His grace. There have been saints of God who were triumphs of divine power both in the order of nature and the order of grace—in the order of nature because God, when He intended to create a saint, gave to that being a strong, a sweet, and a high and perfect nature. And if there be aught in the elements of that nature that may be repugnant to sanctity and to the obligation of His highest creation, He gave to that saint a strength and a power of will and a determination of action by which all that might be faulty or imperfect in nature might be overcome and constantly put away; so that God's work even here, as saints, would be the brightest and most generous and most beautiful of all His creations. But no, this foundation of nature was only the beginning of the works of God in His saints. It was only when they were thus prepared, thus strengthened, and thus chastened and subdued, and made conformable in purity and in all other natural virtues to His heart, that the Almighty God poured out on them the vial containing His holy oil of superior charity and sanctity. And, therefore, He first formed them unto His own heart, and then with His holy oil He anointed them. And what was the unction of which the Holy Ghost spoke? It was the anointing of high charity, of the highest form of all virtue, in which all the virtues meet, as all inferior and partial things are found in the most perfect and complete things. Therefore charity was said to be the law and love of the perfect, the bond of perfection, and he that loveth has acquired all the virtues and fulfilled all the law.

Let us apply all those principles to the man whose name is upon the lips of the Church to-day in praise, in admiration, in benediction to God, because in a dark and dreary age He gave us so great a saint; let us apply those principles to the man whose glory was celebrated by the Church triumphant in heaven, sung by the angels, admired by the saints, and from whom to-day God received so large a measure of thanksgiving and glory for the great St. Vincent.

First of all, he was a man after God's own heart, even after the order of nature. It was towards the close of the sixteenth century, in the year 1575, that he was born, in the province of Gascony, in France. His parents were holy people in humble circumstances, but deriving their nobility from the true source of all nobility—the purity and sanctity of life. He was one out of five children, and they were all reared in the fear and love of God by their pious parents.

All the children were good and pious, but the child Vincent, from the days of his infancy, began to show signs of strange and extraordinary holiness. His idea of amusement and recreation was to steal into some quiet place and there pour out his young infant soul in prayer. He seemed to know intuitively all the principles of divine faith. As he grew from infancy to childhood every grace seemed to grow with him, until at length he came to that age when the passions begin to be stirred by the demons of iniquity. But Vincent was as pure as an angel of God. Whatever faults were in him he painfully and laboriously cast out of his character, until they found him at twenty-five years of age—after years of study, seven of which were spent at the University of Toulouse—fitted for the priesthood in the necessary learning and all other acquirements, but, above all, fitted for the priesthood inasmuch as he had a virgin soul fit to enter the golden gates of God's sanctuary, unsullied by the slightest touch of anything approaching sin. At twenty-five he was ordained priest, and then there remained but one test through which Almighty God must put him and try him before he crowned him with the crown of the most heroic charity by which he rose as a giant in the annals of the Church. This was the test of affliction, misery, suffering, and trial. The sign of the cross had not yet been burned into his heart by suffering, and this was the last crowning test to which our Lord put him.

Consider the capture of the young priest in the Mediterranean by Saracen pirates, and his sufferings as a galley-slave, and afterwards under cruel masters in Africa, until he sang his own misery in the "Psalms of David" and the praises of the Virgin in the "Salve Regina," which, heard by his master's wife and described by her, caused the husband's conversion and the release of the saint, who, by a miraculous intervention of God, escaped to France. Now he was a priest once more in his own land; God had tried him sufficiently, and the sign of the cross of his Redeemer was now on his heart and soul. He springs at once into an atmosphere of higher sanctity, and that sanctity took a treble form, and that was the threefold form in which it flamed in the Sacred Heart of Jesus—a trinity of love in the heart of the Master, and a trinity of love in the heart of His child—and in everything he proved himself a man after God's own heart. Take the three master loves of the Sacred Heart of Jesus—love for God the Eternal Father, love for God's poor in every form of misery and distress, and finally, love for God's holy Church. (He eloquently reviewed the life of our Divine Lord, to show how particularly he brought into practice this threefold love.)

Vincent, chastened, purified, and sanctified by every element of sanctity, entered on his great career of charity, and from him came the evidences of the love that filled the heart of his Divine Master. Intercourse with God became his very life, at all times and under all circumstances. Even when the agonies of death were on him, when eighty-five years of age, the pains of death, the failing of a long and laborious life, and the sorrow of separation from all he loved in this world were on him, with trembling limbs, with a breaking heart, even then he rose in the morning at four o'clock, and for three long hours he prayed motionless, as if he were dead, while every fibre of his aged frame was trembling with the agony of death; still he mastered it and prayed to God.

Next to this was his manifold love for the poor. Every misery that ever came across him was relieved; every sorrow that he ever met was changed to joy; every soul that ever came within the touch of his hand, the sound of his voice, or the glance of his eye was purified by him.

There is not in the roll of saints who adorn the annals of the Catholic Church one whose charity went forth so powerfully, so wonderfully, so universally, whose charity so embraced in distinct action every single corporal and spiritual work of mercy, as the great St. Vincent de Paul. In his day society was in a deplorable state. Little children used to be abandoned in the streets of the cities by their unnatural and wicked mothers, to die of want and hunger. St. Vincent de Paul went out into the streets of the city and found them, took those precious creatures by the hand, and founded large institutions, hospitals, asylums, and refuges for foundling children. St. Vincent de Paul stood by the newly-formed grave where the father and mother were laid down to rest, the grave surrounded by the trembling, weeping, hopeless, defenceless, and abandoned orphan children, and he was a father to them all; he took them all to his noble heart, and founded his great asylums and institutions for orphans.

St. Vincent de Paul spent long days, from morning watch until night, among the poorest of the poor in city and in country, teaching and purifying. Wherever he appeared the light of knowledge went forth from him, and the truth of God sprang up in his presence. St. Vincent found the fallen and degraded sinner the most hopeless of all. The most hopeless of all it seemed indeed, for when Jesus passed away it seemed as if He had forgotten to make provision for the sisters in crime of the woman who crept to His feet. There was no provision made for the abandoned. But St. Vincent was a father to them; he founded Magdalene asylums wherever he went. The fever-stricken, the paralyzed, the leper, all found in him not merely one helping in an isolated case, but a great organizing charity that was able to take in hand all their wants like our Divine Lord. A great war broke out in the province of Lorraine, a war followed by the usual curses that come in the train of war and the most terrible pestilences. The history of the famine found no equal in the history of the world until we come to recollect the famine that fell on dear old Ireland not many years ago. St. Vincent was then a poor man, for everything that was given to him was exhausted in charity; but yet he went amongst the famine and pestilence stricken people, and during his ministrations he spent two million livres, an extraordinary sum in those days. He made provision for the galley-slaves by establishing a hospital in Marseilles, so that the castaways of the world found a supporter in him.

This was his life for sixty years, during which he toiled

night and day; and every year he brought forth some new evidence of his great energy and the power of charity that was in his heart and hand. But there was another love which had taken possession of him, and that was the love for the Church, the Spouse of Jesus. That Church in the days of St. Vincent was threatened by one great danger—the Jansenist heresy in France, a heresy that under the pretence of sanctity would break down Christian law and destroy the purity and virtue of Christian teaching. Against that heresy St. Vincent rose up, and by sanctity outshone the pretended sanctity of Port Royal and other centres of heresy; he cast their light into darkness, and in his own life and teaching he showed fully and completely the difference between the real idea of sanctity that came from heaven and the spurious imitation that came forth from the hypocrisy of man.

There was another danger which in those days was very great, and that was that the Church found it difficult to provide herself with holy and devout clergy: and to this Vincent turned himself with all the energy his great charity was capable of. Everywhere he provided for the preparation of the clergy who were to minister at our altars. At the request of St. Francis de Sales he took charge of the Visitation Order of Nuns, and the testimony of St. Francis was: "I have seen many, and heard of many, but I have never seen or heard of a holier or worthier priest than Vincent de Paul." Thus did his heart throb with the three loves of Jesus. But a man may have all these characteristics, and may do all these things, and in this way receive a great crown in heaven, but yet his work may die after him, and have no permanency. Not so with this saint. With him the promise that was made of the apostles was continued: "These words I have put on thy lips, and the words of the Lord shall not depart from thy lips nor from the lips of thy children after thee." The permanency of the work was the great feature of the labors of Vincent de Paul. Revolutions that had uprooted everything had swept over his work, as well as the works of other men; wars and pestilences, and heresies and infidelities, rapine and cruelty, and slaughter universal had come and gone, and yet through all this did the work of St. Vincent de Paul go on; not a single work which he raised with his munificent hand was destroyed, for they are all flourishing to-day. The nuns whom he founded, his spiritual daughters, and of whom he said when it was objected that he did not give them a veil to cover their faces: "Their modesty shall be their veil"—they had multiplied all over the earth. Wherever the Catholic priest, in the most distant or barbarous regions, had to face the dangers, miseries, privations, which only a man could be supposed to face, the Catholic priest had in all those difficulties the Sister of St. Vincent de Paul with him, suffering with him, laboring with him, going through such trials as no other woman on the face of the earth would think of enduring. But they dared all. The angel of death might stand at the pest-house, and every human being might withdraw in terror from him, but the Sister of Charity swept by him and went in, if need be, to suffer and to die. The armies engaged all day in battle might withdraw in the evening, yet angry shots were fired, and death was in the air; the angel of death was yet at his work; the missiles were sweeping over the well-fought field; even the stoutest soldier might retire to shelter in that reign of death; yet in the midst of that destruction the Sister of St. Vincent de Paul appeared, bound up the wounds of the wounded and consoled the dying soldier. She knew no fear, no difficulty; she knew no thought of danger; she knew no worldly shame. In the midst of the wildest society she received the same tribute of respect from Christian, infidel, and Turk; everywhere her modesty was her veil. Thus St. Vincent put the sign of stability on his own great work, and had the three great principles he had spoken of before him when he founded his great order.

Ireland, in his day, was not forgotten by him. Ireland in the days of Vincent was making her great effort in defence of religion. The Confederation of Kilkenny was formed; Catholic armies led by Catholic generals took their place on Irish battle-fields. The terrible sword of Cromwell decimated them. All was death, destruction, confiscation, and misery, and it seemed as if Ireland was doomed to die. It was then, in the saddest epoch of her history, that Vincent sent some of his first and most holy children to Ireland. "Go," he said, "and help to keep the sacred lamp still burning in that land of faith; go, and, if necessary, add your blood to the blood so gloriously shed by that heroic people." They came, and were angels of consolation and light to us, and their care over us has never failed; for through every corner of the land their voices have been heard resounding the praises of Jesus and Mary, and implanting in the heart of Ireland more deeply those divine principles of grace with which Almighty God had so richly endowed it. Well do I remember when famine passed over that land, when desolation and misery were everywhere, and Protestantism made its last desperate effort to enable the dark angel of heresy to enter through the same gate that let in the angel of God's withering anger—the angel of famine; when they came with their gifts and offered the meats of heresy to a dying, a heart-broken, and famishing people; and when that faith was imperilled, and when it seemed as if the strain put upon it was more than it could bear, when many had fallen shamefully, and it seemed as if Ireland was about to lose her last and only remaining treasure—well do I remember the Vincentian Fathers coming down to that western land, and with powerful words, and with holy sacramental action, and with self-sacrificing labor, almost superhuman, standing there and guarding that faith, bringing back the fallen, raising the renegade from degradation, confuting the adversary, and putting to flight for ever the agents of heresy that had dared to invade this land for the corruption of our children. Even in our own province God has chosen a Sister of St. Vincent de Paul to offer her virgin self in martyrdom. There is one Sister of Charity in heaven a martyr, crowned with a martyr's diadem. And, oh! she must look down surely on this fair church and you assembled here, for it is her brother who is saying the Mass. Blessed be the Lord! O Lord! accept whatever feeble voice of praise we can send Thee to-day. Thou art wonderful in Thy saints! Thou didst find in Vincent a man according to Thy own heart, and with Thy holy oil Thou didst graciously anoint him. We are praising him now whilst the angels around Thy throne are praising him also. O Lord! accept our praise, unworthy though it be, to swell the chorus of joy which shall ring through the vaults of heaven for ever and ever.

ST. CATHERINE OF SIENNA.

In the following panegyric of St. Catherine of Sienna Father Burke has shown how a little child rose from a humble sphere in life to become a great saint. Nothing is more beautiful than the life of St. Catherine, and the reading of it, as portrayed by the matchless style of Father Burke, will produce both profit and pleasure.

AMONGST the many proofs that Almighty God gave of the divine origin and life of the Church there was one that had at all times been put before the eyes of man, and never more clearly than in our own day. The Church of God had always been persecuted, and although we might not be able to fathom the depths of the great Redeemer's reason for permitting His Church to be persecuted, it would appear that it was necessary in order to prove the faith and test the love of his children on earth. They should, however, remember that when the Church was apparently crushed under the strong hand of the world's persecutions, by enemies without in serried array and her traitorous children and false friends within, God showed that she was based on a rock which could never be moved by any tempest that might assail her. Then it was that He showed He loved the mother Church the more because she was smitten by the hand of persecution and trodden down. Nor were any of the dark hours of the Church without consolation, for God said His Church should remain for ever. Even history gave consolation in its records of many epochs, and what greater could there be than that derived from a careful and loving study of the life and characters of the saints of God?

In every land in the world, which knew no accord on any other question, there was a strong and an infernal unity in the persecution of the Church, and in this day there was a great effort being made to destroy the Church. Her principles of faith were repudiated, denied, disputed, and contradicted; the very principles on which the existence of Christianity depended were assailed on all hands, and those who assailed the Church were held up to the world as men of refined minds and of independent character, to whose tender mercies we were called upon to hand over the education of our children, so that they might exclude God from their teachings until they effaced His existence from the minds of children who had the misfortune to fall under their upas influence.

They persecuted the heads of the Church; the holy virgins consecrated to God were dragged from their cloisters, deprived of their means of subsistence on earth, and cast upon the world as waifs, with calumny heaped on them so that they might be shunned by all whom they met, all because they were consecrated to God. So did the world; and people who wished the destruction of the Church turned with a half-pitying expression and said that her sufferings were very great, and they were sorry her end had come. Such people were to be pitied for their ignorance, for to his children on earth God always held up the consolation of their faith, and a glorious epoch in the Church's history was exemplified in the life of our saint. They should go back five hundred years for the name of one of the saints whose memory was enshrined in the heart of the Church, whose name rang through the vaults of heaven—St. Catherine of Sienna.

Five hundred years was not a long time to go back when they remembered that the world was about six thousand years old, and the Church existed from the beginning of all time. Five hundred years ago the world was pretty much in the state in which we behold it to-day. Rome, rebellious and ungrateful, had so worried the sovereign pontiff that he was obliged to quit it in 1308 for

Avignon, in France, where he lived seven years. When the pope withdrew from Rome poverty and famine and pestilence set in, and dissension became rife. Italy was convulsed with dissension and disorder, and, owing to the ravages of the pestilence, grass was growing in the streets of Rome; for the pestilence had swept away eighty thousand people. Contention and strife reigned supreme. Was that to continue? No; for a great and wonderful destiny was reserved for that land, the fruitful mother of saints, blessed with the greatest gifts of Heaven. Even the very house in which the Mother of God beheld the Word made man was by angelic influence transferred to the olive-crowned hill by the Adriatic wave in Loretto, in Italy. In the midst of pestilence and plague, of dissension and bloodshed, a little child was born to poor parents in 1347, in the city of Sienna, in Tuscany; she was one of twenty-five brothers and sisters. The child was called Catherine, after a saint of the same name who had reflected glory on the Church of Alexandria. Amongst so many brothers and sisters the child grew up almost unnoticed. Though the fear and love of God was inculcated into the hearts of the children in those days, the world's learning was not so general, and Catherine was not taught either to read or write. She was taught, however, the Christian doctrine, and was told that the love of Jesus Christ and his Divine Mother were to be objects of her greatest care in life. As soon as she heard the names of Jesus and Mary, even before her mind had learned to apprehend truth as it was in itself and for its own sake, her heart brightened with joy. She grew up comparatively unnoticed until she got to her seventh year, and though she was not what the world would call beautiful there came over her at that age some power which captivated all hearts—a kind of mystic light of loveliness and divine grace. She cast away every thought but one, her heart was so full of love for Jesus Christ. St. Thomas, the great theologian of the Church, had written that when a soul comes to reason it must act and decide for God, not for sin. In her seventh year Catherine made an act of love which she embodied in a solemn vow, by which she consecrated her soul and body in virginity to God. It might be said that the heart thus consecrated was but the heart of a child, but surely God would communicate to infants light unknown to the aged and learned. Did not the unborn Baptist leap in his mother's womb when he felt the presence of Jesus Christ? Then commenced in Catherine's life an abridgment of the whole perfection in the saints.

Under divine love we should first mortify and purge ourselves of all passions, for sin must not exist in the soul. The purging of the soul from sin must be the first act of divine love; that must be preparatory to union with Jesus Christ, for divine grace and wisdom would not dwell in bodies given to sin. When the soul is pure, then may we look for extraordinary manifestations of divine love; and just as the human love is strong in absorbing the mind and in vigorously picturing the object of the affections in a thousand ways, so the love of God places Him for ever before the eyes and souls of those who love Him, making them forgetful of everything else, and giving the soul strength more powerful than death to do things for God with all the strength and passion of love.

The third manifestation of divine love was the zeal it brought to the soul endowed with it. The soul of one endowed with such love burns like a furnace, that it may impart its flames to all around it; it possesses a zeal which stops at nothing; and into this state did Catherine enter in her seventh year, when, in order that her body might be no hindrance to her loving soul, she began to fast and mortify herself in a manner the most astounding, giving up flesh-meat and wine, and limiting herself to such a point that how she lived became an object of wonder to those around her. She spent the night in prayer, and while all the other members of the family slept she was awake, praying to God. She at length brought her vigils to such a point that out of twenty-four hours she only gave half an hour to sleep, and even then she only laid her head on a stone, or on a hard board that served for her couch. One trial was wanted in order to perfect her. The hunger, and thirst, and mortification were self-imposed and voluntary, but domestic affliction surrounded her. Her father and mother and sisters, not knowing what kept her apart from the rest, commenced a system of petty annoyances, and a storm of domestic persecution surrounded her. Every one she met from morning to night chided her, and she only received from them harsh words and actions. She was denied a little room for herself, and she was prohibited from going to church to receive the sacraments, and it was then that she built up a little temple in her own heart, and in it she worshipped God.

In her thirteenth year the father, a hard yet a just man, learning that she had devoted herself to God, said that he should not attempt to contradict her will, and he gave her his blessing. Soon after she beheld St. Dominic coming down in a vision, and he told her to enter his order. Now there was no impediment in her way, and the next few years that intervened she manifested the most powerful divine grace and fidelity. Her prayers became continual, and every night she scourged herself mercilessly until the blood flowed from her body. She visited the lowly sick in their houses, in hospitals, and in jails, and her life before it became public was one manifestation of miraculous grace. On one occasion, before she entered the order of St. Dominic, she attended a woman the ulcers on whose body were of the most sickening and revolting nature, calculated to disgust and sicken any one. Catherine felt a sickening sensation on seeing the loathsome ulcers, and she was strongly tempted to turn away in disgust. But she felt that the temptation came from the devil, and she prayed that she might be able to resist it. On arising from her knees she went and put her lips to the loathsome ulcers, and felt in doing so as if her very soul would die within her with sheer disgust. She again went to pray, and while kneeling down our beautiful Saviour came down from heaven on the wings of His love, and, drawing His robe aside, showed her a bleeding wound in His side; and then for the kiss she gave the revolting ulcer she was permitted to approach and put her lips to the bleeding wound of Jesus Christ.

Though she was a virgin of great modesty, she almost forgot the weakness of her sex, for actually when the people were horrified by the blasphemy of one or two murderers who were in jail awaiting execution, she said, Why should they perish in sin; and she went into the cell where they were in heavy chains, and, throwing herself on her knees before those frightful criminals, she began to tell them how beautiful Jesus Christ was, and how they would love Him if they only knew Him. They were at first astonished, but their feelings changed soon to repentance, and ultimately they knelt down to pray with her and ask forgiveness of the Lord, and the tears which they dropped in her hands she flung up to heaven in an excess of joy. She soon became an object of wonder and veneration. On one occasion, when a young nobleman was sentenced to execution for a political offence, his noble heart revolted at so ignominious a death and at so unjust a sentence, and he went forth blaspheming God and man; but Catherine, hearing him, came out of a house and spoke to him of the higher love of God, and entreated and counselled him, until at last he consented to receive a priest and forgive all, on condition that she should stand beside him on the scaffold and hold him in her hands while the hand of justice severed his head from his body. He mounted the scaffold, and before him stood the executioner with his bright axe upraised. And Catherine, who was there, said: "O Christ! love, fire, and flame of my heart, if that axe only could fall on me that I might fly to you."

The young man was struck with the words, and he died repeating the names of Jesus and Mary and Catherine, whilst she kept whispering hope into his ear; and as his life-blood oozed out and saturated her garments she saw his soul ascending into heaven crowned with the crown of forgiveness and divine love. Yet the moment came when she was to write her name in history and be a saint in the Church. Italy was ruined. Rome was desolate, the curse of immorality was on the people, and a league was made to get rid of the pope and to prepare the way to get rid of his spiritual and temporal authority.

It was a terrible moment, when the crown of Italy's fate was tottering on her brows, but there were some found who thought that before they drew the sword they would try negotiations with the sovereign pontiff, and Catherine was sent from Florence to try and induce him to come back to Italy. She presented herself to Gregory XI., and said: "My sweet father, I kneel at thy feet and ask a blessing and your return to Italy." And he said: "Arise, O daughter! go back to Italy; make what bargain with the people you can. I will leave the Church in your hands, only save the Church from dishonor." Never since the Virgin Mary beheld the Word made man did saint occupy such a grand position on earth—the destinies of the Church in one hand and the fortunes of her native land in the other. She went back, and when she entered Florence she saw blood flowing on every side. She pleaded the cause of the Church in their midst. At the sound of her voice the angry waters of passion and pride and revenge were calmed within the souls of men, and a Pentecost of divine love and peace fell on them, and they made peace with the Church.

She went back to Avignon and she asked the sovereign pontiff to come back to Rome, even though, as she said, "you made a vow not to return." He was amazed, for though he had made that vow no one on earth knew of it, and he asked her how she knew he had made such a vow, and she replied that God had informed her; and she said: "Arise, holy father, and return"; and he arose in wonder and followed her to the City of the Seven Hills, and all Italy was appeased, and peace and grace came upon the land. In 1386 there was a schism within the Catholic world. Clement XI. was elected pope by a faction; cardinals, bishops, and priests were found untrue, and internal dissension prevailed. Urban VI., the legitimate pontiff, was in Rome, and Clement was at Avignon; the world was divided, not knowing whom to obey, though knowing that there could be but one pope, one visible head of the Church on earth. A voice was wanted to point out the true pontiff, a saint whose sanctity could not be disputed. Sweden, Sicily, England (which had always a taste for schism), and many other nations of Christendom heard Catherine's preaching in the streets and the highways, and she pointed to Urban VI. and proclaimed him the true pope, and she proved it by several miracles.

By the touch of her hand she cured the sick, and on learning that her mother died without the sacraments she was deeply grieved, and hurried to her house in Sienna, where she found them preparing for the burial, for she was dead many days. She stood in the presence of the multitude and gave herself up to prayer; she put forth her voice like Him who spoke over the tomb of Lazarus, when her mother's senses awakened, her eyes opened, and an act of heartfelt sorrow burst forth from her bosom. She was restored to life and a long time was granted to her to do penance, and the people heard that the woman who proclaimed the true pontiff in Rome was the author of this miracle, and the whole world did homage to Urban VI. She was now thirty-three years of age, and it was fitting that the fulness of her years should be as His whom she loved so deeply and served so faithfully. She laid her head down, and, fatigued by the burden of the great mission and the fulfilment of all the divine purposes on earth, she looked up to heaven, and in a spirit of prayer her heart went up to God. She was able to smile at all the forebodings of the enemies of the Church who tried to put down the pope. Great was her life and great and lasting her services to the Church on earth, a fact which was acknowledged by the Pope a very few years ago, when he placed the Church of God, and especially the Eternal City, under the special protection of St. Catherine of Sienna. There, amidst the seven hills of Rome, she lies to-day, and when the trumpet shall sound for the disentombing none shall arise more glorious than Catherine of Sienna.

ST. COLUMBKILLE.

In this panegyric of St. Columbkille Father Burke has given a unique sketch of the life of the great saint. It does not claim to be a critical dissertation on the truthfulness of the wild legends that Irish writers have handed down to us, putting them to the account of St. Columbkille, but it is a most entertaining and instructive lecture.

MY FRIENDS: There are two things necessary in order to make a saint: nature and grace must both work out the character of the man. Those whom the Almighty God destines for the high sanctity which the Catholic Church recognizes by canonization either receive from God in the beginning a calm, sweet, gentle nature; or else, if they receive from God a hard, vigorous, obstinate nature, they receive, on the other hand, copious divine graces whereby they overcome this nature thoroughly and make themselves after God's own heart.

But whatever man's natural disposition be, whether it be the amiable, sweet, gentle disposition, easily, unselfishly yielding to others, or whether full of character, full of self-assertion, full of vigor, full of obstinacy—whatever it be, if that man is destined to be a holy man, a man after God's own heart and nature, there is another thing that must come to him from heaven to aid the natural disposition which he has received, and that is the mighty, copious graces of the Almighty God to saints of the Catholic Church.

The saints of whom we read were men like ourselves. In reading their lives nothing is more interesting than to trace the man side by side with the saint. They had the same passions, they had the same difficulties to overcome that we have, the same enemies; the world lay around them, the devil was beneath them, and the flesh was their very selves. But, arming for this contest, whereby they were to triumph, not only over the world around them and over the powers of hell beneath them, but over their own selves, they received from God the highest, noblest, and the most powerful graces, and by corresponding with these graces they elaborated and brought forth their own sanctity.

Now, what follows from all this? My dear friends, it follows that there is a natural and a supernatural side even in the lives of the saints; it follows that we find the man overcoming himself, sometimes yielding so far as to bring out his natural character, but in the end overcoming himself by divine grace. It follows that the lives of the saints are not only the most instructive to us as Catholics, but that they are also most instructive to the historian or to the antiquarian as subjects of natural character. Now, my friends, the world is divided into various nations and races of people, and all these various races differ from one another in the most extraordinary manner. All that you have to do is to travel to see this. I have travelled a great deal—all over the Continent of Europe, I may say, with the exception of Russia and Turkey—and nothing in all these countries struck me more than the difference of the various races.

For instance, I travelled in France, and there I found a lively, passionate, impulsive, generous people, most polite, most willing to go out of their road to serve you in any manner; entering a stage-coach or railway-car, coming in hat in hand, with a "May I be permitted to speak to you, sir" style; making themselves agreeable to you at all times. Passing through France into Germany, there I found a people silent and reserved, with perhaps more of the grandeur of manliness than in France, but no approach to anything like conversation; no apparent external politeness, though a great deal, no doubt, of true politeness.

In a word, as different from all the neighboring country as night from day. So, in like manner, go to Ireland and travel. Let a man who is not an Irishman go there, and he finds a quiet, bright, intelligent, generous, and impulsive people. If he makes a joke, no sooner is it out of his lips than the Irishman laughs, and with his ready laugh shows that he appreciates the joke. If he does not make a joke, the simplest Irish peasant that he meets on the road will make one for him. (Great laughter.) If he wants a drink of water and asks for it, the probability is that the farmer's wife will say to him : "Do not be taking water, it is bad for you. Take a drink of milk." (Renewed laughter.) Impulsive, speaking without thinking, saying the word first and afterwards thinking whether it was right or wrong to say it, perhaps giving you a blow in the face and afterwards thinking perhaps you did not deserve it. (Laughter.) More or less slipshod and imprudent, allowing everything to pass off easily. Pass over to England and you find a country as different as if you had passed from this world into another sphere. Everything is kept in its own place. You may pass through the land and there is neither welcome nor insult for you. If you ask for a drink of water, there is very little fear that you will be offered a drink of buttermilk. So throughout all the world and the nations of the earth, each one has its own character. Don't imagine that I am abusing the Englishman by contrasting him uniformly with the Irishman. My friends, I am one of your race, but I tell you that the Englishman has qualities that are admirable. As a rule he is a brave man, a self-reliant man, a truthful man ; his word is his bond. Only leaving Ireland out of the question and the Catholic religion, argue with him on any point and you will find him a fair man ; but the moment you talk to him on Catholicity or upon Ireland you might as well be talking to the devil. (Laughter.) Now, why am I making these remarks ? For this purpose : the saints of the various nations share in the national character; they are, perhaps, the very best specimens of the national character of each nation and people. Of whatever nation the saint is, you are sure to find the natural side of his character, with this difference, there you find the grace of the Almighty God in its highest, noblest, and strongest form acting upon the natural character of the man, or, if you will, upon the national character of the people as embodied in that man.

I have come here this evening to speak to you of one of the greatest saints in the Catholic Church—a man whose name is recorded in the annals of the Church amongst her brightest and most glorious saints, a man whose name is known throughout the whole world wherever a Catholic priest says his office and wherever a Catholic people hear the voice of their pastor. There are many saints in the Catholic Church of whom we hear but little, many saints, heroic Christian men, exalted in their sanctity. What do you know about them ? You are Catholics, and you have scarcely ever heard the names of some of the great and illustrious saints—of St. Louis Bertrand, a Dominican saint of my order, one of the greatest evangelists God ever sent forth ; of St. Hyacinthe. But there were names of saints who were so great that the whole world is familiar with them. St. Augustine, we have all heard of him ; St. Patrick, who has the most ardent devotion of the Irish race, his name is known to the whole world, and will be known to the end of time. Amongst the mighty saints, amongst the saints who have written their names upon the history of the world, amongst those saints adopted by nations as their patrons, whose names are familiar to every hearth in the lands where civilization and religion have extended themselves, is the name of the Irish Saint Columbkille, known outside of Ireland by the name Columba, but known amongst his own people as "Columbkille." It is of him I have come to speak. Therefore I speak of the national character and the natural side of the saint as embodied in him.

You all know, my dear friends, that it is now fifteen hundred years since St. Patrick preached in Ireland. At that time the religion of Jesus Christ was only known in Italy, in Spain, in portions of France, and throughout the East in the primeval nations. The rest of Europe was in darkness. As yet the voice of the apostolic preacher had not been heard. The forests of Germany still witnessed the rites and ceremonies of the ancient pagans in that great land. The northern portions of Europe—Sweden, Norway, and Russia, amid their snows—still heard the voice of the ancient skalds celebrating in their sagas the pagan divinities of the olden time. England was in the deepest darkness of her Saxon idolatry. A few of the ancient Britons in the mountains of Wales had received the Catholic faith, and their bishops and priests were ungenerous enough and weak enough to refuse to preach the Gospel to the Saxons because they had invaded their land. It was in this almost universal mist and darkness that, in the year 442, a man landed on the shores of Ireland and lifted up his voice and proclaimed the name of Jesus Christ and his Virgin Mother; and the Irish race to-day profess the Catholic faith in all the clearness, in all the exact definiteness of its knowledge, and profess it still more in the sanctity of the national priesthood and the system of monasticism, as it was given to them from the lips of St. Patrick. My dear friends, no matter what men may say, I am here as a Catholic, as an Irish priest, and I defy any man in the world to produce such a miraculous example of conversion and of instant maturity into fulness of love and holiness of life as that of the Irish race.

Now, since St. Patrick passed to his grave more than half a century has passed by. In the year 521 one of the princes of Ulster had a son born to him. He was of the royal house of O'Neill and O'Donnell, and descended from "King Niall of the Nine Hostages," the man who was supposed to have brought St. Patrick as a captive into Ireland for the first time. This house of O'Donnell and O'Neill is so ancient that its origin is lost in the mists of fable in the prehistoric time that goes before any written record, except the Holy Scriptures. There were kings in the northern parts of Ireland from the sixth century. St. Patrick landed in Ireland and found O'Donnell and O'Neill on the throne of Ireland. In the reign of Queen Elizabeth, only three hundred years ago, there lived an Irish prince by the name of O'Neill, and when Elizabeth wanted to make him an English earl he answered her: "No earls for me; my foot is on my native heath," and sent her back her dignities and her honors. No king in Europe had so grand, so royal a title as that crown of the O'Neills of Ulster. From these came St. Columbkille.

The name he received was not in baptism, but in his conversion. The word "Columba" is the Latin word for the "dove"; so gentle, so tender, so patient was he that they called him the "gentle dove" in the Irish language. They went farther, and because he was a monk who loved to read in his cell, who loved to live among his brethren in their cells, they called him Columbkille, which means "the dove in the church, or in the cell." Tradition and history tell us that no sooner was the child born than his prince-father called in the priest to baptize him. No delay, not even for an hour; as soon as the infant opened his eyes and saw the light of heaven the divine adoption and the light of supernatural faith was let in upon his soul by the holy waters of Baptism. No sooner was the child taken from his mother's breast than he was handed over to the care of the priest who baptized him, the father and mother saying to him: "We begot this child as a child of nature, a child of Adam; as he is ours, he came into this world with the curse of God upon him; but thou, O priest of God! thou dost lift off that curse and dissipate it by Baptism. He is more your child than ours; take him, and rear him up for that God whose blessing, whose adoption thou hast brought down upon him in Baptism." So he remained with the priest that baptized him.

As the child grew two things grew side by side, one with the other. The first one belonged to the Irish character, and was as Irish as it could be. The second was the divine grace of God, which was the most wonderful. We can scarcely reconcile the two, as we look upon that beautiful young figure that rises up before us on the pages of history, as we contemplate his life. He grew from a child to a boy, from a boy to a young man. He was the most beautiful youth in all Ireland—tall above all other men, perfectly formed, with the lofty forehead of the king's son; the light blue eye, full of genius, but full of temper; the strong athletic form, delighting in coursing in the fields in the manly exercises of the strong young man. A beautiful temperament, full of imagination, he was a lover of poetry and of music, and his young hand loved to tune the chords of the ancient Irish harp, and then to draw from them, with thrilling grasp, the very spirit and soul of Celtic music.

Full of talent and of intellect, with Irish brains in his head, there was no branch of knowledge or of science that was unknown to him. With him to look at a thing was to know it; he did not require to study it. But he was also full of pride, full of passion. No man dared to contradict him; his temper was roused in a moment, and when that temper was roused the young Irishman did not stop to think of what he said or what he did. With the word came the blow, and then the apology when it was too late. The very soul of the saint, when he looked at anything, decided whether it was right or wrong. Full of Celtic obstinacy, full of pride, side by side with a heart as soft and tender as that of a young woman, if he saw a poor man or cripple on the wayside in feverish misery, his heart seemed to break in pity for him, and, if no one was around to help, he would take him up on his shoulders and carry him to his house, and there feed and clothe him. If, when carrying a poor man or beggar, any one on the way passed by, and he called upon that person to help him and he refused, the temper came up at once—"May the God of heaven smite you!" He always left a curse on them. There was the full Celtic blood.

Noble, gentle, quick, irascible he was, full of character

and determination, even to obstinacy. This was the natural character; yet, strange to say, side by side with this, and whilst thus hindered with a thousand imperfections, there was the most wonderful supernatural reign of divine graces. A thorough Celt, a thorough Irishman, his angel guardian appeared to him when he was between twelve and fourteen years of age, and said to him: "Columba, I come from heaven." The moment Columba saw him, in the form of a radiant youth, he said at once: "Are all the angels in heaven as fair as you are?" The angel answered: "They are all as fair, and many more fair. I come charged by the Christ whom your love so dearly to ask you what gifts you desire from God." Instantly the Irish youth, the young Irish boy, said: "I ask from God chastity and wisdom." The moment he said the words three angels, in the form of three beautiful maidens, appeared before him. One of the fairest of all then threw her arms around his neck. The Irish boy drew back afraid. "Thou hast refused my embrace, Columba; thou knowest not me. I am the angel of Divine Virtue. I come with my sisters to remain with you for ever." These were the three sisters—Divine Virtue, Divine Wisdom, and Divine Spirit of Prophecy—who came to the child as a boy, a boy full of faults, full of the imperfections of the Celtic character, the same imperfections that you and I have; not sitting down and being prudent and quiet, but always loving a contest, always loving to do a generous thing, and to do it on the spur of the moment; always ready to turn around and take up a slight or an insult before it is offered. (Laughter.) Yet, side by side, we have the evidence in the life of the saint of the other portion of the Celtic character—the virtue of purity.

Thus it was most natural that Columba became a monk and was an obedient priest. He gave his light for ever to that grand Irish monasticism which was the flower and the bloom of the glory of Ireland in that wonderful sixth century. The Irish monks at that time were the most learned as well as the most holy men in the Catholic

Church. Everywhere their virtue was known, in every nation professing the Catholic faith. Students came in profusion to Ireland. Yea, even the very pagan nations sent their children to Ireland to the grand university of the world, there to learn every highest science and art, and above all the art and glorious science of loving Jesus Christ and His Church. They entered the mighty schools of Armagh, the island of Arran on the western coast, and Lismore on the banks of the Blackwater; in a word, they entered the mighty schools that covered the whole face of Ireland, and the old historians tell us that it was considered rather a poor effort where there was not at least three thousand students. The old Irish saintly monks in their history tell us that they cultivated every highest art, and above all the art of music. In the ancient life of St. Bridget we read that on one occasion she went into the king's palace, perhaps at Tara, and there she saw a harp hanging up on the wall. Turning to the white-haired and gray-bearded minstrel, she said to him: "Harp me a song on thy harp." And the old man took down his harp lovingly, and, seating himself while the young Christian virgin sat before him, in melody he poured forth the glories of God and the glories of Ireland. So when Columba entered the monastery he found there every highest art and science cultivated; but he found there two great passions that were always burning in the heart of the ancient Irish monk, and these were an overpowering love for Ireland and a love for Ireland's poetry and music. The young prince, ardent, full of courage, who seemed to be marked out far more for a soldier, a sailor, or a captain of armies than for a monk, no sooner puts on the monastic cowl than he devotes his soul to three things—viz., the love of God's divine religion, the love of Ireland, and the cultivation of music and poetry.

No hand was more skilful to sweep the chords of the lyre; and when those ancient monks assembled the ancient chroniclers tell us that they loved to play their harps, even when they came to the church to sing the divine songs—the Psalms of David—in the office they were saying every day. These old men danced to the sound of the harp, and so from the hands went forth the accompanying thrill of Erin's music, while with sweetest voices they melodiously sang the praises of Almighty God. And so rich and grand was the voice of the young novice that we read when he was an old man over sixty years of age, while preaching the Gospel to the Picts and Scots, he would stop and begin to sing the praises of God on his Irish harp. The pagan priests who were around, who did not want to let him preach, but were interrupting him—who, above all things, did not want him to sing, because his voice had a kind of supernatural power that drew the hearts of the pagan people to God—raised their voices and shouted in order to drown the voice of St. Columba. The Irish saint looked upon them with the old Celtic fire of youth in his aged eyes; he pitched the highest note and brought out from his harp the stronger chords, chanting out the Psalms of David and the praises of God, so that, although the priests roared and bawled until they were hoarse, the voice of the saint sounded above them all. He went over all the country, into the houses of the people, singing the glory of the highest Heaven.

Everything went calmly and quietly with Columba until, when he was forty years of age, an incident happened that gave tone to his whole life, although it broke his heart. When the saint was forty years of age he heard that St. Finnian possessed a valuable copy of a part of the Scriptures, the Book of Psalms. St. Columba wanted a copy of this book for himself, and he went to St. Finnian and begged the privilege of the book to take a copy of it. He was refused; the book was too precious to be trusted to him. Then he asked at least to be allowed to go into the church where the book was deposited, and there he spent night after night privately, writing out a clean copy of it. By the time St. Columba had finished his copy somebody who had been watching him at the book went and told St. Finnian that the young man had made a copy of his psalter. The moment St. Finnian heard of it he laid claim to this copy as belonging to him. St. Columba refused to give it up, and appealed to King Dermott, the Ard-righ, at Tara. The king called his counsellors together; they considered the matter, and passed a decree that St. Columba should give up the copy, because the original belonged to St. Finnian, the copy was only borrowed from it; and the Irish decree began with the words: "Every cow has a right to her own calf."

Now, mark the action of Columba—a saint, a man devoted to prayer and fasting all the days of his life, a man gifted with miraculous powers, and yet, under all that, as thorough-bred an Irishman as ever lived. The moment he heard that the king had resolved on giving back the precious book he reproached him, saying: "I am a cousin of yours, and there you went against me." He put the clanship—the "*sheanachus*"—upon him. (Laughter.) The king said he could not help it. What did St. Columba do? He took his book under his arm and went away to Ulster, to raise the clans of O'Neill and Tyrconnell of Tyrone. He was himself the son of their king; they were powerful clans in the country, and the moment they heard their kinsman's voice they rose as one man; for who ever asked a lot of Irishmen to get up a row and was disappointed? Laughter.) They arose, they followed their glorious, heroic monk down to Westmeath. There they met the king and his army, and, I regret to say, a battle was the consequence, in which hundreds of men were slain, and the fair plains of the country were flooded with blood. It was only then that St. Columba perceived the terrible mistake he had made. Like an Irishman, he first had the fight out, and then he began to reflect on it afterwards. (Laughter.)

Now, at this time St. Columba's name was known all over Ireland for the wonderful spirit of prophecy that was upon him. He was known all over Ireland as a very angel of God for his purity. He was already the founder of several famous monastic institutions. In Ireland there were twelve large monasteries, and hundreds and thousands of monks looked up to Columba as their chief. His prophecies were wonderfully fulfilled, almost as soon as uttered. His sanctity was an acknowledged fact; and yet, in the face of all this, the national Celtic character, the rash, quick temper in the proud Irishman, broke out in him so far that he had hundreds of his countrymen slain. And the next day after the battle he was on his knees, by the side of his priest, acknowledging it all a mistake. The bishops assembled and took thought over the matter, and the issue of it was that poor, dear St. Columba, with all his sanctity, was excommunicated. As for the book there was no question; he never got it back. Strange to say, my friends, that very book, written by St. Columba's own hand, remains, and is shown to this day in Ireland. He went to confess, with great sorrow, to an aged monk named Manuel. The saint was broken-hearted for what he had done—for the blood that had been shed, and, if you will, for the scandal of his bad temper. So he had to endure and to accept any penance that would be put upon him. The confessor asked him this question: "What is the strongest love you have in your heart?" And the poor penitent answered: "The love that I have for Ireland, that is the strongest affection in my heart." Then the most cruel penance was put upon him—that he was to depart from Ireland, never to see her or to put his foot upon her soil again.

Sentence passed, the man fell to the earth as if the hand of God had smitten him, as the Lord Jesus Christ fell under His cross, which was more than He could bear. Rising up, with despairing eyes he looked on the face of the terrible confessor to whom he had confessed his sins; then, making one effort, he accepted the great sacrifice, and said: "Father, what you have said shall be fulfilled." Then he wrote a letter to his friend Tyrconnell, in Ulster; he said: "My fall is accomplished, my doom is sealed; a man told me that I must exile myself from Ireland, and that man I recognize as an angel of God. I must go." With breaking heart and weeping eyes he bade a last farewell to the green "Island of Saints," and went to an island among the Hebrides, on the western coast of Scotland. There, in the mist and storms of that inhospitable region—there, upon a bare rock out from the mainland, he built a monastery, and there did he found the far-famed school of Iona. Then began the second grand portion in the life of this man, whom God had determined and predestined to make so great a saint. He came to Iona a man, a prince, a saint of Ireland, full of passion, full of nationality, full of the love of God, unstained, unsullied in his virgin mind and soul as any angel before the throne of God. And there he was destined to remain for thirty-six long years in constant fasting, in unceasing prayer, until the divine grace, descending upon him, made a perfect saint of him who was before so noble a specimen of the Celtic land.

Now, do you know how hard it is for one in exile! Here is an account given by one of the greatest writers of modern times. He tells us of his love that he retained for Ireland, the affectionate tenderness of the exile, a love which displayed itself in the songs which have been preserved to us. It is beautiful. He goes on to say that, amongst other things, St. Columbkille left behind him such words as these:

"Death in faultless Ireland is better than life without end in Albion. What joy to fly upon the white-crested sea and watch the waves break upon the Irish shore! What joy to row in my little boat and land upon the whitening foam of the Irish shore! Ah! how my boat would fly if its prow were turned to my Irish oak-groves! But the noble sea now carries me to Albion, the land of the raven. My foot is in my little boat, but my sad heart ever bleeds, and my gray eye ever turns to Erin. Never in this sad life shall I see Erin or her sons and daughters again. From the high prow I look over the sea; great tears are in my gray eyes as I turn to Erin—to Erin where the songs of the birds are so sweet, where the monks sing like the birds, where the young are so gentle and the old so wise, where the men are so noble to look at and the women so fair to wed."

In another place he says to one who was returning from his Scottish island to Ireland:

"Young traveller, take my heart with thee, and my blessing; carry them to Cornghaill of eternal light. Carry my heart to Ireland—seven times may she be blessed!—my body to Albion. Carry my blessing across the sea! Carry it to the West! My heart is broken in my bosom. If death should come upon me suddenly, it will be because of my great love of the Gael."

That was the Irish people; it was the master-passion of his life.

What can be more tender than the message that he gives to one of his monks? One morning he called from the little cells in Iona to one of his Irish monks there in exile. He said to him: "Brother, go out and stand upon the hill near the east shore. After you are there a while a bird will come and fall at your feet with her broken wing. Take up that bird, dear brother," he said, "and feed and care for her gently, restore her to strength again, for that bird will fly over to Ireland. Ah! my broken heart, that bird will fly back to Ireland again, but I can never go back!"

This was the heart of the man, the grand passion of his life, which became the source of his martyrdom. Exile from Erin was to him the bitter penance that the priest of God put upon him after the great indiscretion and sin of his life. Yet it was an Irish sin. He did not want to glory in anything wrong; and this I do say, if it was a great Irish sin, there was nothing mean in that sin; it was the sin of a brave, passionate man. He felt he was injured, and he called upon his people, and bloodshed followed upon it. It was the act of an impulsive man; nothing vile to be ashamed of, nothing that the recollection of which could bring anything but a manly sorrow to his heart. It was the Irish sin.

Now began a great period of his life. He was forty-two years of age when he left Ireland and landed on the little island off the western coast of Scotland. Here his Irish monks built a wooden church, and here that man lived in the humblest of cells. St. Columba for forty years slept upon the bare ground an hour or two out of the twenty-four. Thus he lay, with a hard rock whereon to lay his head. This island on which the Irish monks landed was destined to be the most holy, the most gloriously historic spot in Western Europe. He brought monks from Ireland with him, and there upon the distant shores of Scotland did he find a people divided into two great nations—viz., the Irish who had emigrated hundreds of years before, in the very time of St. Patrick, who were Christians, having brought their Catholic religion with them, and who possessed the southern and western portions of Scotland. But the northern and eastern portions of the land were in the hands of another nation, the most terrible, the most brave, and withal the most savage that ever the Roman legions encountered. They were called the ancient Picts. So brave were they that when Julius Cæsar conquered the whole of England he never was able to conquer the Picts and warlike savages that inhabited Scotland.

As they were brave to resist invasion, so were they also brave, with an infernal bravery, in resisting the Gospel. Holy saints came to them only to be torn to pieces and slaughtered. The hour of their redemption came from the hour when St. Columbkille landed on the island of Iona. He brought a large colony of Irish monks, and his first mission was to his own Irish people settled in Scotland. They were governed by a ruler subject to the king of Ireland. He went in amongst them not to preach the Gospel, for that they had already received, but to preach that which in the heart and on the lips of the Irish priest is next to the Gospel. He went in amongst his exiled Irish brethren to preach the Gospel and love for their native land. He spoke to them in the language of the bard and of the poet of the ancient glories of Ireland. He told them that, although they were established in a foreign land, their best and holiest remembrance, their grandest and noblest influence, was the recollection of the land from which they and their fathers came. He chose one of their princes to be king. He banded them together into a kingdom, and he crowned that Irish prince the first king of Scotland. And that Irish colony of Caledonian Scots, as it was called, was destined to conquer the terrible, savage Picts, and the first man that reigned was the holy Irish Prince Aden.

Well, my friends, it is most interesting to us to find that the very day that St. Columba crowned the Scotch king he made this speech to him: "Mark my words," he said, "O king! the day may come when you and your children after you may be tempted by the devil to make war upon Ireland—upon Ireland," he said, "the land of my love, the land of my race, and of my blood." And here are the words that he put upon that king. In the midst of the ceremony of the coronation he said to the king whom he crowned: "Charge your sons, and let them charge their grandchildren, that they attempt no enterprise against my countrymen and my kindred in Ireland, the land of God, or the hand of God will weigh heavily upon them, the hand of men will be raised against them, and the victory of their enemies will be sure in the day they have the misfortune and the curse of turning against Ireland." There was the glorious law of the Irish priesthood and of Irish history; there was the true father of the heroic St. Laurence O'Toole, that stood in the gap on that terrible day, when no man in Ireland seemed to have heart or courage enough to strike a blow in the invading enemy's face.

Aden was king. He was not long crowned when the Saxons, who invaded England—that is to say, the country that was south of the Grampian Hills—invaded Scotland also. The king had to go forth to do battle against them, and here again we find our ancient Irish saint coming out. Faithful love for his race and country, which had moved him with compassion for the young Irish kingdom, did not permit him to remain indifferent to the wars and revolutions which were at the time of the Irish Scots. There was no more marked feature in his character than his constant, his compassionate sympathy, as well after as before his removal to Iona, in all the struggles in which his companions and relatives in Ireland are so often engaged. Nothing was nearer to his heart than the claim of kindred. For that reason alone he occupied himself without ceasing in the affairs of individuals and relatives. "This man," he would say, "is of my race. I must help him. It is my duty to work for him, because he is of the same stock as myself." "This other man is a relative of my mother's." Then he would add, speaking to his Scottish monks: "My friends, they are my kindred, descended from the O'Neills; see them fighting," when he would hear of a victory, or perhaps he said it to Heaven before the throne of God in the day when Red Hugh O'Neill destroyed the English army at the Yellow Ford; or when in the day Owen Roe O'Neill, and perhaps O'Donnell, proclaimed before God, and before the angels and all high powers— "How the O'Neills and the O'Donnells knew him to fight!" He was praying one day with his famed companion monk named Dermot, and whilst they were speaking together the saint said: "Rise, O Dermot! ring the bell and call the monks to pray." The monk rang the bell, and all the other monks of the monastery came around the father. Here are his words: "Now," he said, "let us pray with intelligence and fervor for our people, for King Aden, who at this very minute is beginning his battle with the barbarians." They prayed, and after a time Columba said: "I behold the barbarians fly. Aden is victorious." Who were the barbarians? The Saxons of England, the pagan Saxons, the haters of religion and his Irish people, the haters of Aden, the Irish king, and his religion.

Another nation lay before him, and the heart of the saint was touched for them. You have seen what he did for his own countrymen in Scotland. He saw in the north-

ern fastnesses of the land those uncivilized, savage, pagan
Picts, the men to whom no missionary was ever able to
preach, the men whom no preacher dared to address.
And here again see how the character of the saint came
out. He arose and took with him a few of his Irish
monks, and they travelled into the very heart of their
country and the islands of Scotland. He went in order to
preach the Gospel of Jesus Christ to the Picts. Their king
had established himself in a mighty fortress with his pagan
priests. They were noticed, and when from the towers the
king saw the brave missionary, the magnificent form of the
Irishman, coming he admired his manliness and his princely courage. He saw the light of the sun beaming upon
his grand face, and he loved him, but he gave orders that
the gates of the fortress should not be opened. "Tell him
no man shall enter here a guest who is not welcome, and
that if he attempts to preach he will die."

The message was given, but Columba, without hesitation, without stopping to take counsel, without one moment's prudence, the moment he heard the king say he
should not come his Irish blood was up, and it seemed to
him there was no reason why he should not go in. He
went straight to the very door of the castle and dealt it a
mighty blow with his staff. "Open," he said, "in the
name of the Father and of the Son and of the Holy
Ghost." Again he struck it, and the mighty gates fell
open, and St. Columbkille of Iona walked in like a conqueror. There was the king on his throne, angry, thirsting
for his blood. Finding the pagan priests around him
claiming that he had violated their laws, and that he
should be put to death, he lifted up that terrible voice of
his in the Irish language, which was easily understood by
the Gaels or the Picts. He said: "I would here speak today. I tell the king to his face, and the chieftains, I am
Columba of Iona, and would make them take the Gospel,
if I had to drive it down their throats."

Years of sorrow, years of repentance, years of prayer
and of fasting had passed over his head, and just now an

elderly man beyond the prime of life; but the moment opposition comes to him in a just cause, that moment the old Irish blood of his youth and all the terrible ardor of his Celtic nature is raised within him. My friends, he converted the Pict nation nearly as perfectly as Patrick converted the Irish. He left his character upon them, so that they became a stanch, and loyal, and true Catholic race in the Highlands of Scotland, as they continue to be almost to the present hour. Yes! there are villages in the Highlands of Scotland which have suffered for the defence of their faith like in Ireland, suffered by bad landlords; the same scourge came upon them of English Protestantism and bad laws ; but the tradition of Ireland's Columba was with them, and his words remained with them like a blessing. And there are villages in Scotland that never yet lost their Catholic faith through weal or through woe.

Now another nation lay before him. Great was the heart of the man and true. He saw the pagan Saxons of England in their hundreds and thousands. What did they worship? They worshipped the meanest and lowest forms of idolatry; they had not the grace to worship the sun like the Irish. They worshipped Thor, the god of the Scandinavians, a huge fellow, with goggle eyes, no feet, and a big club in his hands. They were Saxons! St. Columba neither loved nor liked them. They were Saxons! Perhaps he, being a prophet, foresaw that they would be the "scourge of God" to the land of his love. They were Saxons! They had assaulted and invaded the land of his own people in Scotland and the king whom he had crowned. But they were men, and they had souls, and he loved them with the mighty love that burned in his heart for the Lord and Saviour who died for him. So, accordingly, we find after his conversion of the Picts that the mighty preacher went south, and, with the aid of his monastic brethren after him, the Irish St. Columbkille converted all the Saxons of Northampton and the middle portions of England.

Badly have they repaid us, *for we gave them faith*, and

they endeavored *to rob us of our faith*. We gave them, through our great St. Columbkille, the liberty of the angels of God, and they have endeavored to deprive us of that liberty which is the inheritance and birthright of the children of men. We gave them light, and they have endeavored to repay us with darkness. And though St. Augustine came to preach the Gospel to the Saxons of England, his labors were only in the south. St. Columbkille and his children had already converted the Saxons of the North of England. They were the true apostles of England.

And now old age was upon him; he was approaching his seventy-sixth year; and we read two things of him— namely, that to the last day of his life he never mitigated or changed his austerities. The old man of seventy-six still lay upon the damp earth with a rock for his pillow. The old man of seventy-six still fasted every day of his life. The old man of seventy-six seemed to have a heart as young, as compassionate, as tender, as if he were a boy of fourteen. And one little incident shows us how much the Irish fire was tamed down in him by the sanctity of the saint. When he was an old man the great feature of his character was that he still continued the holy work as hard as when he was young, writing a copy of the Sacred Scriptures. The great passion of his life was writing books. There was no printing in those days. He wrote books even when he was bent to the earth with old age and austerities. Yet he fired up into the ardor of the young harpist as he took the Irish harp and with his aged fingers swept the chords, his voice pouring forth the praises of Ireland and of his God. We read that when he was an old man some strangers that were there in the land were coming to him for his blessing. And one day a man came into the little room where St. Columba was writing, and in his eagerness to get the saint's blessing he rushed with such vehemence to where the saint was that he overturned the ink-bottle and destroyed the whole manuscript. Oh! if he did that thirty or forty years before. (Laughter.)

But all the old saint did now was to take him and embrace him, put his arms about him, and say: "Have patience, my son; be gentle; do not be in such a hurry." He was seventy-six years of age, and he prayed that he might die at Easter. God sent an angel to tell him that his prayer was granted. Now, mark the Irish heart again. The moment that he heard his prayer was granted he prayed to God to let him live for another month, for he said to the monks: "My children, I prayed that I might die and pass my Easter Sunday in heaven. God said He would grant my prayer; but then I thought that you are after fasting a long Lent upon bread and water, and that you are all looking forward to Easter Sunday as a day of joy; and if I died on that day it would be a sad and sorrowful day, so I asked my God to put it off a month more." The month passed. It was Saturday night, and Columba in the morning told his children, the monks: "This night I will die and take my rest." The monks were accustomed to go into the church precisely at twelve o'clock. The bells rang, and Columba was always in the church at prayer. When he was not studying he went before the others into the dark church. There was no light, and he knelt at the foot of the altar. Dermot, his servant, his faithful man, followed the old man, and, groping about in the church for him, at first not being able to see him, exclaimed: "O father! dear father, where art thou?" A feeble moan soon was heard, and he came to where he lay. The other monks came in and brought torches in their hands, and found Columba stretched out dying, grasping the foot of the altar—dying, with a heart long since broken with love for the Lord Jesus and for the dear land that he left behind him! They lifted him up, and with his dying lips he said: "Come around me, that I may give you my last blessing." He lifted his aged hands, and before the sign of the cross was made the hands fell by his side, the light of human love departed from his eye, and one of the most glorious souls among apostles and martyrs that ever passed into Thy kingdom, O Lord! beheld Thee in Thy joy.

This was our old saint. How grand, how great in his national character! How great the character of the saint in his cell!

THE CATHOLIC CHURCH IN AMERICA.

The following magnificent lecture was delivered by Father Burke in Munster Hall, Cork, soon after his return to Ireland. The attendance was very large, embracing the best society of Cork. Father Burke was introduced by the mayor, who said: "Ladies and gentlemen, it is usual upon an occasion of this kind for the chairman to introduce the lecturer. I am sure you will join me in the sentiment that it is the very merest of formalities to introduce to an Irish-hearted audience such a lecturer as Father Burke, and upon such a subject as the Catholic Church in America. (Cheers.) Without further preface I beg to introduce to you Father Burke." Father Burke then came forward, and was received with cheers and waving of hats. He said:

IT is now some months since I returned from the great land of the West. Whilst I was in America I was in the habit of addressing large audiences of my fellow-countrymen, and they gradually made me brave from the kindness of their reception. (Hear.) I have now spent some time in retirement—preaching only as a priest—and I feel, coming forward here this evening, something of the nervousness, the timidity, which I felt when I first had the honor to address an Irish audience in America as a lecturer. But the kindness of my reception has somewhat calmed and toned it down. I beg to thank you for the cheers with which you have received me this evening. I know that your kind welcome is given me not at all as an Irishman—for as such I would not value it—but that it is given me, first, as an Irish priest, and, secondly, as a man whom Almighty God gave, with high grace, high privilege, the opportunity of speaking in vindication of the glorious land that bore him. (Cheers.) I feel, ladies and gentlemen, somewhat nervous in approaching the subject of this evening's lecture for one reason out of many—namely, that the subject which I propose for your consideration and attention has been already brought before you and before the world by one of Ireland's best and noblest sons—the late John Francis Maguire. (Great cheering.) Wherever I went in America I only followed in his footsteps; and I say more than that, I derived assistance from every page of that very remarkable book which this truly good and great man has left after him in the language of a most enlightened and truly Irish heart. (Cheers.) I pay this tribute in the beginning more willingly to John Francis Maguire because at the time his death spread grief through every true Irish heart, both here and in America, my public lectures in America were drawing to a close, and I had no opportunity given me of expressing in the Western land the feelings of my heart, which would have found an echo in every Irishman's bosom, at the loss of the distinguished fellow-citizen taken away from you.

Now, I say again, addressing Corkmen, familiar with the words of this great Corkman, that I feel I am utterly inadequate to the theme I have undertaken, and yet perhaps there is not amongst them any subject that could occupy the attention of the public lecturer, and indeed the observation of any trained mind, more wonderful as well as interesting than tracing the origin and progress and forecasting the future of the Catholic Church in America. (Cheers.) We know, my friends, no matter what philosophers may tell us of our origin when they ask us to believe that we came from the ancestral ape or the oyster, or tell us of the theory of chance—we know both as reasoning men and as Christians that the Almighty God, with providential mind as well as providential hands, steers, directs, and governs the progress and destinies of all this world of ours. (Hear, hear.) We know that the true philosophy of history lies precisely in this: of being able to trace the mind and the hand of Almighty God's providence in all the events from the tissue of what the world calls history. (Hear, hear.)

Now, it has often struck me that the close of the fifteenth century, famous for so many discords, was remarkable for three mighty and solemn events—the birth of Martin Luther in 1483, the discovery of America by Christopher Columbus in 1492, and about the same time the birth of St. Ignatius of Loyola. Never, perhaps, since the banner of Christianity was unfurled—never were there three men who exercised greater influence upon their age. We have in the year 1492 a man dreaming of the existence of a mighty continent which we now know by the name of America. The nations of Europe, fatigued by the failure of the Eastern crusades, multiplied in numbers, found no outlet but to spend their energies upon vain pursuits of learning and philosophy, which they had yet scarcely learned to understand, and which brought with it what is called the Reformation, or, in other words, the emancipation of the human intelligence from religious and infallible authority in teaching concerning God. But any man who reads the history of the close of the fifteenth century will find that minds were disturbed, some seeking to find foundation for their theories on philosophical speculation most unsound, some in researching through relics of pagan antiquity, and some, again, restless minds like Christopher Columbus and the Castilian of that day, dreaming golden dreams, romantic dreams of yet undiscovered countries, and calling them by the name of El Dorado, or places where there are fields of gold. Then a man appeared who united with the immensity of his genius a remarkable meekness, a gentleness, a piety of manners, together with a wonderful strength of the Catholic faith, and that was Christopher Columbus, whose message was this: "I know there is far beyond the trackless ocean a land yet undiscovered. Give me means and I will open unto you a new and wonderful world." He was furnished with a few small, crazy ships, and it is a remarkable fact that the vessels which first crossed the Atlantic were so small, so badly fitted out, so terribly unfitted for the work cut out for them that perhaps the bravest captain or sailor of the present day would not have the courage to cross the Atlantic in them, those almost open boats in which Christopher Columbus sailed and discovered America.

There was in the heart of Columbus a high and glorious purpose, and that splendid light of faith. He never undertook this task of discovering a strange country for the mere purpose of enriching himself, but for the high, generous faith that was in him. (Hear.) He dreamed of lands yet undiscovered, where he would find peoples, where he would find numerous beings who had never heard the name of Christ; and the saintly Columbus had in his heart only the desire to find them out, in order that he might unfurl the standard of the cross amongst them, and gain millions of souls to heaven through Jesus Christ. (Applause.)

If ever there was a land that owes its discovery to Catholic faith, Catholic ardor, Catholic instinct, that land is America. (Hear.) If ever there was a land which might be said to have sprung into its acknowledged existence from out the mind and heart of a man who was the very type of the Catholic heart, that land was America; and, in fact, Columbus, in crossing the trackless ocean, turning his prow to the West, laying firm hand upon his helm, and whilst the eye tracked the setting sun upon the placid waves, the mind of the great mariner was exalted to heaven, and hope and prayer went forth from his lips. (Cheers.) Seeing no sign of land appearing, going further and further on the ocean of the untravelled, unknown West, his mariners lost courage, and turned to him and said: "Let us return to our home and our kindred."

But the great Columbus, guided by a better light than the setting sun, still went on, until upon that glorious morning he beheld Hispaniola, the island of San Domingo, and his first act was to plant the cross of Jesus Christ. (Applause.) He called upon the priests who accompanied him to bless the land, and he proclaimed that America—its mountains, its rivers, its plains, its cities, and its peoples—was the property of God and of Spain. (Cheers.) He was accompanied by friars of the Dominican and Franciscan Orders—

(cheers)—with whose faith and hope he was identified, for the others who accompanied him looked for gold and wealth.

Now, history tells of the Spanish Federation in South America. History tells us of the depredations committed by the founders, the cruelties exercised upon the simple, hospitable, generous, gentle people; but history also recalls to us what is very glorious, that in South America, wherever the standard of religion was raised by the good friar, no matter how powerful the natives or how intractable the Indians, they always found a glorious protector in the followers of St. Francis and St. Dominic. (Cheers.)

Meantime there were other discoveries going on. Other navigators were plying the Atlantic now in the wake of Columbus; but a great event in the meantime had happened, and here see the providence of God. Luther had proclaimed what is called "the Reformation." Truth was no longer to be respected. It was torn into a thousand fragments. Almost all the northern states of Europe started their churches—Sweden, Denmark, Germany, and a large portion of France even; and England, emphatically and most prominent of all, became Protestant, and separated from the Catholic Church. The consequence was that whilst Columbus and the children of Spain, with their Catholic hearts, were carrying the truth and spreading it in the southern portion of America, the northern portion, which now constitutes the United States, was discovered and colonized by Englishmen. They brought with them, as Bishop Spalding said, strong religious prejudices and bigotry, and the words of this learned bishop are borne out, for they were the first to introduce religious persecution in America. (Hear, hear.)

Instantly that they proclaimed Protestantism in England, that religion, as it is called, brought with it various sects. That was a thing necessary to follow, because, upon their principle, there was no certain acknowledged religious truth revealed to us—that there was something true laid down in a certain book, and that they were to take that book and read it, every one according to the reasoning of his own individual mind, and according to his own private judgment was to discover his whole religion. Whatever discovery he made, whatever his religion may be, he was bound in conscience to follow the deductions of his own private judgment. Now, such a system as this involves two things, my friends: first, it involves an inherent right in every man to choose his own religion according to his own interpretation of that book which is called the Bible, and which is undoubtedly the Word of God. It involves in every man who embraces the principle of private judgment not only a right but an obligation to select his own religion and stand by it; and, secondly, it involves necessarily an utter weakness, for it forces a man to conform himself to your views. Therefore, what the Protestant religion declares is illogical, and it is a fact that since blood first reddened this earth there has not been a fiercer spirit of persecution existing amongst men than we find existing amongst these sects of the sixteenth century.

I say this not in a spirit of disrespect nor in any spirit of religious hatred. I lay it down simply as a logical phenomenon and historical fact. I know that liberal-minded Protestants of the present day detest and abhor the acts of their forefathers as much as any right-minded man can detest and abhor persecution. I know very well that if the history of that period was to be rewritten, and if these men—liberal-minded Protestants—of whom I speak had the rewriting of it, that the blood which stains its pages would not be there. But history is history, and fact is fact. Some Englishmen, using their right, and undoubted right, as Protestants, have disagreed with other Englishmen on the question of religion, and at once they were subjected to the most terrible persecution. There were Dissenters or Nonconformists of the sixteenth and seventeenth centuries; they fled from the persecution which they were not able to stand in England; they fled from the demon of religious persecution and bloodshed; they sought refuge in America, in order that they might there, in a new country, practise and exercise their own religion and opinions in peace, and no longer have to suffer for them. No man denies that they were right, that they had reason, supposing the truth of the principle upon which they stood, not to acknowledge any supreme power upon earth to which all men shall bow down in obedience in matters of religion.

But here again is the strange fact that no sooner were these men landed in America, no sooner had they taken possession of that part of the country which is called the New England States, than the first thing they did was to make laws to persecute every one that disagreed with them. (Laughter.) There was to be no mercy for the Quaker. (Laughter.) I will read some of their prominent laws for you about Quakers. Listen to this: "It is ordered that whosoever shall henceforth bring or cause to be brought, directly or indirectly, into the colonies any known Quaker—(laughter)—or any other blasphemous heretic"—(laughter)—after the Quakers themselves it was any one who should bring them in—" every such person shall forfeit the sum of £100 to the country, and he shall be committed to prison, there to remain until the penalty be satisfied ; and if any person within this jurisdiction shall entertain or conceal any such Quaker—(laughter)—and that he, Quaker, be caught—(laughter)—every such male Quaker shall, for the first offence, have one of his ears cut off, and he shall be kept at work in the House of Correction until he can be sent away at his own charge, and if he go back again, for the second offence he shall have the other ear cut off." (Laughter.) Like the fellow in Galway that was eating the goose : he first took off one wing and leg on one side, then said he : "It is a pity to leave it out of proportion ; I may as well eat the other side." (Laughter.) "Every woman Quaker that shall presume to come into this jurisdiction shall be severely whipped, and that every Quaker, he or she, that shall a third time herein offend, they shall have their tongues bored through with a hot iron."

These are the Blue Laws of Connecticut. What do you

think now about Catholics ? The game laws that were there instituted were very severe. They declared that it was not lawful for any man, under forfeit or penalty, to shoot game of any kind. But it was lawful for any man, wherever he found a priest, to shoot him at once. Their treatment of the Indian was no better. It was ordered that it should not be lawful for any man to fire a gun at any kind of game unless it be at a wolf or an Indian. They were strict men in their way. (Laughter.) Here are more of their laws for you. I will show in what spirit they were : "The court, taking notice of the great abuse committed by persons profaning the Sabbath or Lord's day, ordain that if any one do any unnecessary servile work, or unnecessary travelling, or sports, or recreation"—for example, if a man play a game of ball or take a walk—"he or they that do so transgress shall forfeit for every such default the sum of 40s., or be publicly whipped ; further, if it clearly appears that this sin was proudly, presumptuously, and with a high hand committed against the known command and authority of the blessed God, such person shall be put to death, or punished at the discretion of the court." If a couple of young men went out to say their prayers until they were black in the face—(laughter) —and to go into the church and hear the Puritans "humming and bumming over their heads," and if after that they went out to have a game of cricket or take a walk, and they were asked why they did it, and one of them were to say that they were tired of all they had heard, they would be liable to be put to death.

Now, here are more of their laws : "No one shall run on the Sabbath day, or walk in his garden or elsewhere— (laughter)—except reverently to and from meeting. No one shall travel, cook victuals, make beds, sweep house, cut hair, or shave on the Sabbath day." Why, on that day, of all others, a man would like to appear clean and decent." (Roars of laughter.) "No woman shall kiss her child on the Sabbath or fasting day." (Laughter.) These States were young colonies, under the protection of

British law as British colonies. The Catholic religion, persecuted at home—both in England and Ireland—was persecuted still more terribly in America. We read, for instance, that in the year 1700 the English soldiers who then held New York received a commission, and on that commission they massacred Sebastian Rasle, and his colleagues were scattered and had to fly the country. The same legislation held throughout, for the States were then British colonies. This was about the very last tyrannical act of England; in 1778, which was a memorable year, the American Revolution was then in full swing. At that time America was up in arms. They said: "No more tyranny; we must have our own land for ourselves." (Tremendous and prolonged cheering.) The English soldiers in 1778 were obliged to make a speedy and inglorious retreat from New York. The spot is still pointed out at a place called the Battery where they hung a British flag to the top of a flag-staff, and they greased the pole for fear any one should climb up to pull it down. But there was a little American lad so strong in his knees that he was able to climb the pole, though it was greased, and to pull it down before their ship was out of sight. (Laughter.)

Their last act was to take a Catholic priest, the Abbé de la Motte, a Frenchman, and throw him into prison, because he was guilty of the atrocious crime of singing Mass. Well, my friends, as it was in the Eastern States, so it was further south. The State of Virginia was colonized and was the stronghold of the Church of England, as distinguished from the Dissenters or Nonconformists. There was a society called the Society for the Propagation of the Gospel in Foreign Parts, and they were so anxious for the propagation of the Gospel that the first thing they did was that if they found a Catholic priest they thought they would do a holy and wholesome thing for God to put him into prison or put him to death. Well, there were some Catholics—English and Irish—in that State. They were there in the year 1634, and amongst them there was a noble English family, the head of which was Lord Baltimore, with an Irish title, derived, I think, from your own country. This man, finding his people persecuted, said: "I will not stay here to be persecuted by these vagabonds; there are thousands of miles of territory elsewhere, so in the name of the Father, Son, and Holy Ghost let us go somewhere else."

That year Lord Baltimore landed on the shores of the Potomac, in Maryland, and established the only Catholic State in America. Land was purchased from the natives by Lord Baltimore, from whom the city derives its name. They made their own laws and constitution, and now for the honor of the holy Catholic Church I say that the very first law that Lord Baltimore and his fellow-colonists made was: "In this State of Maryland no man shall ever be persecuted for his religion." (Cheers.) And how was this constitution accepted and received? O my friends! it is worthy of your earnest attention. We are told, on the authority of Mr. Bancroft, the great American historian, that as soon as this new principle of religious toleration was declared the people were astonished to hear it. They came there from all the countries of Europe, and from every colony of America, that they might breathe the air of religious freedom. (Applause.)

These are the words of the historian: "Emigrants arrived from every clime"—(mind, he is a Protestant who speaks)—"and the Colonial Legislature extended its sympathies to many natives as well as to many sects. From France came Huguenots—(Protestants who were persecuted for their religion)—from Germany, from Holland, from Sweden, from Ireland the children of misfortune sought protection under the tolerant sceptre of the Roman Catholic. Bohemia itself, the country of Jerome and of Huss, sent forth its sons, who at once were made citizens of Maryland, with equal franchises." The Quaker who wanted to keep his ears, and who did not like the application of a red-hot iron to his tongue, came to Maryland, and under the flag of religious freedom he found peace and immunity. (Applause.) Many Protestants were sheltered against

Protestant intolerance in the Roman Catholic colony of Maryland.

Now, recollect what I am going to tell you. They came in; they were heartily welcome; they multiplied—small blame to them: they wanted to keep their ears—and in a few years they got numerous. We have the evidence of the great Protestant historian, Bancroft, that they applied for the protection of the English law, and disfranchised the Catholics. I feel my blood boil when I read it. Lord Baltimore died, and though his sons continued his policy, the ruinous influence of Anglican institutions was now to be once more manifested. The powerful influence of the Archbishop of Canterbury was solicited to secure an establishment of the Anglican Church (the precious concern Mr. Gladstone pulled down), which clamored for favor where it already enjoyed equality. Why was it not satisfied with equality? If there are any Protestant ladies and gentlemen here to-night, to you I address myself. Why were they not satisfied with equality? (Applause.) If they had the truth, what does the truth ask but a fair field and no favor? (Applause.) "The prelates demanded not freedom but privilege, an establishment to be maintained at the common expense of the Catholic province. The English Ministry soon issued an order that offices of the government in Maryland should be entrusted exclusively to Protestants. Roman Catholics were disfranchised in the province which they had planted." (Groans.) It is unnecessary I should dwell upon this thing to create bad feelings. I am ashamed of it, and so is every right-minded Protestant in the world. Meantime, how fared it with the Catholics? The Catholics, my friends, were few in the land—few and far between—here and there. Five or six Highlandmen from Scotland of the old class that kept the ancient faith, the Irish family driven by persecution, or by some strange impulse, or by some venturesome spirit, or tired of fighting in a hopeless cause, would go to America, and, bringing their Catholic faith with them, would remain in the wild forests, hewing the primeval trees, ploughing the virgin soil, hunting the elk, destroying the wild beasts, making a little civilization, but sighing in vain for the sign of the cross or for the visit of the priest. (Applause.) The poor Catholic baptized his own children, assembled them at night to say the rosary, taught them, when he might, their Catechism; but beyond this there was no aid whatever, no help whatever, from that religion which he knew and believed to be the only true revelation of God, and with which he believed all his hopes for time and eternity were bound. (Applause.) Occasionally a Spanish priest from South America, from the Southern States, might venture into the northern wilds and forests. Occasionally the poor Irish emigrant, the poor Irish Catholic, might see at early morning a little canoe coming down along the solitary stream, and as he strained his eyes for a time he might see upon the very top of the mast of the frail boat something like the sign of the cross—some French Jesuit or some Dominican priest, committing his life and his all, going down the Ohio, the Missouri, or the Mississippi in search of souls. (Loud applause.) Then great was the joy when the man of God arrived, and when, perhaps for the first time for twenty years, the Catholic, with his children around him, was able to kneel down at the Holy Sacrifice and adore his God. (Applause.)

I need not tell you that in the year 1776 the American Revolution broke out. The British soldiers were defeated, the flag of England disappeared from off the ports and cities, whilst all America and the world beheld for the first time that which I for one honor and revere, the glorious "Stars and Stripes." (Loud and prolonged applause.) You will not be surprised to hear that when this glorious event was accomplished, in the process of which the blood of Irishmen was shed freely, that the immortal George Washington, well, indeed, and proudly, avowed that the strongest force at his right arm was the patriotism and courage of the Irishman. (Loud applause.) Yet in that day there was not a single priest in the whole State or city of New York. The first priest that settled in the city of

New York was Father Francis Whelan, an Irish Franciscan, who came there in 1785, and his congregation amounted at that time to about two hundred Catholics in the city. Further on, in 1808, there were only one bishop and one diocese in the whole of the United States of America; that was the Bishop of Baltimore. It seems to us as it were a thing of yesterday, our idea of antiquity carrying us back to the middle ages. And in America they consider themselves old when we in Ireland are what we call robust men. I knew myself that I was not a bad-looking man, but I was called the old gentleman frequently. (Laughter.) I do not mean old Harry or old Nick, you know, but the old gentleman. (Renewed laughter.) In 1808 there was only one bishop in America, and in 1815—the other day we say; our fathers remember it—the first cathedral was constructed by Bishop Chevereux of Boston. Dr. Connolly, a Dominican, was appointed Bishop of New York in 1822. Many men here may have some recollection of that year. In that year there were only eight priests in the whole diocese of New York. Do you know what the diocese of New York meant at that time? It meant the whole of New York, New Jersey, and Long Island, which then comprised Brooklyn, Albany, Rochester, Buffalo, and Newark, and in the year 1822 there were only eight priests there. California at that time was scarcely known. Some Spanish friars had formed the people into societies, taught them agriculture, and made them a happy people, and everything went on well until the year 1813—so far up to our own time. We find that ninety-five years ago there were thirteen States; now there are thirty-eight. Eighty-one years ago there was but one bishop in America. Seventy years ago—sixty years ago there were but four bishops in America; now there are fifty-seven. (Loud applause.) The population of America at the time of the Declaration of Independence was two millions eight hundred thousand; now there are over forty millions. (Applause.)

In that population did the Catholics keep up with that

immense increase of population? The increase in the population was fourteen hundred and thirty-three per cent. The Catholics at the time were enumerated at twenty-five thousand in America. To-day John Francis Maguire, whose authority I accept, declares that it is a small estimate to say that the Catholics in the United States number nine millions. (Loud applause.) That is to say, more than thirty-three thousand per cent., whereas the increase in the States in the main is fourteen hundred and thirty-three per cent. Some of the statistics of the diocese will give you some more accurate idea of these things. In 1786 there was but one chapel and two hundred Catholics; now, at the present day, there are at least one hundred and fifty-five churches in New York, and two hundred and fifty priests on the mission. (Applause.) In 1822 there were only eight priests in New York and seventeen thousand Catholics in the whole diocese of New York. In 1847 the diocese of Albany, a mere slice of New York, was cut off, and in that diocese alone there are one hundred and seventy priests, three hundred and eight churches and chapels, and a Catholic population of two hundred and fifty thousand. In 1822 there were but seventeen thousand Catholics and but eight priests in the whole State. In 1847 Buffalo was cut off from it, and two years ago there were one hundred and ten priests there and one hundred and fourteen churches and chapels. (Applause.) In the city of Brooklyn there was but one priest twenty-five years ago, and now it contains, besides its cathedral, twenty-five Catholic churches and twelve thousand children attending daily for education at the Catholic schools. (Loud applause.)

I need not go into the details with you, my friends, for it is quite unnecessary. One or two facts such as these give you an idea of the contrast between the America of to-day and what it was so few years ago. I wish now to direct your attention to a few remarks I have to make. In 1834 there was in Milwaukee, in the State of Wisconsin, but a single white man. The place belonged to the red Indian. Three years later an Irish priest, and true man,

Father Kelly, came there, with perhaps only one man for his congregation, so that he could address him as Dean Swift used to address his clerk—" Dearly beloved Roger." (Loud laughter.) Two years later, in 1839, there was one church in Milwaukee; one year later, in 1840, there were two thousand Catholics; in 1844, twenty thousand Catholics; and in 1868, five years ago, there were three hundred and twenty-two churches, sixteen chapels, seventy-five stations, and four hundred thousand German and Irish Catholics. (Applause.)

This was indeed a miraculous growth. Measure it by the growth of some of the religious orders. Take, for instance, the Order of Notre Dame, of which order there are two ladies here at present looking for subjects among the faithful and grand maidenhood of Ireland. I was speaking to one of them, and she told me she was reaping a rich harvest, as I told her she would be sure to do amongst the faithful, pure, and grand maidenhood of the country. (Applause.) Sixteen years ago there was but one convent of that order founded in America; now there are fifty-eight convents and five hundred sisters. In 1847 Dr. Timon was consecrated Bishop of Buffalo, and at that time there were but sixteen churches (mere shanties) there, and sixteen priests. Twenty years later that bishop died, and before he died he left one hundred and sixty-five grand churches and one hundred and twenty-six priests on the mission in his diocese. (Applause.) These facts alone suffice; now let us look for the explanation. How came this wonderful growth? How came it to pass that the Catholic Church, as if she were only founded forty years ago, and as if she had the twelve apostles bestowing on her the blessing of God, produced such a miraculous growth as this? We don't expect such a growth from this old tree, nearly two thousand years old, from which so many fair branches have been lopped off, dried up, and cast away. How comes it that this old Church is able to put forth her branches, to overspread a mighty continent, and out of twenty-five thousand to produce in an inconceivably short time, within the span of one man's memory, nearly ten millions of souls? (Loud applause.) It is a great problem, my friends, and one well worthy of consideration. It is worthy of our consideration as a human fact. We have *data* and evidence for it that, whilst the Catholic Church has been growing in this way, like unto the tree planted by the running waters, every other religious institution, sect, or whatever you may call it, has been decaying and losing its hold upon the minds and hearts of the Americans. (Applause.)

I speak thus upon the evidence of Americans and Protestants. One writer says: "The growth of Popery is simply prodigious." When in Boston I asked what was the proportion the Catholics bore to the entire population in a city where, when a learned Catholic bishop visited the place after the Declaration of Independence, it was said to him: "Now we know you are not the devil, though when first you came we would cross the street and go out of your path, so that we might not breathe the same air with a Catholic." (Laughter and applause). To-day, in the centre of the mind and intelligence of America, the majority of the population is Catholic and mostly Irish. (Loud applause.) I lectured there myself, and Mr. Patrick Donahoe, the able editor of the Boston *Pilot*, brought thirty-five thousand people to hear me. View it humanly, it is an astonishing fact; but, beyond this, it is a supernatural fact. He who founded that religion and that Church declared that His Church and His kingdom were like unto the mustard-seed, which falls into the soil the least of seeds, but when it grows up a mighty tree, and extends its branches hither and thither, all the birds of the air find their nests there. (Applause.) It is a supernatural fact in this: no religion demands from those who profess it such sacrifices as Catholicity. Catholicity at the hands of you, my friends, demands sacrifices intellectual and physical.

As an intellectual sacrifice, Catholicity demands that you bow down your intelligence with humility before the eye of faith and worship God who was crucified. Oh! how often have I found during my career in America men who would say to me : "Give me leave to reason the thing out until I come to a conclusion founded on human reason." But we must not look to human reason for a solution of this problem. As well might we doubt the existence of stars in the heavens which are not visible to the naked eye. It would be folly to look for those stars with the naked eye, but if we take a telescope they come out upon our vision. And so it is with those truths which are far, far removed from the mere ken of human reason, far beyond the scope of human argument. God has furnished the telescope of divine faith, which will remove the cloud which veils the eyes of the infidel and will disclose to his vision the glorious and golden truths of God's revelation. (Applause.) Catholicity imposes physical sacrifices. There is none of us who does not think that a beefsteak is more pleasing than a salt herring. (Laughter.) There are a good many days in the year when you and I have to be content to eat a bit of fish when we would like a bit of meat. (Laughter.) Catholicity imposes sacrifices greater still. It obliges the proud man to go to confession. There is the sacrifice of sacrifices! There is the grandeur of the Catholic faith! God has thrown the omnipotence of his mercy into a commission given to the priest, who tells the proudest man to bow down and humble himself before that omnipotent power wielded by man. (Applause.)

I met a gentleman in America who told me, I believe, all he had to tell me of his life. "Sir," he said, "I am telling you everything, but I am telling it to you as a friend; for I could not, if I were to die for it, demean myself to do so as a poor penitent, believing you could do everything for me." And yet Catholicity imposes that upon us; and how could you account for it except by the supernatural reason that religion was clearly defined in the humiliation of the mind and heart, and the humiliation of the body to accept as law such religious privations? (Applause.) The explanation is, first, by the reason I have given—it is the work of God; secondly, the United States of America have received the superabundant population of the older countries. The energy, physical and intellectual, which found no vent in Europe has found spacious room for its exercise in the vast continent of America. And, above all, America was intended, I believe, by the Almighty God to be the home of the hunted and the refuge of the persecuted, and to open her arms and take to her bosom a race the most faithful, the most gifted, though the most down-trodden of the people of the earth. (Loud applause.) They turned their eyes towards the West; they turned their backs to the pauper's grave; they heard the rattling of the chains that hung upon their fathers for ages; they fled to the West, and brought to the glorious Columbia that wealth of Irish blood, of Irish brains, and Irish heart, but above all, and beyond all, that grand principle which is the only unifying and uniting principle of our race for ages—that of their Catholic faith. (Loud and prolonged applause.) Those have crossed the sea in thousands—ay, I will say in millions. They crossed the sea, and soon the generous hand of Columbia wiped away the tears from the exiles' eyes. They consented, for the sake of the land of their adoption, and for their own temporal interests, to confine her rivers, to cut down her mountains and fill up her valleys, to build her cities, to cover her with that wonderful network of railways which places her in advance of the whole world; they consented to fight in her armies, until the soil of America is reddened with Irish blood, shed on many a glorious battle-field, almost as much as the old land itself is reddened with the blood shed in martyrdom. They consented to do all this, and they did it well; but they demanded from Columbia in return one privilege—to proclaim the Catholic faith and uphold Catholic doctrine, and to cover the glorious land with the grandest churches and the most magnificent evidences of Catholicity that the world beholds to-day. (Applause.)

I do not deny that this great increase in Catholicity is due also to another great element in American emigration —the Germans. From the Catholic states of Southern

Germany they also came in their hundreds and hundreds of thousands; they brought with them faith—a quiet faith. I have observed it carefully and lovingly—a quiet zeal for their own sanctification, a great zeal for the Catholic education of their children. Everywhere, wherever the German community is found, do you find good churches and schools; but when they have built their church and secured the ministrations of a priest they sit down and enjoy their religion. But the Irishman builds not for himself alone; he will not content himself with building a church for Irish Catholics, but will devote half his day's earnings to build a big cathedral for all Catholics; his Irish heart takes them all in. (Loud cheers.) The Irishman, restless himself, perhaps, still will not leave the place where he has earned a dollar until he puts half that dollar into the soil, in the shape of some glorious evidence that the Irish Catholic hand was there. (Applause.) The German will enjoy his religion, but will not fight for it; Paddy will stick up for his religion, and Paddy will fight for it. ("Bravo!") And it would be a strange thing indeed if a race that is said to be so disposed for fighting that they will fight for the fun of the thing—(laughter)—it would be a strange thing if they would not fight when it was a question of God and His holy religion that was at issue. (Hear, hear.) I was travelling in Kentucky, and there were four young gentlemen, with more fun than good sense in their temperaments, came into the carriage. It was the only time I received the slightest indignity while I was in America. These young gentlemen seemed to be coming home from school—four strapping young fellows. At any rate, they commenced chaffing the poor priest. Well, I had met with so much of that kind of thing in England that I didn't mind a bit. But when we pulled up at the station a man appeared at the door of the carriage—a tremendously big King's County man, looming up like Finn McCoul. (Cheers and laughter.) He walked in. Those four gentlemen hushed up, and one of them said in a whisper that I heard: "I guess that's an Irish chap. We had better shut up." (Great laughter.) And so well they might, for after they departed, and I told my Irish friend, he put out a gross exclamation: "Be the mortial," said he, "if I knew that"—(loud laughter, which was increased by Father Burke's pantomime)—"I would not leave as much clothes on the vagabonds as would make a mop to swab the carriage, and I'd break their necks in the bargain." (Applause and laughter.)

The third reason to which I attribute this extraordinary spread of Catholicity in America is a certain attribute of the native American mind of which I am very anxious to speak, for I feel very intensely about it. Strictly speaking, we must draw a broad line between the British colonial America which ceased at the time of the Revolution and the new and glorious States which sprang into existence from that period. The British colonies, as they were called, were legislated for by the home country; they got their laws from London, and these laws were impregnated with the spirit of religious bigotry and intolerance, and the statute-books were stained with Catholic blood. The moment that America dashed to the ground that unworthy banner and raised up the banner of her own freedom she had the generosity to blot out all recollections of the past by splendid legislation, and declared the great principle of religious liberty. (Cheers.) The consequence was that the American of to-day—that highly-intellectual, that grandly-gifted American mind of to-day—is not a bit agreeable to the more ancient opinions and traditions of persecution. They are free from them, as, more than once, gentlemen in America boasted to me: "Father, you must acknowledge our hands are free from blood." The consequence of this is a certain largeness of mind, a freedom from prejudice, a certain willingness to consider fairly the great truths of revelation, a certain logical acumen which keenly and logically perceives the truth. Nothing struck me more than this—the clear, unprejudiced habit of mind I discovered amongst Americans. I will give you a case in point. I was called, during my stay in America, to visit a gentleman who was sick. He was a lawyer of eminence in the Southern States—all the best families are in the Southern States—and a man very highly connected. He was a man, too, who had travelled in Europe and had read a good deal. I went to him and found him with all his senses perfectly clear, and I spoke to him on religious truths. The man looked at me. After a time I felt the moment was come; I concluded my arguments; I rose from the place where I was sitting at the bedside, and said: "My friend, you are dying; it is necessary in order to please God to have some specific form of religious belief. You have heard my arguments; I command you now, in the name of the Father, Son, and Holy Ghost, to ask to be received into the Catholic Church, and to consent to receive the sacraments at my hands." The moment I put it to him the man complied, and before I left the room he was a Catholic. (Loud applause.)

And now, my friends, such is the present of America—a glorious Church, united like one man. The episcopacy, the priesthood, and the Catholic laity in America are the most united of any branch of the holy Catholic Church, for they have less dissension or appearance of diversity of opinion amongst them. Obedience to the holy Church of God; love for the Church's head and centre, the Pope of Rome; rational yet most loving obedience to every mandate of the head of the Church, and docile submission to every enunciation of the Church, their mother—these are received and acted upon as matters of course in America. It is the most glorious in its unity of all the nations that have embraced the truth and the cross of Jesus Christ. (Cheers.) A glorious Church, numbering to-day fully one-fourth of the population of the United States, destined to grow with that mighty, growing country, destined to leaven that country with truth. For of all the converts to Catholicity I have ever met—and I have encountered many of different nationalities—the most intellectual, the most fervent, the most simple-minded and religious are the converts made to Catholicity from the worst forms of New

England Puritanism. (Applause.) They brought all the energy of their Pilgrim forefathers with them into the Church of God; they brought their dogged Anglo-Saxon determination that, having seen the truth, they shall stand by it to the end, and they will fight for it, and, if necessary, die for it. (Cheers.) These converts are multiplying every year. The shrewd, keen intelligence of America has an insight into the truth far keener than those nations whose youth and childhood have been nurtured upon the traditions of bigotry and intolerance. Those converts are multiplying. Protestantism is rapidly disappearing out of the haunts of Puritanism. In Massachusetts itself Catholicity has made such advances that one statesman of America said, a few years ago: "In twenty-five years I believe that the great masses of our population will be Roman Catholic." (Cheers.) I believe it for two reasons. One is a supernatural, the other a natural, reason. I believe it for a supernatural reason. The Church is the salvation of the world. Every Catholic believes it; every Catholic must believe it. If I did not believe that her mission was to save the world, to save society—the human as well as divine society of her own children—I would not remain a Catholic. (Cheers.)

The American mind—coming to the natural argument—is beginning to recognize this fact. They see clearly and distinctly that it is necessary for the salvation of American society that the sanctity of the Christian family should be preserved. They see it is necessary the Christian wife should be the queen of her Christian household; that there should be no power on earth or in hell able to sever the sacred bond that God himself seals—the sacramental bond of matrimony. They see that the purity and integrity of the children depend upon the fidelity of the husband and wife; and therefore they begin to see every day more and more clearly that that religion alone can save them which sanctifies their union, which stamps upon the man and woman the sacramental seal which represents the fidelity of Jesus Christ to His Church. (Loud applause.)

Before leaving America one of the things I received was a book from a distinguished Protestant clergyman. It was a book written against the principle of divorce, and it was written in as sound a spirit as if a Catholic priest wrote it, and with as firm and impressive and as eager an eloquence as if the best Irishman that ever put pen to paper was the author of it. (Hear, hear.) In that book he lays down as a principle that until the law of divorce is utterly ignored and abolished there can be no safety for society in America. The keen American people, who love their family ties, and no people love them more dearly—that excellent people, leavened with much that is excellent in the various nations that supply the elements of its population—the American people, who love strongly and tenderly, are beginning to see more and more that between the lawlessness of the border nations and the rites and intelligence of Mohammedanism—that between the strange practices of this sect and that, all flowing in upon and intended ultimately to destroy them, there is only one great bulwark to defend them, only one capable of standing between them and all that abomination, only one power that can exorcise that demon that would destroy society, and that one power is the holy Roman Catholic Church. (Great applause.) America to-day groans and laments by the voices of her statesmen, her philosophers, her writers, and her press over the awful corruption of official life, the awful corruption of commercial life, and the dishonesty which they publicly proclaim is found in every order of commercial, social, and political life. Nothing impressed me more than this—the universal lament, day after day, in all the papers in America.

Thus we read that a man absconded, having made his "pile"—for they have their special names by which to designate those operations. Another man absconded, having executed a tremendous "job," and taken a couple of millions of dollars from the public. Now a man is brought to bay until he is made to disgorge sums of almost fabulous extent—eight, ten, or twelve millions of dollars; and now some great company is "burst up," to use another American phrase, through the dishonesty and fraudulent conduct of two or three of its head men, and so on. Men see all these facts. Over and over again I have preached, and lectured, and spoken to American audiences on this great truth. "Gentlemen," I have said, "there is only one religion that can save you; that is the religion that begins by making men honest, through sacramental grace; and if they are not honest, it is the only one that knows how to punish the thief by making him make restitution. (Cheers.) Prevent a man from stealing if you can; but if you cannot, the worst infliction you can impose upon him is to take him by the throat and say: 'Make restitution of all you have, or down to hell you go.' (Great applause.) The Catholic Church alone can say this." Here it is that the true, shrewd mind of America sees the immense advantage Catholicity offers over those shams. For it is only a sham and a humbug the religion that is for ever crying: "Lord, Lord!"; that invokes the holy name with blasphemous familiarity; that is constantly spouting texts from the Old Testament, and is always parading before you the sayings of this prophet or of that lawgiver; that is ever flattering men and laying the flattering unction to their souls that they have found the true way to happiness when they learn to believe and "lean upon the Lord." (Cheers and laughter.) Well, my friend the commissioner or my friend the road contractor may "lean upon the Lord," but you may be sure he will bring an addition to his own weight in the shape of a bag containing a couple of million dollars. (Great laughter.)

My friends, one word and I have done. I believe I can afford to wait, for I believe if God give me the ordinary term of human life I shall live to behold Catholic America —a great nation clothed in all the grandeur and strength and pride of the holy Church of God. (Loud cheers.) It is said that when the Son of God was on the cross His dying face was turned towards the West. I know not if the circumstance be so, but it seems as if it were. The tide of sanctity and divine faith receded many ages ago from the very hills that witnessed His crucifixion. The approaching tide of barbarism, Mohammedanism, and infidelity swept in, and every vestige of the Church of God was obliterated there. We have seen that tide sweeping on from Jerusalem to Ephesus, from Ephesus to Constantinople, proceeding westward still, finding strength in Rome; and from Rome the tide of sanctity, retained by her, still swept westward, westward still, until in a far-distant western isle, the island of saints, of monks, and of apostles, the glory of Christendom, the grandeur of Catholic sanctity burst out even upon Christian nations as a still brighter light, and all the world praised God in Ireland. (Great applause.) The surging waves of infidelity are to-day lashing with angry roar the very foundations of the seven hills of Rome; but westward still flows the tide of sanctity, growing and increasing in the light of divine faith; and to-day the whole world gazes upon the portent of American Catholicity, and glorifies God through the means of faith for that which no human reason can account for or understand. (Immense applause.)

I met old priests in America—old men who in their first days of missionary priesthood were obliged to lie down in the snow, and were forced to camp out in the winter on their way of a hundred or two hundred miles from one station to another to say Mass. There may be American priests here, some who, like myself, have heard such words as these made use of by Father Abraham, the grand old Kentucky patriarch. "Father," he said, "I am utterly astonished; I am amazed; I can find no reason on earth for it; I must cast my eyes to heaven." Surely, if there be such things as these—if the spirit of light and grace be there, and if its nature and tendency be to grow and increase—may I not promise myself to behold, ere my eyes are closed in death, this glorious and magnificent sight of the Catholic Church triumphant in America? (Loud cheers.) Oh! in that day, when the great flag of freedom —the flag unstained by blood shed in persecution or injustice, the flag first upreared by Irish hands in the days of the first Revolution, and borne proudly by the same brave hands over a hundred battle-fields from end to end of the land—when that flag shall wave over a people united in their faith, and consequently in every minor relation of life, sanctified by Catholic sacraments, purified by Catholic agency, strengthened by Catholic unity, emboldened by Catholic hope, as well as enlightened by Catholic faith, and all this comes to crown the acute intellect, the strong determination, the firm purpose of the natural American man, where, since the world was created or redeemed, where was there such a sight seen as Columbia will present to the nations? (Immense applause.) I say for myself, and for the men of my blood and of my native land, it is your wish and mine, it is the highest wish and desire of millions of our countrymen in America, who pray day by day at the thousand altars of the land, that in return for all that Columbia gave them God would give to her the grand crown of Catholic faith, Catholic hope, and Catholic charity, till in the strength of divine grace she shall be the light and the glory of the whole world.

(As the reverend gentleman concluded his magnificent oration, the audience rose with one accord and cheered again and again, while hands were clapped and hats were waved, making up a scene of enthusiastic rapture such as has been rarely witnessed amongst us.)

THE CATHOLIC CHURCH THE SAFETY, NOT THE DANGER, OF THE GREAT AMERICAN REPUBLIC.

THE subject of this lecture is one which Father Burke is admirably adapted to discuss, and one which is of deep interest not only to the members of the Church but to all thinking people. It is one of his most valuable lectures, and though it was delivered in America we deem it worthy of the readers of this volume. Let it be particularly recommended to the serious thought of all lovers of American liberty.

DEAR FRIENDS: Any one who wishes to mark attentively the course of the events of this world must recognize in all that he sees around him the hand of God and the hand of the devil—God influencing all things for good, and the devil coming in on every side and trying to spoil God's work. Now, amongst the works of God the greatest is the Christian religion and the Catholic Church; and amongst the many means that the devil employs to gain his end—namely, that of spoiling the work of God— one great evil that he makes use of is to inspire the nations and the people with a kind of dread and fear of the Catholic Church. He says to the nations: "Don't listen to her; don't hear her voice at all; don't have anything to say to her. She is bad; she will corrupt you; she will bewitch you." He gives them no reason for this. He has no reason for it. Nothing must strike one more at first sight than the strange repugnance and unreasoning fear with which so many sectarians, Protestants and others, regard the Catholic Church. I remember, some years ago, a very enlightened, highly-cultivated English lady came to Rome with her daughter. The daughter became a Catholic, and I received her into the Church. Her mother came to me the same day, wild with grief, the tears streaming from her eyes—a heart-broken woman. She said: "What have you done to my child ! O you wicked man ! what have you done to my child ? You have ruined my child and broken my heart." I said: "How is that ?" "Well," she said, "you have made a Catholic of my daughter." "Yes, that is true. Under God, I have been the means of making a Catholic of her. But do you think that is sufficient reason for breaking your heart ?" "Yes, it is," said she. I said to her: "You are a well-educated lady; I simply ask you one question: What point is there in the teachings or in the practice of the Catholic Church that you object to ?" She paused for a moment. "Well," she said, "I don't know; but I know you have bewitched my child and have broken my heart." "Can you find fault," I said, "with any one doctrine of the Catholic Church that your child has embraced ?" She said she could not. And yet that woman acknowledged to me, "If my child," she said, "had renounced God and had declared herself an atheist, I would not be so grieved as I am for her to become a Catholic"; and that without any reason under heaven, without knowing the why or the wherefore, without being able to find the slightest cause. Well, as it happened, within twelve months I had the happiness to receive the mother into the Church and make a good Catholic of her. (Applause and laughter.)

My friends, amongst the nations among which I have travelled, nowhere have I found this distrust and fear of the Catholic Church less unreasoning and less powerful than in America. I generally enter freely into conversation with people, strangers with whom I am thrown. But sometimes I have found people to whom I have said: "Good-morning," and they would move off as if they heard the rattle of a rattlesnake. Sometimes I have been obliged to say : "You need not be afraid of me ; I am a priest, but I will not eat you." "Well, this is the first time in my life that I ever spoke to a Catholic priest. Do you know that I would rather not have anything to say to you?" But I reason with him; I ask him: "What fault have you to find? Why are you afraid of me?"

"Well, nothing particular—but I do not know. It is a subject I avoid. I will not have anything more to say." Then, by a little pressing, I get the man into an argument, and I find that he has not a single idea about the Catholic Church, that he does not know a thing about it, that he is frightened at a bugbear, an imagination, a creation of his own fancy, like the Chinese, who make monsters, which their soldiers carry before them in battle against other Chinese, and at the sight of which their enemies turn and run away. So Protestantism for three hundred years has been making a most horrible bugbear of the Catholic Church—giving it horns, hoofs, and tail, flaming tongue of fire, and great goggle eyes; and it says to the men of the nineteenth century, who boast of their intelligence: "Do not look at it! Run away! Do not speak to it! It will bewitch you. Hate it, detest it. Do not trust the Catholic Church. If you do, she will put an end to your liberties, your happiness, your all." And the big boobies of the nineteenth century get frightened and run away. (Laughter.)

Now, the subject on which I propose to address you this evening is the glorious theme that the Catholic Church is not the danger but, under God, the future salvation of this grand and magnificent Republic of America. (Applause.)

I confess to you, my friends, that as firmly as I believe in the Catholic religion; convinced as I am that that religion is the only true religion; convinced as I am that the Church of God is the only means of salvation—save and except under the mean pretext of invincible ignorance, which means that if men knew a little more they would be damned; they are just ignorant enough to be saved: a little knowledge would be the ruin of them—believing all this, I would not have the heart nor the courage to speak to the people of America and preach Catholicity to them if in the secret recesses of my heart and mind I had the faintest idea that the Catholic religion would be dangerous to the state. In this age of ours men are not willing to accept even the kingdom of heaven at the cost of any great sacrifice. If God would offer them heaven on condition of giving up certain advantages, they would be unwilling to accept it at such a price. But no single earthly advantage is sacrificed, while everything is gained, when a nation rises up, as Ireland rose up under the hand of St. Patrick, and like one man opens its eyes and heart to Catholicity.

First let us reason a little on this great theme. I suppose all men, Protestant and Catholic alike, acknowledge that when Jesus Christ our Lord founded our religion on the earth He founded that religion for the express purpose of saving the world—that that religion was to be the salvation of mankind.

Now, from what did Christ purpose to save the world? What was the evil He came to remedy? Answer: The first evil our Lord came to remedy was ignorance—ignorance the most deplorable, the most profound. Could anything be more terrible than the state of ignorance in which Christ found the world? Men of intelligence, with splendid minds, varied and profound genius, bowed down and worshipped their own vices and their own wickedness, and called those vices God. The whole world worshipped impurity under the name of Venus; dishonesty under the name of Mercury, who was the God of Thieves; revenge under the name of Mars—every vice and passion, even the passion of avarice, that eats the heart out of the miser, which they adored under the name of Plutus, who was the protector of riches and those that sought them. It was bad enough to be ignorant of the truth, but they went further, and they not only lost sight of heaven, but, not content with the darkness of earth, they went grovelling down into hell to find their god there.

The second evil that Jesus Christ found in the world

wide-spread was the evil of impurity sapping and destroying the vital energies, physical and mental, and the power and strength of men. He found as soon as manhood began to dawn upon them, as soon as they began to feel the throbs of virile blood in their veins—He found them yielding to every prompting of the base command, going out ravening to gratify the strong, unreasoning, earthly passion that poisoned the spring of life and destroyed all hope of future manhood. He found impurity all over the world, so that the virtues of chastity were not only not to be found amongst men, but it was not even known amongst them—it had no name. The Virgin Mother, the purest of God's creatures, had her virginity laid as a reproach upon her. From this impurity it would follow that there was no such thing as the family circle, with its blessed and holy influences. The Roman wife was a slave, dependent upon the mere caprice of her husband, whom, when time had worn the bloom off her cheek, he exchanged for another and fairer woman.

In the third place, Jesus Christ found the evil of dishonesty. No man's word was to be depended upon; commercial honesty seemed to have perished. The old straightforward manner of the first republican Romans had departed, and in the tottering, effete empire dishonesty—commercial, social, and international—was the order of the day.

These were the diseases under which the world suffered. Men sinned because they knew no better; they were ignorant. They were steeped in impurity, their manhood was gone out of them ; so that a few thousand barbarians easily broke up and smashed to pieces the mighty Roman Empire, and overcame those once invincible legions that had given law to the whole world. Whilst dishonesty was creeping into every rank of life, society was rapidly breaking up into chaotic elements.

What did Christ say and do ? He told men that He had come down from heaven expressly to teach them, in order that all might know the truth. He emphatically declared that from His lips, and from the lips of those He had appointed to teach, the world should gain—not a spirit of enquiry, my friends; not a spirit of Protestantism looking for the truth—no; but He said: "You shall know the truth; you shall have knowledge of it fixed, clear, and definite, and in that knowledge you shall find your freedom; you shall know the truth, and the truth shall make you free."

And then the Son of God laid His hand upon a little child, and said: "Blessed are the clean of heart, for they shall see God"; and to all men He said: "Unless you become even as this little child, you shall not enter the kingdom." As if He would say: "Behold this child! no impure thought has ever soiled its innocence; no unlawful crime or sinful passion has ever entered its breast; unless you become as this little child, you shall not enter the kingdom of heaven."

And then He declared the sacred principle of conscience, that every man should act to his fellow-men as he would wish them to act to him—that every man who perpetrated an outrage or injury should not enter heaven until he repaid the last farthing. He established the principle of social, commercial, and international honor. Truth, chastity, and honor! behold the three elements of the religion of Jesus Christ—the three grand sanitary powers that He had put into His Church when He declared it to be the salt of the earth. It is by truth, chastity, and honor that the Church has saved, is saving, and is destined unto the end to save the world. Without truth, chastity, and honor there is no salvation for the people.

Reflect first upon the truth. Why is truth the salvation of the people? For many reasons. I will give you only one. I do not know that it is the highest reason, but it is the one that bears most directly upon myself. The salvation of a people lies in unity. To be a unit is the first necessity of a people. Christ our Lord Himself declares that a house divided against itself must fall. And the first element of national existence and national progress is that the people should be united; and the enemy of public freedom and the liberty of the people in all ages has always begun his infernal work by trying to create divisions and dissensions among them. I might point, as an illustration, to Ireland, the Niobe of nations, the martyred mother who bore me. For seven hundred years we have groaned beneath the tyrant's hands, pitiless and unrelenting, unrelaxing in his grasp. Why? Because he governed a divided people. It was but the other day that an eloquent Englishman in New York said to our very teeth that Ireland was a slave because she was divided, and on the day that she was united no power under heaven could bind her into slavery for a single hour. (Applause.)

Union being the first element of national existence and progress, I ask what is the first element of this union—what is the strongest bond that can bind a people together and keep them together? I answer at once: The principle of religious unity. It is the most sacred of all bonds, because it is the most abiding, the most unchanging; it is a bond fixed by Almighty God Himself. (Applause.)

Nations are sometimes made one by the accidental circumstance of conquest. But the union that is effected by the sword must be preserved by the sword, or it ceases to exist. Take the union of Ireland and England. It was effected by the sword—a sword that was never allowed to rust as long as there was Irish blood at hand to keep it clean and bright by the tears and blood of the people.

But that sword has begun to rust to-day. It is no longer the powerful falchion it was once in the hand of a fearless nation. It rusts in its scabbard; the nation that owns it is afraid to draw it; and the people of Ireland are waiting, thinking that the rust will come over the brightness of the blade; and the moment it does, that moment the union which was effected by the sword will be broken by the sword. (Great applause.) Why? Because such a bond is not of heaven, but of earth.

Again, the accidental circumstance of mutual consent may bind nations together. For instance, the various

States of this American Union have agreed and united upon the basis of State rights. So they have been united, and so they are united, and may God in heaven bless that union and inspire every American citizen, great and small, no matter who he be, with respect for the sacred principles which the nation adopted, for it is only by respecting them on the solid foundation of the law that a people can be kept together. (Applause.)

Nations, again, may be bound together by mutual commercial interests. England and France made a commercial treaty a few years ago. But France found the treaty worked disadvantageously to her and dissolved the treaty, and the *entente cordiale* of which we hear so much was broken.

There is only one bond that can bind a people and keep them together in a union that can never be destroyed, and that is the union of heart, soul, mind, and sympathy that springs from one undivided and common faith. (Applause.) Every other bond may be shattered, and yet a people remain essentially one. Every other preserving element of a race may be destroyed, and yet a people will retain their national individuality alive and vigorous, in spite of everything on earth, because their union comes from God. Let us take a case in point: For seven hundred years the people of my native land have been subject to a series of the most terrible persecutions and trials that ever any nation in the world suffered. Her enemies wished to break in pieces the individuality of Ireland, so that the *disjecta membra*, the broken fragments, might be cast into every nation on earth and amalgamate with them, but that the Irish, as a people, might be wiped out from the face of the earth. For seven hundred years, in spite of the fact that the Irish were divided on every other point in councils, in politics, in sympathies, even in race and blood, Ireland preserved her nationality, and to-day represents a compact, strong, individualized nationality, full of life, youth, vigor, intellect, and energy. Why? Because God blessed us in the midst of our misfortunes with the blessing from heaven of religious unity. Now, I ask you, as reasoning men, did Christ say anything about this idea of unity? The night before the Son of God suffered on the cross He had His apostles around Him; at the last supper He lifted up His eyes and hands to heaven and made His prayer for His apostles and His Church and for every man. What do you think He prayed for? He said: "O Father! I pray for these, that they may be one. Keep them in unity as you, Father, and I are one." He repeated this over and over again, and every apostle took up the same message. Then says St. Paul:

"Brethren, let there be no division among you, no schism, no heresy. I pray you in the Christ and the Holy Spirit that ye be of one mind." These are the words of St. Paul. Therefore, that unity, springing out of religion, enters distinctly into the principles of government as it entered into the prayers of Jesus.

The next question is: Where does that religious unity exist? Let us for a single instant suppose that the Catholic Church no longer exists in America. Have you then left a single principle of religious unity? Not one, not one! The Unitarian denies the inspiration of the Bible. You say there is one common idea in the Protestant sect—that is, the divinity of Jesus Christ. Not at all. I can take you to Protestant churches in New York and Brooklyn, and before you are there five minutes you will hear the preacher deny the divinity of Jesus Christ. Not a single principle of religious unity outside the Catholic Church; but in its place you have Shakers and Quakers, and Baptists and Anabaptists, and Methodists and Mormons. (Applause and laughter.) In the midst of them all, in the midst of the jarring discord, the sounds of their bickering and quarrelling, in the midst of their mutual hurling of damnation at each other, one having as much authority to do it as the other, rises the awe-inspiring figure of the Catholic Church, gigantic in her proportions, rising over the whole world, many-tongued in her voice, for her word is heard in every tongue in which man expresses his sorrow and his joy; crowned with two thousand years of undisputed glory, standing upon a pedestal sunk deep into the rock of ages, and built up with the blood of her martyrs, there she stands, speaking the self-same words that she spoke two thousand years ago, preaching the same truth, proclaiming the same authority: "I come from God. My message is from God. I stood by the Saviour at His cross. I stood by His empty tomb on Easter morning. I stood with the fiery flames over my head on the day of Pentecost. I speak the words I have always spoken, and defy the whole world to contradict me in one word of my speech."

She alone can create unity, because she alone will permit no man to contradict her. As she has her message from God, and as that message must be as true as God, who sent it, the man who contradicts her must be a liar; he must be an enemy of the truth and a contradicter of the truth, and the moment he raises his voice against the Church, though he were the first of her bishops, or the most powerful king in the world, the Church shuts his mouth with her hand, and says: "Kneel down and repent, or else let the curse of excommunication be upon you. Begone! to wither and die, and fall into hell."

What is the great difficulty with the nations to-day? For fifteen hundred years the nations were united in their faith. No nation was Christian that was not also Catholic. But Luther came and the nations were divided. One of the most celebrated and greatest statesmen that ever lived, William Pitt, Earl of Chatham, who governed, as Prime Minister, England and Ireland in 1800, the year that Lord Castlereagh, that amiable man, who afterwards cut his throat, made the union between England and Ireland—Pitt was decidedly one of the greatest minds in England; he was obliged to resign the premiership because he declared he could no longer govern England and Ireland, because the people were divided in their religion. He solemnly promised the Catholics that he would grant them emancipation in 1800—twenty-nine years before it was forced—he pledged his almost royal word that it should be done; but as soon as it was known in England, and as soon as Protestant Ireland knew it, there was stirred up such a clamor that the very greatest man in the three kingdoms resigned his position, and declared that it was impossible to govern a people divided in religion. Two hundred years before, in 1640, Charles I. promised to relax the penal laws against the Catholics. He saw their injustice. The moment that it was known in England such were the turmoil and the threats that the king was obliged to break his royal word, and put his broken promise in his pocket, and let the misery go on.

The present Prime Minister of England is a very fair-minded man. He sees the injustice with which Catholics are treated. He sees that every petty Protestant school in Ireland has its endowment and its charter, whilst the Catholic University is refused one. We did not ask for a half-penny, only a charter; Gladstone would be glad to do it, but he is afraid. One of the grandest ideas of this age of ours was the unification of Germany. Bismarck, a man of wonderful genius, conceived that idea and carried it out practically—a magnificent achievement; but he is so short-sighted as to be now at work exasperating sixteen millions of the German people who are Catholics by persecuting their religion, shutting up their schools, driving out their nuns and Jesuits, and shutting their hospitals. He is doing a foolish thing; but he cannot help it, because the nation decided that he must do it. I must say, as a student of history, that while they lay to our doors the charge of persecution, nowhere do we read in the annals of the world of persecution carried on with so much gusto and enjoyment as the persecutions by the Protestants when they have the upper hand. You see it to-day in Germany. The Protestants there have but a small majority, but they exercise their power pitilessly.

How easy it would be for Bismarck to avoid all this if Germany were again all Catholic, as she was under Charles V.! How easy it would be for Gladstone to govern England

and Ireland if they were a unit in religious faith ; for when this great screw in the political union is loose the whole machine is rickety, and is liable to come to pieces at once. The Catholic Church alone can create unity. And yet men say the Catholic Church is dangerous to America. The Catholic Church is dangerous to America when disunion, mutual distrust, and mutual disaffection become one of the elements of the greatness of a nation, and not until then. The next element of greatness, power, and strength in a nation is the virtue of purity. Every evil, every sin, in the long run, tends to the destruction of man, no matter how pleasant it may be at the moment, and every act committed by a nation, as well as an individual, injures the nation as well as the individual in the long run ; and, although a hundred years may elapse, the punishment may be traced back to the crime that caused it.

The vice of impurity has this peculiarity—that it is destructive not only of the individual but of the race ; and it is noticeable that, though in punishing other crimes God visited individuals, in punishing this vice He has afflicted whole nations.

The Flood and the destruction of Sodom and Gomorrha are examples of this principle.

(Father Burke here drew a beautiful picture of the Church, the spouse of Christ, calling her ministers to serve at her altars, but demanding of them as an essential qualification a virgin body, allowing no hand to assist in her holy rites, no voice to be raised in her consecrated service, but those of men and women who could bring to their work purity. He also showed how the Church demanded from all her members equal purity : from the maiden and the young man virginity, and from the married fidelity to the marriage vow.)

To enforce this purity the necessity and use of the confessional becomes apparent; for the knowledge that confession must be made teaches every man to watch his own actions, words—nay, his very thoughts.

Contrast the purity demanded by the Catholic

Church with the impurity licensed, and even made a duty, by Mormonism, the last form in which Protestantism shows itself to the world. This is the last issue of Protestantism, just as the last issue of Protestant philosophy is Darwinism—that we are descended from apes. These are the metaphysics and ethics of the nineteenth century among Protestants.

And finally, honesty is an element in the greatness of a people. It is getting scarcer every day. Some time ago I was in a railway-carriage, and a gentleman quoted the poet: "An honest man is the noblest work of God," when another man cried from the other end of the carriage: "I am sorry to say that God Almighty does not seem to spend much time producing works of that kind nowadays." (Laughter.) I don't speak from experience; I know nothing about society; I don't belong to it, I belong to the cloister. I find those amongst whom I live are honest men. It is easy to be honest among us, for we have not anything that persons could take from us. (Laughter.) But I read the papers, and hear great complaints of commercial dishonesty.

(Father Burke here dwelt at some length on the prevailing forms of dishonesty—adulteration, cheating, international dishonesty, social dishonesty—alluding to the occupation of Rome by Victor Emmanuel as a piece of robbery paralleled by that of a burglar who would make out his title to your effects by virtue of his six-shooter; and showing that the Catholic Church inculcated honesty of all kinds.)

If, then, O people of America! if union founded upon the grand principle of religious unity; if the preservation of strength, manhood, genius, and intellect; if honesty, public and private—if these three things are necessary for you in America, you must come to the Catholic Church to get them, because you cannot get them elsewhere. (Applause.) If, on the other hand, these things are dangerous, then the Catholic Church is a danger to America. If America looks upon these things as dangerous—any nation that looks upon religious knowledge and unity, upon purity and chastity, upon public and private honesty—any nation that looks upon these things as dangerous is already self-condemned. But America does not look upon these things as dangerous. No, the intelligence that has been thus born and cradled in freedom never yet turned away from the glorious light of the Catholic Church, but sooner or later turned to it. The nation that has opened her imperial bosom, irrespective of previous antecedents, to all who have been driven from other nations by religious or political tyranny, that nation sooner or later will become Catholic; and in the day when mighty America becomes Catholic, in the day when the genius of Catholicity, the first mother of human liberty, the guardian of human purity, the proud shield of the dignity of womanhood, the splendid and unchanging voice proclaiming herself the strong preserver of public and private honesty—in the day when this genius of Catholicity enters into the mind and heart of America, when this mighty people will be united as one man by the sacred union of religious unity, based upon freedom, based upon integrity and upon justice—tell me is there any man living, tell me is there any philosopher upon earth, poet, or orator, whose vivid imagination can approach to the magnificent realities, the intellectual, moral, and physical grandeur that America will present to the world in that glorious day? (Prolonged applause.)

THE CATHOLIC CHURCH AND EDUCATION.

THE following discourse is the charity sermon preached by Father Burke in SS. Michael and John's Church, Dublin, November 20, 1870, in aid of the evening and Sunday schools founded in the last century by Dr. Betagh, S.J. The text is taken from the fourth chapter of St. John: "The Samaritan woman said to Jesus: Sir, I perceive that Thou art a prophet. Our fathers adored on this mountain, and you say that at Jerusalem is the place where men must adore. Jesus saith to her: Woman, believe me, the hour cometh when you shall neither on this mountain nor in Jerusalem adore the Father. You adore that which you know not: we adore that which we know; for salvation is of the Jews. For the hour cometh, and now is, when the true adorers shall adore the Father in spirit and in truth. God is a Spirit, and they that adore Him must adore Him in spirit and in truth."

MY dearly-beloved brethren, I need not remind you of the great object for which you are gathered here to-day. It is to strengthen and enlarge, as well as to continue, the Sunday and evening schools which for many years have been attached to this church and this parish. I ask you, therefore, to consider in relation to this great charity three thoughts which I will endeavor to lay before you: first, the necessity under which we all lie of being educated ourselves and of instructing and educating our children; second, the necessity, special and specific, which the Catholic Church, above all other bodies on this earth, has for education; third, the nature of her duty and her dogma in enforcing that necessity. I am come here to-day to speak in favor of education. If you believe the writers of former days, and many of the writers of the present day as well, I am come here to speak to-day against my own convictions and against my own conscience. They will tell me—presuming to know more about me than I know about myself—that as a Catholic priest I am an enemy of education; above all, as a Catholic monk I am the sworn foe of knowledge. It is in vain that I challenge the assertion. It is in vain that I point to the history of centuries, during which the order I belong to, the habit I wear, and the priesthood which Almighty God has conferred on me have been the beacons of light to the world. It is in vain that I appeal against those objections, against this prejudice, to their own experience, to the evidence everywhere around them; they but hug their prejudice and falsehood more closely to their breasts and exclaim: "At least it is certain that the Catholic Church is somewhat afraid of education."

Education is a simple necessity for the high service of the revealed religion. I need not remind you that in every man there is a double nature—the nature of the body and the nature of the soul. Each separate nature has its own wants, its own requirements, and it is only by complying with the requirements of the body and of the soul that each is developed into the fulness and perfection of its natural existence. Therefore does the young child require food that it may grow. It must be nursed, and housed, and clothed, and cared for in all its bodily wants, else it either dies or gradually becomes a stunted, weakly, deformed, and apparently misbegotten and disgusting object. As it is with the body so also is it with the soul. The soul must be nursed and nurtured, and have all its wants attended to and supplied as fully as the body; else though the body may grow and develop to the full perfection of its physical formation, yet the passions of the body will develop with its development, will spring up like giants in their might, and assert themselves in the irresistible craving for every form of the vilest and most despicable self-indulgence.

The neglected soul is not dead. Its nature is immortal, and it can never die. It remains stunted and deformed, an infant in its powers and in its growth, incapable of exercising its noblest faculties, which lie dormant and undeveloped within it, void of all indications or inducements to good, shut out from all hope on earth or in heaven. Man without instruction is powerless to accomplish the purposes of his creation. God gave him reason to guide his will. That reason, stunted in ignorance, undeveloped by education, is utterly powerless. The will recognizes the control, and submits to the control, of those baser passions which the will should govern. The vile handmaid of earth comes and declares herself queen over the soul, and makes a slave of that better part that came from heaven by divine infusion into man. Thus neglected, uninstructed, uneducated, he is not available even for any of the ordinary purposes of human society. Human society demands interchange of thought, communion of mind with mind.

But this man has no mind; his soul is fallow within him. No sunlight of knowledge has ever enlightened the darkness of his understanding. Human society, even in its humblest form, demands some technical knowledge. This man has none. Therefore his companionship must be with the brute beasts, and even they surpass him in physical strength, the only property that his manhood has bestowed. Then by the voice of nature alone man cries aloud for education—light, light! for light is the yearning and the wailing of the soul in darkness. Light was the first gift of the Creator to man. When He sent His "spirit brooding over the water" He began the sublime work of creation by making light. "And God said, Let there be light, and light was made." "Light!" exclaims the darkened soul; "give me light for earth, give me light for heaven, give me light for time, give me light for eternity." Education is the light of the soul. Education is as necessary to the soul as food and clothing are to the body. I need not remind you how completely all hope and joy is blotted out of the life of an uneducated man. Even in this life his fate is sealed. He can never rise; if there be any change in his low condition, that change must be for the worse—change that will lead him down step by step to the lowest stage of misery, and finally fling him into a pauper's unknown grave. No matter how great the genius with which God may have endowed him, the pity is but the greater if that genius be undeveloped by education. Therefore it is that the Catholic Church, from the day that her Divine Lord and Spouse set her up to be light and salvation to the world, has always been the mother, the loving, careful mother, of education and instruction. She has spread light over the world—light not merely of divine but of human knowledge.

During the days of her triumphant reign, during the mediæval history of the civilized world, wherever she set her foot she left the commemoration of her passage behind her in the colleges and universities which she founded. Genius looked to her cloisters and her colleges for its necessary development. Everywhere the history of the world tells us that sanctity in the Catholic Church went hand in hand with learning, as we see by looking to the history of our own mother-land, when it was called for its sanctity the "Island of Saints" and the "Island of Scholars." Never was Ireland's sanctity greater, purer, or brighter than when her learning was at its highest, and when she shone forth as a light to all the students of the civilized world. How, then, could the Catholic Church be said to be the enemy of education, to be the foe of knowledge? To come from her general history—to narrow our views from that retrospect of all homes and lands over the earth—let us come to consider the charity for which I am here pleading to you to-day, and there in that charity you will find the whole mind, the whole genius, the whole mission of the Catholic Church.

This is the oldest educational charity in this city of Dublin, I may say in Ireland. More than a hundred years ago a father of the Society of Jesus came to Dublin. He was already a noted and distinguished member of that great society which has been from the day of its foundation the home of the heroic and of the greatest of the Church's sons. He came loaded with titles and with the acknowledged admiration of some of the greatest of the members of his society and of the learned bodies of Europe. He came at a time when all the iniquitous powers of the world rose up as they rise up to-day—every government, every king and emperor, every revolutionary and popular movement amongst the people—and they all had for their sole object the suppression and destruction of the Jesuits. Oh! if they could only be crushed and annihilated, then the enemy of God and man felt he could stretch out his arm with a free sweep over Christian society, and destroy it. And such was the pressure that the world brought to bear upon the Church that for peace' sake, and for reasons which it is not becoming in me to judge—which God forbid I should judge—the Society of Jesus was suppressed a few years after the arrival of this great Jesuit in Dublin. He had to put off his habit; he had to leave his convent home; and then he himself knelt before the Archbishop of Dublin and asked to be allowed to labor for the Irish people, who were the object of his greatest love. He was sent into this parish.

At that time Ireland was only beginning to breathe faintly under the first timid relaxation of the penal laws. For two hundred years the nation lay as dead at the feet of her enemies. Every impulse of national and religious life seemed to be not only paralyzed but deadened utterly within her. No schools in the land; no priests to minister to the people; no churches wherein to assemble; no altars before which to adore their God! All was proscribed, all was banished, and a desolation the most terrible that the world ever witnessed was seen externally over Ireland, whilst deep in the heart of the people burned the flame of divine faith and charity as bright and as pure as ever. But now the penal laws began to be somewhat relaxed, and the Catholics of Ireland, and especially of this city of Dublin, began timidly to assemble in hidden places, and there, trembling, to worship the Lord God, raised up before them by the hands of His priest. The great Jesuit, coming into this parish, saw among the many wastes around him the most terrible of all—the waste of ignorance. The youth had been uneducated; it was no fault of the Church, no fault of the Irish people, that it had been made for many years a felony and a crime to teach a child to read. They were already grown up in their ignorance around him, and his heart beat with love for them, and his great mind, filled with the knowledge which the Catholic faith produces, taught him that the very first requirement and first want of the people was education, and therefore he cast about to supply this want.

But the youth had grown up; it was no longer the question of educating little children. They had grown into young men and women; they were at their various occupations all day long. How could he catch them in order to educate them? The prolific mind of the servant of God devised means, and he instituted in this parish the Sunday-schools for those who are at work all the week, and the evening-schools for those who are at work all day. He was seventy-three years of age, he was broken down with infirmities, and his heart was broken when he saw his great mother-order scattered and dispersed, although God gave him the consolation to live until he beheld it arising once more—arisen in almost a glorified body at the command of another pontiff in the Church of God. But even at that advanced age this man, seventy-three years old, having labored all day visiting the sick, hearing confessions in the church, performing all the duties of a faithful pastor, when the evening came, and when he might in all conscience and reasonableness seek a little rest for his aged body, what rest did he take? He went down into a cold, damp cellar in one of those crowded neighboring streets, and there he sat night after night for many a year, and spending the hours he might have given to rest in instructing the young. So successful were his labors that, from the time he established the evening-school until the day of his death, in 1811, there passed under Dr. Betagh's hands upwards of three thousand men whose minds, sealed fountains, were opened to knowledge by this almost divine magician—three thousand men sent forth, each one now educated, to scatter around him, as far as influence might, the saving influence of the light which he had received from the aged saint of God. Behold the work in its history!

See the ardor with which the Catholic Church, embodied in the mind and action of this great servant of God, gave itself to the world in education! See the glorious results—thousands of minds enlightened, thousands of souls liberated from the worst of slavery, that of ignorance; thousands of men sent forth in the fulness of their faith, and with no small means of worldly knowledge, to make their way in this world, and to assert for Ireland and Ireland's people that great heritage which God has given to Ireland of genius and intellectuality! The saintly man, crowned with years and with successful labors, passed to receive his reward before God. But, dearly-beloved, the work which he inaugurated was continued by zealous and faithful men, his successors in the priesthood; it has come down along more than a hundred years. Men assemble every night in these schools after their hard day's work, and so they are drawn from all the dangers and the evils which night brings forth. They pass through the crowded streets; the emissaries of evil cross their path; the messenger from hell beckons to them. But they are bound on the high and holy mission of self-education, and they pass the tempters by. The temple of drunkenness flares and flames in their eyes, and those treacherous doors are ominously on the spring. The touch of a finger will open to the ante-chamber of hell; but they are bound upon the high mission of self-education; they turn aside from that which was the most degrading of all that could degrade and demoralize man, and thus they are saved by these evening-schools from the very dangers which surround their path. They go forth with so much human knowledge as puts them in the relation not only of an intellectual kind with their fellow-man but also in relation with the past, opens up to them the thresholds of the discoveries of knowledge, puts before them that technical, scientific knowledge which alone may be wanting to enable them to better themselves in life and to advance in this world, and make for themselves, perhaps, a name. And yet, in the face of all this, whilst her priesthood, as her history tells us, became martyrs to education, we are told, indeed, that the Catholic Church is the enemy of education! She is specially noted for this work of education; she alone—the Catholic Church alone—makes ignorance such a crime as to exclude from the kingdom of heaven. Ignorance alone, in Catholic theology, is such a sin as to exclude man, without any other sin, from the kingdom of heaven. Do you not all know, my friends, and have we not all been taught since our childhood, that there can be no salvation without a knowledge of at least the principal mysteries of faith?

The Church of God is founded on this knowledge; she cannot exist without it, much less flourish and triumph, and pursue her apostolic career amongst the nations. Knowledge is her first principle, because *Deus scientiarum Dominus*—God is the lord of knowledge—and, adds the apostle: "He that is ignorant shall be ignored and unacknowledged of God." Nay, more, the Catholic Church depends more than any other institution—I will not say religion, for there is no religion outside of the Catholic Church; there are forms of opinion calling themselves religion, but religion means the *cultus Dei*, the worship of God, and that worship must be one, it must be true, it must absorb the whole intellect and heart by faith and divine grace, it must take the whole man and put him in the presence of God for the purpose of worship, or else it is no religion—the Catholic Church, I say, depends more than any institution in this world on education, whether we consider her dogmas—that is to say, her belief—or her practice. Think, my dearly beloved, how finely intellectual is the religion which is based and founded upon the mystery of the Incarnation, and demands, my beloved, of its children to grasp the mighty thought that God became man, so that out of two natures, the divine and the human, only one person, and that person divine, sprang forth. This mystery is so great in itself, in its intellectual power, and in the demand that it makes upon our intelligence, that the greatest philosophers of old, the masters of all human knowledge, were unable to grasp it in its immensity; and yet the humblest Catholic child not only receives and believes it but pronounces it every time that he says: "Holy Mary, Mother of God, pray for us." "Mother of God!" Behold the whole mystery of the Incarnation. This mystery, the fundamental one, is followed up by a series of the highest and most arduous intellectual truths.

They come to us, it is true, in the shape of divine assertion; they come to us on the authority of the Almighty God who utters them, and of the infallible Church who interprets them. But tell me, is it no small act of intellectual power to grasp the idea of a God revealing unchangeable truth—that is to say, manifesting his own nature—of a church on earth, unchanging, infallible, bearing witness to that one truth, and standing up for it against all the powers of this earth and all the powers of hell? I might dilate upon this subject; I might go from dogma to dogma of the Catholic Church, and throughout them all we find her making an appeal upon the trained intelligence of her children, and making knowledge absolutely necessary, and the deficiency of that knowledge penal. But let us pass on to the practices of the Catholic Church. Remember again that as she is the only body on earth that teaches with authority, that appeals to authority, that never changes in her teaching, she is the only body upon this earth calling itself religion which prescribes certain specific duties and obliges her children to perform them. These duties are many, as we know by the experience of our daily life. Ah! my brethren, it is no light yoke, it is no small burden, that the holy Church of God puts upon us for the purpose of saving our souls.

Every single duty that the Catholic Church imposes upon her children, with, perhaps, the single exception of fasting, is intellectual—appeals to the intelligence, appeals to knowledge, appeals to the instructed mind and the trained intellect. The first of these duties is prayer. You know we are bound to pray—nay, more, that if a man committed no other sin except the simple neglect of prayer, a prolonged, total neglect of prayer would be in itself a sin sufficient to exclude that man from God for ever. We are bound to pray. What is prayer ? The humblest Catholic child is bound to pray. What does that mean ? "Prayer," says St. Augustine, "is an elevation of the soul to God." Can anything be imagined more intellectual or more elevated ?—the intelligence created in man to meet the uncreated intelligence in God in intercommunion —thought between the thinking soul and the essential thought which is God. Prayer involves a knowledge of God's mercy, as how can we pray to that of which we know nothing ? Prayer involves knowledge of ourselves, of our own wants and miseries, else how can we lay them before Him ? Prayer involves that grand action by which the intellect of man, by the power of grace, is able to go from earth to heaven and put him into communion with God. Yet the only religion, the only teaching body, in the world that so enforces the duty of prayer as even to exclude from the kingdom of heaven those who will not pray is declared to be an unintellectual and unspiritual religion !

Next to prayer—and I will take only one other of the practices of the Catholic Church—is the duty of preparing for the frequenting the Sacrament of Penance. Every one among us Catholics goes frequently to confession. Now, consider what that involves. It is an act not only of living prayer but of magnificently elevated intellect. Man must have knowledge, no matter how simple yet deep and profound, before he can prepare for confession properly. He must, first of all, know the law of God, for he is about to take himself to task as to whether he observed that law or violated it ; and how can he know that unless he knows the law ? Knowing the law, he is preparing for confession, and he then turns from the contemplation of God's holy law and of his own personal duties to God—he turns into himself, he examines himself, he learns to know himself, he reads his own soul and his own conscience like an open book. That knowledge of self was declared by the great philosopher of old to be the very highest point of human intelligence and of human knowledge. And when he has come to know his own shortcomings another kind of knowledge must be then exercised by him : he must know what sin is, what the nature of sin is; he must know somewhat the beauty of the God whom he has outraged, and God's claim upon him for obedience; he must know what the natural, the supernatural, deformity of sin is, else how can his heart be troubled and his eyes weep penitential tears over his guilt? Oh! how manifold is the knowledge demanded of the humblest Catholic in order to perform the ordinary duty of going to confession.

Who, therefore, can deny—either looking with the eyes of nature or with the superior illuminated eyes of faith on this divine institution of God—who can deny that the Catholic Church subsists without education? For four thousand years the world was preparing for the Incarnation and the coming of Jesus Christ, and all that went before was a preparation for it. All the knowledge of pagan philosophy pointed to it; all the sacrifices of the Old Law symbolized it, and held it out in the future as a promise to be fulfilled. Even so, dearly beloved, the Catholic Church demands the right and power to instruct and educate her children. But education, and instruction, and human knowledge she only makes the handmaid of her own divine purposes and religion. She gives, indeed, all that the world can give of human knowledge to her children, but she is careful to send hand-in-hand with that human knowledge the element of divine knowledge by faith, and the infusion of divine grace to create charity, that there may be not only the power of knowledge in the intelligence, but that there may be strength in the will and unity in the aspiration of her children.

Behold, then, the great purpose for which I am here. I ask you to strengthen the zealous pastors and priests of this parish. Already has this charity so grown upon them that the parish priest has been obliged to incur a heavy debt for the purchase of other premises, to enlarge its classes, and afford to the children of labor the inestimable food of knowledge, of which they may have been deprived in their legitimate childhood, either by the neglect of parents or by circumstances of poverty, or, perhaps, by the unthinking wilfulness of the child himself. And when the young man, growing into manhood, realizes for the first time all that he has lost by his neglect of school—then, when his heart might almost despair within him—when, helpless and disheartened, he is almost tempted to give up the race of life as utterly lost—when every door of advancement and promotion in life would seem to be closed in his face by his own neglectful wilfulness that condemned him to a life of ignorance—then the evening-school of St. Michael and St. John opens its door and says: "Here is the refuge; here is still for you the knowledge that will open your mind, and renew for you the promise of your life; here is the knowledge still for you that will enable you to receive all the supernatural gifts and all the divine graces which are in the hands of the holy Church of God."

This is the knowledge out of which is true wisdom. "Wisdom is an inestimable treasure to man," says the Holy Ghost, which they that possess become the sons of God, for it teaches justice and prudence, and temperance and fortitude, which are virtues better than all else in this life. Let us not deny this priceless treasure to the children of toil. Let us open to them and keep open those fountains of holy knowledge, that we may deserve to receive from the Lord the highest crown of all—the crown which no mere human mercy can make its own—the crown reserved for those whose mercy is eternal and divine for the sake of the Lord God. "They that instruct many unto justice shall shine as stars for all eternity."

THE CHURCH AND CIVIL GOVERNMENT.

FATHER BURKE in this discourse handles an interesting subject in a manner which should set at rest the carpings of those persons who find fault with the Church in its relations to government. He shows clearly that good government cannot exist successfully without the Church.

MY DEAR FRIENDS: Before I go any further it is necessary I should put before you some notion of what is the Church, and what is civil government, and what each of them signifies. To do so I must go back to the very beginning. Man was created by Almighty God with most magnificent gifts—the amplest endowments of intelligence, a power of knowledge limitless in its range, and a perfectly free and unfettered will. He who abuses the power of knowledge against his fellow-man makes him an intellectual slave. He who abuses the power of intellect against his fellow-man makes him a bond slave, and both one and the other is the oppressor of his fellow-man. The man who propounds an intellectual falsehood, whether it be historic, philosophical, or religious, most of all if it be religious, is a tyrant, an enslaver, and a debaucher of the dupes who listen to him. He is as unjust and tyrannical in abusing the gifts God has given to him as the slave-driver in South America who has whipped his slaves to death. When the Almighty God created man with these gifts of intelligence and free will, He ordained that where that freedom was there should be a government of truth and of law. And in the submission of intellect by which it recognizes and acknowledges truth, and of the will in which it acknowledges the Omnipotent God, in these two lies the quintessence of human freedom. (Applause.)

Freedom does not consist in writing or doing whatever we please or believing whatever we like, if it be false. That is not freedom. Freedom, as defined by Almighty God, resides in the knowledge of truth and in obedience to just law. (Applause.) Hence the Son of God had said: "You will know the truth, and the truth will make you free." The martyr lying in his dungeon on the eve of execution, with fetters on his limbs, was yet free, because his soul possessed the inestimable boon of truth. So it is that the man who admits the reason and the omnipotence of just law and of authority, and who yields to it a free and unfettered homage of his will, is therefore no less a freeman. He is still more one because he fulfils the duties of a free citizen. (Applause.) Freedom, therefore, means intellect guided by truth, justice expressed by law; and therefore the government which is the expression of authority for intelligence and the will is the guarantee of freedom. Reflect on these things, for in this revolutionary and rebellious age men are apt to confound liberty with libertinism, and freedom with injustice. The government of truth and law, expressed by competent authority, is the very quintessence and guarantee of freedom, and therefore has God made man, and when He did so He made him by necessity subject to government. This government is twofold, because man is twofold. Man is created for time, to arrive at a certain number of years in this world, to fulfil a certain cycle of duties, to acquit himself of certain obligations to society, to his fellow-men, and to his native land—so far man is the child of this world. But man has a higher destiny, that goes out beyond the limits of time. Man was not created for a few years of this present life alone. He has to act, think, live, and exercise all the vitality of his being as long as God is on his throne in heaven, and that is for an endless eternity. (Applause.)

And as Almighty God created His own masterpiece and His own image in freedom of will and of intellect, so also for man, in his temporal and his eternal relations, has He appointed a twofold government—temporal and eternal. The temporal belongs to the state, to the constituted and lawful authorities who govern the state, which enacts laws for the preservation of society, for the regulation of all our citizens, and their temporal relations to each other, and for all that belongs to time. That is civil government, supreme because of God, for it holds the sword which belongs to Him, and its power comes from Him; for all power, temporal and eternal, comes from God. I am a citizen of the state and under the authority of the law, and I ground my obedience to it on the responsible power which was delegated from on high to man. (Applause.) And if I were not so instructed as to recognize in the law the reflex of the divine justice of God—if I were not so instructed by my religion, I would tear to pieces and trample beneath my feet every law that prompted man to fetter his intelligence or his will. (Applause.)

But there is the second and the far greater relation of man to eternity. That is the great duty which deals, not with time, short and fleeting, but on which depends the destiny or doom of man for eternity—the duty he derives from that intelligence he received from Almighty God. Here it was that he entered the higher sphere of his duties, and for it the laws are found in the holy Roman Catholic Church. That Church is a kingdom. He who founded her called her His kingdom—"*regnum meum.*" "Art Thou, then, a king," said Pontius Pilate, "O Man of Sorrow! yet true God?" He answered: "I am, but my kingdom is not of this world. It is of heaven." My kingdom is my Church—my royal kingdom. That is the city which He compares to a city situate on the mountain-side, that all men who stand on the plain will see its grandeur and admire its consistent beauty; that is the city founded on a rock by the hand of God, and that rock is Peter, the Prince of the Apostles, and the central stone of the arch on which Christ built His Church. (Applause.) Being a kingdom, it has its authority and it has its laws. That authority is from God directly. These laws are a reflex of

God's infinite reason and justice ; they are the immediate revelation of God in matters of faith, and they are the selected image of the sanctity of God stamped on Christian morality. These laws belong to the Catholic Church—(applause)—they constitute her government. Thus we find that there are the civil government and the government of the Church. They are both ordained by Almighty God and for the well-being of man. Civil government deals with all matters concerning this world ; the other is for our eternal well-being, and deals with all matters concerning not only time but eternity. The Church holds the conscience of man. Through his conscience is man, by divine light, ruled by faith ; and therefore it was that the apostle said that he preached again and again that Christ should be born in His disciples.

Now, the question arose, Did these two governments clash ? That is one of the present questions of the day. Is one of them destructive of the other ? Must the triumph of one prove the ruin of the other ? That is the great question, and now come forward the great prophets of the day to answer it. One of them is a great philosopher, and says man is not capable of government in the world, because, he says, man is only a well-developed ape. (Laughter.) That is what Mr. Darwin says. Could you get two hundred monkeys and drill them, and make them shoulder arms ? Could they hold a parliament ? Certainly not. If this Darwinian theory holds good, we are all apes *minus* the tails—(laughter)—and nothing remains but for each man of us to take his own branch of a gum-tree and crack his own nut. (Laughter.) His theory resolves itself into its own great absurdity.

Let Mr. Darwin pass on. Another figure moves up—a grand figure, and one that we thought would be a grand historic figure. A man comes out before us over whose grave we had fondly hoped to have erected a statue, and on its pedestal the inscription, "Intellect, justice, religious freedom." But he comes before us to-day blasted and seared with the lightning which he himself, like another Prometheus, called forth from heaven—a fallen angel. It is the figure of William Ewart Gladstone. (Applause and murmurs.) He comes before us with his foul, bitter accusations against the Catholic Church, and says that the two governments are incompatible. He says in effect that if the Catholic Church is to live the state must fall, and on its ruins be built up an overbearing, ignorant, and a domineering priesthood, a tyrannical priesthood, through which the Church will rise; or if the state is to assert its rights and maintain its own independent freedom, it must be built on the ruins of the Church. Oh! what a change. "*Quantum mutatus ab illo!*"

Time was when this once glorious name reminded us of all that was greatest in the spirit of true progress, founded on justice, honesty and freedom, and of glorious ideas of the past and glorious hopes of the future. But to-day what are his dimensions? He has warred against the Church of God, and borne false testimony against it; and, as at the touch of Ithuriel's spear, one far greater than Mr. Gladstone arose and crushed him to the earth. That was the glorious John Henry Newman. He dealt with the Protestant champion—(applause)—and overcame him by the inherent force and power of truth and mighty genius. Time was when Mr. Gladstone's name was beginning to be a household word in the land, and now he is what he is. Of the man we will say no more, but of his public conduct there is yet something to be said. First of all, we hold that the man who says the Catholic Church is antagonistic to the civil government inherently; that she is inherently antagonistic to social liberty in its true sense, and to real progress; that she is an intellectual tyrant, seeking to trespass on the domain of civil government—we hold that man lacks philosophic truth, historic truth, and experimental truth. That he has no philosophic truth can be seen in a moment.

First of all, could it be possible that the Catholic Church, if she be as we know her to be, the true Church of God, can be the enemy of civil government? Can she be incompatible with the rights of citizenship, of progress, or of national liberty ? Can these things be ? Civil government is the ordinance of Almighty God, coming as the reflection of His glorious and greatest authority. Consequently, the only real and reliable claim that the state has to our honor and obedience is that we recognize in it the justice and authority of God. (Applause.) We have also seen that the Church government in things eternal and in things temporal springs from God, and is the subject of his first and greatest love. Consequently, civil government and Church government both spring from God. Therefore they are not antagonistic. If they were, God would be contradicting Himself. His authority in things material would be destructive of His authority in things eternal, and that is impossible. (Applause.) Any man, therefore, who comes forward to say that the existence of the Catholic Church in any state or amongst any people is incompatible with true liberty and progress tells a philosophic lie—nay, more, he tells a historic lie. I am going to make a bold assertion, and I do so knowing that my words will be carried abroad over the face of the earth on the wings of the press, for

"A chiel's amang ye takin' notes,
An' faith he'll prent it."

(Laughter and applause.) I know that what I assert now will be told for years to come, and yet I assert the great truth. Never since the Catholic Church grew up side by side with civil government and with civilization, which she has created, never in any one well-ascertained instance has the Catholic Church intruded on the domain of civil government. (Applause.) Never has she taken on herself to contradict the civil government, or to interfere with it in the promulgation of any just or legitimate law. Never has she been known to tell any people that they had a right to violate any law. Never has she sanctioned any rebellion against known, just, and legitimate authority in the state. She has never told these things to any people who had the grace to listen to her. This challenge I fling out broadly and boldly, and I defy fearlessly the industrious student of history to point out any single part of history that would bring home to the Catholic Church the charge that she was ever an unjust impediment to the course of legitimate civil government. The civil government imposes taxes. When did the Catholic Church ever tell the people that they should not pay fair and just taxes? When the people were taxed, and taxed almost to death, the great preacher of patience says: "Pay as long as you can. If the Government did not want it they would not ask it of you." "Ah!" said a man once to him, "if it were not for you, and the like of you, with all the powers of the law, they would not be turning me out." And now I shall turn the tables on Mr. Gladstone, although the "chiels" are still " amang ye takin' notes." I say it under the same sense of responsibility as I made my former assertion. I would lay down another general proposition.

Since the day the Catholic Church founded the civil government—and I claim that she was its real foundress—it has never been able to stand on its legs independently of her. From the time that civil government first got on its legs it has never been able to work properly without the help of the Church; and yet it has been coming in and taking up matters of which it knows nothing, and in which its action is fatal to man's freedom and man's free will. (Applause.) The civil government is the creation of the Church, and it can easily be proved. The Catholic Church was founded nearly one thousand nine hundred years ago by the Son of God made man, and He told His disciples that they were to live under the civil government and the law of the Church. Here were the words in which He told it to them and in which He tells it to us: They brought him a coin, and said: "Tell us, Master, are we to pay taxes to Cæsar?" And he said: "Render to Cæsar the things that are Cæsar's, and to God the things that are God's." They were Cæsar's subjects and they should pay tribute—that is, the taxes which he has a right to call for from them. But they were also God's subjects, and they must give to Him what He demands and what belongs to Him.

For the first three hundred years after Almighty God founded the Church there was civil government existing. It was a government which was unjust, and which sorely tried the patience of the early Christians. But the Church taught them that they were bound to obey it, and they did so, in accordance with the words of St. Paul: "Be subject to the powers that be." Yet for more than three hundred years it filled the amphitheatres with the blood of the best and bravest children of the Church of God. Still the Christians obeyed it, even when they were strong enough to rebel—when they were strong enough to raise a successful rebellion against that monstrous civil government. (Loud applause.) But that which the Christians did not do, because they were Christians, the Goths and Vandals did. They had no church and no divine government, and obeyed no human law. They destroyed cities; they ravished and ruined palaces and provinces; they sacked and set fire to imperial Rome itself, and not a single vestige remained of the ancient civil government. When these barbarians were satiated with plunder and with blood, and the sword dropped out of their hands crimsoned with gore, the Catholic Church found itself in the midst of the chaos of society. (Applause.) She alone remained pure and powerful during those troubled times, for God had breathed on her and promised to be with her always, even to the end of the world.

For twelve hundred years she taught, wrote, and acted from the necessity of her own existence, and because she could not teach the Gospel to mere scourges of the world. Out of the chaos she created civilization and civil government. (Applause.) And thus, while the Church was forming modern society, obtaining for England one of her oldest and greatest rights, obtaining for the cities of Italy their municipal rights, restraining with strong hand the licentiousness of the mediæval dukes and barons of Europe, and everywhere making herself the interpreter and champion of true freedom, she was founding civil government. And yet, after all she has done for it, civil government has tried to encroach on the rights and dominion of the Church in three ways. Firstly, it has tried to usurp the rights of the Church of God in the matter of education; secondly, in the matter of the most important of the sacraments—matrimony; thirdly, in the internal arrangements of the Church in her sanctuary.

Now, reflect on these three things, and say how far we ought to listen to Mr. Gladstone when he accuses the Catholic Church of trying to subvert civil government. If there is anything specially dear to the Church of God, it is the education of children. Education means to bring the man out of the child. The poet has said that the child is father to the man. So he is; the little child is parent of the future man. Man should be liberated to be formed out of the child, who has within him the seeds of his manhood. Whatever he has in him is to be brought out by education; and if he is to be fashioned in the image of Christ, and to be prepared for the enjoyment of heaven with God, endowed with the glorious attributes of faith, hope, and charity, the Church, the Catholic Church alone, can bring him thus out of the child. (Great applause.) Yes; the man who comes and says that statesmen should educate this child, who says: "You priests, with your message from heaven, stand aside; you priests, with your sacraments and cross, stand aside; I will not allow these sacraments or that cross to touch this young child; you priests, trying to discover the finger of God in all events, I will not allow you to discover the finger of God in any idea"— to such a man I would say that the grossest ignorance would be better for a child than such teaching as he would give him, and that he is training him, not for heaven, but for hell. (Applause.) And yet this is what civil government nowadays is always aiming at.

Seven hundred years ago the German emperor, Frederick Barbarossa, founded the University of Naples for the express purpose of destroying the pope's University of Bologna. The new university was worthy of its mission. Teachers and pupils were alike corrupt; so much so that when Thomas Aquinas—the greatest genius that God ever created in His Church—went amongst them, after a year so much was he disgusted by their conduct and teaching that he left them, and put on the habit of a Dominican and became one of the greatest lights of the Church.

When Elizabeth wanted to establish the blessed Protestant Reformation in Ireland, what did she do? In her apostolic authority, and in that virginal meekness that never spat in a bishop's face or boxed an earl's ears—that queen whose love for heaven was so great that when she was about to die, this worthy daughter of Henry VIII., she could only put her hands into her mouth; this base woman, who wanted to establish Protestantism in this old Catholic country—what did she do? She founded Trinity College. She enlarged its foundations till it became the greatest in the land. She saw very well what education could do, and then she made a law that if any Catholic layman or parent taught a Catholic child he was to be put to death for felony. (Sensation.) When she ascended the throne she found six hundred priests of my order (the Dominicans) in Ireland teaching the grand Thomistic theology, and she passed her maiden hand over them so lightly that when she lay dying in Hampton Court, blaspheming God, only four out of the six hundred remained. (Sensation.) Five hundred and ninety-six died, or perished in exile, under the treatment of that awful woman, who was one of the most awful pictures that rise in the pages of history. She claimed the right of educating our youth in Ireland.

From the time that Patrick placed his hand on the head of Bridget, the women of Ireland had been its pride. But if the power that the queen sought of educating our children had been obtained, what would have become of them? What would become of the womanhood of our country under the training she would select for them? Still further to show how the state sought to obtrude itself into the domain of education, and not only that, but to exclude the Church from teaching the children committed to its care by Almighty God, let me mention a law recently passed in Italy, by which it was declared that if a man had been taught by a priest he was not eligible for any government office. There is, say, the office of county surveyor vacant—(a laugh)—and two young men present themselves as candidates for it. One of them is thoroughly up in his business; he knows all that the requisites of the situation demand. The other is a "stupid," without two ideas in his head. They are examined, and the examiners say to the first: "This is a splendid fellow." The other knows nothing, and they say: "As for this fellow, he is a fool." And they say to the clever man: "Where were you educated?" He answers: "I never went to school; my father hired a poor but good and learned priest, who taught me, and it is to him I owe all I know"; or he says: "I got my training from a Jesuit." To the fool they say: "And, my good fellow, where were you educated?" "Begorra," he says, "I do not know where I was educated at all. (Laughter.) The man that tried to teach me was a Jew, and I did not mind what he said. He told me not to believe in God, and I did not believe in God, and that is all I know." Then they turn to the highly-trained and educated young man, and say: "My dear sir, we are very sorry for you; the fool must be the county surveyor." (Laughter.) What do you think of that?

And the civil government says the Catholic Church is wrong in not bending down to such a system as that— (applause)—and not giving some support to it! And because the hierarchy and priesthood of Ireland will not condescend to take theology from Darwin and ethics from Tyndall, and because they rose up and stood between the people and their peril, Mr. Gladstone has thrown off the mask and said: "It is the Irish bishops who have forced me to write all this." (Applause.) And if it were the Irish bishops who have torn the mask off this man's face and compelled him to put out the poison that was fomenting in his embittered heart; if it were the bishops of Ireland who were able to stand between him and their people, and defeat any scheme of education that would not "educate" the Irish people, that would not train them for God and eternity, then all honor to the Irish bishops. (Loud applause.)

Here was, then, the second matter in which the civil government intruded on the domain of the Catholic Church. The civil government comes in and says to the Church: "You must let me into the sanctuary! You must let me put on the surplice and the stole." For what purpose? To destroy the most important of all the sacraments of the Church of God—the Sacrament of Marriage. Properly speaking, Baptism and Holy Orders were greater than Matrimony; but if we had no real Catholic parents, what use would it be to baptize children in the faith, for who would train them in it? And where would be the subjects for the Sacrament of Orders if there were no Catholic children? Matrimony is the fountain-head of Christian society. (Applause.) Our Divine Lord performed His first miracle for a marriage ceremony, and thus raised it from the position of a civil contract to the distinction and importance of a sacrament. St. Paul, inspired of God, tells us that it is a great sacrament, and why? Because it is the symbol and type of the union of Jesus Christ with His Church. "This is a great sacrament, but I speak in Christ and in His Church." Christ can never be wanting to His Church, the Church can never be faithless to Christ. He said to her: "I will be with you all days, even to the consummation of the world"; and again: "On this rock I will build my Church, and the gates of hell shall not prevail against it." (Applause.) And, therefore, speaking of this mystic union, the apostle said: "Christ loved His Church, and gave Himself up for her." For what purpose did He do so? To present her to Himself without spot or stain, and that while time shall hold she may be worthy to be the symbol of God. Therefore marriage is indissoluble;

for so is the union of the Son of God with the Church; and the Church says: "What God has joined let no man separate." The man who attempts to sunder that bond commits a sacrilege against society, against the Church, and against God, who in the Sacrament of Matrimony makes man and woman one. Then is woman raised to the full dignity of matronhood, and is placed upon that throne from which no hand, save that of God, can remove her. (Applause.)

For this great right and position the Catholic Church has ever contended. When Philip Augustus, the most potent monarch of his age, wanted to put away his lawful wife, attracted by the beauty of a young maiden, he appealed to the pope for a divorce. "Heaven and earth will pass away, and the generations will perish, O king! but the word of God will remain for you, and that word is that, unless death, nothing will separate you from your lawful wife." (Great applause.) So said the pope. "But," said Philip, "I will cast the bishops and priests into prison, and I will drown the Catholic world in blood, or I will carry my point." "Do," said the pope, "but you cannot sever the bond of God." (Applause.) And when, three hundred years later than Philip Augustus, Henry VIII. arose and wanted to put away Catharine of Aragon, his good and lawful wife, and take in her place Anne Boleyn, whose head he soon after cut off, what did he do? The pope would not grant him a divorce, so he applied to the universities of Europe—God bless the mark! (laughter)—and they said of course he could put away his lawful wife, just as Martin Luther had said to the elector of Brandenburg. Clement VII. said: "You will never put away your lawful wife." Henry said: "I will, and I will take England from the Church's fold." The pope still said: "No power on earth can separate you from your wife." We all know what happened. But nowadays nearly every government in Europe is trying to force its way into the sanctuary, and teach that marriage is not a sacrament, but a sort of limited liability affair. (Laughter.)

They say: "My young friend, you have married this young girl; if you are ever tired of this young girl, trump up an accusation against her, and drive her out into the world and take another girl in her place." This was the law in England, but the law of divorce they never dared to introduce in Ireland. Then there is the institution of civil marriages. Those who patronize them go to the registrar. He says: "Young man, are you going to marry this young woman?" "Yes, sir." "Young woman, are you going to marry this young man?" "Yes, sir." "Then, in the name of civil society, I am going to marry you. Pay me half a crown." (Great laughter.) Against this the Church protests. The Protestant Church has bowed down and accepted the law of divorce; and if a divorced English blackguard comes into a Protestant church and asks to be married again, there is not a Protestant minister who would dare refuse to marry him. A Catholic priest would not marry him; but if he did, his bishop would excommunicate him, the faithful people would shun him, and the curse of God would follow him.

Again, the civil government follows the Church into and intrudes on her internal arrangements. Not content with making conscription laws, from which there is no exemption—as a young man said to me: "When a boy is eighteen years of age he is fit to be a soldier"—not content with imposing taxes so great that in Italy a cobbler cannot mend an old pair of shoes without first paying taxes on his awl—(laughter)—the civil governments come in and say to the people: "We have a right to appoint parish priests; we will appoint them, and put you in jail if you do not support them." To the pope they say: "We will appoint bishops, and you must recognize them." The man they appoint may be a real Jew, or a Jew like the blank page that is between the Old and the New Testaments, with nothing written on it—(laughter)—or he might be an atheist; but the state may want to make him a bishop. That is what the pope has nowadays to protest against and resist. There was Bismarck—they had heard of him—or

Beast-mark—(loud laughter)—as some people called him. He is to-day filling the prisons with bishops and priests. If the bishop appoints a good priest to a parish, Bismarck shoves him into prison, and then seeks to put a blackguard in his place, if he can get one ; or if he cannot get such a one, he tries to get one ordained for the purpose. The English Government tried to get a little power of that sort in Ireland when the Catholics were looking for emancipation. They asked for a veto on the appointment of bishops. A man might be a Francis de Sales, a Dr. Doyle, or a John MacHale—(great applause)—and the better man he was and the truer man to God, the Church, and his country, the more strongly would the civil government come in and say —if they had got the veto—" We will not have him at all." But the Catholics of Ireland came forward and said: " We will not have any such veto ; we will not have any such interference with our Church business. We would rather wear our chains for twenty years longer, if necessary, than have the fetters of the veto hanging over us." (Applause.) And the Catholics of Ireland have gotten their reward. It is the purest portion of the Catholic Church ; and if our fathers had not been so true in protesting the veto, the Catholics of Waterford would not have such a bishop to-day as the Most Rev. John Power. (Loud applause.) It was plain, then, that the Church did not interfere with the civil government, but the civil government did interfere with the Church. Bismarck qualifies his doings by saying he is afraid of the Church. He, with his two million armed men behind him, asks : " Who will save me from the cruel bishops ?" (Laughter.)

Is it not clear that the Catholic Church is the truest friend of man for time and eternity ? Is she not the first and greatest necessity for man in this world and the next; the surest, firmest guarantee of his true loyalty, because she founds it on principle ? Is she not his firmest friend for eternity, since she derives her power from God ? And if ever that glorious epoch comes when the two will be combined in their highest philosophical and historical existence, it will be when we have a free Church in a free state. Then will we behold one of the greatest glories in Christendom, such as she had once possessed in the olden days, when Brian Boroihme bore the sceptre of Ireland's nationality on Tara's hills, when Irish princes respected and defended the rights of the Irish Church, the Irish bishops maintained Gospel truths and the greatness of the power of Irish nationality. (Loud and continued applause.)

THE CATHOLIC CHURCH AND THE AGE WE LIVE IN.

THE following lecture was delivered by Father Burke in the Abbey Church of the Holy Cross, Cork, in aid of the fund for discharging the debt on the building. The chair was taken by the Right Rev. Dr. Moriarty, Bishop of Kerry, who said: "My good friends, the ceremony of introduction is a very easy one when friends meet and are welcome, and I am sure that out of the countless army of the Church there is not one of any grade or any order more welcome to you than Father Burke. (Hear, hear, and cheers.) His voice was heard far away. The accents of that voice were borne hither to us across the Atlantic waves, and they fanned the flame of your love for faith and fatherland—(applause)—and nowhere have they been heard with greater pleasure than they shall be heard to-night upon the strand of the Lee. (Renewed applause.) My dear friends, I need not bespeak a kind and attentive hearing for Father Burke, because I am sure you are all most anxious to listen to him." (Hear, hear.) Father Burke then rose, and, when the acclamations which his appearance elicited had subsided, said :

MY LORD BISHOP, LADIES, AND GENTLEMEN: The subject upon which I have the hardihood this evening to address you is "The Catholic Church and the Age we Live in." There may, perhaps, be some amongst you who imagine from the title of this lecture that I am come here to praise the Catholic Church and to denounce the age we live in. I am going to do the one and not to do the other.

One of the common errors of our day is that a Catholic priest, as such, must make it his especial business to denounce this age of ours. I myself received a curious illustration of this when I asked a poor man in the west of

Ireland some time ago what he thought was the proper business of a Catholic priest. He scratched his head, thought for a few moments, and then: "I suppose, your reverence," said he, "the proper business of a Catholic priest is to tell us all we are going to the devil" (Laughter.) Now, I do not denounce the age we live in. I am not such an ungrateful son of the century that bore me. Born within this nineteenth century, destined, in all probability not to see its close, like your bishop, a child of this age, I rather admire this nineteenth century. I find much that is grand and admirable in the workings of this century. I compare it with the eighteenth century, and with the seventeenth, and I hold that this nineteenth age of ours is far more glorious than either of its predecessors. For, if it had nothing else to distinguish it, and to make it a memorable epoch in the history of the world, there are two great facts. The first of these (and the greatest glory of it belongs to the spirit of justice of the nineteenth century) was the Catholic emancipation of Ireland. O glorious emancipation! the upraising of an entire people, all the more glorious that those chains were not stricken from the hand of Ireland by brute force, but that they were shaken off by the peaceful agitation of a united people, by an appeal, which was acknowledged by our age, to the eternal principles of justice. (Applause.)

The second great and glorious fact of this century of ours is the abolition of slavery in the Southern States of United America. Now, when we reflect upon the awful nature of such an institution as this, that delivered a man as bondsman to his fellow-man, reducing him to the level of the brute beast, I hold that the grand sense of justice that prevailed in the utter abolition of slavery, that nerved the arms of the North and prevailed upon the bright intelligence of the men of the Southern States of America—than whom none more cordially accept the abolition of slavery—I hold that this second fact marks our age as an epoch to be considered glorious in all the future history of time. (Hear, hear.) More than this, my friends, I see in this nineteenth century of ours a march through the fields of scientific research the most glorious that the world ever witnessed in any age since its creation. I see the power of the human mind asserting itself over matter in its keenest, subtlest, most terrific, and almost its spiritual form—space annihilated by our railway system; the very elements, so effected for our destruction, coerced under scientific control to be the humble and great servant of man, and of man's civilization; the lightning caught from the clouds of heaven and made the messenger of human thought, when mind speaks to mind by the trembling telegraph wire, which goes round and round the earth and under the depths of the sea. (Applause.) Compare the results of the scientific research and of the inductive philosophy of our age; take the two great facts that I have mentioned—Catholic emancipation and the abolition of slavery—and if our age had nothing more than these to boast of, I hold that this nineteenth century of ours may be written in letters and characters of gold upon the annals of the world's history. (Applause.)

But, my friends, you may admire much of a man—you may have a friend and you may admire his genius, the brilliancy of his imagination, the grandeur of his intellect, the harmony of his voice, the softness and tenderness of his heart; and yet, if you be a true friend of the man, you will not blind your eyes to his defects, you will not allow your friendship and love for him to carry you so far into blind devotion as to set him up as an idol and think him all perfect. You will rather, because of your friendship and because of your admiration for him, all the more keenly deplore the blemishes and imperfections that spoil so fair a character. And even so, child of the nineteenth century smitten with admiration for the age of which I am a son, I love my fellow-men too well, I love the society to which I belong too well, I have too keen an interest in its welfare, to allow that admiration and that love to blind me to the grave faults and serious shortcomings of this age. What are these? They are, my friends, principally to be found in the great leading features of our intellectual life, of our moral life, of our social life, and of our political life; and when I take these four, I think I have exhausted all that makes up the true life of a civilized people. I have grave faults to find with this century in its intellectual life. I have grave faults to find with it in its moral life, in its social life, and in its political life. But I go farther than this; I hold, judging by the light of history and of experience, and without intending to say a word that would offend any man, no matter of what religious persuasion he may be, I am convinced unto the very marrow of my intelligence that the Catholic Church and the Catholic religion is the only remedy for the evils which I am about to put before you, and is the only principle and the only system that can save this nineteenth century from the utter disruption and ruin that compose society. (Applause.)

It is a scientific age; who can doubt it? It is a scientific age, an age of research, an age when every man is trying to push intellectual activity to its very highest summit in whatever walk of life he may be. It is an age of the best engineers, an age of the greatest astronomers, an age of the greatest musicians—I will not say, for I cannot, of the greatest painters and sculptors; but in the more material pursuits of science it is pre-eminently an age of scientific research and of scientific excellence. Every man is trying to be the best man at his own craft, whatever it be. "I remember a time, your reverence," a poor Galway piper said to me, "when half a dozen tunes, jigs, and reels would be enough to keep a poor decent man with a bit in his mouth and a coat on his back; but now if you do not play all the waltzes for them, and all sorts of things, they will not listen to you at all. (Laughter.) I thought, sir, that my father was a great piper entirely, and he never went beyond the 'Humors of Glin.' (Great laughter.) But, your reverence," says he, "it is not alone that I must have all the jigs that ever was known to the people of Ireland, but I must have all the foreign tunes as well." (Roars of Laughter.) So that even the humble musician of the class of which I have been speaking must be a very magnificent piper nowadays even to be able to earn his bread. (Applause.)

But, my friends, we must never confound science, in the exact sciences, we must never confound the material conclusions of science, which tell so powerfully upon the comforts and luxuries of life, with that higher speculative philosophy, without going into the region of pure thought, of pure analysis, that undertakes the investigation of the most serious and most awful questions, such as the origin of man, the destiny of man, the powers of mind, the mysterious harmony of free will, with the agencies acting upon man. These are questions that belong to the highest philosophy, and one of the great mistakes of our age is that the man who is most excellent in scientific research, in judging of nature and of nature's laws, in examining the phenomena that lie around him, in sounding the depths of the realm of material science—that such a man, because of his excellence in this respect, because he is a first-class engineer or a great astronomer, or because he invents some new way of conveying a telegraphic message, or because he discovers a new planet by the aid of a telescope of strange power—that such a man is tempted, in the intoxication of scientific success, to pass into the realms of speculative philosophy, and with perfect freedom judge of matters that lie far beyond the ken of human sense, far beyond the evidences of mere human science. Thus it is that the eminent physicists and scientists of our day, pre-eminent as they are as long as they keep themselves within their own sphere—the surgeon with his scalpel, the astronomer with his telescope, the engineer with his steam-engine, the electrician with his appliances of electricity—excellent as they are in all this, no sooner do they go within the limits of speculative philosophy than we find them stumbling in the most deplorable manner to the most lamentable conclusions. And in this intellectual, purely intellectual, philosophy, in this speculation, in which the human mind labors and strains with eager desire to gain an atmosphere beyond its nature, the nineteenth century fails, and men of our age have asked us to accept, as a solution of the greatest of all problems, the most degrading theory that ever was propounded to man. (Applause.)

One of the greatest and deepest thinkers of our day has come forward and asked the intellectual world to accept the astounding conclusion that man—man with his human language, man with his human intellect, man with his glorious freedom of will, man with his fund of affection, and tenderness, and strength of heart, man with so much that is noble in him, brought out even by the very spirit of our age, man who is asserting the complete dominion of mind over all the material elements of nature—that this man is nothing more than a development of an ugly, brutal, grinning monkey! (Laughter and cheers.) He tells us that if we want to trace our origin we must not look up but look down; that if we do look up at all we must not look higher than the first branches of the forest tree. (Great laughter.) Christian philosophy, enlightened by the light that never was created, the light that comes forth from a height inaccessible, from the Father of light, leads the man of to-day to the man of yesterday, or the day before, and from him to the man who went before him, and so on and on, higher and higher still, to the man of remote ages, who also was descended from another, and he again from another, and another, and another, until we come to the first true and grand man, who, as the Evangelist says, "was from God." (Applause.)

O grand philosophy! partly recognized even by the imperfect light of the pagan of old, of whom the poet said : "Though we know Him not, He who created us has given us a noble countenance capable of looking up." But Darwin says: "No, I will not allow you to look up to heaven; the highest aspiration I will permit you is, if you want a genealogical tree, you must go to the gum-tree." Did you ever hear a song called "Possum up a gum-tree"? (Cheers and laughter.) Look at him in the upper branches with a cocoanut in his paw. (Much laughter.) There he sits, swaying to the breeze that passes through the forest, jabbering brutal, unintelligible sounds, gnawing at the cocoanut until he gets to the precious kernel, or milk, that is inside. His tail is twined round a branch of the tree in order that he may not fall off—a vile, unclean thing. Professor Darwin comes out with a bland smile and says: "My dear philosopher, my dear elegant lady so refined, my dear bishop or priest, this animal does *not* happen to be your grandfather—(roars of laughter)—but he is one of the series of grandfathers. (Intense merriment.) Go back far enough and you will have to say to this creature: 'So you are the one that Almighty God commanded me to honor and to love!'" (Great applause.) Would you like to know what the argument of the professor is? It is simply this: "I have analyzed the monkey," he says, "and I find that his jaw-bones are very like the jaw-bones of a man—(laughter)—that the *os frontis*, or forehead bone, is formed so that it admits the same amount of matter that the human skull does of brain. And so," he goes on, "since they are so alike, I conclude that man is nothing more than the development of the ape." Now, on the same theory, if you take an animal that I suppose I may not name here, on account of so many ladies being present—there is a little animal that sometimes infests people's houses in the summer, and when they are not kept very clean; a small creature that jumps very high. (Laughter.) Now, they say that if you put that little domestic animal under a strong magnifying-glass you will find that he is very like an elephant. Therefore, on the Darwinian theory, the elephant is but a development of the—well, I must name him—of the flea! (Cheers and laughter.) It lies here: to go from the mere material evidence of similarity, from that which is merely material, to climb up into the purely intellectual, the purely spiritual, and, with audacity unheard of, to make a revelation as to the origin of man out of the jaw-bone of a monkey!

My friends, how are we to remedy this gross intellectual

error? For what a degrading system it is! what a degradation for man to be told this; and this in an age when men are so proud that they repudiate with scorn the slightest interference with their intelligence, with their minds, if that interference comes from God, or in the name of God! The man of the day, the intellectual man of the nineteenth century, says to the priest: "What! ask me to go to confession! Ask me thus to humble myself! Nothing of the kind. Ask me to believe in the truths of the Catholic religion, which you tell me you preach in the name of God! I will not do it. My intelligence has been too well matured, too well taught, too well trained to believe such things." But then he turns round and says to Darwin: "I will believe what you tell me in the name of an ape, for I am nothing better than an ape." (Cheers and laughter.) My friends, what is the remedy for this intellectual degradation that enters so largely also into the moral life of man? It is a law of nature, as well as a revealed law, that the child should honor his father and his mother. The God of nature as well as the God of revelation has put this as a first principle into the mind of every child. Does not this theory that I speak of, this degrading speculative philosophy, does it not give the lie to this law of nature? Am I to be called upon to honor those who went before me, father and mother, grandfather and grandmother, whilst my philosophy teaches me that they are a step nearer to the primeval ape than I? (Hear, hear.) According to this theory the human race is becoming more perfect as it goes on; consequently, it must lose all reverence for what is past. No, if I could get my mind to believe in the speculative philosophy of the nineteenth century, in the name of civilization itself, and in the name of my own self-respect, which I believe is due to myself, I would consider it my duty to turn my back upon father and mother and despise them. (Cheers.) How, I say again, are we to remedy this great evil? O my dear friends! what remedy have we for it except the religion which alone, with the authority of God, in the name of

God, with a history traced distinctly up to God made man for us, to our Divine Lord—a religion which comes to us from the open grave that was there in the garden on that Easter morning, when they went to seek for the living amongst the dead—the religion of a Church coming down to us with her credentials in her hands, with the sign of truth upon her both in the promise of her Founder and in the unchanging spirit with which she has preached the same Gospel for generations—a religion which gives proof of the divinity of its origin in the power which it exercises over the minds, and hearts, and lives of those who profess it—a religion coming with all the power of divine revelation, with all the strength of divine authority, and teaching the scientific man that which religion alone can teach him, which no science or wisdom of man has ever been able to fathom and reveal—the mystery of man's origin, of man's history, and of man's destiny in the future? (Loud applause.)

It will, perhaps, be said: "But if the scientific man is also a Catholic, a man of faith, he will not be able to push his researches, he will not have freedom, he will be afraid that he may discover something or other that may upset his religion." My dear friends, this objection is made by those who are without faith, and who presume that no such virtue as faith exists. How can I be afraid, if I am a scientific man, that any discovery or conclusion of mine will upset my religion, if that religion be in my mind as an absolute certainty of divine faith? And if I know more surely than I know my own existence that no form of natural science or natural truth can upset or shake one principle of that divine faith which is in my mind, I am all the more free to engage in those researches. If Professor Darwin, for example, became a Catholic, do you not think he would be just as well able to continue his examinations of the monkey as he is now? (Laughter.) Do you imagine that because he is a Catholic he should have to drop the monkeys and excuse himself from further enquiry by saying: "I must drop this investigation now, for if I go on considering these monkeys, how do I know but I may discover they are men"? (Laughter.) On the other hand, who is so free to go out into the field of scientific research as the man whose mind and intelligence rest with perfect intellectual satisfaction upon the certainty of his faith? In every science the very first thing that is demanded, as a necessary condition to the pursuit of that science, is some first principle that is admitted as such. When Euclid began his investigation of geometry he found it necessary to make two or three postulates. "We cannot go on," said he, "we cannot argue a single proposition, unless you admit something to be true without my proving it."

And so it is of all the sciences. Philosophy itself demands some one admitted principle, some admitted truth, upon which it can build up an edifice of its own truth. So, in like manner, no man is so free, so unfettered, so unencumbered for scientific research as the man whose mind and soul rest upon the certainty of divine faith. (Hear, hear.) He has no anxiety, he has no fear; he says: "Whatever I discover of science will not interfere with my religion; for it cannot contradict that religion, because I know my religion to be true, I know it to come from God, and that God who has revealed that religion will not contradict Himself and His own truth in the sphere of natural and scientific investigation." And, therefore, he is unencumbered with fears and doubts. This is the remark that Milner makes in his "History of Latin Christianity." Speaking of Thomas of Aquin, he says: "No man ever lived that investigated more fearlessly even the most awful questions than did this great saint. No atheist that ever was born went more fearlessly into the question of the existence of God, or threw out more terrible arguments against it than St. Thomas." Well, he explained it in this way: He was fearless, because his own soul rested upon the immutable truths of his religion and his faith. He knew nothing could interfere with them. No discovery or argument could upset them, and therefore he went out with a sense of utter security, and fearlessly pushed his enquiries into the most awful questions ever presented to the mind of man.

If St. Thomas had not that absolute Catholic faith which the Catholic Church alone has, he would be afraid to institute those enquiries; he would say to himself: "Who knows but I may discover some argument or fact or something that may upset my religion!" He would be afraid to go on for fear of disturbing the peace of his own mind. Thus, I say, the Catholic Church is not afraid of scientific investigations. She is the best friend of the age; she is the surest guardian of it; and, therefore, I hold that she is necessary to the spirit of our age, and to the mind of our age, and to the cause of the man of science.

Oh! but it will be said (before we leave this branch of our consideration)—oh! but it will be said: "How do you say the Catholic Church is in favor of science? How can you say she imposes no trammels upon scientific men, upon the researches of philosophers, astronomers, and the like? Why, she put Galileo in prison because he made out that the earth moved and that the sun stood still." My dear friends, this is a big question to go into, and it has been discussed so often that it is not necessary for me here to go into it; but this I will say: The two great facts against the Catholic Church which are lugged in day after day to accuse her of hostility to science are her treatment of Copernicus, the great astronomer, and her treatment of Galileo. With regard to the first, he was a priest of the diocese of Ermeland, in Prussia. He certainly was one of the greatest astronomers—perhaps the greatest—that ever lived. His system revolutionized all that went before it in the magnificent science of astronomy. And men say in this nineteenth century that the Catholic Church was opposed to him; that she fettered him; that she did not permit him to place the result of his researches in the full light of the world, and treated him badly. Now, listen to how Copernicus was ill-treated by the Catholic Church. He was made vicar-general of the diocese in which he

lived, and his name was put forward to be made a bishop
of the diocese. (Applause.) There was no objection
against the man. The two men who protected him and
encouraged him to publish his books and go on with his
discoveries were Cardinal Nicholas Schomberg and the
Bishop of Colomb—a cardinal and a bishop were his dearest friends, and they encouraged him to bring out his
books. He was honored by the Church to the last day of
his life, and I may as well mention here now that it was
in *his* time Martin Luther began to preach Protestantism
in Germany; and one of the greatest and stanchest of
his enemies—one of the first—was Copernicus, the great
philosopher. (Cheers.) So if that man was treated badly
by the Church, all I can say is this: I am perfectly willing to submit to such treatment myself in the morning.
(Laughter and loud cheers.) Now, with regard to Galileo,
I may as well remark at once to you, it is true that Galileo
was put into a kind of imprisonment. He was locked up,
the same, perhaps, as the Bishop of Paderborn, in Prussia, was locked up the other day by Prince Bismarck, the
same as if he had been caught picking pockets or cutting
somebody's throat. (Laughter.)

Now, everybody acknowledges that takes the trouble
of reading history at all that the locking-up of Galileo
and his imprisonment meant simply this: that he was
lodged in a beautiful house with a large garden to it, and
was requested not to go out till the affair was settled.
Then he said his health was bad, and his doctors ordered
him to be removed to Padua. And what sort of a prison
do you think they flung him into there? It was the archbishop's house, and he had the run of it—(great laughter)—
including the run of the kitchen. (More laughter.) But
was it Galileo's scientific opinions and researches that were
condemned? That is the question. I say it was not—(applause)—and I will give you a very simple fact in proof of
it. When Galileo's cause was under examination there
was a very learned man applied to by a Catholic bishop, who wrote to ask him if he thought that Galileo

was right in his astronomical conclusions. The Carmelite came out with a long essay in reply. He said: "He is right; his system is the right one. I know it and can prove it"; and he endorsed every single scientific conclusion of Galileo. He addressed this letter, and he wrote to the general of his order, who was living in Rome under the pope's nose. (Laughter.) The letter was published with the permission of the Roman authorities, and the man that published that letter identified himself with Galileo publicly, and was never censured nor corrected by the Catholic Church. (Loud applause.) What is the true reason of Galileo's imprisonment? Read the Edinburgh "Encyclopœdia." It is written by Scotchmen, and Scotchmen are not as a rule noted for their tenderness to the Catholic Church; but they have acknowledged, though they are Protestants, that it was not for his scientific researches or conclusions Galileo was imprisoned, but it was that he was well known to be a man hostile to the Catholic faith, and that there was that concealed in the spirit of his writings and in the man's conduct that alarmed the Church and alarmed the authorities of the time in his regard. (Applause.) So much for this and many other arguments that are brought against the Church. It is easy to overthrow them. The world has been flinging mud at us for the last sixteen hundred years. The only wonder is that we are not buried long ago under a mountain of this muck of falsehood which they are for ever heaping upon us; and in this nineteenth century men are still ransacking the libraries of Europe, reading history and investigating every single fact in the vain pursuit of some doctrinal lie, that they may put it on the face of the Catholic Church, and so hold her up as a liar before the nations. That lie never will be discovered. (Loud cheers.)

Well, my friends, the moral life of this grand age of ours—which I certainly love, and, in many respects, which I deeply admire—the moral life of our age is injured at its very root by the blow that has been struck at the sanctity and inviolability of Christian marriage. Now, let me remark to you at once, the keystone of the whole arch of human society is the sanctity of the marriage tie. (Applause.) It is in the sanctity of matrimony that the fountains of Christian life are sanctified. The family depends upon the inviolability of the marriage tie; the city, the nation, depends on the family. And what is the world but an aggregate of all nations? When you have traced human society up to its source you must lay your hand upon that most sacred bond that makes the husband faithful even unto death to the wife of his bosom, and that places the woman in the grand and unalterable security of her position as wife and mother.

It is true that, in the pagan times of old, woman was but a slave. In Greece and Rome, before the light of the Gospel came upon them, woman was merely the slave of man—his toy and his delight as long as the fire of youth was in her eye and the bloom of beauty on her cheek; but when she grew old or infirm, the Roman poet describes, in forcible but necessarily brutal language, the male slave or servant of the house coming to the mother of the children, of his master's children, and saying to her on his master's behalf: "Your face has grown pale, and your eyes have lost their lustre—begone! my master has found one younger and fairer than you—begone." She was thrust out of doors, a dishonored and homeless woman, leaving her children behind her, never to see them again, and going out into the world without a home to shelter her or an arm to protect her. Such is her position to-day in the nation that never opened its eyes to the Gospel nor bowed down before the cross. But when the Son of God came He took a woman for His Mother, the Virgin of virgins. He made that woman the greatest of all His creatures in heaven or upon earth; neither in heaven nor on earth was there anything like Mary ever seen before, and neither in heaven nor upon earth shall her equal be found among the creatures of God for all eternity. (Cheers.) And He, for her sake, and in her, raised woman from the degradation of her pagan slavery. He made her the equal and the partner of the husband who gave her his young heart and hand. He sanctified her, and threw over her the ægis of His own divine protection. He sat down at Cana, in Galilee, at the marriage feast, and with His own omnipotent hand blessed the husband and wife, and afterwards ratified that blessing by declaring that the bond thus linked should never be broken—"That which God has joined together let no man rend asunder." Thus woman became the queen of her household; her position was secured; the love of her husband became the inalienable property of the wife. Man was bound to her with a fidelity designated by the love and the fidelity with which Christ is bound by the espousals of divine grace to His Church. She was left the undisputed mistress of her house, as the mother of her children, entrusted with their education and the formation of their character, and she became the mother of the man as well as of the child. The Church of God protecting and sanctifying that marriage tie, and conserving "the Great Sacrament," as Saint Paul calls it, that God put in her hands, the Christian woman rose to the fullest of her rights in the magnificent fidelity of her husband and the sanctity of marriage. (Loud cheers.)

But a change has come upon the moral spirit of the age. Like Samson laying hold of the pillars that upheld the temple, and swaying them to and fro in his blessed might until he brought the great building down, and buried himself and all around in one crash of ruin, so the blind legislators of our age—blind to all the best interests and wants of society—have laid hold of this great pillar that sustained the whole edifice of society and have shaken it to its centre. Desolating by their impious legislation the sanctity and inviolability of marriage by their doctrine and laws of divorce, they have dethroned woman, and flung her back to what she was in the pagan time. and delivered up man to the wild and unbridled indulgences of his own passions, and so destroyed the family, through the family the nation, and through the nation the world. (Applause.) How is this to be remedied? Ladies, I believe you are nearly all, perhaps entirely, Catholics. There is a great

agitation going on in this age, all about what they call
"woman's rights." (Laughter.) They want to get the
right of returning members to Parliament—indeed, I believe they want to get the right of being returned there
themselves. (Laughter.) In America they have pushed
their rights very far—very far indeed—some of them involving the right of shooting a man with impunity.
(Laughter.) It is a dangerous thing, I can tell you, to
pick a quarrel with one of those ladies, to be shot in a
railway-carriage or a tram-car, and to find no jury in the
land so devoid of gallantry as to convict a woman and
have her hanged—(laughter)—such a thing would be unheard of. But while the womanhood outside the Catholic
Church are prating about "woman's rights," they have
permitted their first, their greatest right to be taken out
of their hands, and it is only within the grand walls of the
holy Church of God that woman still preserves the sanctity and dignity of her position as a wife and mother. (Loud
cheers.) I do not mean to impugn the fidelity of husbands
who are not Catholics; I do not mean to lower the dignity
of wives who are not Catholics; but this I must say: that
it is only in the Catholic Church that woman is perfectly
safe from the treachery of the heart of her husband, and
that man is perfectly safe from his own imbecility and
from the dangerous infidelity of his own passions. (Cheers.)

I find great fault with the political life, the legislative
and political life, of this nineteenth century. What is it
that constitutes the security of any nation or of any people? It must be—wherever society is civilized, wherever
the light of God beams—it must be of necessity the justice
of their cause. If a people have their rights founded upon justice, these rights are to be respected, and the respect
the world has for them—the respect that nations in their
international relations have for right and justice, irrespective altogether of power; the respect they have for
treaties, irrespective of their own ability to break them—
constitutes the political and international life of the world.
Take that away, break those treaties with impunity, let

them lose their sacredness, let truth and justice be unavailing where the greater power comes in to suppress the weaker, and you reduce society to the elements of chaos and barbarism out of which Christianity alone brought it forth. (Applause.)

Now, I say that in the political life of this nineteenth century I have this great fault to find: that the spirit of our age is hurrying us back to the first elements of barbarism and of savage chaos. What is a treaty worth to-day? One nation makes a treaty with another. They swear to observe it. What is it worth? Not the paper that it is written upon. After the Crimean war we made a treaty with Russia that she was not to send her war-ships any more into the Black Sea. She swore she would observe that condition, but she was only watching the opportunity, and the moment she saw the Prussians had conquered the French she broke that treaty, tore it into bits, and ordered her war-ships into the Black Sea. Did anybody taunt her with her heartless faith? Did anybody call her a purjurer? No, that is all out of fashion nowadays; it is no crime now for a nation to break its oath or to violate its treaty, if it only has the power to snap its fingers at those it wrongs. (Applause.) The Treaty of Prague, what does it avail to Denmark to-day? Not the paper it is written on. And why? Because Germany has the power to break it, and she has broken it. (Cheers.) The oath of Victor Emmanuel in the Convention of September—he swore before God and heaven that he never would invade Rome; that he would never allow a soldier of his to invade its walls; that he would leave the Pope in possession of his ancient home and city. But as soon as ever he dares he turns his cannon against the walls of Rome, he bombards them, his soldiery rush through the breach, he imposes his sway upon Rome, and actually gives thanks to God because the Almighty had given him the means to break his oath. (Applause.) This is the political teaching of the world. When the war between Germany and France broke out you all know there was a plot hatched between Napoleon and Bismarck to seize Belgium and divide it between them—Belgium, an independent kingdom, its people a free people, offending nobody, its crime that it was a rich prize, and that its only protection was founded on right and justice. It had the misfortune to be small and weak. Bismarck said Napoleon wanted it, and Napoleon said it was Bismarck that wanted it; but between them both it came out that the two thieves had been putting their heads together to rob their neighbors. (Cheers and laughter.)

I ask you, my friends, what remedy is there to-day for this political evil of the age, which everybody acknowledges? Every man—every right-reasoning man—acknowledges that the balance of power is destroyed; that treaties have ceased to bind; that the only law which is now acknowledged by the nations is the law of might against right. *La force contre le droit*, has become an axiom among diplomatists. "Are you able to rob your neighbor? He has just gone down the street, and has a gold watch in his pocket. Are you able to take him by the throat?" "Yes, I think I am the stronger man of the two." "Then go and take the watch." (Laughter and applause.) Nay, more, the nations are speaking of each other as if they were a pack of robbers. Take the *Times* newspaper or any other newspaper any day, and you will find them crying out: "We must make fortifications here; we must build a camp here; we must march an army there, because we do not know the day when Bismarck or somebody else will come and attack us."

Why should he come? Because he is a robber. There is no other conclusion. (Applause.) Germany has become an armed camp. All Europe is obliged to arm like her. The moment every young man becomes eighteen years old he is fit to be killed, and the very first thing the Government does is to make a soldier of him. (Cheers and laughter.) But why is this? Why is France trying to raise an army of upwards of a million? Why has Germany more than a million armed men? Why is Russia boasting of her nearly two millions? Why are all nations armed to the teeth, with their hands on their swords and pistols? Because they acknowledge they have become a pack of robbers. (Applause.) Now, my dear friends, it was not so in the olden time. There was a time when if one nation was going to war with another they would have to explain to the world that the war was a just one—that they could not help it. For many ages the pope was the acknowledged head of Christendom, and if the king of England was going to make war against the king of France, he would go and explain to the pope his reason; and if the pope said, "You must not make war," he was obliged to submit, or if he would not the pope excommunicated him, and called upon all the nations to rise up against him as a malefactor. (Applause.) This was the law of nations; this was the public conscience of Europe for many ages. How are we to save the world to-day unless you get somebody to keep the public conscience? "Oh!" says Mr. Froude, when he was lecturing in America, "the pope was at that time the keeper of the public conscience," and it was quite true, and I am sure if it was not true Mr. Froude would not have stated it, especially with relation to the pope. (Laughter.) Then I asked him: "Would you be kind enough to tell us is there such a thing as a public conscience now, and if there is, who keeps it?" (Great laughter and applause.)

I behold in the age we live in much to admire and much to deplore. I behold the Catholic Church standing to-day, her sovereign head uncovered and dethroned, practically and really imprisoned. Has she lost one tittle of her unity? (Cheers.) Has the Pope ceased to be her head, her acknowledged representative in the grand unity of his jurisdiction, representing in the eyes of the Church the one invisible Head who is at the Father's right hand in heaven? Not one iota has the Holy Father lost of the veneration and love on our part, but rather has he received an increase of it from his temporary calamities. (Loud cheers.) He, the head, represents the unity of the Church. There she stands—one, undivided, indivisible—before this age of ours. The unity that was put upon her in answer to the prayer of Him who said: "Lord, the Father in heaven, let them be one, as Thou and I are one," is upon her to-day. She stands in her robe of sanctity, protesting against the moral evil and against the political evil of this nineteenth century. (Cheers.)

Accepting all the results of her scientific research, glorying in them, making use of them for her own divine purposes, encouraging every man who thinks he can discover some hidden mystery of nature, but in all her sanctity against all the evil around her, she stands before the nineteenth century the only voice that is able to make itself heard and respected, and the only one that can heal and remedy the lusts of our age. (Cheers.) She stands protesting, even though her voice may have lost the tones of temporal power; she protests against the tyranny that would revolutionize, the insurrection, the insubordination and disobedience of the peoples that would rise against all law and revolutionize all society. (Loud cheers.) Oh! the richness of her inheritance. This age denies her powers to interfere, or dictate, or even to advise; but the evils of the world will never find their remedy until this world, and this age, return again upon the old track and kneel down before the Church of God, to receive at her hand the graces of intellectual power without intellectual immorality, of moral virtue, and of the sanctification of its society, until the nations hear her voice once more; and, whether they put the crown upon her brow or not, they will yet admit into their councils and deliberations the only voice that for nearly two thousand years has resounded always on the side of justice, mercy, and clemency, governing the rulers and saving the people from the wild ambition of kings and monarchs. (Great cheering.) When that auspicious day shall come again the world will rejoice. We Catholics know that it is coming—(cheers)—we also believe that man is getting more perfect as he goes on, not only in conquests of scientific research, but also in

the higher march by which the world is approaching nearer
to Him who is choosing and sanctifying His own elect; we
not only believe this, but we believe that it is only through
the Catholic Church, the spouse of God, the one holy, the
one infallible Church of God, the one power which alone
claims and represents and exercises the authority of God
in this world which He has made—that it is through that
Church alone our age and every succeeding age can be
preserved, regenerated, sanctified, and truly ennobled.
(Cheers.) Oh! may that day come; may He who is coming hasten its approach and the triumph of His Church,
when she shall arise again, the glory of the world, as she
was in ages gone by—a glory still remaining to her—that
it may be acknowledged by all men, that the saving cross
may fling its shadow over all the nations, and that the
Great Teacher may be recognized, with the one teaching
that proclaims the reign of prudence, justice, temperance,
and fortitude, which are such noble virtues that no man
loveth anything more precious in this world. (Enthusiastic
cheering.)

THE CATHOLIC CHURCH AND SCIENCE.

This lecture was delivered in Dublin before an immense audience. It is one of the most entertaining and instructive of his lectures, and though but an abridgment it is well worthy of perusal. On coming forward Father Burke was greeted with a storm of applause. When silence was restored the reverend father said :

I HAVE the honor to appear before you this evening to discuss a most important question—namely, the relations of the Catholic Church to science and to scientific men. It is a subject interesting, indeed, to you as Catholics, although you repose in the absolute certainty of your principles. It is a subject so interesting to some of your fellow-citizens that it is driving half of them mad. (Laughter and applause.) Now, as the room is warm, and I do not wish to detain you a moment longer than is necessary, I may as well go into my subject at once. You all know when the summer comes, and people go to bathe, there are two ways of getting into the water. One man sneaks in—a very uncomfortable way. Another man gets on a rock and takes a "header." (Laughter.) You will permit me to take a "header" into the subject. (Laughter.) First of all, I will lay down this principle : that human reason alone is not sufficient to guide man to a knowledge of revealed religion. The proof of this—and the all-sufficient proof—lies in the simple fact that God has made a revelation, and God never would have made that revelation if it were not necessary, and if human reason alone could have guided man into the knowledge and practice of revealed religion. (Hear, hear, and applause.) The student of nature and nature's laws, the more deeply he goes into the subject of his researches, the more thoroughly is he convinced that in the vast creation of God there is nothing unnecessary or superfluous. Everything has its place; everything has its specified office. If, therefore, the human reason of man were all-sufficient to guide him to the revealed religion of God, then Almighty God never would have been guilty of the superfluous act of revelation.

I remember once preaching a sermon when a young priest, and after the sermon was over I met a countryman —it was down in the West of Ireland—and I said to him : "Frank, how did you like the sermon?" "It was very good, sir," said he—"a very good sermon." "Did it throw any light on your mind?" "Begorra, it did not; I knew it all before." (Laughter and applause.) If the reason of man was sufficient to climb the height of divine and revealed knowledge unassisted by revelation from God, then would man be in a position to say to the Son of God when He came down from heaven to teach : "You may go back with your message, we knew it all before." But, in truth, reason was not sufficient for this herculean task. The mightiest intellects of antiquity—the purest, the most subtle, the most gifted minds of pagan civilization—directed all their attention and all their efforts to the solution of the simple question: "Who is God and who is man?" and the greatest philosophers of antiquity, unillumined by the light of revelation, were obliged to bow down and to confess that they were unable to answer the question which the little Catholic child could do the first day he took his Catechism in his hand. (Loud applause.)

It would, perhaps, be asked what place has reason, what use has it? The Almighty God has given you two great guides, each distinct in its own sphere, each distinct in its own operation and in its own source of knowledge. He has given you reason to be your guide to human knowledge, and through the mazes of human science to throw its light forth on the hidden places of nature, to investigate all the wonderful phenomena with which you are surrounded, and to draw from that investigation those high principles teaching the laws which govern the material world and the creation of God. He has also given you in another sphere another guide. Man is immortal. Man is imperishable. He cannot die. The body dies, but the soul shall live; and this truth, primary and essential, even the pagan philosopher of old knew when he said: "*Non omnis moriar*"—"I will not altogether die." If, then, the destiny of man is eternal, if the origin of man be clouded in mystery, if the true essence and existence of man be one of the profoundest mysteries that exists, so that the Grecian philosopher made it the summit of the philosophy of man simply to know himself—it follows that the Almighty God must have provided for us some other guide besides that of mere human reason—some guide coming not from the world but from heaven—some guide illuminated not by the light of time but by the rays of eternity—some guide able to take our hand and lead us through all the mazes of time to the very threshold of our eternal being, and there to show the splendid revelation of all the hopes He has created in our hearts. (Loud applause.) That guide is divine—revealed religion. Each of these two guides has its own great and wonderful work in its own sphere. You can look at the magnificent triumphs of human reason in the researches of modern science. They are children of this nineteenth century—this nineteenth century so full of pride, so full of injustice, so full of resolution from above and revolution from below, so full of contempt for all the sacred and time-honored principles of right, of justice, and of law, yet still a century with so much to admire, to love, and to revere in its magnificent scientific progress. (Applause.) I am a son of that age, born in its bosom, scarcely expecting to see the dawn of the coming century. Childhood, manhood, and prospective age, all are the property of this nineteenth century; and although I wear a habit seven hundred years old, and linked altogether with the traditions of bygone times, yet I am free to say that as a man, as a priest, as a Dominican friar, I am proud of the age in which I was born. (Great applause.)

It is an age that has effected great wonders. It has imprisoned within the valves of the steam-engine a power able to annihilate space and to span the world. It has caught the very lightning of heaven—those destructive elements in which your forefathers saw only the threat in the hands of an angry God of desolation and death. It has caught the fleeting lightning that "appeareth in the east and shineth even unto the west." It has bound it down to a wire, and made it a messenger of thought from man to man instantaneously, throughout the whole face of the world, and even under the sea. (Applause.) This age of ours has caught the air, invisible to the eye, impalpable to the touch—the sensible, grosser touch. It has caught that air, compressed it, expanded it, made it a servant, weighed and measured it, and placed it under rules of scientific discovery and management in a most wonderful fashion. This age of ours has so enlarged the orb of human vision that the eye of man, which naked and natural can scarcely cover the extent of the horizon, and is only able to take in a few objects surrounding him—that eye, under the guide of the scientific genius of the age, is able to pierce the vault of heaven, to call from the far-off recesses of millions of miles planets and stars unseen by their ancestors, and to place the wonders of the ethereal firmament under almost the very hand and touch of the scientific man. (Applause.) In this, and in the ten thousand improvements tending to the comfort and solace of human life, you see a grand work. The art of medicine has progressed so as to lead to the mitigation, in some cases to the annihilation, of fearful diseases that you were accustomed to. The art of chemistry is about to follow, almost like the Almighty Eye itself, the crafty devices of the murderer, to track the secrets of his misdeeds, to take from the decomposed body the evidence of the life and of the death of him who moved in the flesh.

It would require a tongue far more eloquent than that of the highest scientific genius of the age to define, or even to give an outline, of the triumphs of this nineteenth century. But should you deny to the Church her triumphs? Behold the nations of to-day basking in the light of civilization! Behold the nations of to-day advancing with rapid strides in every art and science, and then ask yourselves the simple question, Who brought out of the darkness—out of chaos, out of utter disruption—who drew forth from the awful ruins of the crushed and broken-up world of the fifth century, the glories of the nineteenth century? The angels of the world's history would point to the magnificent figure of the Catholic Church of Jesus Christ. (Vehement applause.) She alone did it, who alone was able to do it. She took the rude savage son of the northern forests—she took the child of barbarism, inflated with the triumph and victory in which he trampled upon imperial Rome, making his blood-stained offerings to his northern pagan gods, unconscious of mercy, unconscious of clemency, unconscious of purity or self-restraint, wild barbarian, all the more terrible because with his barbaric hand he had shattered the great civilization of paganism—and out of such unpromising elements the Church elaborated during many weary ages the civilization which is our pride and glory to-day. (Cheers.) She turned barbaric pride into meekness; she drew from out of a people detestable in their impurity an immaculate priesthood and a very self-restraining Christian manhood. She gathered together all that remained of the universal wreck and ruin of ancient art and science and civilization, and she treasured them in her cloisters; she watched them with zealous care; she brought them forth from day to day in her great universities; she prepared the nations to receive them: she is the mother of that Christendom or Christianity which made the world a civilized and an organized power when it seemed as if nothing short of the creative word of God could have drawn light from so much darkness or order from so much ruin. (Cheers.) Behold her martyrs for three hundred years deluging every province and city of the Roman Empire with Christian blood! Behold her virgins lighting up the lamp, well trimmed and filled with the oil of divine love, and thereby illuminating the darkness of the nations! Behold her missionaries spread into every land, so that their voices were heard on every soil on which the sun of heaven shineth! Behold her penitents, their pride broken, their sin humbled to its own destruction, and the greatest of her saints made lights of the world from being the greatest of sinners—the heresy of an Augustine changed to the light of God's Church, and the great sinner become the Bishop of Hippo!

Of such and such, multiplied indefinitely, were the triumphs of the Church of God, as great and greater in her sphere of that which was divinely revealed, purer in faith, holier in morals, than are the collateral triumphs of the science of an age of which you are proud. And God intended that these two great guides should move harmoniously together over all the universal creation of God, the infinite harmony of whose divine being shines out in the admirable order that prevails throughout. No one force of nature animates another. Light lends to light, knowledge helps knowledge. The abyss of one form of knowledge only calls to another abyss, cognate and collateral to itself. Behold the heavens of God, how harmoniously they move in their infinite movements and variety! Behold the divine law shining forth, so that harmony is found throughout the whole creation of God! It was the intention of God that the two great guides—reason and revelation—should work harmoniously together to bring man to the full perfection of his being, beginning on earth and ending on a high throne in heaven with God.

While the Church to-day says, as she has always said, that she is no enemy to science, that science is no enemy to revelation, that she is not afraid of it, that she loves it, the children of the world, on the other hand, scientific men, the men who spend their days in study of nature's laws, are loud in proclaiming that religion is an enemy of

science. Generally speaking, in this world there is some
great delusion or some great deception always held up
before the world. One time it is a scientific delusion, another time a false system of philosophy, another time, and
indeed at all times, some form of religious error, the most
numerous of all the delusions of the devil. (Laughter.)
Now, one of the great delusions of our day is this: men
imagine, and speak, and write, and seem to believe that the
Catholic Church is engaged in a tremendous and constant
onslaught upon science and scientific men. That is the
great parable of the day. That is the text on which all
the anti-Catholic newspapers are uniting. "Oh! who will
save us from that terrible Pope?" exclaimed big, blustering
Bismarck. (Great laughter and cheers.) "He'll crush us.
I have only two millions of trained soldiers, the grandest
army in the world, at my back, and he has not a single
man." (Continued laughter and cheers.) And then out
came the *Times* newspaper of London on the edifying
spectacle of Bismarck and Germany trying to save themselves from the terrible attacks of Pius IX. and the Ultramontanes. (Cheers, laughter, and some hisses.) "Oh! who
will save us?" exclaims Gladstone. (Laughter, cheers, and
hisses.) "Who will save us from the terrible Vatican
Decrees? They loosened all the bonds of loyalty and allegiance. We cannot trust a Catholic any more, no matter
who he is; I do not care whether he be a lord chancellor
or a postmaster-general or a private soldier. (Loud
laughter and cheers.) They are all gone, no more allegiance or loyalty; if the man sent word to-morrow, they
would be up with a knife at our throats, and who knows
but it is Cardinal Cullen that would be minister?" (Roars
of laughter and vehement cheering.) "Ah! who will save
us," exclaims Professor Tyndall—(continued laughter and
cheers)—"who will save us from that terrible Catholic
Church, these terrible Ultramontanes? They want, if you
please, to make religion a kind of knowledge, and not to
leave it in the region of emotions with Messrs. Moody and
Sankey. (Renewed laughter and hearty cheers.) They

will teach young men the necessity of going to confession instead of leaning on their emotions. (Cheers and laughter.) They will teach their people, if they have stolen anything, that they must give it back. Oh! who will save us from them and leave us to our emotions? Have we not harmoniums? (Loud laughter.) Have we not beautiful hymns? (Laughter.) Have we not grand sermons all about leaning on the Lord and nothing more? (Renewed laughter.) Have we not heaven made easy? (Laughter and cheers.) Oh! who will save us from Catholics saying their prayers and abstaining on Fridays—(laughter)—examining their consciences, keeping themselves pure, restoring if they had the misfortune to take a farthing or a farthing's worth?" It is all very fine. Lean upon the Lord and trust to yourselves. (Continued laughter and applause.)

Meanwhile the great Catholic Church stands there, robbed and plundered in Italy, imprisoned in Germany, fettered and hampered, crossed and contradicted in France, in Spain, in Brazil, held up to scorn and ridicule. The blind fools' cry all the time is: "Save us from her—(loud cheers)—make way until I throw a stone right in her face." (Cheers.) Send a few bishops to prison; send a few priests to prison; take whatever trifle of money they have; take all their churches, sell everything, and then cry out: "What a wonderful fellow I am to be able to defend myself from the people!" (Laughter.) Then, on the other hand, they are told day after day: "Ah! what would not the Church do to those people if she could lay her hands upon them?" Professor Tyndall is a great man in his own sphere, a child of genius, a glory to the land that bore him; he is the scientific apostle of light. According to those truth-telling writers, if the Pope only could get hold of him he would improve his speculations on light by putting it out. (Laughter and cheers.) Professor Darwin is a man of extraordinary talent and research; no one can deny it. His forte is what they call comparative anatomy—comparing different orders and species of animals, and trying to prove the similarity and the analogy between them—and he began very lowly indeed : he took the sea-spittle, a thing that had scarcely any life at all, and on that very soft foundation he went on building and building until he came to man. As a science it is admirable. Now, according to the cry of the day, if the Catholic devils could get hold of him they would make him a specimen of comparative anatomy by dissecting him. (Laughter and cheers.) Now, this is a popular delusion, and in this what are the men of science doing ? They are doing what a celebrated Catholic called Don Quixote once did when he attacked a windmill. (Continued laughter.) The mill was quietly grinding corn and flour to make bread for the laborers about, but the Don, in his imagination, thought it was a grand castle, inhabited by ghosts and goblins, who held knights and fair ladies in durance vile, and, setting his lance in rest, charged it, and broke his head against the walls of the windmill. (Laughter and prolonged cheering.) Here is the Catholic Church quietly doing to-day what she has done for eighteen hundred and seventy years, grinding, as it were, the corn of the Word of God, to make out of it the bread of life for men's souls. (Cheers.) And around her is not one scientific but an entire army of poor, crazy Don Quixotes. Coming on with their lances in rest, one says : "I will prove she told a lie in such a year." (Laughter.) Another says : "I will prove that she cannot coexist with the rights of civil allegiance." All poise their lances and rush on madly to the attack, until, passively resisted by the Rock of Ages, they fall easy victims to their romantic folly. (Loud cheers.)

In the face of all here I assert a very simple proposition, and it is this : The Catholic Church is not the enemy but it is the friend and patron and encourager of all true science and of all true scientific men. (Cheers.) It is all nonsense to assert the contrary, and I will show it to you by bringing the search to the plain, ordinary test of common sense. Let us suppose for an instant that the Catholic Church is what those men declare her to be, afraid of her life of science, afraid of scientific men ; declaring that she could not bear them; telling them to stand off, that if she caught them she would fix them. (Laughter.) Let us suppose that she considers deep scientific research to be inconsistent with the profession of her faith and the practice of her morality, and what would follow? Let us test it by common sense. You have all, like myself, been preparing for confession since you were seven years of age. And did you ever say when, examining your consciences, you opened your prayer-books and went over the table of sins: "Did I press my studies too far, or was I too scientific?" (Cheers and laughter.) Was any Catholic boy ever expected to say this at confession: "Father, I am a medical student, and all the other students are tremendous fellows for science, and, father, I accuse myself that I was inclined to study—that I was inclined and endeavored to keep up with them in their researches; O father! forgive me"? (Laughter and applause.) I wonder if Sir Dominic Corrigan ever accused himself of being too studious or too deep in his application when studying those subjects so great, and so dangerous, if you will, in which he has achieved so grand a triumph. I wonder did any confessor ever say to him (Sir Dominic): "O boy! that will not do. I hear you got the first medal the other day at the College of Surgeons." (Laughter.) Every boy at Stonyhurst, at Oscott, Exshaw, and other great Catholic schools in England, and in Clongowes Wood, and, indeed, our own Catholic University, would do so yet. They boasted how their own pupils succeeded in examinations for cadetship, for the civil service, for engineers, and the rest, and how Catholic boys succeeded in this and in that science. (Applause.)

Now I will put before you two reasons which I would urge as practically and clearly as possible to show that, despite all that has been said, the Catholic Church cannot be the enemy of science. (Applause.) The first is the simple yet high and grand reason that all truth, wherever it exists in the order of nature, or in the supernatural order of revelation—that all truth comes from God. There is nothing true of the things you see in this world, there is nothing true of the things that you look forward to and hope for in the next, except in so far as it coincides with the eternal truth which is in God. (Applause.) To say that one order of truth is hostile to another, that it is destructive of another, is just the same as to say that God contradicts Himself. It should be remembered that everything which the Church of God is accused of to-day she herself has condemned over and over again as a damnable heresy—namely, that any discovery of truth in nature could be opposed to the truth of revelation. In other words, we declare it a heresy to say that God could contradict Himself. They say there are two gods—the god of nature and this material world, and a god of the immaterial and spiritual and purely intellectual world; and then, in order to find employment for these two, the Manichean heretics set them fighting—the most natural thing in the world if they had nothing else to do. The god of matter, the god of the lower creation, has his own laws, his own truth, but they are all so arranged as to be in opposition to the superior god, and, therefore, whenever one of those heretics committed a sin—whenever he robbed his neighbor or committed any detestable act of private sin—he at once excused himself and said: "Oh! I am the subject of the god of nature." The Catholic Church laid her anathema upon this detestable heresy, and yet, strange to say, she is to-day accused of being frightened at the truths of nature, as if they did not proceed from the same God who gave her the truths of revelation. The great truths of science wherever they are found, no matter how wonderful the results of that science, if they are only true, cannot touch one iota, affect one scintilla, of the revealed truths of God in the way of injury. There is no room even for such possible antagonism as this. The great sciences—astronomy, chemistry, natural philosophy, and the like—move in one groove, and religion in another; and, just as two railway trains on parallel tracks can never collide, so these can never clash. (Applause.)

I would invite your attention to the words of one of the greatest men of the day. Dr. Newman (applause) says: "The physicist will never ask himself by what influence external to the universe the universe is sustained, simply because he is a physicist. His basis of observation, what he starts from, what he falls back upon, is the phenomena which meet the senses. If, indeed, he be a religious man" (continued Dr. Newman) "he will, of course, have a definite view of the subject. But that view of his is private—not the professional view of a physicist, but of a religious man ; and this not because physical science is anything different, but simply because it says nothing at all on the subject, nor can it do so by the very undertaking with which it set out." The Catholic Church, therefore, is not afraid of science, nor of the scientific man, as long as he sticks to his own science and his own subject. Nay, more, she encourages him, she protects him, for she knows that every addition to scientific truth, every great discovery in nature, every real and substantial addition to man's knowledge, is a new manifestation of the beauty and wisdom of God, and in itself serves to prepare men's minds more and more to receive the divine message. (Applause.)

When in her history did the Church ever persecute the scientific man as such as long as he stuck to his own particular science? When did she ever impede him, or injure or imprison him, in the days of her power? When did she ever set her censure on him as purely and entirely a scientific man? Never. When did she leave him unprotected and alone? Never. (Applause.) Her history tells you, and, in truth, you owe the greatest results of scientific research to the protection and to the fostering and kindly care of the Catholic Church, as I will endeavor to let you see. Was it not quite natural that the Catholic Church should foster the man of science, while she knew that every addition to real truth, even of the natural order, every addition to the mighty store of man's real knowledge, was but a new revelation of the depth of the riches, the wisdom, the power, and the beauty of her God? (Applause.)

What better preparation could a man's mind have to receive her divine message than the preparation of science?

The more a man entered into the great mystery of nature the more did he behold in the admirable order and arrangement of those truths which he discovered, by habitual and deep study of the awful hidden power, the admirable hand of nature's God. (Applause.) You are told that sailors as a rule are the most reverent and religious minded of men, because, it is said, of their constant intercourse with the vast ocean. Now they beheld it slumbering in its vastness—it was like a giant asleep; now they saw it in the gloom of night, hurrying and rising in its wrath, and amid the thunder of the elements the terrible force of nature was at work around them, and it revealed to them, in a great measure, the power of God and the terrors of His wrath. And I will ask, Would not the same influence naturally be at work in the mind of the astronomer, of the student of the stars, as he sat night after night silently contemplating the mighty "orbs of heaven around him"? It was a clear night, there was silence around him in his watch tower; with his powerful telescope he called to him the planets revolving millions of miles around; he saw in space their vastness and their number, scattered like snowflakes, and yet he knew that the least of these was perhaps greater than the world in which he dwelt. What was more calculated to bring home to his mind the full power and wisdom of the guiding hand of God? What more calculated to fit his mind for higher truths of revelation, and to receive them reverently—to bow down and accept them gratefully—than the profound and supreme study in which science has prepared him for a higher and better light? (Applause.) "The heavens proclaim the glory of God, and the firmament tells the work of His hand." Therefore, as long as the scientific man adheres to the true principles of his study and does not travel outside them, he will find in the Catholic Church a friend and an encourager. I will give a proof or two of this. One of the great questions of the present day is the opposition which the Catholic Church appears to have shown to the new and modern, and, I would add, the true system of astronomy. For many hundreds of years the scientific men of the schools of this world, not having the powers of the telescope or the aids of modern science, held that this world was the centre of the whole creation of God—that this world or orb of ours was fixed and stationary, and that the sun, moon, stars, and planets of the heavens moved round it as their centre.

Now, this is a mistake—a scientific mistake. It was held for hundreds of years; the holy fathers and doctors of the Church held it. They interpreted the words of Scripture in its literal sense to confirm it. The Scripture told them that the Lord had established the world upon its own basis, and would not be moved for ever and ever. Elsewhere it was written: "He hath established the world, which shall not be moved"; and unaided by science and on a question which had no direct or immediate bearing either on faith or morals, the vast majority, if not the whole of them, interpreted those words of Scripture in their literal sense to mean that this earth was one vast plain—not a globe, but a plain fixed in its place, and that all the orbs of heaven revolved around it. Well, by degrees men began to observe the motions of the stars, to observe the aberrations of certain planets, to observe certain familiar phenomena in the earth itself, as, for instance, that a heavy weight thrown from a very high place would not descend to earth in a straight line as it would if it fell on a plain, but would fall slightly towards the west, because the earth was moving meanwhile eastward; when men discerned these things the theory was started that the earth was not immovable, but moved, while the sun was immovable and fixed in its place. This was a great novelty —perhaps the greatest scientific discovery of any age. And this was brought forward as a proof by these scientific men that the Catholic Church had no welcome for them, that she hates them, and is an enemy to the progress of science; and why? Because she opposed that theory.

Now, the first man who opposed this theory was a young German, born at Coblentz in 1401, who had turned his attention to astronomy. His name was Nicolos of Pusa, and he published a book in which he laid down the principle that the earth was round; and, according to the doctrine of the day, he ought to have been throttled. (Laughter.) But he propounded this theory simply as a theory, for every philosophical truth must, at its inception, be propounded as a theory. It would be contrary to every principle of science and philosophy to take it as an absolute certainty until its truth was proved. If he, with his theory, had gone into Rome by the northern road and entered by the Flaminian Gate, he might have been asked: "Where are you going? You are going, my friend, where there are inquisitors who will pull the windpipe out of you." (A laugh.) However, not having met a kind angel guardian, I might ask what became of this young man. They brought him to the pope—Nicholas V., one of the most eminent of our pontiffs—who heard him prove his theory in the garden of the Vatican, and, would you believe it? he was immediately made a cardinal, with liberty to pursue his scientific studies. (Applause.) He was succeeded in his scientific investigation by a man to whom the world is indebted for his system of astronomy—Nicholas Copernicus—who, having been born at Grauenberg, became one of the greatest astronomers of his day. There was at that time a celebrated Italian astronomer named Cileo Caliagnini. He was a friend of Copernicus and a student, and when Copernicus died he came to Rome and there developed his system under the very eye of the pope.

About the same period there was a celebrated German Oriental scholar, Widmanstead. He, too, came to Rome, with his head full of the new system of astronomy. What happened to him? He was called into the Vatican palace, and there in the presence of Clement III. and of the cardinals, and surrounded by all the learned ecclesiastics of Rome, he explained the system of Copernicus, and subsequently bore away with him from Rome magnificent presents given to him by the pope for his learning. While all this was going on at Rome there was another scientific man who entered on the scene, a man as great as Copernicus, as great as Galileo, the famous Christopher Columbus—(applause)—the man who opened a new world to Europe, who first set his eyes upon the grand shores of the vast continent of the West; the man who, in the providence of God, was the angel sent forth, amongst other purposes, to prepare a home, a glorious and a generous home, for the descendants of the old race of the island in which we live. (Enthusiastic applause.) The noble citizens of his native republic of Genoa laughed at his projected enterprise. He came to Spain. He applied to Ferdinand and Isabella, the Catholic sovereigns of Leon and Castile; but they were too much engaged with other affairs to attend to him, though he put before them, with the simple eloquence of genius, the great things he would do if they only gave him money and two or three ships. A deaf ear was turned to all that, and it was a memorable historical fact that when no man would listen to Columbus a Dominican friar, Egeboso, took him in hand; genius spoke to genius, the friar said to the mariner: "No man seems to understand you, but I do"; and shortly afterwards, when he was made Archbishop of Seville, the richest and highest dignity in Spain, he placed his purse at the service of Columbus; and, humanly speaking, they owed America to the zeal and discrimination of the Dominican friar who aided Columbus in his great enterprise. (Applause.) Another arose after Copernicus—a man celebrated for his scientific discovery and more celebrated system, because he was made the hobby of those who attacked the Catholic Church, although he was himself a Catholic.

Twenty-three years after the death of Copernicus Galileo was born. He became convinced that the earth moved round the sun. So far there was no harm done. Yet, strange to say, the Catholic Church, which did not condemn Copernicus, which did not condemn Di Chusa, condemned Galileo, and for this they were all to lie down and be humbled the moment Galileo's name was mentioned. Books and books have been published of the history of Galileo, and if they read them all they should study for six or seven years. Every assailant of the Catholic Church said: You may boast of the Church's antiquity, of the Church's unity, of the Church's sanctity, of the submission of the Church's members, but wait, what about Galileo ? Down on your marrow-bones. (Laughter.) Now, I will in a few words explain this seeming difficulty. When Galileo came to the conclusion that the sun was stationary and the earth was moving around it, instead of writing a book like Di Chusa's, or seeking additional proofs or reasons to convince the scientists of the day that his theory was correct, what did he do ? The very first thing Galileo did was to lay down the system of the earth moving round the sun as an undoubted fact, as an incontrovertible fact— to call everybody that did not believe it asses and fools. When he was told that the words of Scripture seemed to be opposed to this in the common acceptation of them, he laughed at it and said: "O my dear friends! the Scriptures in a great many things are inaccurate. You call it the Word of God. If it is the Word of God, you must explain it so as to fit into my philosophical theory, or you are all asses and fools." Now, what was his philosophical —his astronomical theory ? It was this: that the earth moved round the sun. *That* is known now to be the fact; but we have sufficient reason to know it; Galileo had not.

Galileo did not know from Adam the laws of gravitation; he never heard of such a thing as atmosphere—pressure upon the globe; yet he asserted that the earth moved round the sun. What reason did he give ? "Oh!" says he, "do you not see the tides come in and go out; sure that shows the earth is moving and wabbling about" (Laughter.) "That cannot be," said another celebrated man, "the motion of the tides is produced by the influence of the moon." "You are a fool—an ass," replied Galileo. That was his usual answer. When the pope and the cardinals heard that the Scripture was to be made subservient to Galileo; when they heard that, with the exception of the texts that bore directly and immediately on faith and morals, all the rest was to be treated as allegory and myth, to be explained according to the whim of every man, at the very moment, too, when Protestantism in its outbreak left the Scriptures in the hands of the multitude, who were running wild with them; when the pope and cardinals heard all this they properly called on the bold Galileo and asked him what he meant. And why should they not? What did Cardinal Bellarmine say to Galileo? These were the words: "We cannot so bend the interpretation of Scripture as to suit your style of astronomy; for this I tell you: when the demonstration shall be found to establish the earth's motion, it will be proper *then* to interpret the Holy Scriptures otherwise than they have hitherto been in those passages which mention the moving of the heavens and the stability of the world." There was the answer of Rome to Galileo. The idea that the earth moved around the sun was an established scientific fact. It moved, as they knew, with enormous velocity. They knew, moreover, that its motion was essentially controlled by the laws of gravity and of attraction. Galileo, who declared the Church should submit to bend the Scriptures to his theory, never heard of the laws of gravitation in his life, and he was three years dead and in his grave when one of his disciples discovered that the air could be weighed, and that it pressed down on the earth with tremendous pressure, and moved with the earth. He spoke disrespectfully and ungratefully of Urban V., but what was his condemnation? He was absolved from all censures; he was then told that he was to be kept in mild imprisonment during the pleasure of the pope, his friend. That imprisonment lasted four days, and on the evening of the fourth day he was told to go to the Florentine ambassador, after which he was sent to his country-seat. Yet Galileo was called a martyr!

IRELAND'S CATHOLICITY, AND WHAT SAVED IT.

The following lecture was delivered by Father Burke in the Assembly Rooms, Wexford, Ireland. It is a glowing tribute to the faithful sons and daughters of the Green Isle.

MY LORD, LADIES, AND GENTLEMEN: The subject on which I presume to address you this evening is, in my opinion and mind, the grandest, the most interesting, and most wonderful that could occupy your attention, or that of any lecturer, in this age of ours—"Ireland's Catholicity, and how it was saved." This subject, I say, is interesting to you Irishmen; for nothing can be more dear, nothing can offer itself for consideration with equal recommendation to the thoughtful mind, or possess such attractive interest, as the study of your religion and how it was saved. Now, this proposition involves three great truths, which immediately present themselves to me when I say, "Catholicity in Ireland, and what saved it." The first is that Ireland is Catholic; if not, how on earth could we talk of its Catholicity? It is true all Irishmen are not Catholics; it is also true that from difference of religion is produced, from time to time, dissension and strife at which the Catholic spirit must revolt. There is no evil over which our country has greater cause to shed tears than the strange hatreds and dissensions produced amongst us by religious differences. All Irishmen are not Catholics; yet Ireland is Catholic. All Englishmen are not Protestants; yet England is Protestant. All Italians are not

Catholics—I wish they were—and yet Italy is Catholic. In the same manner other countries take their religious denomination from the religion of the great majority of their inhabitants. Whatever religion the sweeping majority of a country's inhabitants profess, that country claims it as the religion of the state. Surely it requires no argument to prove that the sweeping majority of Irishmen are Catholics.

A reverend friend of mine was lately called as a witness on a trial, and when he got up on the green cloth to give his evidence a counsellor, who was a bigoted Protestant, asked him first what was his name, and he replied : " Rev. Charles Davis, commonly called Father Charley." The next question was: "How many Protestants in your parish ?" To which Father Charles replied: "Not one, thanks be to God!" (Laughter.) So that in this parish at least it would be true to say that the sweeping majority was Catholic. The same is true in respect of Ireland. The second involves a plain truth. When speaking of Ireland's Catholicity, and how it was saved, we see by that sentence that it must have been at some period or another in peril or danger ; that it must have been attacked by its enemies, and that it must have been rescued from that peril or danger. You sometimes say that is a wonderful man ; his life has been saved. When you so speak you take it for granted that his life must have been in great danger ; that he was nearly drowned, kicked to death, or killed. So Catholicity, like that man, was assailed with dangers, when its enemies stood up against it and thought to uproot it from the hearts of the Irish people; they thought to destroy it and crush it under the earth, and it must have found a refuge in some place.

The third great truth involved is, that if it was saved there must have been some great agency to save it, either from earth or heaven (I will not say hell) ; for I take it for granted that the Catholic Church, preaching as it does the humanity and divinity of our Saviour—that He was God as well as man, that in His boundless love He came down from heaven to redeem man, and that He left behind Him certain great truths to be acted upon, which great truths are in direct antagonism to hell and its agencies—it would be impossible that any agency of hell could have saved Ireland's Catholicity. The agency must, therefore, have been of earth or of heaven, or of both. I ask you to accept these three truths as principles which do not require proof. You are aware that in every science there are what are called postulates, or *axiomata*—simple things that do not require proof, but are evidently true. A lecturer on natural history who kept his audience for an hour in proving that a dog wagged his tail would not perform a more unnecessary or tedious task than in proving the postulates which I have just laid down for your acceptance. It is as true as a dog wags his tail that Ireland is a Catholic nation, and that her Catholicity has been assailed over and over again; that no power has ever been able to root that Catholicity out of the hearts of the Irish people or to extinguish that torch of faith, even though it was plunged into the ocean of a nation's blood. Nothing, then, remains but for us to consider the two parts of the proposition: Ireland's Catholicity and what saved it.

One of the greatest writers and deepest thinkers of our age has left behind this testimony of the stability of the Catholic Church: "Never since the world was created was there a human institution so wonderful as the Catholic Church." So said Mr. Macaulay; but he was mistaken. If it were a human institution it would not be here to-day; it would long since have been swept from the face of the earth, like other great human institutions whose destruction we find recorded in history. Even those which God Himself made and beautified with His own hands are swept away. Who can point out now the boundaries of Paradise—that garden of delights where man in the joy of his newly-created manhood walked abroad; that garden blooming beneath the perpetual smile of the glorious sun, where the voice of sinless man was heard by all his creatures with obedience, that voice which arrested the proud eagle in its flight, brought the spotted tiger and the striped leopard in tame submissiveness to the foot of their lord, to whom God gave them as obedient subjects? Where is now that lovely garden? Can any traveller point out its limits? Can any adventurous explorer tell aught of its whereabouts? No; not a vestige of it remains. Where are the ancient nations once so powerful? All swept away in the mighty waves which it has pleased the Almighty God to send upon them. Where are the ancient cities where the prophets lifted up their voices? They are gone; the very ruins of them have perished. Where are the beauties of Greece? Where the glory of her kings? Where are the ancient systems of philosophy? It seems as if nothing in the order of nature is capable of endurance or escaped destruction; but the Catholic Church has flourished from its foundation, and is at the present day as strong and vigorous, as fresh and beautiful, as it was in its youth, and yet a philosopher of the present day will call it a human institution.

No doubt this old habit would naturally induce you to consider my words as being uttered in my priestly character. It is an old habit. It appeared before Ireton at Limerick on the person of Terence O'Brien. I should like to address you as a priest, but I speak to you now as a lecturer of the nineteenth century. A lecturer of the nineteenth century has no respect for right, justice, nor principle; he is a sincere admirer of Garibaldi and Prince Bismarck, of powder and ball, but who would probably be the first to run away from the latter on account of his belief in them. And in the simple capacity of a lecturer I confidently assert that if the Catholic Church were a human institution it would not be in existence to-day. Why, if the four Gospels were consumed—if the Sacred Scripture itself were destroyed—Ireland would be sufficient to furnish full and efficient proof that the Catholic religion has a divine origin.

The essence of Catholicity is contained in the belief in the mystery of the Incarnation, and every heresy which has sprung up from the time of Nicholas the Deacon to the last and strangest form of intellectual monstrosity can be traced either to the denial of the divinity or the sanctity of God made man. Without full and thorough belief in this mystery there can be no Catholicity. Any doubt, any wavering, is fatal; the intelligence and the heart of man must be filled with the effulgence of the belief in that truth; there can be no room for doubt, nor can there be any hesitation or wavering in this belief. A Connaught man proudly boasted to me once that he knew more than the whole of them (meaning the "Jumpers"); for he said he knew Dr. Gollogher's Catechism. And so he did, for this contained all the saving truths of religion. Referring to "jumpers," it might be truly said that intellectual gymnastics were always dangerous, and spiritual jumping, unless from darkness to light, was damnable. In estimating the progress of religion in different nations the quality of the soil upon which the seed was sown must be taken into account. It was remarkable that the Teutonic or Sclavonic nations never received the faith gratefully nor produced abundant fruits, and the only instance which existed of an order of knights to spread the Gospel with the sword in one hand and the Bible in the other was that of a Teutonic knight who went, sword in hand, to spread the Gospel amongst the Russians. The Gospel itself, which was a two-edged sword, was not enough for them; the material sword should be also employed in a violent effort to convert an obstinate nation. Other nations were wanting in Catholic instinct and feeling. It was remarkable that England in her best days was wanting in loyalty to the pope of Rome. Though England held the Catholic faith for centuries, she never warmed to the pope; and amongst the Eastern nations, in which every dogma and every little point of doctrine were very minutely examined and were fully discussed, yet the spirit of Catholicity was never able to produce a celibate amongst their priesthood.

Never since Christ founded his Church did the seed of

divine faith fall upon so rich, so deep, so congenial, so grateful a soil, or produce such abundant fruit, as in Ireland. What are the characteristics of Catholicity? The virtues which proclaim most directly the triumph of grace over nature. There were many magnificent virtues in which nature and grace are blended—in which it is hard to draw the line between the action of nature and grace. For instance, prudence was a very estimable virtue, and yet a man might be prudent, keep his eyes open, never take a leap in the dark; he might be a cute, cunning, long-headed fellow, an astute Scotchman, that one should get up very early in the morning to get at the blind side of—I wish the Irish had more of this prudence—but you will observe, after all, that this prudence stopped at cunning. There was another virtue—truthfulness, one which he greatly prized; but the natural feeling of honor and self-respect may prevent a man from practising deceit. The man of honor says: "My word is my bond." But though these are very fine virtues they are merely human, and there is no triumph of grace over nature in their exercise. There are virtues peculiar to Catholicity which require the action and co-operation of grace. That of virginal purity is one—a grand virtue, which purifies all the faculties and senses, elevates man to God, turns away his heart from human propensity, and centres his mind in heaven, upon Him who came down from heaven to become the Virgin's Son.

There is another grace peculiar to Catholicity; it is a gift, a grace, a faculty for realizing the unseen. Nature demands the exercise of the senses and the reasoning powers to assure itself of a truth. The philosopher may, on very slight grounds, elaborate a system of philosophy, and discover scientific truths which will one day startle the world, as in the case of Sir Isaac Newton discovering the law of gravitation from the falling of an apple, or him who, from seeing the deadly action of lightning upon an animal or a tree, is enlivened with a desire to direct its rapid action and utilize it for the carrying on of communication between man and man. These things are the result of human intelligence; but the first feature of the Christian character is the realization of the unseen by the graces of faith and hope. The essence of Christianity lies in a belief of the presence of God. When Christ asked the apostles: "Whom do people say that I am?" and they answered: "Some say that you are Elias, others that you are Jeremias, one of the prophets," He answered: "But whom say ye that I am?" Peter immediately fell down upon his knees and said: "Master, you are Christ, Son of the living God." Our Lord said to him: "Blessed art thou, Simon, son of John, for flesh and blood never taught you this, but my Father who is in heaven." This is the first feature of the Christian character—the unseen power of realizing the unseen, the power of knowing it, the power of feeling it, the power of substantiating it to the soul and to the mind, until out of that substantiation of the invisible comes the engrossing, ardent desire of man to make that invisible surround him by its influence in time that he may enjoy its possession in eternity.

Consequently the man of faith, in addition to being honest, industrious, truthful, and having all these human virtues, is a firm believer. It costs him no effort to believe in a mystery because he cannot comprehend it, because he has never seen it. He knows it is true; he stakes his own life upon the issue of that divine truth which he has apprehended by the act of the intelligence and not by the senses. Every man who disputes this great principle of faith as realizing the unseen, if he pushes it to its conclusion, must be an infidel. Therefore, the Spanish, French, Italians, and continental Catholics generally, when they fall away from the true faith, go directly into infidelity. There is no medium between Catholicity and infidelity—a belief in the divinity of the Son of God as man and a denial of that great truth. Where humility is absent there can be no hope; for the proud man raises up his arm against the power that crushes him. These, then, were the distinguishing characteristics of Catholicity, and no country ever realized them so fully as did this island; for amongst no people did the virtue of original purity rule to such an extent, and never was there people whose faith and hope were more sorely tested. Ireland once was called "Insula Demonorum," owing to the savage and unsparing character of its inhabitants. The volatile, the electric spirit of the Celtic character, which prompts to rush with lightning speed from thought or feeling to action, was the means of embroiling the Irish, so terrible in their anger, in so many pernicious wars that they were the dread of other nations. History, which was a faithful and impartial record of events, was not written to flatter. I have been accepted as a lover of my country, but I have never flattered my countrymen, or looked kindly upon their faults. Before the light of Christianity overspread this island the inhabitants of it were the terror of other countries, as none could tell the moment when they might rush upon their neighbors with fiery sword. But when Patrick brought the message of faith amongst them its light and influence spread all over the land; virginal purity in the cloister, maidenly purity in the convent, matronly purity—which combined the modesty of the virgin with the love of the mother in the household—was the immediate result of the spread of Christianity in Ireland. The fierce passions of the men became subdued. The bards no longer attuned their harps to sing the praises of their kings, or celebrate the glories of their warriors. On one occasion, when the king, chieftains, druids, and bards were assembled, up rose the archminstrel (Dubbac) of the royal monarch of Tara, in the might of his intellect and in the glory of his voice and presence, and, lifting up his harp on his hand, he said: "Hear me, O high kings and chieftains of the land! I now declare that the man who comes to us speaks from God, that he brings a message from God. I bow before Patrick's God. He is the true God, and so long as I have this harp, it shall never sound again save to the praises of Christianity and its God." And the king and people and bards and warriors alike rose promptly, and never in the history of the world was there a people that so embraced the light of faith, took it into their hearts and souls and blood, as did Ireland in the day of her conversion. The belief in the great mystery of the Incarnation and love for the Blessed Virgin were remarkable features in the early Irish Christians, and to this day we have evidence of the inculcation of that love by Patrick, when teaching that mystery, in the phrases of the Irish language by which our Lord and His Virgin Mother are spoken of as "*Muire Mathair*"—"Mary Mother," and "*Mac na Maighdure*"—"The Virgin's Son." It is important to bear in mind that these ancient pagans were not gross idolaters; they had too much nobility of character to bow down before a Venus, a Saturn, a Mars, or a Mercury. Pagan Ireland scorned to worship stocks or stones, whether they represented beauty as Venus, or theft as Mercury. It would as soon bow down to a butterfly or a magpie. It scorned to worship anything except the glorious sun, whose rising was hailed by the clash of harps, whilst the bards sang his glories and the people all bowed down in adoration to him who gave them light and life. But when Patrick spoke to them of the Eternal Light which never changed and never set they joyfully embraced the faith. The respect and love for purity was a remarkable feature in the Irish character, and it was the cause of the English invasion. Wexford had reason to be proud of many things, but she had no reason to feel any pride in Dermot MacMurrough. The moment he violated the sanctity of the marriage tie, that moment the people rose up against him, stripped the crown from his brow, and shattered the sceptre in his hand, as one guilty of this crime should never make or administer the laws of the country.

And then why did the Irish rise up against the Dane? He did not come amongst them to make war for the purpose of conquest; he came to ask, as he had asked in Brittany, for permission to be a settler for purposes of trade and commerce. But he came in the name of a false God, Thor; he came denying the divinity of the Son of God and mocking the Virgin Mother; and that is why the Irish rose up against him, fought on hillside and in the valleys till the country became almost depopulated and savage; and never did they lay down the sword till on that Good Friday at Clontarf, following the crucifix, which was held aloft, they hurled the foreign unbeliever in the Incarnation into the sea. (Great applause.) Though the Irish drove out the Dane, they were never able to repel the Saxon or Norman invaders, and this I attribute to the fact that the Irish were not united among themselves. What saved Ireland's Catholicity? I characterize as blasphemy the assertion that it was saved by opposition to England, or by any human agency. I attribute the salvation of Ireland's Catholicity to the divine power of God alone. The principles which were rooted in the heart and soul of Ireland were attached in denial to the divinity of God made man, in the rejection of the Virgin Mother as being entitled to honor, and in the attempt to overthrow the authority of the pope of Rome. To these principles Ireland was ever true from her earliest conversion to Catholicity. The Church had saved herself. The ant might as well come out of the molehill and say the sun shines for me alone as for any man to say the Church was saved by mere human agency. Ireland's faith was saved by God, and by no other agency could it be saved.

A Plea for Catholic Education.

THE following sermon was preached in the Cathedral of Killarney, Ireland. It was preached in aid of the schools under the care of the Presentation Order of Monks in that place. The desire to listen to the inspired eloquence of Father Burke, if not also to assist an important and meritorious charity, gathered into the large edifice an audience so vast as to throng every part of the building. The sermon is one of the most powerful of Father Burke's discourses.

In the name of the Father, and of the Son, and of the Holy Ghost. Amen.
The Gospel of this the twenty-second Sunday after Pentecost is taken from the Gospel according to St. Matthew, 9th chapter:

"*At that time:* As Jesus was speaking to the multitude, behold a certain ruler came up and adored Him, saying: Lord, my daughter is even now dead; but come, lay thy hand upon her, and she shall live. And Jesus, rising up, followed him, with His disciples. And behold a woman who was troubled with an issue of blood twelve years, came behind Him, and touched the hem of His garment. For she said within herself: If I shall touch only His garment, I shall be healed. But Jesus turning and seeing her, said: Be of good heart, daughter; thy faith hath made thee whole. And the woman was made whole from that hour. And when Jesus was come into the house of the ruler, and saw the minstrels and multitude making a rout, He said: Give place; for the girl is not dead, but sleepeth. And they laughed Him to scorn. And when the multitude was put forth, He went in and took her by the hand. And the maid arose. And the fame hereof went abroad into all that country."

"And he took her by the hand, and the maid arose."

DEARLY BELOVED BRETHREN, the miracle recorded in this day's Gospel of the raising of the ruler's child to life is beautifully indicative and symbolical of the great charity and the great cause for which we are assembled here to-day. We are come together to take thought for the proper education of the children of our poor;

we are come together to consider how necessary religion is us forming an element of that education, how utterly worthless their training would be without religion; and, consequently, we are come together to record, by our gifts and by our charity, our determination that the children of our people shall have the first and the greatest of all blessings—namely, a thoroughly religious and Catholic education.

Now, consider, dearly-beloved brethren, the circumstances of the miracle which I have read for you as recorded in the Gospel. A young girl, the daughter of a prince in the land, sickens and is brought to the very point of death. Her father, who was a very rich man, no doubt tried by every means to preserve her in health, to heal her in sickness, and to restore her. He called in, no doubt, the ablest physicians in the land; but they could do nothing for his child. Gradually her strength decayed and the light faded out of her eyes, the pulsation of her heart ceased, and all men said she was dead and beyond all remedy now. Her father, finding that human physicians could not help her, bethought him, in a happy moment, that there was a divine Physician in the land, one before whose action death itself was obliged to yield, one whose word was potent not merely to recall the sick to health but to recall the very dead to life; and to Him, under the coercion of his sorrow, the father went, and, adoring Him, said: "My child is dead, O Lord; but come Thou and lay Thy hand upon her, and at the touch of Thy hand she shall live." Christ our Lord entered the house and said: "The maiden is not dead, but only sleepeth. The element of life," He said, "is in her still." And, therefore, putting out those who filled the house with the noise of their vain lamentations, He entered in, He took what appeared to be the dead hand of the child, and, looking upon her, He commanded her mentally to arise; and the moment that His hand touched her her eyes, opening, saw the light again, her hands quickened into life, the warm blood throbbed around her reviving heart, and she arose in the fulness of her health and strength, restored by the touch of the hand of the Lord.

But, O dearly beloved! how different was the life to which she now rose to that which she enjoyed before—how blessedly different was the new life upon which she entered to that from which she appeared to have bade adieu by death! She had lived the years of her youth and maidenhood in joy; yet she had never known the Lord God; she had never seen the face of God, she had never heard His voice, nor felt the touch of His hand. But now, when she opens her eyes to her restored life, the very first object that she sees is the face of the Lord Jesus Christ; and the moment that the glance of her eyes rested upon Him, that moment a divine faith sprang up within her soul, and she exclaimed with the prophet: "*Vidi Dominum*," "I have seen the Lord with my eyes, I have beheld my Saviour." She felt the touch of His hand as it grasped hers, and a thrill of divine love penetrated her heart, and she found the object of her love in the divine Person of our divine Lord Jesus Christ; a new knowledge entered her mind, a new passion entered her heart; and that knowledge and that divine love became the very substance of the happy life which the Son of God restored to her in that hour. In vain would any other hand have touched her save His; in vain would any other voice have spoken to her save His.

That young girl lying there—not dead, yet apparently dead, and declared by all men to be dead; not dead, though dead to others yet only sleeping in the sight of the Lord—was a symbol and a type of our human nature. Gifted by Almighty God in its first creation with a glorious life—a life described to us in Scripture as a life of knowledge, for the unfallen man knew all things; as a life of empire, for unto the hands of unfallen man God gave the earth and the fulness thereof; as a life of immortality, for no sentence of death was yet recorded against him; as a life of sanctity, for the graces of God were upon him, and his conversation was with the Most High—thus gifted,

… man lived a glorious life till there came upon him a fatal sickness and the death-stroke of sin. Then all the supernatural was lost, the divine knowledge faded slowly away; truth was diminished amongst the sons of men, as the light faded slowly with the sickness away from out the eyes of the young maiden; strength and power were lost to him, and his hands fell powerless by his side; ignorance and error, darkness and idolatry settled in upon his mind; the slavery of sin came upon his will and the powerlessness of sin came upon his hands. In vain did philosophers age after age prescribe for the darkness of that intelligence and for the weakness of that enslaved will. In vain did earthly physicians come with their remedies of earthly knowledge and of mere human civilization. They could not raise the apparent dead. Yet the nature was not dead, it was only sleeping—the long sleep of four thousand years—awaiting the quickening voice of its Saviour and the touch of His God-like hand.

He came. He breathed upon the face of that dead nature, and out of the breath of His lips, out of the creative sound of his voice, light came into those darkened eyes, and they beamed again by divine faith and looked upon the face of their Saviour; love came into that long degraded and pulseless heart—the first love returned, the love long forgotten, the pure love of God. Grace came to quicken those dried bones, dried up from the furnace-fire of passion and of sin, and where sin abounded grace came to abound still more; and under the presence of our divine Lord, at the touch of His hand, at the sound of His voice, our human nature arose to something even greater and grander than that from which it fell in Adam. For from the primeval innocence of the unfallen Adam it arose to the infinitely higher grandeur of personal union with the Son of God, who seated it upon the throne on his Father's right hand in heaven.

Moreover, that young maiden, lying there apparently dead, but only sleeping, is also symbolical of the human soul, created by Almighty God for such grand and holy purposes—for the life of knowledge, of love, of perfect, of true freedom as a child of God; created by Almighty God with such noble powers—with the eye of knowledge penetrating and mastering all the laws and all the mysterious powers which govern this world, but looking far higher, and with the eye of faith penetrating the clouds and realizing the unseen God; with the power of love enduring in its human form, because of its chastity and its fidelity, worthy even in its human form to be associated with grace, made the channel of divine influences, and consequently consecrated by the sacramental seal of marriage—worthy even in its human form to typify that highest of unions, the espousal of the Son of God with His Church; and capable of far higher flights of love—capable of the strong divine love of which God the Holy Ghost tells us that it is powerful and strong as death—capable of the love of a life-long consecration—capable of divine love so pure as to make man upon this earth even as an angel of God; so powerful as to be able easily not only to restrain, but almost to annihilate the strong and terrible passions of a nature which though healed is still corrupt; gifted by the Almighty God with a freedom the most perfect, a freedom which is a reflection of the very action of God Himself, which is essential and eternal freedom, a freedom capable of the noblest resolves and of the mightiest sacrifices under the light of faith and under the strong impulse of divine charity.

Such are the powers, dearly beloved, with which Almighty God endows the human soul. But, like the maiden sleeping, as recorded in the Gospel, these powers lie dormant in the soul of man. The power of knowledge is there—the craving for knowledge may be there; yet that power may never develop itself unless the hand of the educator be there to lead the child on from light unto light. The power of love—the holiest in its human form, the holiest in its divine form—is there, yet that power will never develop itself into the grandeur of the higher human, much less divine, love, unless the hand of the educator be there to point out the eternal laws and the high principles which should govern the heart and the affections of man ; that power will only develop itself into the brutal development of selfish sensuality, unless the hand of the educator be there. Freedom of will is there ; but that freedom is, perhaps, the very first attribute of the soul that will be crushed and destroyed by the overmastering slavery of the passions to which it falls the first victim, unless the hand of the educator be there to develop that freedom, and to preserve its integrity by teaching the true and beautiful, which is God.

And now as the very first necessity of man is to live— as the very first and absolute necessity of that young girl in the Gospel was to have her life restored to her, which the vain lamentations of those mourners never would have given back—so, dearly beloved, the very first necessity of the soul of man is to develop its power by education. Deprive it of all instruction, deprive it of education, leave it untouched and undeveloped—the eyes are there, but they shall never open to the light ; the heart is there, but it shall never feel one throb or impulse of holy love ; the will was there, but it has almost utterly perished, under the mastery and the enslaving influences of the sinful passions. Leave that soul untouched by education ; leave it utterly uninstructed, and follow the process of life as developed in the child. The body grows apace with its passions, with its instincts, with base, brutal inclinations, and corrupt nature cries loudly for its food of sin. The eye beholds the lurking mystery of iniquity in all things, the taste seeks for its own gratification, even in the most beastly indulgence ; every sense of the body, matured to its action by years, cries out for its own enjoyment. The soul, meantime, remains in the grown man, not growing with his growth, not developing with his development ; it remains an embryo of all that was great, an infant that has never learned to think and speak, to use its members, to use its powers, an infant spirit in the body of a gigantic man— gigantic in all the beastly and inferior proportions of his nature, a giant of iniquity, a giant of dishonesty, a giant of impurity and sensuality of every kind ; and why ? Because the body becomes all the more developed in its passionate and evil inclinations from the absolute want of the corresponding development of soul. Oh ! there are passions, there are brutalities sufficient to make the greatest criminal that ever cursed the earth, and not a single ray of knowledge to guide him in the management of those passions, no vivifying hope for the future, no restraining power, no generous impulse to anything high, unselfish, or holy ; no regrets for sin in the past, no hope for the future, no consolation in his sorrow, no soothing remembrance even in the blank and vacant halls of his memory. Man is worse than the mere animal, because all that is divine and spiritual in him has been allowed to perish, and nothing but the mere brute has been developed.

Such is man without education. He is the natural enemy of his fellow-man. For all human society is based upon an intercommunication of intelligence, of mind with mind, intellect with intellect, and the reason why there is no such state as society amongst inferior animals is because they have no intellect, they cannot communicate one with another, they have no intelligence, and therefore each one leads its own mute and isolated existence, concentrated upon its own individuality, and in the fulfilment of nature's laws. But nature has imposed no such strong laws, no such unvarying instincts upon man, because man is to be governed not merely as an individual but as a member of society, by communicating intellectually with his fellow-man. Now, the man who is utterly uninstructed is incapable of such intellectual communication. Consequently he is flung back upon his solitary self, in which he finds so little that is good, so little that is holy, that the very idea of goodness and holiness is a stranger to him ; and the greatest criminal on the face of the earth, the greatest enemy to human society, is the man who is utterly and entirely ignorant.

How shall we heal him ? There is the patient before

us. Who shall heal him? Shall we, like the father of the girl in this day's Gospel, call in the mere human physician and ask him: "Can you give life to this seeming death? The soul is not dead but sleepeth. Arouse its dormant powers, bring forth its hidden faculties, open them to the glorious light of knowledge! Can you do this? Can you bring out a man where now there is only a child? He has not yet grown into that giant of iniquity which he is sure to become. He has not yet grown into that mere brute which he is sure to, if left in utter ignorance. Body and soul are alike still young, still in their infant state. Will you bring them out; will you bring them to the fulness of their being?" And the world answers: "Oh! yes. I will educate the child. I will bring him to the fulness of his manhood. I will make a man of him. I will give him all knowledge that is necessary for him." The world says this to-day with unusual confidence. And the Church stands up and says to the world: "You cannot do it. Without the element of religion largely blended in with your education, without the element of divine truth and divine grace going hand in hand with all that you teach of worldly knowledge, I tell you you never can educate the man in the child."

And here it is, dearly-beloved brethren, that the great contest begins which is raging all over the world to-day in every land and in every clime—the Church of God on one side crying out: "Let me get to the children," and the world on the other hand saying: "I will educate them; do you stand aside, stand aside!" The world seems to say to the Church of God in this our day: "Stand aside! There was a time when you were able to educate the world, yet infant in its civilization. To-day it has outgrown you; the child has grown to be a man; he is emancipated from his mother." "Stand aside, then," the world seems to say, as it drives the Jesuit from his college and closes up seminaries of learning which were held and supported by the Catholic Church in many lands. As school after school was closed, a standard is unfurled, and floats over every city in the world to-day, with these words upon it: "Education without religion! Education without God! Education confining itself to the wide horizon of human knowledge!" There is the great heresy of to-day, with which the Church of God is contending with might and main. But, dearly beloved, the Church has never been afraid of investigation and argument. The Church of God calls upon her children for a reasonable service, for a loyalty founded not upon ignorance, but upon a thorough knowledge of the subject and investigation of the truth. Which of these two is right: the world, that says, "I can make the child a man for every purpose," or the Church, that says, "You cannot do it without me"?

First of all, what is this world that so proudly claims to-day, in the form of the state or in the form of some societies or corporations—what is this world that so proudly claims the primacy in all knowledge, primacy in all wisdom, and consequently the right to educate the people and their children independent of and without connection with the Catholic Church? What is this world? For fifteen hundred years of its first Christianity this world was content to sit down and to learn at the feet of the Church. In those days there was no talk of separation of education from religion. In those days the monk or the priest was the schoolmaster as well as the minister of religion all the world over, and men were content to be taught by him. The Church found the world plunged in the worst form of barbarism. She found the world in all the civilization of the ancient time, crowned with worldly wisdom, yet in its wisdom not knowing God; and that very Augustan era which beheld the birth of our Divine Lord into this world and the foundation of His Church, although it was the brightest and most civilized epoch recorded in ancient history, it was at the same time degraded by crimes so infamous that the apostle will not trust himself to name them, and by excesses so terrible that the world itself was unable to bear the burden of its own sins. Then came the disruption of the Roman Empire—the bursting of that mighty empire, inflated with pride of power and with sin, and stained with the blood of countless martyrs of God. On the disruption of that empire came private chaos and barbarism, from which the world has emerged slowly and by the action of centuries; and the Church of God was called upon as the only existing power in the world to do in a few centuries what men had taken, by their own efforts, four thousand years to accomplish so imperfectly.

She began her work of civilization; she brought the nations out from chaos and darkness to order and into light; she established the principles of right and justice, and obedience to law. She established nations and kingdoms. She led the world on to that high point of civilization and human refinement at which it had arrived at the very moment when the signal for revolt was given and human intelligence broke loose from the Church of God. Three hundred years have now passed since Martin Luther declared that the intelligence of man should no longer be held in obedience to the Catholic Church, for men had now a sufficient knowledge to institute a philosophy for themselves, to choose their own theology, to establish their own principles of politics and of government; and for three hundred years they have tried their hand at this mighty experiment. Let us see what the results are.

The results are to-day, at the close of the nineteenth century, that the work of intellectual emancipation, as it is called, has produced its fruits; men boast of the glorious work which they have done; men found upon it their claim to educate the whole world, and to tell the Church of God to stand aside! But let us see, by examining briefly for a moment, what these boasted fruits are. In speculative philosophy as long as the world was under the guidance of the Catholic Church, in her schools and universities, philosophy—speculative philosophy—led up through every light of human knowledge, and brought man to seek the origin of his being in the action of the creative hand of God, and in the inspiration of a spiritual and immortal soul from the very mouth of God into him.

Oh! how grand was that philosophy which taught man the true nobility of his being by tracing his origin to God, which taught man the obligation of every highest virtue by showing him that he was a divine image, and that that image should be brought out in him. Now, for three hundred years they have speculated on this great question, and at length the new evangelist of the nineteenth century mounts into the pulpit of modern philosophy and gravely tells the learned world that man is nothing but the development of an ape, that his ancestor was a monkey—that he is but the image of an improved ape, and not at all the image of God! Oh! degradation of thought and of mind, following, and following justly, upon that pride of intellect that broke loose from the Church of God. And those men who advocate this theory—the men who come before us, on their own showing, as but a better kind of ape—they ask us Christians to hand over our children to them to be educated by them and taught the observance of the fourth commandment—" Honor thy father and thy mother "—by being told that that father and that mother are one step nearer the ape than the child who is commanded to honor them! In moral philosophy what have their speculations brought them to ?

They have brought them to the last development of the principle of private judgment in morals, to a return to the worst form of the polygamy of by-gone times, and the consecration of the principle that man's passions are not to be controlled, or that they are to find their fulfilment in the utter trampling out of every light of Christianity, and of grace, and of godliness! What are their principles of government ? They have arrived at this sage principle, that it is no longer the justice, that it is no longer the truth, that it is no longer the sanctity of a cause that is to uphold it ; but that brute force—the force of the stronger —is the one justifying principle of government in this our day ! And how have the people responded who have been educated in this school ? They tell the governors who represent brute force that if such be their idea of government, the people's idea of obedience is revolution, and the upsetting of all authority. And to this intellectual and spiritual chaos they have brought the world; nations know not what their future may be; every nation and every man must guard his own by the brutal strong arm and sheer force of the sword. Is there anything in the issues either of their legislation, which has demolished the sanctity and fidelity of marriage by introducing divorce; in their principles of government, which have annihilated justice and substituted force; in their principles of morality, which have gone back to seek their justification in that which the Lord Himself declared was only permitted on account of hardness of heart; or in their speculative theology, that drags man down from every thought of God as his Creator, and makes him look to his ancestral ape ?

Is there anything in all this to command our respect or admiration ? Is there anything to justify those impious men—impious in their pride, for they tell the Church of God they have no longer any need of her influence, grace, or sanctity—in their demand to be entrusted with the work of education? But are they able to bring out the man in the child ? Even if their principles were sound, even if they were guiltless of these grave charges of intellectual imbecility and degradation, of spiritual and moral crookedness which I have brought home to them; even if their principles were sound, would they still, as mere earthly teachers of men in this world, be able to bring out the man in the child ? I answer, No! Every human soul that is to be educated, every child that is to be instructed, has two sets of powers within him, both of which must be brought forth and developed equally. There are the intellectual powers—the mind which can be taught, which requires to be taught, which is capable of receiving every form of human knowledge, and the higher forms of divine knowledge. But together with that mind there is the heart of the child, which must be taught how to love and whom to love. There is the will of the child, the centre and source of his moral life, the will upon which depends whether that child will grow into a good, virtuous, unselfish man, or a monster of vice. Now, the world, in its training and education, does not even pretend to deal either with the heart or with the will of the child, only with its intellect. It does not pretend to form his heart to any higher love than that of this earth. It does not pretend to be able to communicate to him one single restraining influence which will coerce his passions, which will purify his life. Nay, it refuses to open before him even the vision of God awaiting in judgment with His rewards and His punishment as the issue of this life.

Then what education can it give? It can make an intellectual monster. For remember, dearly beloved, that being is a monster any one of whose parts or members is unduly developed whilst the others remain without any development whatever. That man is a monster whose head grows to the full size of a man's head and the rest of his body remains as an infant, and that soul is an intellectual monster which is crowded with every species of knowledge without a single accompanying grace, a single restraining influence or power to moralize and spiritualize life. They say, to be sure: "Oh! give him knowledge, and knowledge will bring with it principles that will make him a good man." I deny it. I appeal to history. Who were the very worst men the history of the world tells us of? Were they not men pre-eminent for knowledge and for intellectual acquirements? A great living authority has said, and said truly: "Quarry the granite rock with razors, or moor the vessel with thread of silk. Then may you hope with such delicate instruments of human knowledge and human wisdom to restrain those great giants, the passion and the pride of man." That passion and pride of man, the corruption of his depraved heart, the selfishness of his fallen being, the proneness to everything that is evil, that natural distaste of every restraint that is good—ah! these only can be touched and remedied by the powerful hand of religion—a hand that will purify the young soul and preserve it in its baptismal graces, a hand that will stamp upon the young heart, while that heart, yet young, is capable of receiving the impression, the divine image of God, who became man for love, and for the purity of our race died upon a cross. That hand that can build up a grand edifice of faith, and of divine and highest knowledge, upon the foundation of hope, which it opens before the young eye, speaking to the child of heaven almost before he knows anything of earth—upon this foundation builds up a grand edifice of divine charity, making the young man pure and chaste as a virgin; making the servant honest as if that which was in his hands were his own, not his master's; making the language of the young man pure as that of the consecrated priest who speaks to God; making the reliable friend who will not lead his friend into misfortune or to sin; making the strong, faithful, chaste husband and holy wife, who shall be the father and mother of a future better and more perfect people. Religion alone can do this. Religion entering into the school with the child, the angel of divine knowledge unfolding the mysteries while the angel of human knowledge unfolds the things of earth—the angel of divine grace sending the sacramental influences into that young soul, teaching the secret of divine horror and hatred of sin and of everything unworthy of man, teaching it the divine instinct of supernatural sorrow for sin, teaching it humility that bows down before God and before God's authorities, divine and human, upon this earth. Religion alone can do this. She must be let into the school with the child. If she is told to stand outside and let the mere genius of human knowledge itself play upon the intellect, in a short time the knowledge that was thus acquired will be turned into an instrument and means of evil.

And now tell me, you fathers and mothers, are you prepared to receive your children from the hands of such educators and instructors—to receive them highly gifted and splendidly endowed? Filled with every branch of human knowledge and every accomplishment, the brightest and the most highly cultivated, they come home to you only to sneer at your ignorance, if you are not as learned as they; without a single element of reverence, without a single element of obedience, or of submission to your word. Then, as their character develops under your astonished eye, you find that the young man is without purity, that the young maiden's modesty is but a veil thrown over corruption. You find that no principle of honesty or honor is there, when honesty or honor would interfere with the enjoyment of selfishness. You find that no principle of divine simplicity, or of child-like obedience is there— scarcely a recognition of God's existence and no practical recognition at all of the obligation of God's law; no sacramental influence, and no purifying grace. Tell me, if the child of any one amongst you return to you thus, would not you say that you received a monster into your house, and curse the day when you gave him to such teachers? And yet such is all that this world can make of him, unless the world is prepared to shake hands with the Church of God on the great question of education, to allow the graces of faith, of purity, and everything that is in the Church's hands to give to go hand in hand for the child with every element of temporal education.

But our sage philosophers, our legislators, our fathers of chaos of the nineteenth century, our bearded fathers of intellectual and spiritual confusion, charge the Catholic Church that in her system of education she gives too much to God and too little to man—that she teaches the child too much about his religion and not enough about the things of this world. To the first part of the accusation I have nothing to say. We all know a man cannot be taught too much concerning God, that a man cannot be made too religious; but in making him all that God created him to be, in making him a true, pure, and self-restraining Christian, I ask, does the Catholic Church sacrifice one iota of temporal advantage, or temporal and worldly education? I appeal to her history. She taught the world for nine hundred years in great part. Where have greater or brighter geniuses ever been seen? Where has the mind of man ever been carried to a higher point of human culture than in the halls and colleges and universities of the Catholic Church? Who were the greatest inventors? Were they not her children? Who was the astronomer upon whose learning and vast knowledge modern science has built up its present glorious structure? He was a humble priest, saying Mass at the altars of the Catholic Church. And to-day those who are charged by the state with the supervision of our national education have the honesty and truthfulness to recall and to confess that the very best schools in this land are the schools conducted by our consecrated monks and holy nuns, that the children in those schools receive quite as much of this world's knowledge, and more, than in the schools in which religion receives only a secondary place, if a place at all.

Nay, more, that whilst they are thus taught everything this world demands of them, they receive that unknown power that reveals itself even before the eyes of the misbeliever in the purity and modesty beaming in the eyes of the boy and the young maiden, in the gentle, natural, inborn courtesy brought forth from them and in them; on the principle of divine humility, and of imitation of a God made humble and lowly for the love of His fellow-man. Therefore the Church of God, the Catholic Church, does not yield one inch, either in her primary or her superior education—not one inch does she yield to any worldling in zeal for human knowledge, in capacity for imparting it, or in the glorious results her schools are able to bring forth; and here she is able to vie with the world, even though that world condemns her.

And now it is for this great cause that I address you to-day. It is for the cause of education—not of a grovelling, imperfect education—not of an education of this faculty or that, to the exclusion of the rest, but of the education of the children of this town, of this parish—the education of your own children in every sense of the word, that they may have that knowledge, that human knowledge, that human instruction which will fit them to take their place in the ranks of human society, perhaps to better themselves at home or in foreign lands, that they may bring with them, wherever they go, the inestimable boon of a matured and enlightened intelligence—that which will enable them to vindicate both at home and abroad that attribute of intellectual genius, of intellectual power which, thank God! has ever been one of the distinguishing marks and features of our Irish race. For amongst the human endowments that Almighty God gave us with lavish hand —perhaps in reward for and to counterbalance the many good things which we lost—He showered upon His own faithful Irish people the gift and principle of an intelligence grand, shrewd, keen, and penetrating. When we consider the laws which made education penal and enforced ignorance upon our fathers who have gone before us, it is plain that if they had not bright intelligence, capable of drawing great results from few causes and little application, we, their children, to-day would be a generation of savages, the most barbarous upon the earth, instead of being what we are, able to hold our own in every walk of intellectual knowledge and of improvement. I call upon you by your contributions and your zeal to-day to give to the children of this town and this parish—to give to your own children—that far greater and higher boon than that of mere human knowledge, that wherever they go, at home or abroad, they may illustrate it in themselves and spread it by the power of their example as a people of traditional faith, of traditional purity of life, of traditional obedience to the Church, which is the most sacred inheritance that the Catholic people of Ireland to-day have received from our martyred fathers who went before us.

They had little to leave us. They lost their all for God. But they left us a faith which no power on earth could conquer; they left us an altar which no power on earth could pull down and utterly destroy in the land. Where the material altar disappeared, an altar was built up in every Catholic heart and in every Catholic home in Ireland. They left us a faith which they sealed with their blood and handed down as a most precious inheritance to their children, a faith which has made the Irish name at home and abroad symbolical of all that is highest and grandest and holiest in Catholicity. They left us purity, which in our Irish women became the glory and the splendor of our own afflicted land, and made our women to be the admiration of the whole world wherever they went. For wherever the daughter of Ireland goes, full of divine faith and full of divine love, she presents to the eyes of an unbelieving world that image and that attribute of Mary in which the tenderest Heart that ever throbbed was united to the purest soul and body that ever were sent upon the earth. They left us the tradition of our manly chastity and purity, which has preserved this most ancient race in a strange integrity, vitality, and strength of mind and body, which has enabled us, wherever we have gone in our various paths of emigration, even to the ends of the earth, to show signs and leave traces of our undying strength and energy in the mighty works which mark the exodus of the Irish people in every land.

And it is for all this I call upon you to-day. If you wish your children to be worthy of their martyred forefathers, to be worthy of their national traditions, to be worthy of that grace and blessing which has followed their fathers before them through every vicissitude, sanctifying every sorrow, and brightening still more every joy; if you would make them to be worthy of the Church of God which has always loved them, as it loved their fathers before them, who devoted themselves to it as holy priests and martyred bishops; if you wish to preserve all that makes Ireland dear to us, and that makes us dear to the Church of God, and through her to our Divine Lord, you must ensure to the Catholic youth in this blessed land of Ireland a true, sound Catholic, and, at the same time, most perfect human, education. For this do I plead; for the community that represents here this sacred principle ; for the men who are contented to live upon the barest pittance with which your charity will supply them, provided that you will enable them to continue their glorious work, to make your children who are daily received into their schools all that God, all that the Church, all that their motherland would wish them to be—perfect men and perfect Christians. I leave the cause, I leave the monks, I leave the schools, I leave the children now in your hands ; and with all my heart and soul I pray that God may send down upon you the angel of His enlightened mercy, that you may be made zealous for those little ones in whom Christ our Lord is to grow, to live, to suffer perhaps, but to rise also into everlasting glory.

The Music of the Church.

This sermon was delivered by Father Burke in St. Fintan's Church, Mountrath, Ireland, Sunday, July 8, 1877, on the occasion of the opening of a new organ. It abounds in poetic passages, and is altogether one of the most charming and interesting of the discourses in this volume.

"Praise ye the Lord in His holy places; praise ye Him in the firmament of His power. Praise ye Him for His mighty acts; praise ye Him according to the multitude of His greatness. Praise Him with sound of trumpet; praise Him with psaltery and harp. Praise Him with timbrel and choir; praise Him with strings and organs. Praise Him on high-sounding cymbals; praise Him on cymbals of joy. Let every spirit praise the Lord."

THESE are the words that form the 150th, the last of the inspired psalms of David. Dearly beloved, this duty and obligation of high-sounding and solemn praise the Almighty God laid upon all creation, simply because He is the Creator of all things; for the Holy Ghost tells us that all things unto the end of time shall be resonant of the praise of Him who made them. Nor can Almighty God create, devise for Himself any other motive, nor was it possible that anything that was created should have been made for any other purpose than the praise of the eternal God; for thus God tells us that He made all things for Himself and that all things may praise Him. And what manner of praise is this which the Almighty God demands from all His creatures? It is, my dearly beloved, a solemn, highsounding, resonant voice of praise, a voice that is never to be silent, a voice which is never to be weary in the burden of its perennial thanksgiving. And in the day that God created first the angels in heaven, the moment that the first of those glorious spirits sprang into existence at the commanding and creating voice of God, that moment he took up the song of praise which is never to die nor fade away from his immortal lips. And then as the nine choirs of God's angels were formed around Him the silence of God's awful eternity was broken by the glorious hymn begun in heaven: "Holy, holy, holy, to the Lord God of Sabaoth; the heavens and the earth are full of Thy glory." Thus the voice, the living voice of heaven began in praise, until the very atmosphere of God's upper heaven resolved itself into song, so that the blessed Saint Hildegarde, in her vision of heaven, tells us: "I beheld and I heard, and the air was music." Forth from the throne of God came the voice of the higher angels; forth from the four-and-twenty elders harping upon their harps of gold came the glorious rolling of praise; forth from those high seraphim and cherubim, those upper spirits who are nearer to God, came the exclamation of joyful praise; forth from archangel and angel, principalities and powers, each in his own sphere, came the commanding note of praise, and all heaven seemed as if it was one very atmosphere of music around the great throne of the eternal God. This is the vision of the saints when they were lifted up to behold how things are in the invisible world.

Then, dearly beloved, the Almighty God created this lower and material creation. After the lapse of ages, perhaps, unknown to man, the visible world and the universe sprang forth, from out the chaos of nothing that preceded it, at the command of God. God stood upon the virgin threshold of His own bright kingdom, and He looked out into the mightiness of space, into the eternal darkness of space that had never yet been illumined by a ray of light, where all was nothing, and God said, "Let there be light"; and the moment these words came from His lips a sun sprang up in that dark void and beamed forth light and illumination unto all things. Countless thousands and millions of glorious stars and planets sprang out of nothingness, and each, catching from the great centre, the sun, its own portion of light, spread its silvery radiance around him, and they all began to move each in its own orbit in that glorious firmament the contemplation of which is the highest study of man. But the moment that sun began to shine, the moment the moon caught up her nocturnal light and entered into her office, the moment the stars began to move in their orbit, that moment was heard, according to the philosophy of the ancient world, "the harmony of the spheres" of God; the moment a celestial voice was made resonant through the movements of those great bodies they moved to the music of the harmony of the mind of God. All the higher nature took up its lesson in praise; the heavens began to tell the glory of God, and the firmament to proclaim in most melodious accents the work of His hands and of His power. Then did God turn to the material creation, and He said: "Let the earth be made and produce every green thing"; and at the moment that this word came from the almighty lips of God, that moment this earth, which was *inanis et vacuus*, empty and void, was covered with the beauty of its verdure, and every tree blossomed into the mid-summer of new life, and every fruit-bearing tree bowed down before God, paying the homage of its fulness. Even this act took place to the music of God's divine will; the very leaves which burst forth upon the newly-created beech and oak tree crept into existence to the music of praise. This earth took up its portion and its song in the great choir of creation, and every breath of air—from the softest murmur, through the howling of the midnight storm that sweeps over the troubled ocean, to the rolling of those awful storms of the night that lift up the huge ship and send her down, with all who are in her, unto the depths of the sea—all, all speak of God. It is the music of nature, it is the rolling voice of the melody of a divine purpose and a divine will which finds expression in every element of God's creation. And therefore, when all this is praise—every creature in its own way, in its own sphere, according to its own capacity, is praising the Lord—the things inanimate are praising Him inanimately yet truly ; the things that live praise Him with living voice, yet unconsciously ; the things that live and feel and understand are called upon to praise Him with a higher voice, the voice of reason, the voice of adoration, and the glorious melody of faith.

If the birds upon the trees could speak, the nightingale charming the dark solitudes of night would tell us that he was singing his night song of praise to God. The lark takes up his lauds in the early morning, and, shaking the dew from his active wings, soars aloft, gathering his song together as he goes, and charming the ear of the early-rising husbandman as he watches the bird rising from the meadow, and hears him gathering his song together, stronger still, as if the little bird were conscious he was coming nearer to the throne of Him who made him, until at length, lost in the ambition of his flight, his form is no longer seen in the air, but he who watches him can catch a note or two of the resonant singer that, in mid-air, is throwing his voice to God, until with wearied wing does he descend again to find his nest in the meadow; but even to the last moment he is scattering around him the broken fragments of the song that was so strong. And thus all nature is performing its office, and with its highest voice is, in its own way, praising the Lord God, and it was for this all things were made ; and therefore the Scripture says : "O Lord! Thou hast made this world, and all things are full of Thy praise."

If such, dearly beloved, be the action of God in the order of nature, we can easily imagine how grand must the praise be, how splendid the song of thanksgiving, that the Almighty God expects to hear from our hearts and from our voices in the higher order of divine grace. Not satisfied with the hymning of His angelic choirs, God wished to create, on this earth, man to His own image, to His own likeness. And to that man He gave powers of mind and of voice—of mind that God might be known, acknowledged, and adored ; and of voice that man might spend himself in the days of his unhappy life in the praise of the Lord God, his Creator. Behold, then, the purpose for which Almighty God created us, that we might know, that we might appreciate, His uncreated and infinite beauty; that we might love Him with all the power of love which He has given us in these hearts of ours; and that the mind that knows Him and the heart that loves Him might find a vent and power of expression of the praise and adoration that goes forth from the willing and loving lips. Therefore it is that as soon as man was created Almighty God imposed upon him the burden of praise. "Praise ye the Lord, O ye sons of men; praise him in all places, praise him at all times." "Let thy mouth," says the Holy Ghost, "be filled at all times with the praise of thy God." Therefore, my beloved, as soon as man was created another voice was added to the choir of universal harmony and praise. But, oh! how distinct, how marked is this new note in the creation of God. God in heaven from His angels was getting pure spiritual praise; God on earth from his inferior creation was only receiving the necessary tribute of unconscious adoration and glory; but now another voice is added to this choir—it is not the voice of a pure spirit, for man is not an angel; it is not the voice of unconscious adoration, for man knows, feels, and appreciates the objects which fill his mouth and his heart with praise. Therefore, midway between the angels in heaven and all material creation upon earth—midway amongst these is the choir of humanity that takes up its glorious song, and in that voice of faithful praise and of constant tuneful adoration heaven and earth unite and are blended together in the harmony of divine praise and the service of God.

This is true of all men from the very necessity of their being, from the very composition of their nature. This was true from the beginning. But, O my beloved! if this was true of all times and of all classes and societies of men, how much more true is it not of that living Church that Christ our Lord established upon this earth to perpetuate His praise, the knowledge of His name, and the adoration of His divine, uncreated majesty—of that Church which He created that she might not only preach His word and make His name known to all the nations, but that she might in her choirs express every emotion of love, of joy, of ecstasy, of profoundest sorrow, every emotion that springs from faith, and express it in the solemn language of song! Hence it is that Almighty God, as soon as He undertook on earth to found a Church, founded it to the note of music. The pagans of old, the philosophers of Greece and of Rome, great statesmen of the ancient times, whenever a great temple or a great public edifice was to be built, laid the foundation stone, raised the walls, and crowned the edifice with its last touch of beauty, but all, all to the accompaniment of sweetest song and music. Sackbut and psalter were there, timbrel and trumpet were there; and so at the foundation as at the dedication of the Temple of Jerusalem all was done to the harmony of music. And when we behold the Son of God laying the foundation stone of His Church on that tremendous night when He ordained His priesthood in that upper hall of Jerusalem, when He gave them the mystic power of evocation of the Eternal in the sacrifice of the Mass, when he gave them jurisdiction of the word of authority, saying to them: "As the Father sent me, so do I send you"—all this was done to the sound of music, for the evangelist expressly tells us that whilst all this was going on, it was interrupted from time to time with the singing of hymns and it closed with music. *Et hymno dicto*—and having sung a hymn, the Lord God stood up and went forth from that upper hall of Jerusalem to begin His passion and his sorrows in the garden of Gethsemani, and that voice of praise that He put upon the lips of His Church was never to die. This was the word of God: "The word of praise, the resonant voice of song that I have put on thy lips, shall never depart from thy lips or from the lips of thy seed after thee, henceforth and for all eternity, says the Lord God." Hence what do we find, my dearly beloved? We find that the instinct of praise, and, indeed, of vocal praise, of sweet, musical, melodious praise, began with the very life of the Holy Church of Jesus Christ.

For three hundred years that Church of God was persecuted, and she had to hide her fair head in the catacombs and caves of the earth. The blood of her children was flowing everywhere; the cry of the nations was, *Christiani ad leones*—" Get us Christians, that we may cast them to the wild beasts." The highest, bravest, and the noblest were destroyed wherever they were found, if only they professed the name and religion of Christ. Yet in the midst of those very persecutions the Church night and day was engaged in her song of praise. Under the ground of that proud imperial city of Rome, under its palaces and public places, under its streets and its imperial thoroughfares, ran corridors and great, vast spaces that were dug out in the earth; they were called catacombs. There they are to this day, miles and miles of passages underground; and for what first purposes they were constructed or excavated no man can tell. But there the Christians were accustomed to hide, and there they were accustomed to pay their devotions to God. And we read that whilst their pagan persecutors were seeking for them everywhere, whilst they were going on their mission of blood through the streets of Rome, every now and then they stopped electrified, for it seemed as if there was music in the air, and it seemed as if the music came up from the very bowels of the earth. Their pagan ears were touched; their cruel eyes were melted to tears; their fierce, sensual souls were shaken and subdued within them. It seemed as if new gods had come from Olympus, and they were all like Apollo with his lyre. Whence came that music, whence came that glorious blending of voices? With the manly chords of a Valerian or a Damasus there came intermingled the sweet, heavenly notes of a Cecilia or an Agnes. These voices came from the catacombs. It was our Christian forefathers carrying out in that darkest day of persecution and blood the mission of the Holy Church of God, and paying to God the tribute of their praise in the office of song. When that persecution ceased those choirs that had hitherto sung deep in the catacombs of Rome came forth; and when the pagan world beheld the troops of Christians coming forth—of holy confessors, of meek and most pure maidens, of aged men grown old and venerable in the period of their sanctity, of little children reddened with their baptismal graces—when this great troop came forth from the bowels of the earth, and walked the earth proclaiming aloud the name of Christ, then throughout the world there sprang up on every side choirs of music—choirs of music the most delicious, the most melodious that ever was heard. Nay, more, it may be said, as far as we know of the traditions of the pagan world, that they had no music, and that their every science and art seem to have sprung from the inspiration of Christianity on the mind and voice of man. Then throughout the whole Christian world, wherever the Church preached truth and converted a people, her very first act was to establish in the midst of that people an undying, perennial voice of melodious praise.

The monks filled the deserts and made the desert air resonant with the vocal choirs of God; the consecrated virgins in every city and every land were gathered together in their cloisters, and the keynote of that divine, undying song of the Church's praise in her office, set to the glorious Gregorian tones that came from out the heart of one of her greatest popes—that keynote throbbed all through the very air. Here, only four hundred years after the day of Calvary, Patrick came; he came into this land of ours, and he came not only to bring the light of divine truth, not only to plant the banner of that faith, which banner has never been lowered by the Irish nation, but he also came to establish the tuneful choirs of praise and thanksgiving to the Lord. And among the various parts of Ireland that he evangelized, one of the very first and one of the most famous places where the song of praise began is in the very midst of you and in your diocese. Under the oaks of Kildare, Bridget, the consecrated virgin, gathered her virgin sisters around her; and just as they lit a fire the flame of which was not for centuries to be permitted to expire, just as they lit up lamps which, like wise and pure virgins, they ever kept replenished and trimmed and bright and burning before their Lord, so in like manner they began that voice of praise and adoration, set to musical notes in their office, which for many a year, ay, for many a hundred years, even when the air was filled with the sounds of battle and strife, still spread the voice of praise around the hillsides and villages of favored Kildare.

After a time persecution imposed silence upon the tuneful voice of Ireland. After a time, and whilst the choirs of Ireland's monks and nuns were still sustaining their glorious burden of harmonious praise, there came the voice of a persecutor, and there came a hand wielding a sword, and there came a cloud darkened with blood, and it burst over the nation, and the voice said: "Be silent; let the praise of God no longer resound in this land"; and the sword said: "I will put an end to every voice that praises Him." The cloud burst, and the whole land was deluged once more with persecution and blood. The nuns were driven once more from their choirs and cloisters, the holy monks were driven from their cells and churches, the bishop from his cathedral, the parish priest from his church, and the people were left desolate. A desolation seemed to fall upon Ireland which fell upon Jerusalem in the sad day when the prophet came and said: "The young man no longer sings in the choir, the aged man is no longer found in the gate of the city, the people are silent, the praise of God is no longer heard amongst them." And thus for two hundred years and more Ireland was silent; the grand, harmonious voice that was heard in every land for ages, leading wherever glorious melody was required for God, leading every choir that harped and sang to His praise—that glorious voice was silent, and "the mother of sweet singers," as well as of saints and scholars, sat down in the midst of her bleeding people, and there kept

silence over what seemed destined to be the grave of her
faith.

But the silence was only that of the tongue; the heart
was musical as ever to God. The voice of praise ceased to
go forth to the pealing accompaniment of harp or of organ;
but the voice of praise went forth from the silent yet faithful heart. The voice of praise was heard in the murmur of
prayer in every cottage in the land. Every Irish father of
a family, every Irish mother, took their rosary beads with
them, and in the rosary and prayer in which its mysteries
and glories were commemorated by vocal prayer the faith
of Ireland was saved. Now the faith has come back, and
Almighty God, smiling upon His people, who have been so
long faithful to Him, seems to say in the language of
Scripture: "I will put thine ancient song on thy lips once
more; she shall sing to me as in the days of old; she shall
sing to me as in the days when she came forth from the
land of Egypt." And behold through the length and
breadth of this mother-land of ours choirs are taking up
the song, and the voice of Ireland to-day, in rendering up
her duty of praise, is as fresh and strong as in the day
when the head minstrel of Tara rose up, and after listening
to the language of Patrick, and holding up his harp with
the strings of gold, cried out: "O ye chiefs! hear me.
Patrick's God that he preaches is the true God; and I
vow that this harp of mine shall never vibrate or sound
again save to the praise of Jesus and Mary that Patrick
preaches." And here, dearly beloved, this fair and magnificent church was built up, an eternal monument to the
undying faith and to the imperishable spiritual strength of
this community. Here this grand and stately temple,
cathedral-like in its proportions, aspiring in a spiritual
ambition to pierce the heavens in the loftiness of its beauty,
grand in every conception from the day that the mind of
the Christian architect devised it until the day when a perfect and accomplished thing it rose, a thing of beauty, upon
this earth, to make glad and joyful the hearts of men for
ever—this grand church is a monument of the faith that

can never die, for it is the church of a resurrection; it is a church that has sprung out of a soil once adorned with as fair a church; but the first things have passed away, and if the elements of death were in them they never could have risen again, but like the fabled bird of old that sprang into a new life from its ashes, so out of a soil reddened with the blood of the people, out of a soil encumbered with the ruins of all ancient forms of beauty that once crowned and adorned it, rose this thing of beauty, this joy for ever to all men. But no matter how fair and stately the Catholic church may be, no matter how entrancing the majesty of strength and lightness combined in pillar and arch, no matter how refreshing to the eye the storied pane that puts out to the light of God the transparent figure and form of Ireland's saints, no matter how fair the altar, how beautiful the service is, the Catholic church is still silent until the great organ is provided for her, which gives her a voice. She is like a beautiful woman—perfect in every feature, entrancing in every movement, robed in all the authority of a queen, but not able to speak—voiceless.

She is like the fair statue which the great sculptor of old made, on which he expended his whole soul; and when he had completed it and made it a thing of wonderful beauty, the very image of life, he then threw down his chisel and burst into tears. "Ah!" said he, "I have done all that I can, but I cannot make my statue speak." But to-day the beautiful queen has found her voice, to-day this stately spouse of the Lord, this temple of the living God, has made perfect every purpose of her construction and of her beauty when after piling up splendor upon splendor around it, when after expending her art in providing for Him the golden gates of His tabernacle, in scattering around Him all the earth has of fairest and most beautiful, in culling the most fragrant of her flowers that they may expire yielding their perfumes before God, in gathering the labors of the mother bee and the fatness of the olive that these too might die in silent adoration before their God—she has crowned all this to-day when she has provided the voice of that great instrument which will bear aloft higher and higher into the heavens every emotion of joy, of sorrow, of adoration, of delight, of triumph, of glory, or of prostration in which the Church of God will speak her love and her faith to her Divine Spouse. The Church has spoken to-day in the traditional language of song which her Lord put upon her lips, in which she is destined unto the last day of her existence to pour forth her soul before Him on earth, and then, when the existence of time is over, to take up in the choir of heaven the eternal song which she has only ceased for a time to sing on this earth. Have we not, therefore, reason to rejoice that the Almighty God has blessed Ireland again in the preservation of her ancient faith, in the strength of her resurrection, such as the world has never seen; have we not cause to rejoice that the sons and daughters of our land have found their voice again, that the young are in the choirs of the singers, and that her honored prelates and priesthood are at the gates of the Sion of Ireland's faith, and her faithful people thronging the house which is called in the Scripture "the gate of heaven and the dwelling place of the Most High"? That joy has come upon us, my brethren, and the very instrument which we are offering and consecrating to God to-day, that instrument which has pealed forth its message—that very instrument has its own significance and meaning, and a deep one it is. Mark, of all the musical instruments, the organ is the queen and the greatest of all; it is so large that it is able to embrace a striking imitation and the sweetest notes of all other instruments together; more than this, it is so formed in the conformation and style of its build and beauty that it is unfit for any other building or purpose than those of the Church of God. It is an instrument that was invented in the Church, by the children of the Church, and for church purposes, and its very notes— pealing, loud, solemn, impressive—seem to be incapable of adaptation to the lighter melodies and the foolish harmonies of this world. It is an instrument that in itself is a striking figure of the Catholic Church and the Catholic congregation, made up of thousands of pipes, from the greatest to the smallest, made up of so many stops and so many different and apparently contradictory component parts, a very complicated little world in itself; yet, touched by the master hand, out of all those various pipes and stops there comes a rushing of sound and a harmonious blending of song in which all are united, yet each one bearing its own part in the harmony that proceeds from the whole.

And so the Catholic Church is made up of millions of men, each one different from the other and each having his own natural keynote and sound, his own opinion, his own voice on every subject under the sun; yet when this varied multitude meet together as we are met to-day, and when the master hand of divine faith sweeps over them, forth from the manifold elements that compose the crowd comes one voice of praise, one voice and one note of faith, all believing the same thing, all adoring the same God, all expressing the same faith and love, each one adding to the strength of that expression and the greatness of that melody by the contribution of all that is in him of mind to know and of heart to love the things relating to Almighty God.

What wonder, then, that the Church should make so large a use of this great instrument in her liturgy and her devotions? The Church has for her object two things; for two great purposes was the Church of God created. She was created for man, for us—she was created for man, for his mind and for his heart; she was created for us, for our minds, to give us all the knowledge of God, to give it in its purity, to give it in all its integrity, to preach it and proclaim it in that wonderful unity of divine truth and in all the majesty of its proportions. But she was also created for our hearts as well as for our minds; it will not do for us merely to accept her message and make it our own by faith; we must go further, we must open our hearts to her and let her move us and sway us to the Lord our God by charity. Therefore she has her seven sacraments, like so many two-edged swords, creating channels of divine grace and pouring that grace into our hearts to sanctify us and meet every want of our spiritual being. Now, among the elements and the means that the Church has for reaching the heart of man, and one of the most powerful, is the splendor of her liturgy, the grandeur of her song, and the resonant accompaniment of her organ music—for, my friends, we would be belying our nature, and would not understand ourselves, if we did not admit how largely the heart and the spirit of man is swayed, is touched, is influenced for good or evil by music. When the King of Israel was troubled; when the good God left him, and reprobated him, and cursed him; when the Prophet of God came and said: "O King! thou art lost, thou hast despised the Lord, and now the Lord God will take away the sceptre from thee, and His Holy Spirit is gone from thee and will never come again"—then came a devil and took possession of the unhappy king, and filled him with the rage of hell and every most unruly passion; and, above all, he filled his soul with gloom and despair, and the man laid down his crown and sceptre with a broken heart.

When these fits of rage would come upon him his servants came and told him to get some one to play upon the harp, and David, then a boy, was brought; and when he saw that despair was heavy on the king, and the rage of hell in his heart, and his lips foaming, and that he was trembling in the convulsions of his awful despair, then would David take his harp and with skilful hand sweep its strings and bring forth notes of tenderest music; and the spirit of music would come upon the ears of the king and soothe him, and those eyes that were burning a moment before would melt into unaccustomed tears, and that heart that was troubled even to despair would begin to think that there was some hope yet in a God from whom there came sweet harmony. He had lost heaven, but the very echo and vision of heaven seemed to come to him again as the young man played upon his harp, and so he found peace and calm, second only, but infinitely second, to the peace and calm which he had lost. And many a troubled spirit will come into this church now and at future times —many a poor man oppressed with poverty, many an infirm one troubled with disease and pain; many a worldly-minded man disturbed in his visions of earthly prosperity and preferment; many a young heart yielding, or on the point of yielding, to the blandishments of a fatal world; and they will come in here to pray, and whilst kneeling before this altar of God, oh! as if touched by an angel's hand, the air around them, the very air they breathe, will begin to tremble to successive waves of melody, and it will seem to them as if God Himself was speaking in the magnificent song which is His own, and the troubled spirit will be calmed, and the down-hearted will be cheered, and those who are suffering will be comforted for a time, and the worldly-minded will be reminded of heaven, and the crafty, cunning man will begin to get a glimpse of the higher world; and the organ will bring all together, with heart open to the voice of prayer, and that prayer will go up to heaven on the notes of the organ. Rejoice, therefore, that you have found your voice to-day; rejoice that the zeal of your holy and devoted pastor is crowned to-day with the last embellishment of his glorious church and the fulfilment of his hopes; rejoice that the Church has found in its new voice another guarantee that it will be handed down from age to age, and generation to generation, among a people the most melodious and gifted in the world. Oh! let us rejoice that Ireland to-day can praise her Lord with all the solemnity of her praise, and that she can give Him thanks according to the vastness of His graces and the multitude of His mercies.

GOD OUR FATHER.

This discourse is one of the Christmas novena sermons delivered by Father Burke in the Dominican Church, Dublin, 1876. It is an eloquent and forcible argument on the mercy of God. It will be read with delight by the sinner who has strayed from his Father's house, and who, wearied of the ingratitude of the world, seeks the consolations of repentance. It is also a masterpiece of theological acumen, and worthy of study and meditation.

"Brethren, we have no longer received the spirit of bondage unto fear, but the spirit of adoption of sons, as of children, crying *Abba*, father."

THESE words, my dearly beloved, are to be found in the writings of St. Paul the apostle. We have already been engaged in the contemplation of the attributes of God. We have considered the mercy of God, and have considered the truthfulness or the reality of God as manifested to us in the mystery of the Incarnation. But in our consideration of these attributes, my dearly beloved, we looked entirely to God, scarcely at all to ourselves. It is necessary now that I should invite your attention to another grace or blessing that comes to all men through the mystery of the Incarnation, and in the contemplation of that grace or blessing we have to look unto ourselves rather than to contemplate Almighty God. That grace and blessing to which I call your attention is the grace of adoption, whereby we are made to be, through the Incarnation, the children and the sons of God. Reflect, dearly beloved, if you please, upon this. By the creation we were made the creatures of God. He has over us the same absolute dominion that He has over all the other animals that He has created. By His continued preservation and providential government we are become the subjects of God. His government, His laws, His guidance are made apparent in every action of our lives if we only submit to His commands. But neither the creature nor the subject can possess the dignity or the glory of the Son. Oh! how different, my brethren, is the position of the child in his father's house from that of the servant by whom he is attended; of the eldest son, the heir apparent of the crown, from that of the lowly subject who lives in subjection to the monarch's government and law. One enters freely and fully into the domestic life of the sovereign, breathes only the atmosphere of love. The other lives in the complete subjection of a subject to his ruler, obliged to perform every duty, to fulfil every obligation that his lord imposes. Now, such is the love of God for man that, not content that man should be His creature by creation, His subject by divine preservation, government, and guidance, God in His infinite love determined to raise up this rational being to the privileges, joys, and glories of his own Sonship. I am not satisfied, the Lord seems to say, that this work of mine should be merely my creature; that this servant of mine should exist as a mere subject of my rule. No! I will raise him to something higher, more noble, more glorious than this. I will make him my son. For this purpose it was necessary that the real eternal though consubstantial Son of God should come down from heaven to earth; that He should become incarnate by the operation of the Holy Ghost in the womb of the pure Virgin Mary.

Christ, by becoming the child of an earthly mother, as really and as truly as He is the child of His eternal Father; by His living on the earth as a man still retained every perfection of His divinity—the sanctity, the purity, the power of God. Thus was the mystery accomplished, not leaving in heaven one single attribute that belonged to His divinity; infinite in His own perfections, beloved by His heavenly Father with an infinite love, taking to Himself a human body from the womb of Mary, taking to Himself a human soul from the inspiration of the Holy Ghost, assuming both unto His divine personality, absorbing both in God. From that union of a human body and a human soul God came forth—Jesus Christ, the man-God, undivided and indivisible. The moment that this great mystery was accomplished in Mary's womb, the moment the earth beheld the union of Mary's Child with God, that moment all the relations between man and God were changed. Man no longer remained merely the creature of the Creator, the subject of the Ruler, the servant of the Master. For Mary's Child was the Son of God, the figure of His substance, the splendor of His glory. God lives and moves in Him. If He suffers pain, it is God that suffers; if He experiences sorrow, it is God that grieves. If those eyes are melted into tears of sympathy with man's sufferings, or by expiation of man's sins, it is God that weeps, they are the tears of God. When Mary's Son lays bare His back to the stripes of the scourger, it is the Son of God that is scourged. When on His sacred head they plant and press down the wreath of thorns, it is on the brow of the Son of God that they set this crown of agony and derision; and when the hammer of the executioner drives the nails through His sacred hands, when He bleeds and faints, and dies on Calvary, it is the Son of God that suffers that agonizing death.

In all that relates to His eternal Father, in all the privileges and power and glory that relate to Him, He is the Son of God, the eternal Son of God, the all-high, the all-holy, the all-adorable Son of God, and yet He is true man. He is the son of the virgin woman, Mary. When she sought Him for three days in Jerusalem, when He was about twelve years old, it was the anxious search of a mother seeking for her child. It was a mother that at length found Him in the temple; it was a mother that took home with her her son. On that terrible morning of Good Friday, when, in the intensity of her sorrow, to her tender eyes was denied the relief and privilege of tears, it was a mother that followed her son to the place of execution and saw Him die, and that son was still truly, really God. The first and greatest privilege of this assumption by Jesus Christ of man's nature into His own is that it makes man by adoption what Christ was by nature; it makes man by direct grace what Christ was by essential glory—the Son of God. We are all entered into the sonship of God by the incarnation of the Eternal Word. We are no longer only the servants of the Master, the slaves of the Lord. We are now the children of the Father, living in the Father's house, entertained at the Father's table, admitted to all the great inheritance that the Father can bestow, the infinite legacy of His love—enjoying, in fine, all the affection and the privileges that a true child can claim from the father that begot him.

For four thousand years man has been the servant of a divine Master, the subject of a divine Ruler, but there was nothing divine in man. He lived in bondage under the law of fear. When God spoke to him it was as a ruler to his subject, an awful master to his lowly slave. The Scripture tells us how the clouds of heaven veiled His face, how the thunder shook the hills, and the lightning flashed across the plains when God stood on Mount Sinai, and the people of His choice lay prostrate and trembling in the valley below. And when, in all His terrible splendor, God flashed before the eyes of His prophet, that prophet exclaimed aloud: "Woe is me, for I have seen the face of the Lord." Oh! how different was the coming of the Lord which we are now preparing to commemorate! He sent no thunder and lightning before His face; His coming was soft, silent, and gentle as the dew to the parched earth. "Send forth your dew, O ye heavens!" says the Scripture, "and ye clouds rain down the justice of God." There is no anger in His face to-day; it is all mercy, meekness, and love. "Behold, Jerusalem!" saith the Scripture; "the King shall come to thee, clothed in magnificence and gentleness. His voice shall not be heard aloud; His spirit is sweet beyond compare." "I will not," He Himself tells us, "bruise the broken reed, and the smoking flax I will not extinguish." Oh! there is indeed a change in the relations between God and man, in the coming of God on Mount Sinai, and the coming of Jesus Christ to Bethlehem. Almost in His first lesson to the world, in His first Sermon on the Mount, He taught His brethren in the flesh that their relations with God were changed. He told them that they were no longer to pray as servants to a Lord of whom a prophet said: "O Lord! thou art a God of fear, a terrible God, and who shall withstand Thee?" But thus, He says to them, shall you pray: "Our Father who art in heaven." We all enter in virtue of this humanizing of God, in virtue of this assumption of our fallen nature, into the infinite sanctity of the divine person of Christ; we all enter into the privilege of the sonship of God; we all bask in the sunshine of His divine paternity. The baptized man is for ever the son of God. He may sin; he may be covered with offences; he may be the worst sinner that this earth contains; God may deprive him of His grace; he may forget the kingdom of God; but there is one thing he can never lose, in heaven, on earth—aye, in the lowest depths of hell—and that is the sonship of God. Once God's sons we are His sons for ever; His sons not merely that He has created us and that we are thus the offspring of His omnipotent power, but possessed of that substantial sonship that comes out of the adoption of God's infinite love, that raises man in the divine person of Jesus Christ to be the real true child of his Heavenly Father. Let this simple truth, my brethren, sink deep into your hearts.

We are preparing next morning to meet our newly-born Saviour, our divine and eternal Brother, than whom heaven could produce nothing greater, whose like earth has never beheld before, for he is both God and man. Oh! my brethren, how shall you greet Him? In what words will you address Him? In what character approach Him? I answer: We shall come not merely as creatures to the throne of their Creator, as servants to the foot of their Lord; we will approach Him as Jacob approached Esau—

when he came to him in the fulness of his love after a parting of many months—when he flung his arms round his neck, and pressed him to his breast and said: "My brother." He is our brother—our eldest brother, begotten in the Father from all eternity, begotten in Mary's womb on Christmas day upon earth. The apostle speaks of Him as the first-born amongst many brothers. We are the brothers of Christ, who is the Son of God; we are the sons of God, who is the Father of Christ our brother. Christ is our true brother; He has admitted us to brotherhood on the terms of the perfect equality of our common nature. The inheritance which He has in heaven and through His humanity comes to us upon the earth. Oh! exclaims the inspired writer in accents of exultation, we are become the heirs of God and the heirs of Jesus Christ, who is the Son of God. And now, dearly beloved brethren, I might dwell upon this glorious subject, and indeed if I were to yield to the wishes of my heart and give vent to the thoughts of my mind, I would behold this mystery of divine adoption in the higher aspects it presents, the higher privileges it confers, in the free intercommunion of prayer and blessing which it admits between ourselves and God. But I will dwell on one special grace that is conferred upon us by this divine adoption. Now, I take it for granted that you are all preparing for a good confession, preparing with pure hearts to meet your Saviour on Christmas day, and therefore I will fasten on this one point, this one great grace and blessing conferred by God's adoption—the perfect ease and facility with which we can, if we choose, turn from our sins and be reconciled to God. The truth is embodied in the parable of the Prodigal Son, that wonderful parable which we are fond of contemplating, but into the deep hidden meaning of which perhaps we do not enter. A certain man had two sons; he was a rich man, perhaps a great lord in his own country. The elder son remained always faithful to his father, but the younger, coming to him, said: "Give me my inheritance, give me whatever is coming to me, and let me go." And when he had received

his portion he turned his back upon his father and his
father's house and went forth into a foreign country, and
fell among evil associates, and squandered his inheritance
in debauchery, licentiousness, and gross sin, and he fell
into abject misery, and his associates abandoned him and
he became a feeder of swine, and even with the husks on
which the swine were fed he endeavored to satisfy his hunger; but he could not do it, says the Scripture, and then
he reflected within himself, and he said: "Well, fallen as
I am, ragged and naked as I am, starved and degraded as
I am, abandoned by all my friends, those friends that were
so loud in their professions in the days of my prosperity,
I am still my father's son. I have no resource, no hope
left but this: I will arise and go to my father, and perchance he will take compassion on my misery." And he
arose and went to his father, and while he was still a great
way off he was filled with reproaches and apprehensions,
fearful in his heart, and covered with confusion and shame,
and he thought he would say to his father, "Take me as a
servant and no longer as a son." At the door of the house
was the old man, the father, and from a long way off he
saw the son approach the house, and his eyes were blinded
with tears of joy at his approach, and he rushed from the
door and met him half way, and put out his arms like a
blind man, blinded with his tears, feeling for his son, and
he took him to his heart and embraced him, and said to
him no words but these: "My son, my son!" And he
ordered that the fatted calf should be killed, and that
there should be rejoicing in the house because the son
had returned. Oh! how wonderful the affection of the
offended father, how strange the confidence of the fallen
child. If he had been a mere servant who had deserted
his master, a vile slave who had run away from his owner,
he would never have dared thus to return. He would
have known that he would have been hunted with ignominy from the door. But he was the son, and he returned
and he was received with all the father's tenderness and
love.

We are the sons of God in virtue of that adoption by which He makes us His children in baptism. We are the wild olives of Adam's growth, but we are engrafted on the sweet, the true, the faithful, the heavenly olive of Jesus Christ. By baptism we have received the *radix*, the root of eternal salvation whereby we may hope to be saved. The root is the essential to the life of the tree. No matter how stunted its growth, how poor its branches, how withered its blossoms, how bitter its fruit, while the root remains there is still hope. So it was with the tree in the Gospel, with the fig-tree that bore no fruit. The master said: "Let it be cut down, for it is barren." And the skilled gardener said to the master: "Lord, not so; but let me dig round the root and tend and water it, and perchance it may yet bear fruit." And the Lord suffered him to do what he desired with the tree, for its root was still there, and while the root remained there was hope of its productiveness, otherwise it would have been cut down at once, for it cumbered the soil. Sons of God we are by baptism; no matter how we may abuse the grace of adoption, still God regards us as His children, and as the brothers of Christ, His eldest and eternal Son. We may, indeed, as perhaps some among us have often done, as men are doing every day, we may go to our eternal Father and say: "Give me my inheritance; give me what belongs to me as the portion of a child."

And God gives us the rich inheritance of a cultivated and enlightened reason capable of knowing Him, of a pure soul capable of loving Him, of a free will capable of executing His commands. And we may take those gifts like the prodigal, and turn our back upon our father and our father's house. We may go forth into the wide, desolate country of sin and cast our lot among the sinners upon this earth; we may debase our intellect, pollute our souls, enslave our wills, till we have nothing left of all the rich inheritance which we have received, and have become poor, degraded, and deserted upon the earth. Then the false friends that took us by the hand in the days of our incipient impurity will turn us from their doors and command us to be gone. The clothing of our souls, of baptismal purity and innocence, is defiled and torn in shreds, we are naked and despoiled, we grovel amongst the swine of our own debased passions and filthy inclinations; we seek in vain with the base food of sensual gratifications to satisfy the cravings of a hungry soul, that disappointed spirit that was created for God, and that can never be satisfied with all that this earth can afford of sensuality or sin. Then nothing remains but for us to do what the prodigal did, to remember that we are the sons of God, and to arise and return to the house of our father. Oh! sweet and consoling thought. I may be scarcely able to recognize myself in this changed and fallen condition; but our Divine Father in heaven knows us. Upon the soul, so degraded and despoiled, He sees the sacred stamp that has been impressed upon it by baptism—the image of the Divine Son, who has a nature common with ourselves. Let me but remember, fallen and degraded as I am, I am still the son of God and brother of Christ. Behold, then, how easy it is to return to God. I may be full of sins, but I need have no fear for my reception. It is not the subject returning to allegiance to his ruler, it is not the servant returning to his lord; it is going back to a father and to a father's house. In olden times by what awful suffering had men, aye, even the man who was called after God's own heart, to do penance for their sins and to win back the pardon and the friendship of God. David, the king, has left us in the Scriptures the inspired record of his penitential suffering. "I have watered," he said, "my couch with my tears; I humbled my soul, and broke it with fasting; my tears were my drink night and day." And great as was his sorrow his pardon was not without conditions. God gave him his choice of war, of famine or pestilence. By suffering and humiliation was the prophet king obliged to expiate his sins. Still he was not sure that his expiation was accepted, that his pardon was granted. "Who," he says, "will give water to my head and a fountain of tears to my eyes, that I may weep my sins night and day ?"

But in that we have received the spirit of the adoption of the sons of God, in that we live under the love of Him rather than that of fear, all that we have to do is to rise up with the prodigal in the Gospel, and say: "I will go back to my father and to my father's house, and my father will receive me as a son. He will not demand from me the labors of a life—of a life of sorrow. He will only ask one sigh of contrition—the tribute of a single tear." The first tears that Magdalen shed, when she fell weeping at the feet of Jesus, blotted away all her sins, for the weeping woman was the sister in Christ, and the daughter of God. The perfect ease with which we can go back to God after we have left Him arises from the fact that we are His sons. The son may be ungrateful to the father, the father may be offended with the son; but the moment he shows signs of sorrow, the moment he shows the wish to be restored to his father's love, that moment he is forgiven. The father's love, the father's heart, is moved within him at the sorrow of his son, the blood of his blood, the bone of his bone, and the flesh of his flesh, the offspring of his loins. Never, or scarcely ever, do we find in revealed or profane history, in any age or any climate of the globe, a father deaf to that loud cry of the nature that is within him. No; when we turn to our Father, though our sins are numberless as the sands upon the seashore, they shall be wiped away—though they be as red as scarlet, they shall be made white as snow. Our atonement is in the blood of Christ. There is this common link between ourselves and our God. It belongs to the Father, because it is the blood of His Own Divine Son—it belongs to us because it is the blood of the Child of Mary, true man, true brother of our nature. His heart was broken, His blood was shed for sin he never had committed, that through His infinite repentance the way of reconciliation with God might become easy to us, His brothers. Now, are we going to refuse the inestimable privilege which He has so dearly purchased for us? Is there one in this church that will say at this Christmas time that is approaching, "It is many weeks, it is many months, since I was at confession or communion. Without any strict examination of my conscience I can accuse myself of sin, of grievous sin, of mortal sin. I know that I am an exile from my father's house, I know that I am an enemy to God. But I will not return; I will try, though I must try in vain, to satisfy the craving of my hungry soul with a surfeit of the gross sensuality which the beasts themselves use only in moderation. My God Himself comes down from Heaven to offer Himself to me in the high banquet of His eternal love. I will not accept His invitation; I will not return to my Father's house; I will not sit down at my Father's table; I will make my Christmas feast of the husks of swine." Is there one amongst you that will pursue this course of shame and sorrow? Oh, no! No; you will prepare this blessed Christmas time to enter upon the road of repentance, of return to God; that return that is so short and so easy, because it is the return of sons to their Father's house. The way from God was long and toilsome; the way to God is short and easy. Scarcely have we turned our faces toward home when we find our Father coming forth to meet us half-way upon our road, and take us to His bosom as the father took his repentant son in the Gospel. He will take us to His embraces in the Holy Sacrament of the Confessional. The moment God thus clasps us in the arms of His mercy, that moment we are completely reconciled to our Heavenly Father, that moment we regain the divine character of the sons of God, pure as the angels that never sinned and never can sin before the Lord, dear to our Father, aye, almost as our eldest brother, Christ, whom He sent down from Heaven for our redemption. God will sound the keynote of the glorious melody of reconciliation and of love in Heaven. He will say to the nine shining choirs of his angels: "Rejoice with Me, My angels, for My son was lost and he has been brought to life, and great will be the joy in Heaven at the return of the repentant sinner." Thus by the grace of adoption we live under the law of love, and free from the bondage of degradation and suffering we enter into the privileges of children of God, crying *Abba*, Father.

The Attributes of God.

On Monday evening, December 18, 1876, Father Burke preached the following sermon in the Church of St. Saviour, Lower Dominic Street, Dublin. It is a faithful delineation of its subject, and contains much profitable food for meditation.

"Send down your dews, O ye heavens! and ye clouds rain the Just One."

THESE words, dear brethren, formed the subject of our meditation on a former evening, and I have also chosen them as a theme on which to address you to-night. If you remember, I told you that we should consider, during these nine days of preparation for Holy Christmas, the attributes of Almighty God as they are revealed to us in the mystery of the Incarnation. Now, dear brethren, what do I mean by the attributes of God? I mean that there are certain virtues, certain qualities, that belong to Almighty God essentially and necessarily because He is God. Every man among us has his certain virtues or his certain vices—certain qualities, whether they be good or bad, which mark him, which designate him, and which form his character. One man, for instance, is good-tempered, another man is an ill-tempered man; one man is generous and hospitable, another man is close and avaricious; one man is meek and patient, another man is violent and revengeful. And just as we all have our qualities and virtues or vices, so there are certain virtues or qualities which belong to Almighty God, which belong to Him essentially and necessarily because He is God, which form His nature; and these are called the attributes of God. I need hardly tell you, dearly beloved, that among those attributes there are no vices, because God is all holy and all perfect. And now, among the attributes of God, the very first, which I take as the subject of this evening's primary meditation, is the attribute of justice. And why? Because, if you remark, when the prophet prayed in the words of my text for the heavens to rain down a Saviour, he called him a Just One. "O ye heavens!" he said, "send down your dews, and ye clouds rain down the Just One." It is therefore lawful, and it is suggested by the theme, that I should treat first of all of the justice of Almighty God as revealed to us in the incarnation of our Lord and Saviour Jesus Christ. What do I mean by justice? Justice, dearly beloved, is that particular virtue which either in God or man gives to every one according to his desert; which pays to every one what is due to him. When we speak of human justice, we speak of the virtue which, embodied in the public law, rewards the meritorious man and punishes the criminal man. When we speak of commercial justice, we speak of that sacred virtue which pays to every laborer whatever is his due, whatever he has earned by the sweat of his brow. When we speak of civic justice, we speak of the justice which promotes to any honorable position in the state only the man who is fitted for that position. And the moment the laborer is defrauded of his hire, the moment an unworthy and incapable person is put into any position which he does not deserve, or one for which he is not qualified, we all exclaim against those vices and call them injustice.

Now, whatever there is of justice to man in the human mind, in the human heart, in human society, or in the human law, it is only the merest reflection of that infinite, essential, and unchanging justice which is the very nature of Almighty God. Therefore, speaking to God, the inspired ones of Scripture always hail Him as the Just: *Justus est Domine et rectum judicatum tuum*—"O Lord God! Thou art just, and Thy judgment is just." And when the prophet proclaimed the coming of the Son of God, the very first attribute that he assigned to Him was the attribute of justice. "He shall judge the world in judgment, but in justice." When, therefore, we look to Almighty God, whether we regard Him in heaven in His dealings with His angels, or whether we regard Him in His dealings with man upon earth, one thing is certain, that we are sure to find in the action of Almighty God essential, unchangeable, and eternal justice: "*Justitia tua justitia in eternum*," exclaims the psalmist—"O God! Thy justice is eternal justice." It may seem to us, dearly beloved brethren, a hard thing when we contemplate the justice of the Almighty and Eternal God; it may seem a hard and terrible law this justice, I grant it. I for one am much more pleased to reflect upon the mercy of God than on His justice. The moment I turn to His mercy I at once get into the region of Divine love. I find my dear Father, I find a compassionate and considerate heart, a kind and bountiful hand; but all that we can say or think, dear brethren, of the mercy of God, should not cause us to shut our eyes to His justice. God is first of all just. He would not be the infinite and all-perfect being that He is if those attributes of justice were not among the very first of those essential and eternal virtues that form the nature of God. And therefore it is that no matter how hard may be the judgment, it is still compatible with justice.

When we see the criminal sentenced to death, when we are horrified by hearing the sound that proclaims that a soul has been sent into eternity, when the expectant crowd see the victim immolated upon the altar of public justice, or when they see that ominous black flag held out to tell that the man is gone, that his soul has fled, we are terrified at the majesty and awfulness of the law. But is it not just? The man who has been thus sacrificed has shed blood; the man who has been thus sent into eternity has violated the most sacred laws. He is a murderer, and he only expiates the foul crime he has committed; and whilst on the one hand we shudder at the punishment, on the other hand we are strengthened by the thought that the law is not only powerful but is just, and is founded upon justice. And, dear brethren, when we rise from the contemplation of mere human justice, and come to regard this attribute in the Almighty God, oh! how terrible it is—how terrible is the justice of God. Our faith tells us that the millions and millions of angels were created around Him pure-spirited, in happiness, in glory, almost in contemplation of the undisguised vision of God. Yet they sinned, and the moment they sinned two-thirds of the angels of heaven—every one of those sacred spirits in whom the sin was found—were cast forth in an instant, in the twinkling of an eye, from heaven. God arose in the terror and awfulness of His majesty and sent them down to the eternal abyss of hell—howling demons, despoiled of all their glory, despoiled of all their brightness, condemned for ever and ever, never to see the light, never to see the face of the Almighty and Eternal God. And so, when our first parents sinned, an intelligence as bright as that of the angels refused to admit the light of God's holy law, a heart as pure as the angels refused to love God, a will as free as that of even the seraphim and cherubim of God refused to obey Almighty God. All this was when Adam committed his sin. And I tell you, my brethren, that if you or I this night, or at any other time, consent to commit mortal sin, that in the act, whether it be an act of the will, deliberately indulging in impurity of the appetite, deliberately indulging in base sensuality of the passions, deliberately indulging revenge of the intelligence, deliberately embracing infidelity—that in that moment you and I commit a mortal sin we commit as great a crime before God as when Lucifer, the light of heaven, refused to love and acknowledge his God and was damned for ever.

An intelligence illuminated by the light of faith refuses to act by its love, refuses to acknowledge God; a heart opened by grace refuses to love God; a will as free as that of God Himself refuses to obey the Almighty God. And God is as much dishonored in you or me when we commit mortal sin as He was dishonored in the angels whom He sent out of heaven into the eternal hell. And so it was with Adam, the father of our race; and when he committed sin he called forth that primary attribute of Almighty God which is eternal justice. God loves mercy more than He loves justice. There is not one amongst us who has not some one passion that overpowers all the others; there is not one amongst us that has not some corner in his heart where there is some particular love that is dearer to him than all others; and so has the heart of God. Mercy occupies the first and dearest part, and God loves His mercy more than He loves His justice. But when that mercy is abused, and when the justice is challenged, then the Almighty God rises up in all the majesty and awfulness of this His first attribute, and the God of mercy, the God of love, the God of redemption disappears, and the God of justice alone remains. And so it was with God in His dealings with Adam. Adam committed the sin in which he not only sinned himself, but in which he implicated all his race; for we who live six thousand years after the creation of our first parents, we sinned in Adam. If you ask why I am tormented by angry passions, why I am swayed by evil desires, why do I find it so difficult to do that which is good and perfect and so easy to do that which is sinful and bad, I answer because you and I sinned six thousand years ago when Adam, our first father, sinned. In that sin the fountain of our being was poisoned, the very fountain-head of that stream which has flowed down to us was polluted, and then the justice of God was challenged for the first time. And now consider the evil that was committed. It was an evil infinite in itself; for, my brethren, there was no measure, no limit to the evil that was committed when Adam committed his first mortal sin. And why? Because he offended, forgot, and violated the God of infinite majesty, the God who had infinite claims upon him, a God to whom was due all the service man could render him, either in mind, heart, or hand—in other words, by intelligence, love, or will.

God is our Creator. All that we have He has given us.

All that is in us belongs to Him. He has given us a mind capable of knowing, and He demands that knowledge by divine faith. He has given us a heart capable of loving, and He demands that that heart be never polluted by unholy or impure affections. He has given us a will free and able to serve Him. He demands that they will never serve another master, never observe another law but His. And, dear brethren, when the mind, the heart, and the will rebel against Almighty God, then the supreme, the infinite, and the eternal Being is outraged and violated. His holy law is broken to pieces, His will is contradicted, His attributes are denied to Him; and this is the effect of a mortal sin. Then, dearly beloved, the question is no longer, "What reward can my love give him?" He deserves none, he is no longer a child worthy of love, he is an enemy. What may mercy do for him? There is no compact between God the just and this sinner, this man permeated with sin; it is only a question of justice revolving itself into simple issue—What penalty is due to this criminal who has broken the law of God? Is it not so in human law; should it not be so in the divine law? If a man steal anything, if a man commit highway robbery, if he obtain money under false pretences, if he be riotous and offend against the law, if he shed the blood of his fellow-man, if there be murder on his hands, it is no longer a question what position of honor shall be given him, what rewards shall be heaped upon him, what high station shall he be placed in. No; he is in the dock, a criminal; and the only question that remains is what amount of punishment is he to receive for his crime; and that punishment is to be inflicted in proportion to the enormity of the crime. But so it is between God and man—so it was between God and the whole race of man when Adam committed his sin. The divine justice of God had only to consider two things. First: What amount of punishment is to be given to the criminal? Secondly: Is he to be let off; if another is to take his place to receive his penalty, what manner of victim will satisfy the justice of God?

Behold the two things which were resolved in the Incarnation!—two questions relating to the justice of God, that show forth in the awful mystery of becoming man. First of all He became man in order to provide for the justice of his Eternal Father—a victim capable of satisfying that justice. Secondly, He became man in order to take upon himself the punishment that was adequate to the crime that was committed. That crime, as we have seen, was infinite, without end, without limit. My brethren, hear me. We are capable of very little; the best amongst us can do but very little; the greatest and holiest amongst us can do so little for God or for man that our best efforts are but vile rags, as the Scripture speaks even of the justice of the holiest. The greatest man that ever lived upon this earth—saint or sinner—did but very little. We are not capable of much; but there is one infinite act of which the least amongst us is capable, and I am sorry to say that this is the act of committing mortal sin. There, indeed, the powers which are so limited for good become infinite for evil. I can do scarcely anything for God, but if I choose to do anything against God I can do something of which no man in heaven or on earth can comprehend the enormity, but only the mind of God Himself. For I can crush the Almighty God, I can violate and tear to pieces every law of God, I can bid defiance to His omnipotent divinity, I can deny His wisdom, I can outrage His sanctity, and laugh at His pretensions of human beauty; and I can turn to the vilest and basest passions of earth, and say to that foul impurity, to that vile drunkenness, to that dreadful revenge, "Thou art fairer to me than God; I will take thee instead of God; I will hold thee, I will serve thee, I will clasp thee to my heart; let God depart, I will not have Him nor His ways." Such is the nature of sin, and then the Almighty God launched out on every attribute of omnipotence, of divine wisdom, and of mercy despoiled and contradicted, and all are absorbed into one assertion of God's awful and terrible justice; and so it was between God and man when Adam sinned. Therefore, the evil being infinite, two things were necessary, my beloved; first of all, if God's justice is ever to be appeased, it must be with a punishment equal to the injury which is done to Him, it must be with a punishment equal to the crime which is committed; if the punishment inflicted is not equal to the crime which is committed, then justice is never satisfied.

Justice is only blinded, and justice is only set aside; the exact measure of justice is never filled up unless the punishment is equal to the crime. Mercy and the other attributes may come in, God may still be merciful and good and loving, but He ceases to be just unless the punishment be equal to the offence. More than this, if the justice of God is ever to be satisfied it can only be satisfied by one who is equal in his own sanctity to the sanctity which was outraged and violated by the son of man, one who is as holy as God Himself, one who is as powerful in expiation as man was in violation of God's law—and behold the mystery of the Incarnation. It is a question now of providing a victim able to atone for the sins of man—not merely for the sins of Adam, but for the sins of all the children of Adam for four thousand years, and as long as the world shall last. It is a question not only of providing a victim able to do this, but a victim who will consent to take upon himself a punishment perfectly adequate to the crimes committed. Look up, look up to the highest heavens, O ye sons of man! We are a fallen race. God wishes to save us, God wishes to redeem us, but God cannot do it unless the measure of His justice is satisfied. Look up to heaven now, and tell man there are nine choirs of angels there: there are the shining seraphim, the adoring cherubim, and thrones, powers, and principalities, archangels and angels—is there one among them, nay, more, if among them combined, will they be able to satisfy the justice of God for your sins and for mine? Ah! no; ah! no. They might expend themselves and annihilate themselves, they might cast themselves down to suffer for eternity in hell for our sins; but they are only the creatures of God, and all that they can do is finite or circumscribed by the fact that they are only creatures; the debt is infinite, and the satisfaction which is not infinite can never pay the debt.

Nay, if all the angels in heaven were to combine and annihilate themselves into the nether hell for all eternity, would that eternal punishment wipe out our sin? No, no; because the sin is an infinite evil, and all the punishment that can fall upon creatures even for the eternity of hell is bounded by the mere fact of their finite creation, and cannot pay an eternal and infinite debt. One alone can do it. One alone can pay this debt. One alone can bear the fulness of the anger and the fulness of the wrath of the Almighty God. One alone can do it, but oh! the thought is blasphemy; how can we think it, that one is the eternal God Himself—God Himself! Can God become a victim; can God take upon Him our punishment; can God take upon Him what is worse than our punishment—our sin; can God take upon Him all the grief, all the sorrow, all the misery that is necessary for the work of expiation! All that seems too terrible for our minds to entertain; but that which is too much for us entered into the mind of God. The Second Person of the Adorable Trinity rose up and said: "Behold me, O Father! behold me. At the head of the book it is written of me that I should do Thy will. Sacrifice and oblation Thou wouldst not; Thou hast prepared a human body, for I will go down from my high place in heaven; I will become a child of an earthly woman upon the earth; I will become as true man in times as I have been true God in eternity; I will bring with me all the infinite holiness of my divine nature; I will bring with me the fulness of my divinity; I will go down to earth; I will bare this sinless bosom and hold out these immaculate hands of mine, O Father! to receive the awful brunt of Thine anger, and the full and the awful torrent of Thy wrath; I will take blood that I may shed it; I will take a human heart that I may break it; I will take human members and senses that I may crush them under the weight of Thine anger and Thy vengeance; I will bear the iniquities of all who have ever sinned against Thee"— and behold the mystery of the Incarnation. God Himself provided a victim able to bear the full tide of divine and infinite wrath—God Himself provided a victim, whose every prayer, whose every sigh, whose every word, whose every suffering, whose every drop of blood was of infinite value, because they were the prayers, the sighs, the words, the sufferings, and the blood of God Himself. And so He came, the Virgin's Child; so He came, beloved, whom we shall greet upon Christmas night, beholding Him as our only Saviour; so He came, a little child, to grow into youth, and from youth to manhood, not for joy but for suffering, not for enjoyment but for torment.

Every member, every sense of His body, every faculty of His human soul, impressed within Him, preserving in the infinite unity of the hypostatical union all the integrity and the fulness of His divinity, and ripening and maturing only that when He comes to the fulness of His manhood He may be stretched out on the cross, and then die, immolated by the wrath of God and the malignity of man, and by the shedding of His heart's blood wipe away the decree of eternal death. He only was fit to plead and suffer for us, because He alone could bear our offences. "The Lord put upon Him the iniquities of us all," exclaimed the prophet. He alone was fit to expiate our offences, for He alone, by every act of humiliation, by suffering and by rising, was able to give more glory to God than even man could deprive Him of by his sin; and so He came. And now mark: the justice of the Almighty and Eternal Father was completely satisfied in the mystery of the Incarnation by the humility, the prayers, the suffering, and the death of His Divine Son—completely satisfied; not a single claim remained of that justice upon Him. Let me drive this into your minds. Christ our Lord took upon Himself all our sins, and He so expiated those sins that the Eternal Father completely forgot His justice, as if it never had existed, as if Adam never had sinned, as if mankind never had fallen. The Eternal Father was completely satisfied, the last farthing of the debt was paid by our Divine Saviour, and we were baptized unto God. We, the children of God through His Holy Church, do not live at all under the reign of God's justice. There is no such thing. I proclaim to you a consoling Gospel. God has retained for us the attributes of His mercy, of His love, and of His fathership; for, as we shall see in a subsequent meditation, we have all become the adopted children of God through Christ our Lord. But I deny that His justice exists. There is no such thing. That justice was satisfied, that justice was completely appeased, by the incarnation and the life and the sufferings of Jesus Christ, my Brother and my God. You never can experience it; it never will touch you; it never will come home to you; it will never exact one single account from one of you, unless, indeed, by your own sinful acts you choose to go out of the region of mercy into which our Redeemer brought us, and come back again to the region of justice. God has no justice for you, only mercy, only love, unless by your own act you prefer justice to mercy, and the anger of God to His love. The Christian law is a law of love. The child baptized receives such graces in baptism, such fellowship with Christ our Lord, such sonship of God, that if that child only preserves the graces of baptism, if that child only keeps what he gets, there is no justice for him, nor for you nor for me if we only consent to abide in that holy atmosphere of mercy into which our Divine Lord led us. There was justice, and terrible justice; terrible and heavy was the hand of that just God that spared not His own Holy and Immaculate Child, but forced the Blood from every pore of His Sacred Body in Gethsemani, and that Blood that flowed forth next morning from every open and terrible wound under the scourge, and finally broke His heart upon the Cross. God's justice could go no further; there is no justice for you or me, unless, indeed, as I said before, we choose of our own free will to go out of mercy and challenge the justice of God by our sin. Ah! dearly beloved, if we do this, then the justice that awaits us is far more terrible than if Jesus Christ had never paid our debts—far more terrible. We read in the Gospel that a servant-man who owed his master ten thousand talents was brought before him, and, kneeling down, he said: "O master! have pity on me and give me time, and I will pay the last farthing." He got the time; his debt was forgiven; not only did he get the time to pay it, but he was absolved from all payment—the master forgave him all. But in a few hours that servant was brought back, and he was put before the same master, and he was accused of other crimes; he was accused of his mercilessness to his fellow-servants. Then there was no more mercy in the master's heart. "Take him," he said; "take his wife, take his children, sell them as slaves; bind him hand and foot, and cast him into a loathsome, dark dungeon. I forgave him the ten thousand talents he owed me; now I declare and swear that I will never let him go unless he pays his last farthing." Why was the master so terrible in his second interview? Because he had forgiven the debt at first, because it was already remitted, and it was only taken back by the wickedness of this servant.

And so, dearly beloved, when you or I commit sin, I care not what sin it be, it is a thousand times worse than if Christ our Lord had never come down from heaven to pay the debt for us. "Woe unto you, Jerusalem, woe unto you, Naim!" says the Lord; "'twere better for thee I had never come amongst thee." Why? Because Christ our Lord in his Incarnation paid our debt; He made Himself responsible for it, He paid it, He shed His heart's blood to pay it. Now, any man that incurs the debt of sin again not only incurs the debt of the act of Christ, but aggravates the malice of that act by abusing the Sacred Blood that was paid in ransom for him, and by trampling upon our Lord and Saviour Jesus Christ. Yes, yes, dearly beloved, that Son of God has laid Himself down upon the Cross, a broken heart in a dying body, and He lies between us and hell. Of old, before He came, the gates of hell were wide open, that every man might freely enter there, but neither you nor I can enter there any more unless we walk over the dead body of Jesus Christ. He has put Himself between us and hell; He has closed hell by the shedding of His blood, and any man who wishes to go down into nether hell by mortal sin must not only commit sin, but he must make a mockery of the Son of God and crucify Him again before he can attain his infernal end. Let us, my brethren, in our great gratitude to Him who paid an infinite debt by sustaining an infinite punishment— if for no other reason, for the sake of our Divine Lord who has come into the midst of us, coming a man into the midst of His fellow-men, coming Himself a son unto the children of woman, coming to take all the weakness and the miseries and the suffering of our own upon Himself, coming to make Himself familiar with our wants, with our sorrows, to bear them all that He may understand them the better, and touch them, as it were, with the more scientific hand,—if for His sake alone, let us make this resolution to-night, dearly beloved: that we shall never again offend Him by sin; that, no matter what shall come to us, one thing at least we must not allow to come to us, the guilt of mortal sin; that no matter what we may do, and what act of folly we may commit, we will never commit the act of cruelty, of trampling upon One whose love is tender, whose omnipotence was made into weakness, whose brightness was made into obscurity, whose infinite beauty was made into deformity, "a worm and not a man," whom no man recognized as a man because of the deformity that His sufferings cast upon Him. Have pity upon Jesus Christ, have pity upon Him! He is coming to you this Christmas; He is coming to be born again upon earth. Give Him a place in your hearts and let him be born in every bosom amongst you. Do not close the gates of your hearts, as the foolish people of Bethlehem closed their gates against Mary when she came and asked them for a night's shelter. Ah! my brethren, let Him be born amongst you.

The stable was poor and humble, but there was no sin there. No matter how humble our hearts may be, or how unworthy, at least let us by a good confession and a preparation for a subsequent communion purge these hearts of anything that is sinful, that so the Son of God may be born freely and really in every heart of ours by Holy Communion. For so every man amongst us may become a Bethlehem to the Almighty God, that He may be born in us, that he may grow in us, and come to the fulness of His manhood in us, and when the hour of death comes that our dying may find us with Jesus Christ. "Blessed are the dead who die in the Lord."

The Mystery of the Incarnation.

THE following is one of the series of Advent sermons preached by Father Burke in the Dominican Church, Dominic Street, Dublin, 1877. The Mystery of the Incarnation is depicted in language simple yet eloquent, and the discourse is a masterly one, on a theme which cannot be too clearly understood by all faithful Christians.

VERITAS de terra orta est, et justitia de cœlo inspexit—"The truth hath sprung up from earth, and justice hath looked down from heaven." In these words again, my dearly beloved, the mystery of the Incarnation is unfolded and put before us in the prophetic language of the Scripture. We have already considered two attributes of God that shine out and are made manifest to us in the adorable mystery of the Incarnation—in that Word Eternal who was conceived of the Holy Ghost, born of the Virgin Mary, and made man. The first of the attributes to which I invited your pious attention was the attribute of the eternal justice of Almighty God, so completely appeased, so entirely satisfied in the Incarnation and Atonement of His Divine Son. The second attribute you considered last evening—namely, the infinite mercy of God as manifested in the Incarnation of the Eternal Word. Now, this evening we come to consider the third great attribute, or property, or virtue, or quality of Almighty God that shines forth bright and adorable on us in this great mystery. That attribute is the essential and eternal truth of Almighty God. When, then, I come to consider that truth more closely, when I ask myself what it is and where it is to be found, I find, strange to say, that I need not look up into the high heaven to behold it. I need not mount upon the wings of contemplation or of prayer to grasp it. The prophet of God, illumined by the Holy Ghost, lays it at my feet. Truth, truth eternal and essential, has actually sprung out of the earth. These words mean, dearly beloved brethren, that the eternal truth of God, abiding in God from all eternity, from the very nature and the essentials of the being of that Almighty God who never had beginning, has come down from heaven to earth, has taken its place upon the earth, has sprung out of the earth, made manifest to us who are the children of the earth, earthy, in the manhood and the divinity of Jesus Christ, our Lord and Saviour. In other words, the clearest and the most glorious manifestation of God's eternal and divine truth that was ever made by Him, that ever could be made by Him to angel in heaven or man upon the earth, was made when the truth itself became incarnate in the Eternal Son of the Virgin Mary—our Divine Lord Jesus Christ.

Let us once again consider the words of the prophet: "Truth has sprung out of the earth, and justice hath looked down from heaven." In simple explanation or paraphrase of this great sentence, truth had sprung out of the virgin earth of Mary in the sacred humanity of our Divine Lord and Master, Jesus Christ—the truth that drew aside the dark screen that hid the light from the world. Justice looked down from heaven; the searching eye of God beheld His Son upon the earth, and the justice of God could find no error, no fault, no blemish in the light of that truth that sprang from Mary. God's essential and eternal truth was upon the earth. That truth had been hidden from men; it had, as we shall presently see, almost disappeared from the vision of the sons of man, until the time of that advent when Truth the Eternal appeared upon the earth in the person of the Man-God, Jesus Christ. Truth is an infinite and an essential element of God. Consider, my dearly beloved, what this word *veritas* means. It has been defined, by one who holds the highest rank in the Church of God, St. Thomas Aquinas—one who also stands high in the estimation of the world among those geniuses whom God gives from time to time to the sons of men,—truth he defines to mean the exact correspondence with the fact that it represents.

There are facts of many and various kinds; some are eternal and divine, some are merely temporary, accidental, and human. That God exists is a divine and eternal fact. That God is all that He is, is a divine and eternal fact. Whether we choose to believe it or not, it remains the same for all eternity in all the integrity and grandeur of its existence. The existence of God, the existence in which His divine and infinite attributes are grouped, is a fact eternal and divine, existing entirely independent of our knowledge, appreciation, or love. If all the men upon the earth were infidels, God would still be what He is. If all the angels in heaven had joined in Lucifer's rebellion and become demons in hell, it would not diminish one iota the reality of God's eternal holiness, of His wisdom, of His mercy, of His power, of any one of those attributes that surround His being. As there are in heaven facts eternal, uncreated, and divine, so there are on earth facts created, accidental, and human. That you or I should exist is the merest accident in the creation of God. God so willed it, and we exist. But not to will it was free to Him. If God had not so willed to draw us forth from the infinite mass of possible being, we could never have sprung into the conscious existence that we enjoy before God to-day.

Truth means the exact correspondence with the fact which it represents, whether it be word spoken by the lips, or a thought conceived in the mind, or an action of a man's life; the truthfulness of that word, thought, or action depends upon its exact and faithful representation of the fact which it professes to interpret. You will pardon me if I lead you somewhat aside into the more abstruse reasons of metaphysical argument. Truth means nothing more or less in thought, word, or action than simple reality. When we talk of men as truthful or untruthful—when we say of such a one, I know him, he is a true man, we mean only that he is a real man, a man whose every action is based on the principles which he professes to guide him, a man who has seen intellectual facts, who acknowledges their breadth, their strength, their importance, and who gives in his life a representation of the reality of his principles and belief. When we say of a man that his language is truthful, it means that he is a man that never by the words of his lips gives a false interpretation of the belief of his heart. The liar is the man whose words are not in accordance with his thoughts, who may by superior knowledge be acquainted with facts of which others are ignorant, but who misinterprets them in his words and tells them as they are not. Reality is truth. God is essential truth and essential reality. Reflect, my dearly beloved, upon this. Take, for instance, the mystery of the Adorable Trinity. God is one in His essential substance and nature, not only undivided but undivisible—incapable of division. He is not merely one, but He is unity itself. He is not one by any form of union or coalition of different individuals or substances. We, for instance, are one nation. We are the Irish people, one as a nation, yet divisible into millions of individuals. This is not unity but union. God in His aggregate of His infinite perfections is also unity. To diminish one iota of His eternal and divine perfections would be to destroy the existence of God. God is infinitely perfect and infinitely beautiful. He is essential and eternal action. Almighty God, who is without beginning, of necessity from all eternity contemplated His own divine beauty. The moment He looked upon Himself He saw the vision of His own infinite, divine, and uncreated beauty. This very conception of Himself assumed the proportions of the Eternal Son. The conception of God in the mind of God is the Second Person of the Adorable Trinity. God is of such eternal substance that the very thought of His mind at once assumes substance too in the form of the Second Person of the Adorable Trinity, the Word of God, the same in nature, the same in essentials, the same in sub-

stance as the Father, from whom He springs, bearing to
the Father, who conceived Him in an eternal generation,
an infinite love, which that Father returns with an equal
love, and such is the reality of God that the very love of
the Father for the conception of Himself, and the love of
the Son for the Father that had begotten Him, assumed the
personality of the Holy Ghost, the Third Person of the
Holy Trinity. The very essential life and action of God
from His reality in this, that one in nature, indivisible in
essentiality and substance, God the Son and God the Holy
Ghost are the offspring of action inscrutable and inconceivable, infinite and eternal—the offspring of the reality
of God. Passing over the intervening actions of Almighty
God, the creation of the angels and of man, we come to the
mystery for whose fitting contemplation we prepare ourselves by this novena—the mystery of the Incarnation.
Here God, the only God, the selfsame God in the Father,
the Son, and the Holy Ghost, infinite in action, infinite in
power, infinite in wisdom, infinite in mercy, infinite in
love, undertakes an act, great, solemn, and holy, but, in
the language of scholastic theology, a personal action towards Himself. It is no longer a question of the action
of God in Himself, but of God taking a new element to
Himself. The Incarnation did not make God other than
He was from all eternity, but it added a temporal (after its
assumption eternal) nature which He had not before. The
Word was made flesh, God became man; He was a real
and true man, as real and as true a man as ever was born
of woman upon this earth. Let us try to realize, my
brethren, what this means. It means that God, who
was incapable of suffering or sorrow, made Himself capable
of sorrow the deepest, of suffering the most intense that
ever mortal man endured. God became man! It means
that Life essential and eternal made Himself capable of
suffering not merely pain and sorrow but the bitterness of
death, the ignominy of the grave. He remained the same
God truly and entirely that He had been from all eternity;
as truly did He become man, as truly was He conceived in

Mary's womb and born unto Mary's arms as ever man was conceived and born on this earth. God carried His own truthfulness down with Him from heaven to earth.

Remember what I said—truth means reality. It was a question, then, of redeeming man from his sins, of atoning for the past and future transgressions of our race, of satisfying the justice, of wiping away the handwriting of death which the hand of an angry God had written against the name of man. For that task suffering and sorrow were essential.

The spilling of blood was necessary for our redemption. But God might, if He chose, have assumed such a body as the Archangel Raphael took when he came down from heaven to Tobias. The angel, indeed, appeared in the form of a man. His body was in all outward semblance the body of a man: a form that a man could touch, with eyes to see, and ears to hear, and tongue to speak, and hand that could grasp the hand of a friend. But his body was not a real human body after all. When the matters were performed for which he had been despatched to earth, and when the will of God had been accomplished, his body resolved itself again into the atmosphere of which it was compacted, and the archangel sprang back to his place among the blessed spirits the same as when he left it. He brought no vestige of humanity back with him to heaven; the angels, his companions in glory, beheld him the same on his return as at his departure. The body he had taken was redissolved in the elements from which it had been drawn. God might have entered into such a body for all the necessary purposes of expiation. He might have lived and labored in such a body even as Raphael journeyed and labored with his young charge Tobias; and then, when, by the spilling of one drop of blood, by the shedding of one tear, by the utterance of one prayer breathed from the lips He had himself created, expiation was performed, he might have returned to heaven, man's redemption accomplished, the same, unaltered in substance or in nature, as when He left His Father's bosom.

Such a body might God have assumed as the Angel Gabriel wore when he appeared to Mary at prayer in the temple. "*Apparent angelus ei,*" saith the Scripture. Now, an angel is a pure spirit, and the bodily-created eye of man cannot behold him; God, therefore, created for him a body cut out of the surrounding ambient air, that he might become manifest to the Virgin, that he might give to her the message of God, that he might say to her: "Behold, thou shalt conceive in thy womb, and thou shalt bring forth a son, and shall call his name Jesus." And when his mission was accomplished, when the Eternal Word came down from the highest heaven to take up his abode in the pure womb of the Virgin, for a moment the angel knelt in prostrate adoration of the present Deity, and then flew back to heaven, his body redissolved into the elements, to announce to his celestial companions that the work of man's redemption was begun, that God had become man upon the earth. But it was no body compacted of the air that his God had taken; no mere appearance of a human frame temporarily formed for the occasion; no body to be afterwards taken from Him as an unworthy thing to be redissolved into the elements from which it sprung. And why? Because such a course would be inconsistent with the truthfulness, the reality of God. Wherever God immediately and personally acts there must be the quintessence of truth itself in its highest, noblest, purest, and most potent form. When an angel comes on a mission of mercy, individual and temporary, he assumes the appearance of a man; when God comes on a mission of mercy, divine, eternal, He becomes a man indeed. God in very truth entered into Mary's womb. His body was formed of the blood of her blood, the flesh of her flesh, the bone of her bone. He took a real body in that Virgin's womb, formed of that Virgin's blood and flesh and bone. Into that body as it lay in Mary's womb He breathed a human, a created soul. But when that body and soul were united no human personality such as you or I possess arose. God said to the human personality, "Stand aside." He took that human body and that human soul, created by His own breath; He assumed it into His divine personality, and out of this mysterious union of a human body, a human soul, and God came Jesus Christ, the Man-God, the Redeemer of mankind, Mary's son—mark that—Mary's son, as truly as ever man was son of woman in human generation. Mary's son, her own natural substance, coming with all the claim of a child upon its mother for love, tenderness, and maternal sustenance, clothing her with all the claims of a mother on her child for obedience and respect. Yet the person that was there was a divine person—was God. He is man indeed, but His personality is divine. A human body is formed in Mary's womb; a human soul is breathed into that body; and body and soul are assumed and absorbed into the divine personality of Christ, the Second Person of the Holy Trinity, that liveth and reigneth for ever. Oh! how magnificent, how glorious the reality of this incarnation.

But is this body, real as it is, taken only for a time? Oh! no; it is taken for ever, dearly-beloved brethren—for ever. So long as God shall reign in heaven, so long at the right hand of God, equal to the Father in all things, the very figure of His substance, the very splendor of his glory, the God-Man, Jesus Christ, shall sit. But assumed as it is for eternity, perhaps it is capable of temporary divorce from the divinity? That body was assumed for so many purposes of humiliation, of sorrow, and of pain that we can scarcely associate it continuously and eternally with God.

We can scarcely bring our minds to conceive that God is prepared in His divinity to go down to the lowest depths of sorrow and humiliation with the humanity of Jesus Christ. But such is the reality of God that He has taken that man's body and soul to Him by a personal union so lasting, so indissoluble, so inseparable, that even when the human soul was parted from the human body by a cruel death—even then, while Christ's body hung a dead thing upon the cross, and Christ's soul went forth into that mysterious region where met the anger and the mercy of God before the expiation of sin—even then the Godhead departed not from the dead body on the cross, or from the human soul in limbo. The Divine Person, the God whom the angels adore and the heavens reverence, was with that body as it hung suspended 'twixt earth and heaven on the tree of shame. The Divine Person was still in that body when it was taken from the cross, when it was laid in the dark tomb to whose mouth the great stone was rolled round which the Roman soldiers watched. The divinity was with the human body, the divinity was with the human soul, when they met in glory on Easter morning for eternity, never to be separated again. The divinity was never an instant absent from the body or the soul from the moment that human body, that human soul, and God became one Divine Person in the womb of Mary. Oh! how different, beloved, was God's assumption of humanity from the assumptions that the angels made from time to time of human form. How easy was their task, how hard was His! There was no pain, no sorrow, no humiliation in the task of the angels that came in human form to Mary or Tobias, of the angels that visited Abraham as he sat at the door of his tent in the "spring of the day"—Scripture's beautifully poetic expression for the early morning. The patriarch invited them to his tent; they partook of his generous hospitality, they performed the mission with which they were entrusted, and they departed. No sorrow, no humiliation to the angels who were sent in human form to Lot, to tell him to fly from the impure city, upon which the floodgates of God's anger were about to open. Their assumption of humanity was apparent and temporary; His was real and eternal. To prove how real, how substantial, how eternal that assumption is of our nature by God, the belief in it is made necessary for our salvation. It is as great, as necessary, as essential a truth to believe that God is man as to believe that God is God.

And now, my dearly beloved, let us apply this great truth to ourselves; for in these our Christian meditations, while we contemplate the highest and the most adorable mysteries—the nature, the attributes, the life of God—we should contemplate them all with a practical application to ourselves. God became man, says Saint Augustine, in order that man might become as God. The Child of heaven became a child of earth, in order that the children of earth might be as the children of heaven. He came in the reality and truth of His divinity upon the earth, to stamp upon His disciples the stamp of reality and truth. There is no room amongst the disciples of Christ for the hypocrite or the liar—the man that knows the truth and speaks a lie—the man that knows the truth and lives a lie. There is room amongst God's disciples, there is room in the Church of God for the lowliest, the vilest, the most abject sinner. For God has likened His Church to a net which is cast into the sea and sweeps up all kinds of fish, the good and bad together. The day of separation comes at last, to receive the good, to put the bad away. But in the net which God has cast for the souls of men there is room for all but the hypocrite and the liar, for all but those who condemn, who scorn the great lesson of truth and reality taught in the Incarnation. Nay, such is the power of truth, of reality, that if falsehood itself be taken for truth it is no longer falsehood amongst men. The false man knows the truth and contradicts it in his words or life. The true man, the real man, believes what is false; he has been told it, and he had confidence in the word of another; his own reason has led him to an erroneous conclusion. He believes what is false because he knows not what is true. He clings to it because he has no means of ascertaining its falsehood, for if he knew its falsehood he would abandon it at once. He is in irremediable, in invincible ignorance; but he speaks, he lives by his belief, and in the midst of falsehood his truthfulness, his reality is preserved.

The Catholic Church, the Church of God, does not

say that man is excluded from heaven. He may die still clinging to that invincible error, that error whose clouds make falsehood appear as truth in his eyes. But there is no room in the Church of God on earth or in heaven for the man who, knowing the truth, speaks or lives as if he knew it not, for truth, reality, and faith are the only passports to heaven. I would rather, dearly-beloved brethren—oh! far rather—take the chance of salvation of the man outside of the Catholic Church, the honest and the truthful man, who acted up to His lights, and could get no better lights than those which he possessed, who died indeed in his ignorance, but died in his adherence to and observance of the principles of his belief, than the chance of the Catholic who knew the truth and contradicted it in his words, in his actions, in his life—who knew the truth and was ashamed or afraid to confess it—who belonged to the only body from whom the truth can be known and abused the inestimable advantage he possessed.

The only body from which the truth can be known—speaking from this pulpit, I am bound by my truthfulness as the accredited minister of God to say it, I am bound by my responsibility to myself and my God—there is no channel of divine truth, no saving faith in God, outside the ark of the holy Roman Catholic Church. She alone is the ark of salvation to the race of man. If a man can be saved outside her folds by invincible ignorance, by honesty and sincerity of purpose, by willingness to adopt the truth, by strict adherence to the principles he believes are true, his salvation is exceptional, abnormal, accidental. There is no ordinary, normal accredited way to salvation save in the Church of God, of which God Himself has said: "Unless a man will hear the Church let him be to thee as the heathen and the publican." But, dearly beloved, there are, even in the Church of God, many that are thought just but are not, many that are not real men, that are not thoughtful men. Dearly-beloved brethren, there are many who believe in the Church of God, who have been born and baptized in her fold, or who, by some extraordinary grace—and it is indeed an extraordinary grace—were called from the ranks of infidelity, darkness, and error into the admirable light of God. They belong to God's holy Church, but they seem actually ashamed of what should be their proudest boast. If they go out to a dinner-party they are ashamed to do this—to make the sign of the cross —this glorious sign that in the day of judgment shall shine upon the foreheads of the elect of God, that cross through which alone, the Scripture tells us, the joy and glory of heaven can be obtained. But there are others who are fervent, loud, blatant in their lip-professions of Catholicity, who are zealous, furious in their denunciations of all outside the Church, even of those whom the Church herself absolves. But look at their lives. How do they correspond with their professions? Do they frequent the sacraments of the Church? Do they approach the confessional? Do you ever see them partake of the sacred banquet of the Holy Communion? No, my dearly-beloved brethren, oh! no; they are a mockery and a triumph to the heretic and the infidel; they are a stumbling-block to the believer. They are spoken of as the criminal classes; the debauchee, the drunkard, the fraudulent tradesman, the dishonest servant are all to be found in these ranks. The careless, ignorant, vicious Catholics are loud indeed in their profession of Catholicity, but careless of every injunction the Catholic Church imposes. Are they truthful, are they real in their lives, they whom Christ himself describes as who with their lips, indeed, confess His truth, but who in every action of their lives deny Him. My dearly-beloved brethren, the very first essential of the true Catholic, of the true man, is reality.

Do you believe the Catholic faith? The Church, unlike anything else calling itself a religion on this earth, puts the professors of its doctrines to rude tests. Do you believe in the Church? If you do you will have to starve yourself on the days of fast which she imposes. You will have to submit to pain and to humiliation. Are you a proud man? are you an intellectual man? Well, you will have to go to some poor priest, who perhaps does not know half as much as you. You will have to kneel at his feet, you will have to confess to him, you will have to speak to him of things that you would rather die, rather commit suicide, than reveal to any other living being. If you be a true man writhing in sorrow and humiliation you will have to reveal to him the darkest secrets of your soul. You will have to acknowledge to him your sins, your excesses, your baseness, your falsehood, your dishonesty, your filthiness of soul. These, my brethren, are indeed rude tests. Where there is reality there must be rude tests. Contemplate the Eternal God born in the stable on Christmas morning: His Mother hunted from house to house, driven as a last resource to a stable, the Child-God brought forth amidst beasts and cradled in the straw of their manger—was not this a sufficiently rude test of the truth, the reality of God as He entered the world? Contemplate Him as He leaves it, nailed to a cross, a hard, rough bed for a dying man; His head lacerated with thorns; His body torn with scourges, His lips parched with thirst; with wounded body and broken heart, dying for the sins of men! These were indeed rude tests that God's reality endured. He came into the world a man. He took upon Himself the heritage of misery. He proved Himself a true man, and from the moment of His birth to the moment of His death He never shrank from agony or sorrow. Outside the Catholic Church there is no test to which those that call themselves members of the body must submit. The Protestant minister that steps into the pulpit in the trim black robes of his ministry to preach the doctrine of perfection is a married man; he has a wife and children of his own, he has the luxuries and comforts that his life affords, he denies himself nothing; who asks him to deny himself? But the Catholic priest must resist his human inclinations and passions—must resist them, ay, even to the letting of blood. He must, if necessary, lay bare his own back to the discipline, and cut the flesh and draw the blood that would rebel. But before he can come into the pulpit, before he can stand at that altar, he must be like the angels of God in his personal purity. Is not this a rude test? The true Church must impose rude tests, and true men must endure them. The Catholic that will not submit to the Church's guidance—the Catholic that is a Mohammedan or a Mormon in his sensuality, do not tell me that he has any other claim or title to the name of Christian than that baptismal robe of innocence and adoption which he has not merely defiled but torn into shreds by his offences. *Veritas de terra orta est.* It sprung forth from the virgin earth of the pure womb of Mary when Jesus Christ, our fellow-man, was born into the world, and none can claim fellowship with Christ except by true conformity with the principles His life and character display —conformity not merely by the words upon our lips, but by the actions of our life, in all the truthfulness and reality that are manifested to us in this adorable mystery of the Incarnation.

The Sacred Heart of Jesus.

THE following passages comprise an extract from a sermon delivered by Father Burke at the laying of the corner-stone of the Church of the Sacred Heart, at Courtwood, County of Queens, Ireland. By those who love the Sacred Heart of Jesus these fragments of a beautiful sermon will be highly prized.

"I saw the holy city, the New Jerusalem, coming down out of heaven from God, arrayed as a bride adorned for her bridegroom," words found in the twenty-first chapter of the Apocalypse of St. John.

MAY it please your lordship. Dearly-beloved brethren, we are assembled this evening under the bishop and pastor of our souls to consecrate and to lay with prayer and benediction the corner-stone of this new temple of God, which is about to be erected under the title of the Sacred Heart of Jesus, and as the Scriptures tell us that all things in the works of God are harmonious, and fit one unto another, I ask you to consider this evening how fitting this church shall be for the title which it is about to receive, and I ask you to consider what that title means --the Sacred Heart of Jesus. "O Heart!" exclaims St. Bernard, "the thought of Thee is balm to my inner soul; the sight of Thee, contemplated by the mind, is a joy to mine eyes, and the sound of Thy name is as the music of heaven to mine ears"; for, dearly beloved, when Almighty God vouchsafed to become man, and for us men and for our salvation vouchsafed to be incarnate of the Holy Ghost and of the Virgin Mary, in that hour of His greatest mercy He showed the greatness of His love for man in that He took to Him a human heart like yours and mine

THE SACRED HEART OF JESUS.

—a human heart indeed in its capacity for joy and for sorrow—a heart most human in the depths of its sympathy, its tenderness, and its love, but at the same time a heart which was divine, and the object of all adoration in heaven and upon earth, and even in hell, where the devils, trembling, still believe, because it was the heart of a divine person, Jesus Christ, in whose bosom it was—the bosom of God. But that human heart which the Son of God took to Him He took for all the purposes for which He creates the hearts of ordinary men, and just as our minds are made to know, so our hearts are created to be receptacles of the affections and to be the home of love. Even so when the Son of God took a human body and a human soul, that Sacred Heart of His He took for the purposes of loving, and the heart of Jesus became the great vehicle and the great receptacle of that infinite love of the Father, Son, and Holy Ghost which was shown to man in the incarnation of the Eternal Word.

And now I ask you to consider the words of my text. St. John the Evangelist beheld with prophetic eye the glories of the Church, which was to be the bride and lamb of God, and he described her as she appeared to him in the heavens coming down from heaven, from out the very mind and heart of God, but coming all robed in splendor and majesty, coming clothed in the very highest form of loveliness and beauty, like the young bride of a king arrayed and adorned to meet her royal bridegroom. What was the beauty of the Church of God of which St. John here speaks? what was the perfection of beauty of which we read almost in every part of the inspired Scriptures, God at one time saying to His spouse: "Thou art all fair, O my beloved! and there is no stain in thee"; again the apostle, proclaiming, says: "Christ loved the Church and gave Himself for her, that He might present her to Himself without spot or wrinkle or any such thing, but a glorious Church, perfect and worthy to be the bride of the Lamb of God"? What is the beauty which belongs to the Lamb of God? It is, my beloved, none other than the beauty of

God Himself. Thus saith the Lord : "Thou wast made exceeding beautiful because of my own beauty which I have given to thee, saith the Lord thy God on Zion." This church, rising here amongst these historic plains, will fling up towards heaven the loveliness of pointed arch and wall, traceried window, and a spire climbing with a holy ambition high into the clouds, until the setting sun of the world's Redeemer—the cross of Jesus Christ—shall be flung broad and wide over many a road around, until that gilded cross shall catch the first rays of the sun rising in the morning in the east, and shall be the last object to receive the adoring rays of the same luminary as he sinks in the western horizon in the evening—a "thing of beauty and a joy for ever" to every eye that beholds and every heart that comprehends the mystery of its beauty. What shall be the beauty of this church? How shall it participate in the loveliness which will make it to be as a bride arrayed for her bridegroom? I answer, Its beauties are intimated in its title—the Church of the Sacred Heart of Jesus. Consider the beauty and loveliness of the Sacred Heart of our Lord, and see how faithfully that beauty which is of God shall be put upon this church, His spouse. One of the great wants of our age is not so much faith as tenderness and love for Jesus Christ.

Oh! is it not strange that Catholic hearts should be cold towards the Sacred Heart of Jesus, whilst the heart of the Church their mother ever burns with the fresh bridal love for the Sacred Heart of her Bridegroom? Is it not still stranger that many outside the Catholic Church should imagine that we Catholics have not a proper, or sufficiently ardent, or sufficiently adoring love for the Sacred Heart of Jesus Christ? Oh! how little they know the thoughts of our faith—how little they know the yearnings of our hope, the strong emotions of our Catholic charity, else in their honesty, in their kindliness, they would never think such a thought of us or speak such a word. Most beautiful of all that ever was created in heaven or upon this earth—most beautiful of all the works of God is the Sacred Heart of Jesus Christ, and its beauty is mainly 'threefold. First, the beauty of His infinite holiness; second, the beauty of His vast tenderness and large bounty, which knew no limit to the greatness of His mercy; and third, the beauty of His immortal, imperishable, eternal divinity, reigning in the Sacred Heart of the Redeemer. I take these three, and ask you to consider them, first in the sacred humanity of the Sacred Heart of our Lord, then we will apply them to this very church within whose incipient walls we are assembled this evening. First of all, the heart of Jesus Christ, the Virgin's Son, was the most beautiful thing that God ever made, because it was the holiest. Formed out of the most pure, the most immaculate materials, elaborated with the most thoughtful care of the mind of God, and joined by a personal union with the eternal divinity of the Word, that heart of the Man-God had become the heart of God Himself in Jesus Christ. How pure and holy that sweet heart of Jesus was! formed out of the blood of Mary the Blessed Virgin—Mary, the Virgin of whom it was said, under the inspiration of the Holy Ghost, that it was one of the privileges of humanity to be able through all generations to call her blessed—Mary, the Virgin whose graces were so abundant and so excellent and so unique in themselves that the very archangel who came down from before the throne of God bowed down before her as one of an order of grace superior to his, and declared that she was "full of grace," and that her name was blessed among all women, for the Lord God was with her. That sacred blood that was in the Virgin's veins was preserved from the slightest shadow or thought to sin allied. Where all sinned Mary alone was immaculate. Enshrined in the omnipotent and eternal decrees of the Lord God, her Maker, the ocean of original sin, surging up like the flood of old, and sweeping over the whole face of human creation, touched all, defiled all, spoiled all, but God said to its waves at their very highest: "Touch not my immaculate one—she is my love, my star, and my dove, and there is no spot nor stain in her." Why did Mary receive this grace? "In order that the veins of her bosom, unstained and unsullied by the slightest shadow of sin, might be worthy to give the materials of that human but most sacred heart of Jesus Christ, which was for ever a living chalice of the Precious Blood. Thus, pure in its origin, God made for Himself out of Mary's blood a human heart, so large, so simple, so strong as to be able to bear the rushing floods of the infinite sanctity of God that came upon Him. For that heart was united in the sacred humanity of our Lord to the divinity, so that the result of the union was not a human person but a divine person, and the heart that was throbbing in the bosom of Jesus Christ was the heart of God. Secondly, consider how unique in its beauty was this Sacred Heart of God. All other men had hearts narrowed by selfishness, defiled in some way or other by sin. Mary herself, though immaculate, had yet incurred the debt of original sin, and was as much saved, and as truly, though differently, by the blood and passion of her divine Master as your or my soul. But even the man after God's own heart, even the royal prophet, left behind him the record of a heart open to temptation—a heart easily inflamed by impure love. Jesus alone of all men had a heart of infinite holiness, but to that holiness was added the other beauty of infinite tenderness and largeness of mercy. He took that human heart to Him for the same purpose of loving his fellow-men, and loving them with all that mighty heart. What were the wants that that Sacred Heart of His failed to feel? Were the people hungering around Him, He spoke to His apostles and said: "I have compassion on this multitude; my heart is moved for them; and I will not send them away fasting." Were the people ignorant, He went out and led them out to the mountain, and for three days and three nights there did He speak and teach till the clouds of ignorance rolled away from the eyes of their souls, and from the darkness of their ignorance He brought them, through the compassion of His divine heart, into His own admirable light of knowledge. Were they sorrowing, He hastened to wipe away their tears.

It is now a sister weeping, or a brother's grief. Tears are falling over the grave of Lazarus, and he is rescued from the very jaws of death. Is it a weeping mother as she follows her only son to the grave? Seeing her, as St. John the Evangelist says, He was touched, and moved, and shaken with pity. Weep no more, He said, and He gave back with His own sweet hand that child to its mother's bosom. Is it the sinner crawling to His feet, heart-broken with sorrow—a sinner whom all men will avoid, a sinner so despised that even the priest and Levite, Scribe and Pharisee gather their robes and say: "Begone, touch us not; we are clean." One only could she come to, and from Him she derived the sanctity of heaven by her repentance. Did He refuse her when Magdalen crept, marking her humble course by her tears? Oh! no; His divine heart was moved by compassion, and when she arose from His sacred feet she was pure as the Angel Gabriel was when he saluted Mary. Nay, more, the sinner not drawn to Him in repentance, but caught red-handed in her sin, was not condemned by Him, but rather she went away like an angel of God in her restored contrition. In fact, every spiritual and temporal want found its safety in drawing upon the infinite fountain of the mercy and tenderness of the Sacred Heart of Jesus Christ. The moment that our Lord fashioned and formed that Sacred Heart for Himself out of the heart's blood of His Virgin Mother, from the moment He took it to Himself, never for one instant of time did the Son of God separate Himself from that heart. Never for an instant did His all-holy and adorable divinity—never for all eternity shall the heart of Jesus Christ, be without the love of God throbbing with a divine love in it. Even when He was dead on the cross— even when the Sacred Heart, so easily moved, so abundant in its care, so tender and anxious in its own mercy—when the Sacred Heart, so forgiving that, with upturned eyes, He prayed to His Eternal Father in heaven that those who crucified Him might be forgiven—even when the sweet heart ceased to beat and was dead—even though the human soul had fled, the divinity of God never left it, and the angels in heaven were adoring this pulseless heart of Jesus Christ during the hour he remained on the cross. Behold, then, the three beauties of the Sacred Heart.

Behold these walls to-day. The corner-stone is laid in prayer and benediction, and within these walls shall rise up prayer and benediction for all time. Everything around these walls in future shall be the most precious that the mind of man can conceive, the ingenuity of man discover, the elaborate cunning of the artificer's hand form into shape and beauty. All the richest marbles torn out from the heart of the earth, gold and silver, orient pearls, the fairest flowers of the earth, the labor of the mother bee; all that the earth has, all that the depths of the sea can render, all that the hills contain, all that the green face of nature can produce, shall be selected and gathered here; and when we have done all this, and more, yet shall we fail infinitely from the beauty and loveliness of the house in which God vouchsafed to dwell. These walls shall be eloquent as they resound to the Word of God for many a day, and within them will be found the same mercy, the same powerful means of intercession, the same ready pardon, the same strong omnipotent grace of absolution that Magdalen received at the feet of Jesus Christ from His Sacred Heart. All shall be found within these walls, and the three-fold beauty of that Sacred Heart shall not be wanting. It was an eternal heart from the moment of its creation, taken unto God, assumed unto the Divinity to be no longer the heart of man, but to be the heart of God, and to abide there for ever and ever. Even so these walls shall abide for ever and ever. As long as man remains on earth to cross the threshold of that sacred door so long shall that door remain open to him. These walls may, indeed, perish; time in its relentless action, the malice of men, and the thousand accidents of flood and of storm may demolish them; but these walls will arise again as the fabled bird arose from its ashes—they shall arise again as they are arising to-day where the more ancient walls perished, or, if they still remain, are only supported by the loving ivy that first trained itself around them. Venerable and beautiful in their ruin we see them throughout the land, these evidences not of a faith that has gone by but only evidences of the action of time and of man, renewed as the strength of the eagle is renewed in buildings like this. Monuments of the faith shall never perish on this earth as long as human intellect remains to believe and human hearts to love Jesus Christ. Therefore we may well apply to this temple the words: This is my resting place, said the Lord, for ever and ever. Here shall I dwell, because I have chosen it for myself. You see the Lord has chosen this place. God was looking down from heaven upon this very spot, and said, There shall I dwell for ever and ever, there shall I dwell among the children of mine, for I have chosen that spot. We know it to-day, and we shall know it better when, still more generous in our efforts, still more munificent in our charity, we shall have it completed and beautified. Entering with joy, according to the words of the Psalmist, into the courts of the New Jerusalem, we shall here upon the altar on the day of the consummation of its beauty behold the tabernacle of God, and He shall here dwell with them, and they shall be His people, and the Lord God in the midst of them shall be their God. This is the object of our hope to-day. Our faith has begun the work, our hope shall continue it, our love for our God shall consummate it and make it perfect in all its loveliness and beauty, and with God's blessing great shall be the reward in heaven for all eternity.

THE ALTAR OF THE SACRED HEART.

This magnificent sermon was delivered at the dedication of the new altar of the Sacred Heart in the Augustinian Church of SS. Augustine and Paul, Dublin, November 3, 1876. It is worthy of a place among the most excellent sermons, and can be read with profit and pleasure.

"How beautiful are Thy tabernacles, O Lord—Thine altars, O Lord of hosts!"

THESE words are taken from the eighty-third Psalm. Assembled as we are to-day to assist at the consecration and solemn dedication of an altar of a Catholic church and that altar crowned with the image of our Divine Lord and Saviour, and dedicated to Him under the title of His own most Sacred Heart, our thoughts, dearly beloved, naturally turn to the Sacred Heart of Jesus Christ. To the subject of the altar, for, as the apostle pithily and forcibly expresses it, "*Habemus altare*"—we have an altar—not merely a place of prayer, not merely a table whereon to commemorate in a shadowy and most inefficient manner the recollection of the greatest act that ever took place upon this earth, but a true and real altar of sacrifice, solemnly consecrated with the outpouring of oil and the voice of prayer—an altar on which the blood of a victim flows in real sacrifice, an altar before which an accredited and anointing priest, sacrificing, takes his stand—an altar whereon is consummated the highest and the great central mystery of our religion—an altar, therefore, of all places on this earth the most holy and the most solemn—an altar of the holy Catholic Church. And, dearly beloved, when we come to consider this subject we are forcibly reminded of the intimate and essential connection that exists between the altar and the idea of sacrifice. "For," says the great Saint Augustine, "never have any body of men assembled in the name of religion who did not embody their homage and their adoration of God in the form of sacrifice." Sacrifice enters naturally into the idea of homage, for the moment that man puts himself in spirit in the presence of the Almighty Creator, the moment he acknowledges his own unworthiness and his own debt, and desires to testify to that unworthiness and in some manner, no matter how inefficiently, to pay that debt, that moment the idea that necessarily comes to his mind is the idea of immolation or sacrifice. He wishes to express his conception of the greatness of that God who is enthroned aloft before him, and in whose hands are life and death ; he takes a victim and he sheds blood, thereby attesting that all things belong to God ; he conceives his own sinfulness and his own unworthiness, and he wishes to put himself as a suppliant before the Almighty God, and to testify to God the great idea that suffering must necessarily atone for sin ; therefore he takes to him a victim, if innocent so much the better, and sheds the blood of that victim in testimony to these great ideas that fill his mind. Hence it was, and is, even amongst the most barbarous nations, that an idea of sacrifice, no matter how faint or shadowy it may be, is almost invariably found ; and the Lord God Himself from the beginning, from the day that man sinned and incurred the debt of sin and the obligation of reparation, the Almighty God, I say, enjoined upon him the natural as well as the legal obligation of sacrifice. Therefore it is that we find the children of our first parents collecting, one the first-fruits of the earth, the other taking the firstlings of his flock, and offering them to the Lord God. Therefore when Noe came forth from the ark his very first act of gratitude and of adoration to the Lord God, who had saved him out of the wreck and ruin of the world, which had perished, was to erect an altar and offer a sacrifice of living victims to the Lord. Therefore the patriarch who lay down at Bethel, with a stone for his pillow, and in the darkness of the night beheld the vision of angels, and rose trembling with fear in the morning, and saying: "Truly this spot is holy, for it is no other than the house of God and the gate of heaven," immediately gave vent to his feelings and testified to the holiness both of God and the place whereupon he had lain down by building up an altar, pouring oil upon it, and then offering sacrifice to the Lord God. And when the people came forth from Egypt, and God gave them their laws, He again enjoined legally and specifically the obligation as well as defined the manner and the matter of sacrifice—sacrifice for sin, sacrifice for every form of legal uncleanliness, sacrifice of victims and first-fruits in gratitude, and sacrifice to obtain mercies and graces in the time to come; and hence, dearly beloved, a whole book of the sacred writings is occupied with defining and specifying the manner and matter of these sacrifices. Therefore the Almighty and Eternal God, before whom not time only but the infinite eternity is present as one point, and who sees all things, the past, the present, and the future, immediately under His own all-seeing eyes, determined that all these sacrifices of the olden law were merely as so many shadows of the great sacrifice which was to come, and as so many reminders to His people of the Victim that He was one day to provide in heaven and to send on earth, whose immolation was to be the redemption of all mankind. Therefore it was that all things, said the apostle, were shut up in figures and in mere significance and promise in the Old Law; for, says the apostle, "without the shedding of blood there was to be no remission."

The blood that was shed from the beginning of the innocent victims of the flock was but a type of the sacred blood of the innocent Son of God, which was to be poured out upon this earth for the sins of all mankind. And, dearly beloved, striking, indeed, and vivid were those images of the future great sacrifice. The innocent lamb is taken out of the flock, and its sinless blood is poured out, and is sprinkled upon the people, and signed upon the lintels of their doorways, and lo! the angel of God sent forth on that terrible night upon his awful mission of divine vengeance is stayed, and he respects the blood of the paschal lamb, and passes by, and neither wailing, nor weeping, nor tears are seen in the houses of God's chosen. The little child, on the eighth day after his birth, sheds personally innocent blood, and in the shedding of that blood obtains the remission of original sin in circumcision. Oh! what were all these things but figures and the foreshadowing of that sacrifice which took place in the fulness of time, when He who was eternal, the eternal Word of the Father, co-eternal, consubstantial, co-existent with the Almighty and Eternal Father, begotten indeed, but begotten of all eternity, was incarnate of the Holy Ghost and of the Virgin Mary. He came into this world and was made man. He took a human body and a human soul in all the fulness and reality of our human nature—took a human heart and fed it with human blood, took every member of our body, so that He was *habitu factus ut homo*. He was made in body and form as a man, true man as He was true God; true man in all, yet not a human person, but a divine. I insist upon it in the name of Christianity, in the name of truth, and in the name of the Eternal God, who did this for our salvation. I fling out as an answer to all the blasphemous assertions of our day, that Christ our Lord was true God and true man, and the manhood in Him was assumed into a divine personality. He was only one person, as I am only one person, but that person in Him was divine, and Mary, the Mother of that person, was the Mother of God. And any man who asserts that she was not the Mother of God, but only the mother of Jesus Christ, is a blasphemer against the hypostatic union by which the two natures were united in one person; he has not taken in the very faintest conception of the divine mystery upon which all Christianity is built up—that God became man, and that God and man were united in the one person—not a human person, but a divine. Why did He who was God take a human body, take a human heart, throbbing with the pulsations of human blood? Why did He take out of the stainless and immaculate veins of Mary that blood? Why did he take flesh that suffered and writhed under the lash when that lash fell upon Him? Why did He take that sacred head which was pierced with thorns? O dearly beloved! it was not for joy, it was not for feasting, it was not for gladness that He came. He took our humanity, that in that humanity He might suffer and die —offer Himself to His Eternal Father a bleeding, torn, dying victim, and pour out every drop of the blood that circulated in His Sacred Heart, and wipe out the handwriting of that decree that was registered against men, and make Himself the Lamb of God who takes away the sins of all mankind. He came therefore for sacrifice. Now, sacrifice involves three things. First of all it involves a victim to be immolated; secondly, it involves a priest who is to immolate the victim; thirdly, it involves an altar upon which the victim is laid. Thus it was when God commanded Abraham to take his only and best beloved child Isaac and to go forth; He told him at the same time to take the wood for the altar, to be himself the priest, and in Isaac He provided the victim. When in His mercy He sent His angel to stay the father's hand then did He find another victim, the altar and the priest remaining the same. And so when the central hour, towards which all things, from the eternity of the past and from the eternity of the future, looked —when the great hour came, the central hour in all the designs of God, in all the hopes of man, when that hour had arrived the altar was provided upon the hill of Calvary; that altar was the cross, which waited, with its outstretched arms, for the victim to be laid upon it. The victim was provided—that victim was the Son of God, the Eternal God made man, the child of Mary. And the priest was there, who was no other than Jesus Christ, offering and immolating Himself to be the victim for the sins of mankind.

And, dearly beloved, when that last loud cry went forth from His dying lips, when the last drop of His precious blood, necessary for redemption, was shed, when the meek, thorn-crowned head bowed down in death and the spirit, the great spirit of our Lord, went forth from Him, then, in that instant, all the sacrifices that foreshadowed Him in the past were fulfilled, all necessity of future sacrifices were completely abolished, for the one great, perfect sacrifice was made, the one great purpose of redemption was achieved. The altar bore indeed still the Victim dead—yet, though dead, still God. For although the human soul was separated from the human body, the divinity that dwelt in Him corporally was never for an instant separated from either the one or the other. Christ our Lord, dearly beloved, might, if He so willed it, have left no trace of Himself upon the earth save in the truth of the Church's teaching, and perhaps in some striking and pious commemoration of His death. But because He was God, because all things in Him are real and substantial, because in God there is no mere shadow without substance, no mere words without the essential truth which it expresses—as, for instance, in the procession of the Holy Ghost, the love of the Father for the Son, and of the Son for the Father, taking a substantial form, there is the Third Person of the Blessed Trinity—so also when Christ our Lord, impelled by His infinite love, determined to perpetuate unto the end of time the commemoration of the great sacrifice which He made upon Calvary, assuming to Him all the reality of His Omnipotent Godhead, He established that commemoration in a continuation of the sacrifice itself—no mere form, no mere commemorative exhibition of the death of the Lord, no mere form of words telling the people of the love of Him who suffered and died for them, no mere feasting, recalling to their minds the recollection of the wonderful supper in the upper chamber at Jerusalem ; no, but the self-same sacrifice, perpetuated and continued, the same Victim, the same Priest, and all but the same altar.

The manner, indeed, if you will, of sacrifice is changed; it is no longer the forcible, visible, material shedding of blood; it is no longer the violent tearing of soul from body in that terrible death as on the cross; it is no longer the drooping head, the scourged body, the breaking heart, slowly fainting away before the approach of the Angel of Death; no, but the body and the blood of the Lord are there, but the body and the blood are mystically separated, and the body and the blood that were offered on Calvary are offered again and again, the same Victim and the same Priest and all but the same altar. The same Victim; for the night before He suffered He took the bread into His holy and venerable hands, and He put the chalice with the wine before Him, and He said to His apostles: "Remember that I have told you again and again that without me you can do nothing (*sine me nihil potestis facere*). Remember I have told you again and again that you must abide in me, and I in you, if you must be saved. Remember that I have told you again and again that you must be united to me as I am united to my Eternal Father. Remember that I have told you again what the manner of that union is to be—that you must eat of my flesh and drink of my blood if you would have life in you; that all your hopes in a future resurrection are bound up in that eating of flesh and drinking of my blood. 'He that abideth in me I will raise him up at the last day.' Now that the moment is come, behold the means of union which I am about to put into your hands. This bread that I hold in my hand is my body." And then, taking the chalice, He said: "This is my blood that shall be shed for the redemption of the world." Peter, James, and John, and the others, looked on with anxious eyes and beating hearts when they heard these awful words of their Divine Lord and Master. They, perhaps, in their ignorance expected to see a startling miracle before their eyes, but no apparent miracle took place. He held aloft that which He described to be His own body, and the eyes of the apostles saw nothing but what appeared to be bread. He put the love and admiration that was centred around this mystery entirely upon their trust in His truthfulness—the argument of things that do not appear—and they bowed down and adored it. Oh! what awe, and at the same time what love and gratitude, must have thrilled their hearts when they heard from His lips those strange words: "What I have done now, the same do ye in commemoration of me." Then, dearly beloved, the great Christian sacrifice was inaugurated, and on the morrow to be made perfect in the sacrifice of the cross, and henceforth to the end of time to be renewed and done in all its reality, as if Christ our Lord was visibly present doing it on every altar of the holy Catholic Church until the last days of the world.

The victim, therefore, of the holy Mass is no other than Jesus Christ; the scene of Calvary is renewed in its reality, though in a different and mystical form. The same body and blood, soul and divinity, are there; the same separation of body and blood mystically takes place for the purpose of sacrifice; but as a sacrament He remains abiding upon our altars for His people, and the word of the Evangelist is fulfilled: "Behold the tabernacle of God with man, and He shall dwell in the midst of them, and they shall be His people, and He in the midst of them shall be their God." He as a Victim is the same; so the Priest is the same.

O my dearly beloved! I am about to announce to you a great mystery. When the Eternal God became man the eyes of men only beheld one who appeared to be a mere man like others. He said to His apostles: "Whom do men say that I am?" and they answered and said: "Some say that Thou art Jeremias, John the Baptist, or Isaias, or one of the prophets." "Whom do you say that I am?" And Peter, dropping down upon his knees, raised up his hands in admiration and cried out, in the name of all his fellow-apostles: "I declare that Thou art the Christ, the Son of the living God." Then did our Lord answer him and say: "Blessed art thou, Simon Bar-Jona, for flesh and blood"—the eyes of the body—"have not revealed this to thee, but my Father in heaven." They beheld only the mere man, yet that man was the true God. In virtue of His incarnation He received the priesthood. "This day have I begotten Thee," says the eternal Father; "Thou art unto me a priest for ever, according to the order Melchisedech." He was ordained a priest the moment that in Mary's immaculate bosom he took our flesh and blood, the moment that Mary, bowing down her head, said, "*Fiat*" ("Be this done unto me"); that moment she was the Mother, not only of the eternal God made man, but she was the Mother of the priest Jesus Christ. Now, dearly beloved, when our Divine Lord said to His apostles: "This do ye in commemoration of me," He passed unto them mystically, but most really, the mysterious power and character and attribute of his own priesthood. The priest, therefore, as a priest, is the representative of Jesus Christ. In the pulpit, speaking under the supervision of a watchful and infallible Church, responsible to that Church for every word that his lips utter, he represents the Word of God Incarnate, and instructing the people in the language of truth. But when he clothes himself in the sacred vestments and ascends the holy altar he is something more than a mere representative of Jesus Christ. He is there as a priest only, scarcely any longer as a man only so far as the man is necessary for the purposes of the priesthood, but the man is altogether priestly; in other words, the action is altogether that of the Son of God, the priest Jesus Christ. Therefore it is that from the moment that he ascends that altar and enters upon the canon of the Mass, and especially at the moment of consecration, the individual man who is there seems to disappear; he no longer speaks as a man, but as the Son of God. He speaks in the elements before him to be consecrated as if they were of his own body. He speaks the words of consolation as if it was his own body and his own blood he was speaking of. He takes the bread into his hands, reminds the Eternal Lord and Everlasting Priest of His promise and His mission, and then, entering entirely into the very person of

THE ALTAR OF THE SACRED HEART.

our Divine Saviour, he says over the bread: "This is my body"; that moment it becomes the body of the Lord. He says over the wine: "This is my blood," and that moment it is the blood of Jesus Christ. Behold, therefore, how, although a man may stand there, yet the priest is still Jesus Christ our Lord. The words are His, the action is His, the power and the efficacy is His. Oh! would that the sanctity of that unworthy celebrant were only as that of Jesus Christ. If, then, such be the Victim, if such be the Priest, what shall we say of the altar? How holy must it be! What wonder if from the beginning the choicest woods of the forests, the choicest marbles and precious stones of the earth, are gathered together carefully and thoughtfully by the Church of God, wherewith to build her holy altars? What wonder that prayer and supplication should be poured over it; that all the angels and saints of God should be invited and invoked to assist at its dedication; that the holy oils that ordain the priests, consecrate the bishops, anoint the dying, should be freely used upon its sacred surface? What wonder when we consider the high purpose for which it is raised? There are all our debts paid. We owe unto God first of all a debt of adoration and of praise, but how shall we pay it?

The word and the command of Scripture is: "*Laudate Dominum secundum multitudinem misericordiæ Ejus*"— Praise the Lord, O ye people! and praise Him according to the measure and the multitude of His greatness. That is to say, give Him infinite praise, for His greatness is infinite; and who can pay this infinite debt? The sadness of despair must come upon us. We are like the poor servant in the Gospel who, not having a penny, was indebted to his master for ten thousand talents, and with the same servant we can approach the altar and say: "O Master! have patience with me, and I will pay thee all." Yes, let the priest approach, let him put forth the mystical words of consecration; presently there is One there, one brother in our human nature, who will pay to His Eternal Father for us all the debt of infinite adoration and praise to the

Lord according to the measure of His greatness. We owe unto God the debt of propitiation for our sins. How many are those sins, how deep the dye of their iniquity, each one can answer for himself. Perhaps those who are accounted the best in the midst of us, when they kneel alone before God are obliged to say, with the Psalmist: "My iniquities are superabundant; they are as the sands of the sea of God." Yet one of those sins, even one, brings with it so much guilt that we incur an infinite debt of satisfaction and propitiation. How shall we pay? We must turn again to the holy altar, and there the language is spoken, and the cry goes forth of blood, crying out more loudly for pardon and mercy than the blood of Abel, the first innocent victim, cried out for vengeance upon his destroyer. We owe unto God the debt of thanksgiving; for, oh! how much have we not received from Him, and how unworthy have we been of His graces? A thousand fall daily at our side, and ten thousand at our right hand, and yet God keeps the punishment of death away from us. Graces and blessings have anticipated our youthful faltering steps. Where many have fallen God has enabled us to stand; where many nations have gone away from the faith and the truth, our fathers received in the day of their dire necessity the holy and the high grace of fortitude even unto death for the faith of God, and that precious faith is the grace of our inheritance. How much, then, have we received both as a people and individually from the Lord our God, and how little have we deserved His gifts! Therefore may we exclaim with David of old: "*Quid retribuam? Quid retribuam?*" What shall I return to Thee? What return shall I make to Thee, O God! for all that Thou hast given to me? Call the priest to the altar, put him there vested and clothed in the character of the eternal priesthood of the Son of God, and he will place upon the altar One whose simplest word is infinite thanksgiving to God. He will place upon the altar One who, worshipping and adoring, commands the attention of all heaven, and whose words fall so sweetly into His Father's ears and upon His Father's heart, and a voice comes from heaven and cries: "This is my beloved Son, in whom I am well pleased." And thus all our mighty debts are paid, all our hopes are centred, all our joys of life are purified and sanctified, all our sorrows are lightened and smoothed; all that we look for in the future, all that we hope to remedy of the past—all find their centre upon an altar of the holy Catholic Church. Well, therefore, may we exclaim with the Psalmist: "How beautiful are Thy altars, O Lord of hosts!" But there is a beauty altogether its own attaching to the altar which we have dedicated to-day. It is the altar of the Sacred Heart of Jesus. It is the altar where all those, the faithful, all those who believe, when they come to ask for light in darkness, for strength in weakness, for comfort in sorrow, for help of any kind for soul or body, it is to that altar that they will naturally turn their steps. For the Sacred Heart of our Divine Lord and Saviour is the home of eternal, undying love; it is the home of that infinite mercy whence came forth all the redemption of mankind; it is the living chalice of the Precious Blood that was poured out so generously for us; it is the Sacred Heart that throbbed with infinite compassion when He beheld the widow of Naim weeping over her son; it is the Sacred Heart which troubled within Him, stirred up the fountain of His tears, which flowed freely and mingled with those of Mary as she wept over her brother's grave. Oh! it is the heart of infinite forgiveness, that, whilst it was fading and dying and breaking on the cross, still found words of joy, reconciliation, peace, and eternal promise for the thief who was hanging at His side. Let us, therefore, rejoice in the beauty of this new altar, as well as avail ourselves of the Sacred Heart and all its love and mercy. Therefore let us, O my beloved! above all remember that there is an altar dearer unto God even than that upon which the blood of His own Divine Son is poured, and that is the altar of our heart. Let us consecrate these thoughts to Him; let the unctions of His divine charity pour, let the lamp of Christian love burn brightly there, let the charity of God and cleanliness of the true Christian reign there; then, indeed, shall we be, in the words of the apostle, "the living temples of the Holy Ghost," the living, breathing statues of representation of Jesus Christ; then, indeed, shall we put Him on who is our peace, our hope, our joy, our consolation in life, in death, and for eternity, to whom be all glory, with the Father and the Holy Ghost. for ever and ever.

THE VIRGIN MOTHER.

THE following eloquent sermon was the last of the series of Advent discourses delivered by Father Burke in the Dominican Church, Dublin, 1877. It is a most beautiful and earnest tribute of love to the Virgin Mother.

"Drop down your dews, ye heavens, from above, and ye clouds rain down the just one; and open thou earth and bud forth a Saviour."

THESE words, my dearly-beloved brethren, taken from the forty-fifth chapter of the Prophecies of Isaias, were the text to which I invited your attention and consideration when we began our novena, and to the same words I turn this evening at the conclusion of our Christmas devotions. I told you that in this divine and adorable mystery of the Incarnation we had to consider the action of heaven and the action of earth—the action of heaven, because it was a mystery accomplished first of all in heaven, and through heavenly influence in the person of the Divine and Eternal Word; the action of earth, because it is also a mystery of earth, consummated on earth, consummated in a child of man, a true child of a mortal woman, the infant Son of the Virgin Mary, as truly human as He is divine. Up to the present time in all the reflections that I have put before you I have only spoken to you of the heavenly aspect of this mystery, the attributes of God as they are revealed through it to us, and the advantages resulting to man from the revelation of the divine attributes of God. But neither you, nor I, nor the angels that are listening to my voice, nor God Himself, that is about to be born this night into the midst of us, would be satisfied if we were to conclude these discourses without special allusion to the Virgin Mother of our Saviour. To her, therefore, and to her part in the adorable mystery of the Incarnation, I invite your particular attention this evening. "Drop down your dews, ye heavens, from above, and ye clouds rain down the just one," says the prophet, but he adds, "And open thou earth and bud forth a Saviour." The virgin womb of Mary was the earth from which the Saviour sprung. Mary's connection with the mystery of the Incarnation may be viewed in a double light: first, her relation to God, next her relation to man. In her relation to God we will consider what she received, in her relation to man we will consider what she bestowed. From the moment that Mary was born into this world, from the moment she lifted her virginal eyes to heaven, her sweet and pure relations with God commenced and His gifts and graces were showered upon her head. Her relations with man began with the Man-God, Jesus Christ, her son, and it is then no longer a question of what she received but of what she gave. Into these considerations I will divide my discourse this evening—Mary's relations to God and Mary's relations to ourselves. There are many who ought to be here to-night to celebrate the mercy of God who are worshipping at another shrine and imagine they are paying some homage to the Christmas festival— strange homage of mortal sin to be offered to God in this holy time that brings the Eternal God into the midst of His creatures. They turn away from their Creator; they admit the demons of drunkenness, of gluttony, of immorality into their midst; they make them their Christmas gods, kneel down in the dust and worship them.

First, then, I invite your consideration to Mary in the mystery of the Incarnation in relation to God, in relation to what she received. Every gift of God, dearly beloved, whether it be vouchsafed to the pure and spotless Virgin or to the lowliest sinner upon the earth, takes the form of divine grace. In whatever form God's gift may come, however much God's gift may be abused, it was originally intended as a grace. One may receive great natural talent and genius, wonderful intellectual endowments; he may turn these gifts against Almighty God, as so many of the highest and noblest of our geniuses have done; but they were given with the wish, with the intention that they should be employed in the service of God, of society, and of fellow-men. Reason is a noble inheritance, a great fortune bestowed on man; he may use it for purposes of dissipation, vile licentiousness, and degrading debauchery. He may employ it to sneer and gibe at the power of the God who gave it. He may offend his God in a thousand ways by means of the very genius wherewith God has endowed him. But though man may misdirect and may abuse the highest and the holiest gifts of God, it still remains true that whatever God gives man He wishes and intends that it shall revert and return to Himself again, through the reasonable homage of man's soul. The gifts that Mary received from God were intended as a preparation for the divine and crowning grace which she was destined to receive, the gift of a divine maternity. And she most faithfully corresponded with the graces she received. You have seen how every gift of God resolves itself into its highest and most privileged form of divine grace, and every grace is increased and enhanced by the correspondence of the recipient.

Mary's graces, and Mary's correspondence to those graces, began even in her mother's womb. God, in view of the high designs He had upon her, began her life with a grace more grand than was ever vouchsafed to man before, than any ever granted to the highest angel in heaven. She was conceived in her mother's womb free from the taint of original sin. But you may ask are not the angels free from the taint of sin, and are not the angels pure through the same power that made Mary pure? I answer, yes. In what, then, does the gift that Mary received transcend the gift granted to the angels? In the language of theology, their gift was general, Mary's was exceptional.

The angels were purified by a universal law made by Almighty God that all His angels should be faithful, and they that were unfaithful were the exceptions to that law. The demons were damned exceptionally, the angels were saved according to the law. But the whole human race sinned in Adam. No man after the time of Adam, no matter how holy he might be, was exempted from that sin. Adam defiled the fountain-head of our nature, polluted the sources of our being. Sin, then, became the rule with man, exemption from sin the exception. Mary is the one solitary exception to the rule. For the forgiveness of original sin was needed the atonement of the Victim. But for Mary the mystery of the Incarnation was anticipated, the merits of the Saviour were applied before His time. For her and Him the guilt of original sin was anticipated before it was incurred. Oh! one grand, glorious, wonderful exception to the law of sin introduced by Adam's crime. Here, then, the grace of Mary's immaculate conception places her on an eminence of instant and pre-eminent purity. All the men upon earth, all the angels in heaven, must look up to her. Even at her conception in her mother's womb she surpasses all the angels in heaven in the extent of the graces which she has received. The graces of the angels end with the grace with which she began, perfect purity, sinlessness, and acceptability to God. From her birth she was sinless before the Lord; she basked in the bright sunlight of God's grace and favor. Her virginal bosom was the only home on earth worthy of a God, and she alone of all God's creatures might truly say: God Himself is come to me, and I am become the Mother of my God. That wonderful and adorable mystery of the Incarnation, inscrutable to the angels, inconceivable to man, is accomplished in Mary. When the Almighty bade His holy prophet go forth and announce this mystery to man, even he, the inspired of God, was confounded and amazed, and exclaimed: "Spare me, O Lord! and send me not forth with such a tale, for if I shall say to the sons of men, Behold, a virgin shall conceive and bring forth a Son, and His name shall be called Jesus, and He shall be the Son of God, what man will believe me?" Yet it was all accomplished in Mary.

For over four thousand years darkness overshadowed the world, and the face of God was hidden from His creatures. Mary was the bright day-star that was to herald the rising of the glorious sun of justice upon the world. Sixteen years, according to the best authorities, were spent in ardent preparation for the great mystery she was destined to accomplish, and every moment of her existence was an accumulation of God's graces in her soul. Oh! wonderful are God's dealings with a faithful soul. The soul that corresponds to God's favors receives graces a hundredfold—a thousandfold—receives graces in an inconceivable addition known only to God. From the moment of Mary's conception she received grace after grace from God. Oh! how wonderful must have been that superstructure of grace in Mary, when the first gift bestowed upon her surpassingly exceeded the highest favor conferred upon man or angel. God's favors are over, but the preparation for some crowning favor which he intends to bestow, if we merit it by faithful correspondence, will surpass and consummate all that have gone before. It is so in our lives. I have had the happiness of administering the Holy Communion to many whom I see here to-night. God could give no higher favor than this, for it was Himself He gave; but many graces thankfully received, faithfully improved, must precede the worthy assistance at the table of the Lord. Great grace went before the horror of sin, the spirit of repentance, the grace that made you resolve that you would die rather than that you would again offend the Almighty. All these were necessary to fit you for the crowning grace of communion with God. Even so it was with Mary. Sixteen years of saintly sinlessness, of exalted purity, were her preparation for the crowning favor of God; and oh! how marvellous must have been that preparation, of which the consummation was so high and noble, the highest and the noblest that God Himself had it in His power to accomplish. Surely might the archangel of God exclaim: "Hail Mary, full of grace, the Lord is with thee"; for she indeed abounded in grace.

The crowning gift of God to Mary was God Himself, the eternal Son of God, the light of the Father's glory, before whom the purest and the highest in heaven kneel in speechless admiration, and who came down from His throne in heaven, from the bosom of the Almighty, to dwell in her pure bosom, to be her Son for ever. There had been pure and holy women on the earth before Mary's time, but to none but her had this great grace been granted, for none but she was worthy.

There was Mary, the sister of Moses, the friend of God, she who led the virginal choirs of the chosen people; but she was not worthy. There was the daughter of Jephte, who, when it was announced to her that she must die, for her father had sworn it before the Lord, asked for a little space of time that she might mourn among her maidens, not the life she sacrificed in obedience to her father's vow, but the life she must forfeit, she that might be the chosen Jewish maiden who would become the mother of the Messias. Even to the strong woman and the valiant, the mother of the Machabees, who died seven deaths in the death of her seven sons for the faith of God, even she was not deemed worthy of this crowning favor. For Mary, and Mary alone, was reserved the highest, the grandest gift that an omnipotent God ever did or will ever bestow upon His creature. Such were the favors that Mary received from God. Let us consider now the favors that Mary conferred upon men.

"Drop down your dews, ye heavens, from above, and ye clouds rain down the just one; and open thou earth and bud forth a Saviour." It is the latter part of the text that we are now to consider. Earth as well as heaven, Mary as well as God, had her part in the glorious mystery of the Incarnation—that mystery by which man was redeemed from bondage and from sin and restored to the hope of heaven. We must consider now the essentials in the atonement, the essentials in the victims for this great sacrifice. Man has outraged the eternal majesty of God by sin. The offence is infinite; the atonement must be infinite to satisfy the justice of God. The offence was committed by a man, and a man must be the victim. An infinite and a human victim is necessary for the sacrifice. God is necessary in this work of our redemption, for God alone is infinite. Man is necessary, for man alone has offended. The victim must be human and divine, true God and true man—as truly God as he is man, as truly man as he is God. Well, then, might the prophet exclaim: "O ye heavens! send down your dews, and ye clouds rain down the just one"; and well might he add: "And open thou earth and bud forth a Saviour."

For the purpose of the Incarnation, therefore, the human element was as necessary as the divine. The victim must be God, that he may offer to God's justice an infinite atonement for an infinite offence. He must be man, that he might suffer and die for the sins of man. In Jesus Christ, the Man-God, that victim was found. He preserved in His person all the power, all the wisdom, all the glory, all the infinite merit of God; but He took to Himself a human nature, capable of sorrow, shame, suffering, and death. That assumption was real, that assumption was eternal. This is difficult to conceive, this is difficult to believe. There were heretics that recoiled from this; they could not believe that the great and eternal God could associate to Himself for ever this debased and degraded nature of ours, and some said: "Oh! yes, he was a good man, he was a just man, he was a holy man, but he was only a man, he was not God"; and they are burning in hell, for they denied the divinity of Christ. And there were others who said He was God indeed, His life proclaims it, His words proclaim it, but He was not man; and they, too, are burning in hell, for they denied the humanity of the Redeemer. Belief in His divinity and belief in His humanity are equally essential for salvation. It is as necessary to believe that Jesus Christ is the son of Mary as it is to believe that He was the Son of God. Mary was an essential instrument in the hands of God to effect the redemption of the whole human race. She gave the blood of her blood, the flesh of her flesh, the bone of her bone to form the humanity of the Saviour. In her womb the Second Person of the Blessed Trinity assumed that human form that was necessary for Him to work out our salvation. "And the Word was made flesh and dwelt among us." Of all the human beings that lived upon this earth Mary alone was pure enough to become the Mother of God. Oh! how perfect must have been the purity, how spotless the sinlessness of that humanity of Mary, from which the all-pure and all-holy God did not disdain to assume a body to Himself. Remember, Mary's free consent was necessary for the consummation of this sacrifice. God never did, and God never will, coerce the will of one of His rational creatures. He sent His angel to announce to Mary the honor that was intended for her, but she was free to refuse that honor if she chose, and her consent was necessary for our redemption.

"Behold," said the angel, "thou shalt conceive in thy womb, and thou shalt bring forth a son, and thou shalt call his name Jesus." And Mary answered: "How can this be, for I know no man?" Even for the dignity of the Mother of God she was unwilling to sacrifice the virginity to which she had vowed herself before the Lord, and the angel eased her fears and told her that by the instrumentality of the Holy Ghost should the mystery be accomplished, and then indeed the Virgin cried out: "Behold the handmaid of the Lord; be it done as the angel hath spoken." God that instant became man in Mary's womb. Her free consent was given, and the work of man's redemption was begun. In this wonderful mystery, in which God Himself disdains not to ask the consent of His creature for the great work which He was about to accomplish, we have before our eyes a wonderful proof of Mary's purity and Mary's grandeur. Mark the language in which the inspired prophet speaks of the Queen of Heaven. Who is she, he exclaims, that comes like the morning, rising fair as the moon, bright as the sun, terrible as an army set in battle array? Yet she is humble and loving as she is beautiful and glorious. Reflect, dearly beloved, what Mary has done for man in the mystery of the Incarnation. By that mystery, in which her part was so large, salvation was purchased for us all. We may scorn and trample upon the priceless gift if we will, but salvation is offered to us all, and there is no soul to-day in the abyss of hell that might not be in heaven if it chose. Oh! how much, my brethren, has the Incarnation of Jesus in Mary's womb given to man. It gives us the right to hope that when our dying eyes close for ever upon this world they may open upon a world that is brighter far than this, that in death we may behold our Redeemer. It gives us the right, this holy Christmas season, by confession and communion, to approach our Saviour; the certainty that if we be but faithful to the graces we receive, we shall never know death, but shall live for ever in the kingdom of our Father. All these priceless privileges were conferred upon us when Mary said to the messenger of God: "Behold the handmaid of the Lord; be it done unto me according to thy word." Behold, then, the position which this wonderful woman holds amid the human race! Behold all she has received from God! behold all she has given to man! God has made her His Mother; we have become her sons. She is our Mother.

When our Redeemer was expiring on the cross, and His Mother stood at its foot in speechless agony, our Saviour in His dying words said to her, indicating His beloved disciple John: "Woman, behold thy son!" and to St. John He said: "Son, behold thy mother!" St. John stood thus the representative of the whole human race. That moment we became sons of the Mother of God, that moment all the intense love in Mary's breaking heart was poured out upon us. We are commanded to love and honor our parents. The same God that demands our adoration for Himself demands our reverence for them. The same God that has said: "I am the Lord thy God, and thou shalt not have strange gods before me," has said also: "Honor thy father and thy mother, that thy days may be long in the land." We must honor our fathers and mothers in the order of nature because God has commanded it; but God requires a reasonable, not a blind, obedience, and it needs no command to induce us to honor the mother who bore us into the world. We honor and love her instinctively, we honor and love her because of the untiring care and the tender love she has lavished upon us, because of the fierce throes of her maternity, the agony she endured that we might be born in the world. But if we thus honor our mother after the order of nature, how much higher should be our honor, how much deeper our love for our Mother after the order of grace! Our mother brought us forth to this material life. Mary brought us forth to life eternal. With much suffering and with many prayers did our natural mother give us birth; but Mary suffered for our sake such affliction, such agony as woman never before endured. We are the children of her agony and of her grace. She has proved her affection by the depth of the sorrows she has suffered for our sake, by the priceless value of the benefits she has conferred. But above all, at this sacred season when we commemorate the adorable mystery in which her share was so large, we should turn to our sweet and gentle Mother with renewed reverence and love. While we adore the Son, the Mother should not be forgotten, and in the temple of our hearts, purified by the holy sacraments of the Church, we should erect for her an altar where we may offer our humble homage to our glorious Queen, our earnest gratitude to our munificent benefactress, and our warmest love to our tender Mother.

THE FEAST OF THE IMMACULATE CONCEPTION.

THE Feast of the Immaculate Conception was observed in the Cathedral, Marlborough Street, Dublin, December 8, 1876, with particular devotion. The sermon was delivered by Father Burke, who preached from the words:

"Who is she that cometh like unto the morning rising?"

MAY it please your eminence. Dearly-beloved brethren, it was thus that the inspired one of the Scripture described the coming of Mary the Mother of God. He contemplated the sad night of four thousand years, and, looking towards the Orient, he saw there a vision of divine beauty rising before him, and he exclaimed: "Who is she that cometh like unto the morning rising?" That was the prophet's vision, and behold we are celebrating to-day the first coming of Mary the Mother of God, our Lord and Saviour Jesus Christ—the first moment of her existence, when she was conceived in her mother's womb. Behold the dawn of that day of which she was the day-star, the precursor, and the promise! Now, observe the language of the inspired one. He calls her *aurora consergens*—the approach or first dawn of day springing up. In the order of nature, dearly beloved, the aurora or dawn gives promise, and is a sure harbinger of the day that is to follow. When a man who is keeping the night watch over his flocks and herds in the fields, or when the sailor who stands during the night watches at the wheel, or when any person who has to keep a vigil during the darkness turns his eyes at the approach of day towards the eastern horizon, he gathers with truth from the dawning of the morning what manner of day is to come. If, my dear brethren, on that eastern horizon he sees the early dawn and the breaking of the orient light crossed by angry clouds, if he sees there marks of atmospheric disturbances, then he concludes that the day will be stormy; but if, on the other hand, the dawn comes mild and pure, and the day-star rises limpid and beaming with undisturbed light—if he notes no cloud across the eastern vista—if no sign of angry atmosphere be there—then is such a dawn the promise of a day unclouded in the beauty and wealth of its sunshine. Even so is it in the order of grace. The dealings of God with man were divided into two great epochs or days. The first is the day of Adam, of whom the apostle says: "The first man of the earth and earthly." The second great epoch is the day of Jesus Christ, "the Second Man, who was from heaven and heavenly." Of others the apostle makes no mention. He divides our history into those two great days, and thus each had an aurora, or dawning, in a woman. As soon as we turn to the first historical evidence of our race—when we turn to the East—which tells us of the origin of our being, there do we see the aurora or dawn of our history in Eve. But scarcely does she appear upon the horizon when we see hanging and clustering around her head the angry clouds of God's bitter vengeance, and we hear besides the voice of that angry God in tones of condemnation and reproach, like the mutterings of the morning thunder, and we are struck with terror to think how awful the day must be that was ushered in with so much promise of storm and of anger. And sad surely that day has been—a day of earth, a day of sin and of darkness, of which the prophet mournfully exclaims: "There is no truth, there is no knowledge of God left in the land; cursing and lying, theft and adultery have prevailed, and behold! blood has touched blood." But, my dear brethren, the second day is approaching, the day that will bring the "Man from heaven, heavenly"— the day that will behold God and man united in one Divine Person, united in our Lord and Saviour Jesus Christ—the day that will behold an unclouded age, darkness dissipated, the reign of sin destroyed, and the mild sway of God's love and grace inaugurated—the day that will behold the terrible decree against man erased, the bolts of heaven withdrawn, and the golden portal opened wide to us all. And this day—this day of peace, of happiness, and of benediction—had its aurora and dawn, and that dawn was in Mary, the Immaculate Mother of the Man-God. Oh! how different from the coming of the first mother, Eve.

Mary came in all the calmness and gentleness, in all the splendor, and in all the purity of the highest grace and the highest love of God. No cloud of anger hangs over her head, no lowering shadow of divine wrath falls before her. The hereditary and traditional sin is stayed by the omnipotent hand of Him who redeemed her; she is untainted by the breath or thought of sin. She rises to tell the world that the sun of eternal salvation is about to break upon us; that the darkness of ages is to be dispelled for ever; that the true King is coming to take up his own, to secure his own inheritance in the hearts and love of man. And she rose calmly and serenely, shining like a lovely morning star, with a brightness not indeed her own, but a brightness coming to her from the Sun which follows in her wake—the brightness of divine grace, transcending all the forms of divine beauty that ever God's grace took in any of His creatures in heaven or on earth—a brightness and a glory of divine grace surpassing the united glory and the united brightness of all whom God has ever honored, or intends to honor, in His holy kingdom; and all this in the one grace of her glorious Immaculate Conception—a grace supreme indeed, for it brought with it to Mary perfect sinlessness.

No shade, no thought of sin was ever allowed to approach to the Virgin, either as a personal sin or as an hereditary sin. A supreme grace of perfect sinlessness carried Mary at once to the very climax and summit of all that every other saint of God aspired to in life or in death; for every form of holiness in man or angel aspires as to its perfection to perfect sinlessness, and consequently to perfect acceptability before God. When they attained to this then were all their aspirations achieved. To this, therefore, tend all the graces of earth, to perfect sinlessness. To this tend all the merciful purgating punishment pronounced even upon the elect of God—to perfect sinlessness—and it is this, the climax and perfection of virtue, that is crowned in heaven by the rewarding hand of an all-just God. Mary began with this perfect sinlessness. The Lord hath cast the foundations of her upon the summits of the holy mountains. This supreme grace was thus supreme, not only in its excellence, but in that it was a solitary grace. A thing may be of no intrinsic value, but if it be unique—if there be nothing like it in the world—from that very fact springs its preciousness and value. Now, of all the children of Adam, of all those who were ever born into this world, of all who ever will be born into it to the end of time, of all those who shall ever enter into the kingdom of God, Mary alone was conceived without the taint of original sin. In that universal corruption which, like a mighty river, proceeded from the sin of Adam for all his posterity, Almighty God took her into His own hands, enshrined her in the sanctity and omnipotence of His own divine counsels and His own heart, and there kept Mary preserved from every taint or stain of sin. It is, moreover, a grace supreme, in that it contained the germ of all other graces that crowned her life. All those terrible consequences of original sin—the promptings of unruly passions, the uprising of all foul desires, the loud calls of a base and fallen nature—all these things were unknown to Mary. The other saints have become saints by overcoming themselves. Mary became the saint of saints, fitted, as St. Thomas says, to be the Mother of God, by simply taking up her enormous graces and corresponding with them. And now, perhaps, it must suggest itself to you or to me that whilst this grandest of all God's creatures is the object of our admiration—for surely we must admire that which God made so fair and noble; nay, more, we are called upon to admire her, for the Scripture says: "God is wonderful in His saints; praise ye the Lord in His saints as in the very firmament of His power"—that whilst we are thus admiring her, and giving God thanks frequently for all He has done for her and through her for us, the very greatness of her graces may seem to lift her so far above us that we find no example, no lesson for ourselves in the life and graces of Mary. But it is not so. She is not only admirable, but she is imitable, and I would fail in my duty to you to-day if I were simply to place the Blessed Mother of God before you as an object for your admiration without also endeavoring to show you how the least and humblest amongst us may imitate Mary, and do in our own sphere and measure what she has done for God. In order to show this I take the graces of Jesus Christ, first of all, as the triumph of God in Mary, and, secondly, as the delight of God in Mary. As to the triumph of God in Mary, it is worthy of remark that Almighty God, who makes all things fair and acceptable to Himself, and who, in the beginning, looked upon all that He had made and saw that it was good, still, out of respect for His own laws, out of respect for the intelligence and freedom of will with which He endows His creatures as their very nature, permits the devil to spoil His works, and in a great measure to frustrate His own designs. It would seem to us an incomprehensible matter how the Almighty God could permit this, were we not to remember that intelligence and freedom are the nature of man; that if he chooses to pervert his intelligence and abuse his freedom, Almighty God has such respect for the nature of His creatures, and for His laws, that He will permit that abuse rather than save man by infringing upon the essential character of his nature and freedom. But though God has thus at times allowed His enemy apparently to prevail against Him, still He has never given to that enemy the complete and absolute triumph. Wherever the enemy seemed to prevail, God in some portion or other of the battlefield asserted His own victory, and put His enemy to confusion. Thus, although the iniquity of man spread all over the earth at the time of the first deluge, yet still the Almighty God preserved Noe and his family, making them pure and holy and good, and so our humanity was saved through them in the ark.

Afterwards, when God opened the heavens once more to rain down living fire on Sodom and Gomorrah, amidst the universal iniquity Lot and his family were found pure and worthy to entertain the angels of God, and so were saved. In after-times, too, when idolatry spread over the land, when every one bowed down to idols, do we not invariably find some one man or one family preserving the worship of the true God, and His or their own purity and innocence; and even in the dispersion of the children of the Lord the Lord asserted Himself in Tobias, nor did He ever permit His enemy a universal triumph. So, dearly beloved, when the devil tempted our first parents and prevailed against them, and in their sin succeeded in tainting and poisoning the very fountain-head of all human nature, it would seem, indeed, that for years, at least, he had asserted himself in a complete triumph over the Almighty God. Adam and Eve fell—all humanity falls with them. Never shall child be conceived in its mother's womb without the taint of sin; never again shall a human being behold heaven save as a penitent, with the taint of original sin at least once incurred; never again can a creature arise to show the angels in heaven, and man on earth, what man would have been if God's work had not been utterly spoiled in him. But did God give this great triumph to His enemy? Oh! no; He asserted Himself—He preserved one unpolluted, one unspoiled specimen of that humanity which so lovingly He had created, and that one was the triumph of God. Mary was always the triumph of God. "Behold! a woman shall crush the serpent's head with her heel." "I saw a great sign—a woman clothed, with the sun and the moon beneath her feet, and around her head a crown of twelve stars"—and before her the enemies of God were drawn out. The *aurora consergens*—the springing up of the day—came to pass in Mary's Immaculate Conception; and yet, dearly beloved, even here is the object of our imitation, for every one amongst us in his or her own sphere, no matter how humble it may be, ought to be, and with God's grace will be, a living monument of the triumph of Almighty God, and of God's grace over His enemy, as often as we endeavor, by holy repentance, to shake off our sins—as often as we say a prayer heartily and fervently to Almighty God—as often as we turn our eyes from that which might by suggestion of evil thought influence us towards the commission of sin—in every such action it is God that triumphs over His enemy. When the Christian man is able to put a constraint upon the passions within him, to defeat the powers of hell at work beneath and around him, God triumphs over His enemy. And God glories in this triumph, even as He gloried in the Immaculate Conception of His Virgin Mother. It is the assertion of the kingdom of God; it is the telling to all hell, and to all the enemies of God, that God has only to put out His little finger to scatter all His enemies—to communicate an act of His divine will by divine grace to scatter them to the winds. But Mary, in her Immaculate Conception, is not only the triumph of God, but the delight of God. God, my dearly beloved, loves Himself with an infinite love, and that love, infinite and eternal, with which He loves Himself is diffused also in His creatures, and those He loves in proportion as they rise to a resemblance to Him.

That resemblance to Himself is found in sinlessness and purity—perfect sinlessness of soul and body; this is the first great means by which His creatures can rise to a resemblance to that Almighty God who is sinlessness and holiness itself. Whenever, therefore, God beholds this, His heart rejoices, and this sinlessness is the delight and joy of the Almighty. Therefore it is that whilst God loves all the just, loves His angels and saints in heaven, loves those who are endeavoring to serve Him on earth with a love altogether His own; yet because Mary gathered to her own soul a more perfect holiness than all, therefore Mary, more than all the saints, was the delight of God— *delit a Dei*. He speaks to us in Scripture of the delight He feels when He beholds virtue and grace triumphant, and therefore she is especially "the delight of God." In this also may we imitate her. Oh! what untold consolation to think that we also can give joy and gladness to the heart of God. "Unto my heart thou shalt give joy and gladness." What a consolation to think that even the least of us can return to God His own gifts. Out of Thine own, and that which Thou hast given us, we give Thee back again. Thou hast given us joy and gladness, and we, O Lord, will give joy and gladness to Thee. O dearly beloved! let us put away our sins, and let us enter on this holy time determined and prepared to meet our new-born Saviour with hearts inflamed with love for Him, cleansed with repentance, that He may be born into the soul of every one of us—by cleansing our souls from sin. There is joy in heaven for one sinner that doth penance, and the joy in heaven begins in the heart of God Himself; therefore out of our very misery, humiliation, and folly can we find material to make ourselves the delight and joy of God. In these two great respects, therefore, is the Immaculate Virgin imitable. We can, my dear brethren, behold another Mary to guide us in the repression of our passions, in asserting the triumph of divine grace—another Mary to guide us by the joy and gladness which our repentance and true contrition will assuredly give. Second only to the joy with which He contemplates perfect purity —and great is the joy of God to-day when He contemplates the Blessed Virgin in her Immaculate Conception—second only to this was the unction that swelled the divine heart of Jesus Christ when He looked down at Mary Magdalene, and when her first tear fell upon His sacred feet. Oh! if we cannot give Him the perfect joy of perfect purity, perfect charity, perfect goodness, at least let us give Him the joy of perfect, true repentance, and so rise in some degree towards the perfection of the Mother of God. Let us do that, my brethren, and this will be for us the *aurora consergens*—upspringing and dawn of the day that shall know no ending—of the day in that bright heaven, that kingdom, in which the sun and lamp is God—the day that shall never know an evening—the day spent in the contemplation of the infinite loveliness of our Lord and Saviour Jesus Christ, and in sight of Mary the Immaculate Mother of God.

THE STATIONS OF THE CROSS.

In this discourse Father Burke has treated with great power a subject of deep and singular interest. It was delivered in the Church of SS. Augustine and John, Thomas Street, Dublin, in aid of the fund for the Stations of the Cross.

"There stood by the cross of Jesus, Mary, His mother, and the other Mary"; words taken from the Gospel of St. John.

YOU know, dearly beloved, that all we have worth estimating in this world, and absolutely all that we hope for in eternity, is derived by us from our Lord Jesus Christ. You know, moreover, that by His sufferings and death He not only took away the sin of man, washing it out in His own precious blood, He not only cancelled the handwriting of the awful decree which consigned us all to eternal banishment from God, but He opened up, on the other hand, to us all the treasury of His Father's kingdom and His Father's love, and He obtained for us, through the merits of His suffering and passion, every good and every perfect gift that cometh down from the Father in heaven. Now, there are two sets of Christians in this world. There are those who love to contemplate all the results of the passion and sufferings of our Lord, who love to think that He has taken their sins upon Himself, as in fact he has done, who love to think that He has delivered them from the slavery of that old law which He accomplished and abolished in His own Divine Person, but who in their joyous recollection of all that they have received from Him turn away deliberately from the contemplation of the sufferings and the death and the humiliation and the sorrows by which they obtain from the Almighty God so many good and glorious gifts. They are those who, calling themselves Christians, and professing a belief in Christ, do not belong to the Catholic Church. To those the feast of Christmas and Good Friday is all the same, an equal rejoicing. They rejoice on Christmas day that a child is born who is to redeem them, but they will not enter the stable nor contemplate the child's sufferings and humiliations; they call that superstitious. On Good Friday they stand indeed under the shadow of the rood, but they will not lift up their eyes to Him that suffers there, but, like the soldiers who were casting their dice at His feet and rejoicing that he had left them a few garments, so they cast and shuffle their dice of mutual congratulation under the cross, whilst they are rejoicing at what they have obtained by those sufferings. They refuse to contemplate them, much less to sympathize with them.

But, dearly beloved, there is another class of Christians in this world, and they are the children of the Catholic Church, which was founded by the Son of God, dowered with His eternal dower of truth and of divine grace, sanctified by the blood that fell upon her head as she stood at the foot of the cross, looking on fearlessly, though with agonizing eyes, and she exclaims, like Sophonias of old: "Oh! Thou art a spouse of blood to me this day, and our espousals are consecrated by sufferings." And for these, the children of the Church, the passion and the sufferings of the Son of God are a daily theme proposed to them by their holy mother to be the subject of their daily thoughts.

Is it not strange, dearly beloved, that wherever we turn in a Catholic church something or other reminds us of the sufferings of Christ? Over all her altars we see the crucifix. It would be a mortal sin for one of her priests to celebrate the Mass unless the image of the Crucified were there, raised up before him, that whilst he commemorated the sorrows he may look upon that which will remind him of the original. The Church of God loves constantly to commemorate the passion and sufferings of our Lord, and when the day of days comes which brings back the hour that beheld Him raised up on Calvary, oh! all is grief and sorrow and desolation in the Church; no light must glimmer upon her altars, the very lamp of her sanctuary is extinguished, as if put out by the tears of sorrow that have fallen upon the perennial flame; all is draped in the deepest black, all speaks of sorrow, of the broken heart, of the empty house, of joy departed—all brings as powerfully as the senses can before the minds of the faithful the sufferings and the desolation of the Son of God. And now, it may be asked, why does the Church of God put this sorrowful view before us, rather than the joyful? Surely our Lord has gained for us everything by His sufferings; why should we not, therefore, consider our own gain with joy, rather than consider His sufferings with sorrow? I answer, dearly beloved, that the Church of God, in this as in every other spirit that animates her devotions as well as judges her dogmata—the Church of God, I say, in this is moved by the mind of God on the one hand and the nature of man on the other. The mind of God is clearly put before us. He will not have us be forgetful of what He has suffered for our sakes. Christ our Lord never dreamed of such forgetfulness. He will not permit it. When He instituted the greatest of all His mysteries and performed the greatest of all His miracles— namely, the mystery and the miracle of His own Divine Presence in the Blessed Eucharist—He expressly tells us that He did this in order that the memory of His sufferings and of His passion should never pass away nor be forgotten.

When He had changed the bread into His own most sacred body He declared: "This body is about to be broken and given up for you"; and when he took the chalice and changed the wine into His own most precious blood He declared to them: "This is the blood that is about to be shed for many unto the remission of sins." This is not a feast of joy, but a commemoration of sufferings. The mind of the Son of God Himself was perpetually engaged in the contemplation of His own sufferings, of His own passion. The word of the prophet is: 'My grief and my sorrow are always before me"—" *Dolor meus in conspectu meo semper.*" As the Child of Nazareth grew from childhood into boyhood, from boyhood into manhood, He grew only to the fulness of His age for the purpose of suffering and of agony and of sorrow, and the thing was always before His eyes. So did this suffering occupy, not only the mind of the Father in heaven, who saw in them not only satisfaction to His justice, but they also occupied the mind of God made man upon the earth, who dwelt constantly upon the contemplation of them ; and so also it was with Mary His Mother. In the first days of the fulness of her joy, when we may well imagine that no shadow of sorrow could fall upon the brightness of her delight, when she brought her child into the temple that she might give him to God, and then purchase him back again from God, as her first-born, by paying for him the little tribute of two turtle doves, Simeon, the high-priest, said to her: "Thou art the mother rejoicing in a son of whom David spoke of old, but I say unto thee that this child is raised up for a sign, that shall be contradicted ; that thy soul the sword of sorrow shall pierce through and through, that the thoughts of many hearts may be revealed." And the Evangelist tells us that Mary, having received her prophetic message of sorrow, laid it up in her heart. "And Mary," says the Evangelist: "laid up all these things in her heart." And from that hour until she saw the mystery fulfilled the passion and the suffering of her Divine Son were ever present to her mind. But it is not only, dearly beloved, that the Church interprets the Word of God, but she also interprets the deepest feelings of the heart of man. And now I must appeal to you not so much in the language of Scripture, nor of authority, but in the language of plain, common reason and experience. Suffering is the test of love. Take the mother that loves her only-begotten child with all those depths of love which only a mother's heart can know. As long as

the child is well, in rude health, as long as he is able to
move about freely around her, no matter how deeply she
loves him, she never can test or know the depth of her own
love. But a day comes when the fair blooming child is
smitten with disease, and now his mother sees him under
the doctor's knife, or writhing in agony which cannot be
explained, much less relieved; then, and only then, for the
first time do the hidden and deeper depths of her love
well up and be moved within her; then, and only then, she
knows in the agony of her anxiety how great is her love
for the little suffering babe before her. If you had a
friend, a friend who is dear to you, a friend whose voice is
music in your ears, the very sight of whom is a light to
your eyes and a joy in your heart, a friend whom you have
tested in a thousand ways, whose friendship has never failed
you when you wanted it most, whose voice has always
cheered and sustained you, whose hand and whose heart
were ever open to you, whose very heart was yours—you
love him, of course you love him, but you do not know the
depth of your own love; it is not whilst you are receiving
benefits from him, it is not whilst you are rejoicing in his
company that you can ever sound the depth of your own
love; but when the hand of death comes in and removes
him, and the loved face is seen no more, and the sound of
the cheering voice is heard no more, and all that you so
loved and prized and could find in no other is gone in him,
then, oh! it is then that the heart of man feels in the
depths of his sorrow how deep his love, and hence there is
no more common saying amongst men than when a friend
dies and is taken away from them to say to each other:
"Well, I never knew how much I cared for him until I
lost him." Why is it said: *Nil de mortuis nil nisi
bonum*—let nothing be said about the dead except what is
good? Why, because as a rule love asserts itself in sorrow,
and the failings and the faults of the deceased one are forgotten in the love which remembers only his virtues and
his perfections; and this is the nature of man, and God
Himself recognizes this, for He makes suffering in the

Scripture the test of love and death; it is the climax of sufferings, and is precisely what He has taken by the mouth of His prophet to compare with love to say: "Love is as strong as death."

When, therefore, brethren, we recollect that we are the children of the kingdom and the children of the new law, that we are called not to a law of fear but of love, that we have received the spirit not of "bondage unto fear," says St. Paul, but as of children crying, "Abba, Father," when we consider that love or charity is the perfecter of the law, when we consider that Jesus Christ our Lord, in return for all that He has done and suffered, only demands the reward of our love, saying to us in the language of Scripture: "O my son! give me thy heart," what wonder, then, that the Church should put ever before our eyes and before our thoughts these deep and terrible sufferings of the Son of God in His passion and His death, in order to stir up the deeper love which is in our hearts, in order that grace may be helped by nature, and in order that every one may find not only a test of his love but also his affection in his sympathy with the sufferings of Jesus Christ? For, dearly beloved, sympathy with our Divine Lord in His sufferings—or, in plainer language, devotion to the passion of Jesus Christ—is at once the countersign of the children and the elect of God, and their pious privilege. Ask yourselves now, my dearly beloved, here—you who fill this church to-day—let each one ask himself: "Have I devotion to the passion and sufferings of Jesus Christ? Do I often think of them? Do I ever reflect upon the strong young man, thirty-three years of age, in the full bloom of His manhood, in all the grandeur of His majestic beauty, stripped of His clothes on that early morning in the month of March, and His hands taken rudely and tied behind His back to the pillar, and then the cohort of soldiers closing around Him, every strong man with a sharp scourge in his hand, scourging Him from head to foot, right and left. They struck Him across the face, they struck Him on His breast, they struck and mangled Him until His flesh was torn and the blood streamed forth, until He hung from that pillar senseless with the loss of blood—until the very scourges, sodden with blood, have to be thrown aside, in order that new ropes may be taken, still to injure and lacerate the broken body; until at length from the top of His head to the sole of His foot there is not a sound place in Him. The very Virgin Mother who bore Him could scarcely recognize in the figure streaming with blood the form of her fair Son. Do you ever think of this? Do you ever think that after the sleepless nights, with the soul drooping until it was made sick unto death, with those other wounds open from the interior energy of His sacred spirit, until every pore of His sacred frame became a wound pouring forth blood, that He was brought out in the early morning, and seventy-two long, strong thorns driven into His head—driven until they touched the fevered and the aching brain, driven until, were He mere man, He would have been maddened by the agony they inflicted? Do you ever reflect, my children, on the strong man, thirty-three years of age, hanging for three awful, desperate hours by two huge spikes driven into His hands and two driven through His sacred feet—hanging out from that cross, every throb of His heart weaker and more faint, the thirst of death upon His lips, unable almost to speak, the film of death upon His eyes, the streaming blood from His thorny crown blinding Him, the strain upon every nerve and muscle breaking His heart and agonizing Him, the sorrows of all the anger of Heaven piled upon Him as mountains? Do you ever think of this? Yet I tell you that devotion to all this—for it is the Lord God made man who endured it all—the devotion to all this is first of all the countersign of our election, and it is also our best and our dearest privilege. The sign by which we may know whether we are the sons of God and the elect of God, dearly beloved, is charity, the charity of God which is revealed through the cross. "They shall have His name and His Father's name as a sign upon their forehead." What is the sign, I ask, if not the sign of the cross that bore aloft upon its strong limbs the suffering victim for the sins of man? Wherefore St. Paul said: "The Gospel that I preach, Jesus Christ crucified." The word that is upon my lips, the word of the cross, behold the true Gospel of Jesus Christ. Wherefore, if any man would have it, he must have it impressed upon his soul, impressed upon his forehead and upon his lips by devotion to the passion and the sufferings of our Lord. Therefore it is the countersign of the elect of God. It is, moreover, our greatest privilege. This is a great mystery which I am about to propound to you in a few words as clearly as may be. My dearly beloved, suffering, which must come sooner or later, sorrow, which must at one time or another make itself felt, and perhaps often, frequently, is the lot and the portion of every one of us. If any man thinks that he can pass through life as through a pleasant dream, as through a hall lighted up by sunshine, uncheckered by shadow, he deceives himself.

There is no life for sin or the sinner without suffering and sorrow. But the Almighty God has given us this comfort in our sufferings, the greatest comfort that can be —He has given us the privilege of comparing our sorrows with those of His own Divine Son and of the sacred Virgin Mother that bore that Son into this earth, and of all those whom He loved and whom He chastened, that out of the depths of our faith we may derive strong help in our hour of trial and great consolation in our hour of trouble. For unto the Blessed Virgin the Church applies the words of Scripture: "All you who pass the way," she says, "come and see if there be sorrow like unto my sorrow." She does not speak to those who pass the way of joy, she does not speak to those who come with laughing eyes and rejoicing words, who have never known sorrow; with them she has nothing in common, for she is the Queen of Martyrs and the Mother of Sorrows. But it is to those who are in grief that she speaks. "All you who walk the way of tears, all you whose path is strewn with thorns, all you who carry the heavy weight of a broken heart within your bosom, come, oh! come unto this mountain of sorrow and compare your sorrow unto mine. See if there was ever a child like unto Him whom I beheld agonizing and complaining in my ears of his death-like thirst, and I could not open my breast or hand to relieve Him. See if there be sorrow like unto this." It is true the Blessed Virgin in that hour of sorrow knew well how holy and necessary these sufferings were. Oh! yes, we all know that, and any one amongst you who has ever sat by the bedside of a suffering and dying friend also knows how good and salutary and necessary these sufferings were, for "those whom God loves He chastens."

But tell me how much did that knowledge avail to lighten the weight of your grief; did you not grieve all the same when you saw the face distorted, the look of agony in the dying eyes, the brow clammy with the perspiration of death, faintly looking for some friend to give relief, when you heard the heavy, labored breath of that breast which was so soon to be silenced by death—oh! what then, though you knew that those sufferings were good and necessary, what relief did they bring to you when in your love you were unable to help them? And now I say unto you that it is one of the principal reasons for which the holy Catholic Church puts up in all her churches the commemoration of the passion of our Lord and His sufferings that those who are steeped in sorrow, that those who are afflicted and in suffering may come in and find some consolation in viewing the greater Calvary and the grander sorrows of Mary. Moreover, these devotions to the passion are not only the privilege and the refuge of the suffering heart, but they are also the strongest arguments of our faith. It is as necessary to believe in the humanity of our Lord as it is to believe in His divinity. It is easy to believe in either one or the other when that one is exalted and shows itself. It is as easy for us to believe in the divinity of our Lord, as it was for St. Peter to believe when he saw Him shine like unto the sun upon Mount Horeb, and when he cast himself down in an ecstasy of faith which was almost changed into a vision, and said what he afterwards said in heaven: "Lord, it is good for us to be here." It was easy for him to confess His divinity. So, in like manner, it is easy to believe and confess in His manhood, in its reality, in its true existence when you find Him dying, nailed to the cross, looking down to the earth, and saying to His friend: "O friend! take this poor afflicted woman and be a child to her; she is your Mother"; and to His Mother: "O Mother! behold thy son; don't look to me any more, for I can do nothing for you nailed to the cross." It is easy to believe in His humanity when we hear a faint murmur come from His dying lips, parched with the thirst of death: "I thirst; will no one give me to drink?" And so, dearly beloved, this holy recollection and constant memorial of His passion typifies the faith, animates the hope, but above all deepens the love of the soul in its devotion to Jesus Christ. Far away in the west of Ireland, where her ancient language and holy traditions are most jealously and faithfully preserved, there was a mother who went every Friday in the year, her growing son by her side, to perform the Stations of the Holy Way of the Cross, and it was during the first year of the famine, when great misery was upon the land, and when the angel of death stalked abroad and struck terror into every heart. And this mother and the child were going around the Stations of the Cross when two strangers entered the Franciscan church.

One of these, a Protestant, said to the other, for the woman was weeping freely—she, with that demonstrativeness that belongs to our genuine race, she not only wept freely but she sobbed aloud—and this stranger said: "Why is this mother weeping?" The other answered: "She is weeping over our Lord Jesus Christ, over His sufferings, over His death." "What!" said the strange man, not a Catholic, "why, it is nearly two thousand years ago since He suffered and died." "No," said the other, who was a Catholic, "no, He dies every Friday in the year before that mother's eyes, and she is weeping over

Him as if she were amongst those Marys who stood upon Calvary. He is a living presence and a living reality to her, and she is teaching her boy to weep." So it is. It was not for the misery that was around her, though it was great; it was not for her personal sufferings, though she had to suffer with our people; but it was that she came to the mountain of sorrows, and there in the contemplation of the miseries of Mary she measured her own grief with that of the Virgin Mother and found that the greatest sorrow of life, even of the mother's heart, compared with the sorrows of Mary, is but as a drop only to the mighty ocean. And now, dearly beloved, all this that I have spoken to you is but to lead your minds to the subject for which we are here to-day. You know that the fathers of St. Augustine, who have built this magnificent church—not yet completed and in all beauty, but a promise of the perfect thing which soon I hope will gladden our eyes and make your hearts to rejoice—have resolved, even before their church be completed, to set up at once here the Stations of the Holy Cross—that is to say, fourteen elaborate pictures in which all that the pious mind of the Church could conceive or the deft hand of the artist execute will bring out before the eyes of the faithful the various stages of the passion and sufferings of our Lord. The expense of these works of art is great. Most willingly would the good fathers have them executed nearer home, most joyfully, if they could only nearer home produce the same thing at the same expense. But, bound on the one hand to consult the requirements of high art, and on the other hand to consult their own modest means, they were obliged to get them abroad. But these stations are about to be erected here, and much if not all will depend upon the generosity with which you enable the fathers thus to decorate their church by your offerings to-day.

You may ask me what is the history of this devotion. There are fourteen Stations of the Holy Cross—that is to say, fourteen phases of the suffering and passion of our Lord—put before the faithful for their contemplation in this devotion. Some of these are recorded in the Gospel, and are consequently articles of faith; some of them are recorded only in the Church's traditions, and, if I may use the words, they are articles not of Christian faith but of Christian love. For instance, we are not told in the Gospel that our Divine Lord fell three times under His cross whilst He journeyed the sad *Via Dolorosa* from Herod's court to the Hill of Calvary. We are not told that Veronica came and offered Him the tribute of a woman's devotion, and that He wiped His bleeding and perspiring face in the handkerchief which she gave Him. But these are amongst the earliest traditions of the Church's love. And their history is simply this: You all know that when our Divine Lord and Saviour was dying He left His blessed Virgin Mother in charge of St. John the Evangelist, telling St. John to regard her as a mother, and telling her to regard him as a son. After the ascension of our Lord unto heaven John remained some time in Jerusalem before he departed for Ephesus to take charge of the churches of Asia Minor, and during his stay in Jerusalem, whilst his new Mother was with him, her delight was to go out from her house and silently and privately to go over the scene of that Good Friday morning. She went and stood before the entrance of Pilate's palace; there she recalled that she saw Him crowned with thorns, and with the old purple garments clinging to His wasted and blessed limbs, and heard Him proclaimed, "Behold the Man." She followed from the Prætorian Court out over the steps, bending down and kissing those particular marks of her own, where she knew His blessed feet had left traces of His blessed blood. She followed Him until He came to the spot where she, unable to restrain herself, came before Him and knelt down and cried out: "O my Son! O my Son!" She followed in the same way until she came to the spot where she said to herself: "Here I saw Him waver and tremble under the cross, and I heard a great noise, and I saw Him fall to the ground and that mighty cross crash down on Him. Here I saw those brutal soldiers lift the cross and then strike Him with their swords until He rose, more dead than alive, to take once more upon His lacerated shoulders that heavy burden."

And so she went on step by step until she came to the Hill of Calvary, and there this brave woman, the Queen of Martyrs, stood for three hours again, and went through all the agony of her mother's heart. This was Mary's life, according to the Church's traditions, in Jerusalem. And the other Mary, the other Mary who represented Christian womanhood and manhood, and Mary of Salome and the Magdalene, and the Magdalene's sister, Martha, and other pious women, gradually observing their Virgin Mother going forth on this way, went with her and mingled their tears with hers. Then as the Church was gradually spreading throughout the nation, the newly-converted Christians naturally turned to Jerusalem, and were anxious to see the places where our Lord had lived and died, and they came and found Mary and the women going through their daily devotions, the Stations of the Cross, and they joined them —Roman senators, the noblest of the land, generals of armies, the marshals and conquerors of the world, the greatest of Rome's statesmen, the greatest of Greece's artists, painters, and sculptors, bowing down before the Mother of God, and with wondering eyes and pitying hearts joining in the procession and accompanying Mary and the women on the *Via Dolorosa*. And the Church crowned it with her indulgence, and Mary departed to Ephesus, and from Ephesus to heaven; but the devotion spread on, and that which was confined to Jerusalem was spread by the beneficence of the Church, and wherever the fourteen Stations of the Cross are erected there is a new Jerusalem, a new Calvary waiting for its Mary, waiting for its pious souls to come and pour out at the feet of our Divine Lord the tribute of an undying love. Behold the history of the Stations of the Cross. And now this devotion is about to be raised in the midst of us. O my friends! you who are able to contribute largely help those good fathers to-day, that you may have a consolation in life and at the hour of death, and that the poor and the afflicted may have a refuge here. For, dearly beloved, unto the troubled soul, unto the sorrowing heart, the Church must ever be like the pool of Bethsaida, where, no matter what disease was upon you, if you entered and descended into its waters you were presently relieved. And so those who come into this church bending under their weight of sorrow must go forth erect through the misery and the sufferings of Jesus Christ. It is, therefore, for them that I specially plead when I ask you to-day for the sake of Him who suffered and died, and whose sufferings are thus commemorated, to be large in your charity, and enable these good fathers, who are already all but crushed under the tremendous effort of raising such a church as this, to give to that church its most necessary embellishments, and to make it in the midst of you a *Via Dolorosa*, leading from the heart of every family in the neighborhood here, leading up to Calvary; for, brethren, in the Christian's progress Calvary is the necessary height from which the soul must spring to the Horeb of the eternal heavens.

THE PASSION OF OUR LORD.

THE following very remarkable and beautiful sermon was preached by Father Burke in St. Saviour's Church, Dublin, after Tenebræ, on Good Friday evening, 1877. It is one of the most faithful portrayals of the passion of our Lord that has ever been given to the world.

DEAR BRETHREN: I suppose that in every family among you there is a copy of the Holy Scriptures, the Bible. The Catholic Church loves that her children should read and meditate on the Holy Scriptures. It is a calumny and a falsehood to say that she is opposed to the reading and the meditating upon the Word of God. I therefore take it for granted that you have all in your houses a copy of the Bible. And now I ask you when you go home this evening or to-morrow morning, whilst the thing is still fresh in your memory, to read the fourth chapter of the Fourth Book of Kings. There are four Books of Kings, and in the fourth chapter of the fourth book you will find the following incident or fact related: The prophet Eliseus by his prayer and his blessing obtained for a certain woman, a Sunamitess, the gift that she should bear a child, a son. Great was the woman's joy in the possession of her son, but, to her great sorrow, when the child was growing up strong and healthy, and was assuming the proportions of manhood, he sickened and died. And his mother came to the prophet and implored him that he would restore to her by his prayer the son whom he had obtained for her by his prayer. Then the prophet Eliseus arose and he went to the woman's house. And now comes the portion of the miracle to which I invite your special attention. He went into the house and he found the child lying dead upon a bed. He prayed to the Almighty God, and when he had prayed he stretched himself out upon the dead child, placing his hands upon the child's hands, his mouth upon the boy's mouth, his eyes upon his eyes, and his heart upon the heart of the dead one. And thus stretched out, leaning and lying upon the dead child, the Scripture, as you will see—for I ask you to read it—the Scripture tells us that by degrees he warmed the flesh of the dead child. But the child did not rise to life ; he remained dead, though warmed by his contact with the prophet. Then the man of God arose, and, still praying, the Scripture says that he walked through the house once, walked through the whole house, went into every room, went into every closet, and when he had walked through the whole house and had seen it all he came back again to the chamber where the boy was lying dead, and once more he stretched himself out upon the child, first stretching out the child's hands, and so he put hand upon hand, mouth upon mouth, heart upon heart, and when he had thus leaned over the child and stretched out upon him the dead boy opened his eyes and looked ; presently he opened his mouth and cried out with a voice. And then the prophet called his servant, a man named Giezi, and he said to him : "Go call the Sunamitess" (this was the mother) "and bid her to take her child." And she came, and she found her child living, and she prostrated herself before the man of God, and she gave thanks for the gift that he had given her.

Now, there is the fact to which again, for the third time, I invite your attention. I ask you when you go home to open your Bible at the fourth chapter of the Fourth Book of Kings, and you will find recorded word for word the fact as I have stated it to you. Now, dearly beloved, you are come this evening into a temple and into the presence of an altar where on every other occasion of the year you see some sign of worship and of joy—some sign of life, the lamp burning before the Blessed Sacra-

ment, the fatness of the olive exhausting itself in a tribute
of light unto its God; some sign of joy, the candles lit
upon the altar, and the fresh fair flowers among the sculp-
tured saints and angels that stand around watching the
sanctuary and the tabernacle. But to-night no sign of life,
no sign of worship or of joy is there; the lamp is extinguished before the Blessed Sacrament and yields no light;
the doors of the tabernacle are thrown open to show you
the empty place where He who usually dwells, dwells no
more, but seems to have fled from His dwelling-place. No
flowers adorn the altar, no lights brighten it; all seems as
if the God of the temple were gone and as if the abomination of desolation has fallen upon His very holiest places;
and so it is. It is Good Friday night. Three o'clock on
Good Friday heard the last cry of the dying Man upon the
cross. The next moment beheld Him dead. In an hour
or two He was taken down from the cross and buried in
the tomb. Mary went down from the Hill of Calvary, leaning upon her newly-found son, John the Evangelist, with
a hand thrown carelessly round the neck of the loving
Magdalene, who still supported her. She goes home to a
desolate house, a widowed and a childless mother. Jesus
Christ lies in the sepulchre, darkness has closed upon Him,
death has asserted its dominion over Him; hell has had its
victory over Him.

Ah! but let us consider the victory, let us consider the
combat and the triumph which seems to be of hell, and we
shall see how glorious the combat fought by the hand of
God, and how magnificent the victory was of that God
over the devil, of life eternal over death, and of all that
heaven contained over the powers of hell. The prophet
came into the Sunamite's house, and there he found a dead
child. The child was once living, full of life, full of all
the grace, full of all the growing sweetness of his childhood, the delight of his father's heart and the light of his
eyes; but now he lies dead, unable to see with those young
eyes of his, unable to move his hands, unable to return the
love of the father, who comes caressing him even upon his

death-bed. But humanity, dearly beloved, was born of God ; our nature was the creation of God ; whether in body or in soul, it was still the work of God's hands, and whatever comes of God is instinct with life, instinct with beauty, and has the perfections that belong to it, simply because it is God's work. And, therefore, when man was first created he was created in the integrity of a perfect nature ; a body which, though formed of the slime of the earth, yet stood erect among all the other creatures of God and looked to heaven as to its last and eternal home ; a soul created by Almighty God for that body, inspired by the very breath of God, the very image of God, filled with knowledge, filled with love, and dowered with a glorious freedom to serve and love the God who made it unto His own likeness. And thus our first father came from the hand of God, worthy of that God that made him, and the very image of the Eternal Life which had created him. But he sinned, and "by sin," says St. Paul, "came death into this world," and death reigned supreme. Adam sinned, and in his sin he died. He died—his eyes closed to the vision of the eternal life and beauty of God ; his hands were no longer lifted in grateful sacrifice of prayer ; he sank lifeless to the ground, his feet no longer bore him along as during those mysterious walks in which he communicated familiarly with God in the shades of Paradise before his fall ; his tongue no longer spoke words of praise ; he was dead, and in his death we all died. The child of God is dead—the son of the Sunamite has ceased to live. How shall he ever be revived again ? How shall he ever open his eyes to behold the same God again who is now shut out from him by the cloud and the darkness of sin ? How shall his hands ever be raised again by his own action in sacrifice and in prayer ? How shall his heart beat again for God ? How shall his lips move ever again in words that will penetrate the skies and fall like music upon the listening ear of the Most High ? Who is to give him life ? Ah ! dearly beloved, the life eternal, the life essential, the life which is the very essence and quintessence of life, the eternal Word of God; in Him was life, necessary and eternal, and from Him in the act of creation went forth life unto all things that live. "For by Him all things were made," says St. John, "and without Him was made nothing that was made." This Life Eternal came down from heaven and came upon this earth; He looked with pitying eyes upon the face of the dead, and, not content with that looking upon our dead humanity, but, like the prophet in my text from the Fourth Book of Kings, He stretched Himself out over the dead and put His hands upon our hands, His eyes upon our eyes, His mouth upon our mouth, His heart upon our heart, and he warmed the dead child, not yet vivifying, nor yet recalling to life, but He warmed the dead flesh. And this He did in His first stretching out over us in the Incarnation—in the Incarnation in which the Eternal God made Himself like to man. "*In similitudinem hominis factus et habitu inventus ut homo,*" says the apostle—he was made in the likeness of man, and in form found like a man. Hands like ours, eyes like ours, mouth to mouth with ours, heart to heart with ours, for His were human hands that delighted in the labor of man, His were human eyes that looked upon an earthly Mother and loved her with a true filial love, His was an earthly mouth that moved in prayer and in supplication, just as you and I can pray. His was a human heart beating with human affection, yielding to the high and glorious impulse, now of tenderness, as when He wept with Martha over her brother's grave, now with a no less noble and grand passion of Christian indignation, as when with hasty hand He made a scourge of little ropes, and, lifting His hand, scourged the buyers and sellers out of the Temple. True man, as true as you and I, like to us, He stretched Himself out in all His divinity over our humanity in the Incarnation. And, strange to say, although God became man, and there was a Man-God upon the earth, yet our humanity had not begun to live. It was only warmed into a preparation for life.

The flesh of the dead child was warmed when the prophet first stretched his living body over it; the flesh of the dead child was warmed, and there was hope of life there, and any one coming and feeling the hands or the face of the dead would say: "Perhaps he may return to life, for the warmth of life is slowly returning into him from the man of God." And so, dearly beloved, in the Incarnation we began to be warmed into life, not yet to live. He spoke for thirty-three years in the midst of us; the sight of Him, the example of Him, the words of knowledge that He poured out, the faith that those words created prepared our dead humanity to be resuscitated, but it had not yet begun to live. We did not begin to live in Bethlehem, we did not begin to live in Nazareth; no, nor in Jerusalem, even though he taught us in the Temple. Our life must be postponed, we only began to live elsewhere, as we shall see presently, but we were prepared to live under the contact with Jesus Christ. Then when the prophet had stretched himself out and warmed the flesh of the dead child he arose, and, says the Scripture, "he walked through the house once." So our Divine Lord and Saviour stretched Himself out upon us, and laying hold of us, hand to hand, face to face, heart to heart, in His Incarnation, then He rose up and went through the house of our humanity. Ah! for thirty-three years He went through the house. He beheld us in all the phases of our being, He met us in all the stages of our infirmity—the blind, the lame, the paralyzed, the leprous, the sinners, the woman willing to return who came to His feet to wash them with her tears, the woman unwilling to return and brought sullenly before Him with her fair arms tied with rope, for she was caught in her crime—every form of human need, every form of human, physical, mental, spiritual misery, was brought before Jesus Christ, and He made Himself familiar with all. He went through the house. He went through the house, He left no part of the human heart unexamined, no corner of the human spirit unexplored: He saw with scientific eye every turning and twining and twisting of our perverse nature. He followed the Pharisee in his cunning jealousy, He followed the publican in all the windings of his depraved avarice; but not only did He look with scientific eye, but He touched with medicating and tender and scientific hand every form of our nature; and so He went through the house, and this career took Him thirty-three years. And now He has made the round, the searching, penetrating round of all the house of His world and of our humanity, and the prophet returns to-day, to-day the man of God returns to stretch Himself out once more upon the dead child, and this time, in this second stretching, to raise him up, to open his eyes, to open his mouth, to give him back life, blood to his heart, pulsation to his pulse, voice to his lips, sight to his eyes, hearing to his ears, and joy to the Sunamitess, his mother. How did Jesus Christ do this? This second outstretching of the Son of God is the mystery contemplated on this evening. My brethren, I will use bold, adventurous, but, I am confident, orthodox language when I tell you that as the prophet went through the house after his lying down on the dead child and warming it, and then, having gone through the house and seen it, came back and lay upon the child once more and vivified it, so it was necessary that Christ our Lord should go through the house of our humanity, should examine us in every detail of our weakness and of our depravity before He came to stretch Himself out a second time upon us and give us life. And why? For the simplest of all reasons.

The first outstretching of the Son of God upon our humanity was an act of divine love, divine condescension, divine mercy; but it was not a mercy fulfilling in itself alone the act of our redemption. For remember that if it pleased our Divine Lord on the very Christmas night when He was born at Bethlehem, if it pleased Him to anticipate His resurrection and His ascension, and, rising from the manger in which Mary laid Him, to take her with Him, and the Mother and the Child to ascend into heaven, God—the Son of God made man—could have done it. But if He did it, we should remain as we were before His coming—unredeemed. If He had done it He in heaven would be glorified even as Man, glorified for the act of obedience, for the act of submission to His Eternal Father. He would be glorified, Mary would be the Mother of God, two human beings would be in heaven, but not another child of Adam could ever have entered there. The second act was necessary; it was not enough that He outstretched Himself over us in the humiliation of the Incarnation, but He must do it in the still greater humility and pain of His sufferings, of His passion. He must come to us not only with the hands of an infant, outstretched in love, but with the bleeding hands of a man outstretched in expiation.

He must bring to us, and place heart to heart on our hearts, not merely the sweet, loving heart of the innocent Babe of Bethlehem, or the beautiful heart of the growing Child of Nazareth, but He must put upon our heart a heart bleeding and broken for our love. He went through the house; He made himself familiar with every form of our human depravity, with every human weakness, in order that when the hour came for the second outstretching of himself upon our humanity He might be able to offer distinct suffering and a distinct offering to God for every single form of human depravity. Now the hour for that second contact between God and man approaches. Christ our Lord has made His prayer in the garden, and He has gone through the agony of His voluntary acceptance of our sins. Christ our Lord has given the gift of gifts in the Last Supper. Now He rises up from the garden after His prayer, and He delivers Himself into the hands of His enemies. Ah! He is embraced by Judas, and the heart of the Son of God feels chilled, like the heart of the mariner who, sailing upon the northern seas, suddenly finds his ship between the icebergs, and a chill of northern ice goes over him, and the very blood in his heart seems to freeze. So froze up the heart of Jesus Christ when the blood mantling His face, the blood that was streaming down from that divine face, came in contact with the lips of Judas.

He is dragged across the brook of Cedron, brought that night before Annas and Caiphas, and when they had questioned Him and struck Him, and buffeted Him and humiliated Him in every form, He is then handed over towards midnight to a company of Roman soldiers, pagans—they were called archers, the archers of Pilate's guard—and they took Him. He was a godsend to them, a prisoner given up to their hands. They took Him, and from midnight to the early morning He sat in their guard-room, and they amused themselves the whole night long by voiding their obscenities and their wickedness and their reproaches upon the person of Jesus Christ. We may well imagine how the night passed. The brutal jest from man to man, the horrible allusions to their excesses and impurities falling upon the ear of the Virgin's Child. Then, by way of diversion, we can imagine one of those archers of Pilate's guard untightening his bow and removing the string, and then for mere pastime striking the Lord Jesus Christ right and left across the face with the bow ; making bets with each other who would offer Him the grossest insults ; spitting upon Him, striking Him upon either cheek, blindfolding Him, and then going and striking Him on the face and saying to Him : "Oh ! you are the Jewish prophet; tell us the name of the man who struck Thee." And thus He passed the night until the early morning. Ah ! think of that night. Ah ! you—let me speak to you candidly—ah ! you man, if there be one among you, who is a sinner, and who watches until the shade of night begins to fall to go out and seek his unlawful pleasures, his lustful enjoyments, until the morning, think of the night that the Eternal Son of God spent among the impious Roman soldiers. That night was spent in penance for your excesses, and to make some atonement to God, and to shield you from the anger of an awful God, before whose eyes the midnight is as the noonday, and who watches you in all the passages of your iniquity, and takes terrible note of your sins.

The morning came, and our Divine Lord is brought

forth from the prison in which he spent the night, wearied from want of sleep, tired and bruised from all the insults that He has received, horrified from the obscenities that He has heard, heart-broken for the dreary day and the awful work that is before Him, abandoned by His apostles and disciples. He is led forth; He is carried before Pontius Pilate. Now, now, He lies down the second time upon our dead humanity, hand to hand, eye to eye, heart to heart. But it is quite different from His first contact with us in the Incarnation. Now He comes, after having walked through the house, examined and seen our infirmities, touched our evils, experienced our baseness and our misery, He now comes matured scientifically, by his outstretching and outcovering of us to bring us to life. And in the walking through the house He found that the great sources of all human evil and of all the sins of man were the concupiscence of the eyes—that is to say, the love of wealth, the love of riches, the love of glory, the love of self—the concupiscence of the flesh—that is to say, the love of pleasure, sensuality, lust, impurity—and the pride of life—the pride of will, the pride which a man takes in his own reputation, in his own glory, the ambition for distinction and titles, or at least the ambition to be considered a man of talent, a man of genius. These were the three evils which Christ our Lord found whilst He was walking through the house.

Now He comes in His passion to lie down upon us, to stretch Himself out over the dead child, and by contact with Himself to heal us and give us back our life. And what does He do, dearly beloved? In His passion He first of all comes in contact with the concupiscence of the eyes, the love of self, and He meets it by His own abject poverty. He comes in contact with the concupiscence of the flesh, and He meets it by His own personal sufferings and mortification. He comes in contact with the pride of life, and He meets it with His own humility and abnegation. I ask you to consider these three. Hand to hand, eyes to eyes, mouth to mouth, He came upon us. He came and found the hands of the dead stricken by the spirit of avarice or grasping for wealth. He came and found the eyes of the dead blinded by pleasure, longing for fame, glory, independence, and pride. He came and found the heart of the dead lifeless and motionless, because Asmodeus, the demon of impurity, had touched it with an impure and lustful love, and every higher and holier emotion had expired within us. And, therefore, in His passion, He came by His poverty to atone for our avarice—hand to hand; by His humility to atone for our gazing after pride and honor—eye to eye; by His sufferings, bodily mortification, and rending of the flesh He atoned for our sensuality, self-indulgence, self-pampering, and impurity—heart to heart. He had not much to lose, poverty was always His companion in life; He was born in a stable, He lived among the poor, He cast His lot in with them, and even in death He died naked, and charity opened another man's grave for Him. All that He had in this world when His enemies found Him was, first, the affection of His friends and apostles, who up to that moment were saying to Him: "Master, even if we are to die for Thee we will never abandon Thee or deny Thee."

Secondly, He had the love of His Blessed Mother, Mary; thirdly, He had the few garments that clothed Him, the seamless robe which He wore; and fourthly, and above all, He had the love of His Eternal Father in heaven. Now He must be stripped of all this. He had nothing else to lose; He had no money in His purse, He had no lands or possessions to be robbed of; He was poor, but He must be stripped even of the little He had. And, therefore, in His passion His disciples and apostles gave Him up and ran away and abandoned Him. He stood alone. His mother, whose love was so much to Him, He gave up by His own act, saying to St. John: "Take this woman, take her for thy mother; behold thy mother!" And to the woman He said: "Behold thy son! Do not think of me any more, leave me here alone." The few garments that He had, the seamless robe, and the few other articles of clothing, before He died on the cross He saw the Roman soldiers cutting up with their swords and dividing them, so much for the one and so much for the other. And when they came to the seamless robe which Mary's hand had wrought for Him, they said: "We will not divide this, we will cast lots for it"; and presently He heard the rattling of the dice, and one man won it and took it. And He remained naked. Nothing remained for Him on earth; oh! but the riches of heaven were His. But even these He must lose. Therefore before He died He lifted up His eyes, heavy with the heaviness of death. He raised by a great effort the drooping head, in which seventy-three thorns were planted, each one sending forth its stream of blood; He raised to heaven that divine face, now pale with death, His lips quivering in His agony, and faint with thirst, and He cries out to His Heavenly Father: "O God! why hast thou forsaken me?" The Lord Jesus Christ! His Mother His no longer, as He has given her to John; His few garments are no longer His, they have been raffled, they are taken away; His friends are no longer His, they are gone from him; His God in heaven, His Eternal Father, seems to have forsaken Him, for He cries out with faint lips: "Why has thou forsaken me." What remains? Behold Him outstretched over our humanity, outstretched hand to hand and heart to heart with that humanity of ours that is always looking for friends, and for good clothing, and for love, and for favor both from Heaven and here. He gives them all up. He stretches Himself out, eye to eye. It is not enough that they plunder, it is not enough that He is forsaken of friends, deprived of the little insignificant property that He possessed, deprived of all consolation from Heaven, and surrendering Mary's love to another upon the earth; He must go further than this. There are some things that belong to Him, and it seems as if no man could take from Him, and they are that which seems the interior and peculiar inheritance of every man—namely, His reputation.

Even though Mary be already in the arms of her second child, even though Peter and the rest of them be shivering with fear far away in the city or at the foot of the mountain, even though the soldiers have taken the few robes that belonged to Him, He is still robed in the crimson mantle of His own sweet blood, and He may still fall back upon that which no man can take away from Him—namely, His magnificent character for sanctity, for wisdom, and for power. He had a great reputation for sanctity. When the blind man whose eyes He opened was brought before the synagogue, and they said to him: "Do you know anything about this man who opened your eyes?" "No," said he, "I know nothing, only this: I know that I was born blind, that I never saw one ray of light until Jesus of Nazareth laid His hand upon me and gave me sight, and I swear to you that that man is holy who has done this for me." And all the people acknowledged His holiness. "Master," they said to Him—we know the very Pharisees said—"Master, we know that Thou teachest the way of God in holiness and truth."

Grand as was His character for sanctity, His character for wisdom was equal. When He was only twelve years old He went into the Temple at Jerusalem, a little boy, sat down among the doctors, and not a man of them was able to answer His questions, and they were struck dumb before Him. Nay, more, we read in the Gospel that when they brought Him the coin of the tribute and asked Him if it was lawful to pay taxes to Cæsar or not, He answered so wisely and penetrated so keenly into their inner souls that "from that day," says the Evangelist, "not a man was able to ask Him a question," He had such a reputation for wisdom. Finally He opened the eyes of the blind and bade the paralyzed to walk, and the people all said: "This man speaks not like the Pharisees, not like our priests; this man speaks like one who has power." Very well, now at least He has all this. No, my friends, reputation for wisdom, reputation for sanctity, reputation for power, all these belong to the dear aspirations of every man among us, and Christ our Lord must surrender them, and before He dies upon that cross He must be stigmatized as a man without sanctity. They brought Him to Pontius Pilate, and when Pilate said to them : " What accusation do you bring against this man ?" they answered him : " If He was not a malefactor we would not have brought Him to you." When he pushed them and said : " But tell me what He has done," they answered : " He is a blasphemer, and according to our law He must be put to death." And actually the Son of God so lost His character for sanctity that He was condemned by the Jewish Church, and His condemnation was ratified by the Roman governor, as a blasphemer, as a man who had risen in rebellion against the Eternal God, as a man who was unfit to pollute the air He breathed by being allowed to live and breathe in it. And as such He was put to death. You know, my friends, that there are certain deaths that are very honorable. When the patriot, the man of immaculate character, the man whose virtues are upon every lip, when the patriot, animated by noble thoughts and great designs, draws an untimely sword and strikes an imprudent blow and fails, he may be put to death, but his memory goes down in honor, and the very men who assist in his execution are worshipping the glorious character of him who is taken away. Not so with Jesus Christ. Nay, the mob that followed Him to Caiphas, the crowd that beheld Him when He was lifted up on the cross, they hissed and slunk away from Him ; the very women with children in their arms looked upon Him, and if they had any courage at all it was only the courage to advance a step and spit on Him who was crucified ; and they taught their children to look upon Him as the greatest malefactor that was ever crucified in Israel. Jesus Christ our Lord had still His character for wisdom —the Pharisees were afraid to speak to Him, He was so wise. And in the hour of His passion Pilate sent Him to Herod, and when He came to the court of Herod what did they do to Him ? My brethren, they put a white garment upon Him, a white robe, and they put some foolish emblems upon His head; they brought Him in among the lords and ladies of the dissolute court of Herod and began to play with Him as children would play with a fool. They asked Him to work miracles. "Do something," they said, "for us." And then some courtier, in all the bravery of his court dress, of his gold and fine linen, would come forward and playfully slap our Divine Lord in the face, and there was a great laugh among the lords and the ladies.

They sent Him back to Pilate through the streets of Jerusalem, dressed as a fool with a white robe and the foolish head-dress upon Him, and the people came to their doors and looked, and said: "Is this the madman? Oh! the poor fellow. And so they are going to crucify Him. Well, perhaps it is as well; there will be one fool the less." And the little boys followed Him and plucked at His garments, and some struck Him from play and some from malignity. He was led through the streets as a fool, and as a fool He was brought up to Calvary and crucified. Not a soul remembered that this was the man whose awful knowledge confounded and silenced their Pharisees and priests; His reputation for wisdom was gone. Well, they may think He was a malefactor, and may say it was through Beelzebub, the prince of devils, that He wrought His miracles. They may think He was a fool—it was not the first time in this world that real wisdom was mistaken for folly—but at least there was one thing they cannot be mistaken in: they cannot rob Him of His attribute of power. His power He has proved by so many miracles, His power He has put before them in so many and such astonishing ways, that surely no man among them can think, whether He be man or devil, whether He be wise or mad, no man among them can think He has not power. They saw Him raising the dead; they saw Him commanding the blind to see, and they saw; they saw Him commanding the paralyzed to walk, and they walked; they saw Him cure the demoniacs raging with fury; the moment He stretched out His hands and said: "Be still," the devil was humble and meek before the face of his God; nay, more, they saw

Him upon the bosom of Genesareth's lake, when the stormy winds tossed it into fury ; they heard the cry from the apostles: "O Lord ! save us or we perish ; our little barque will sink beneath us," and they saw the strange, mysterious figure of a man standing in the prow of the boat and saying to the angry winds : " Be still," and to the threatening clouds : " Depart," and at His command the tempest died into a calm like the peace of God, and the clouds, as if they were ashamed to have thundered over the head of their Lord, suddenly disappeared, and the blue vault of heaven appeared above. And yet He is now lifted up upon a cross, nailed with four nails, bleeding and fainting, and from time to time during the three hours letting fall some little faint word of love, of recommendation, or of wailing ; and—would you believe it ?—the Pharisees and the priests of the people they actually came to the foot of the cross, and they looked up in the face of the dying Man and they said to Him : " We know that You called the dead to life, and we saw them rise out of their graves ; now, now, Thou malefactor, and Thou fool, save Thyself if Thou canst ; come down from the cross if Thou canst, and we will believe in Thee." And he died without a shred of reputation left to Him. The proud Pharisee, with his sweeping robe, came up, the priest in all the grandeur, in all the abominable assumption and pride of his wicked soul, defied our Lord—"Come down if Thou canst, come down and we will believe in You"; and when he got no reply from the Victim he turned to the people and said : "He was able to save others, He is not able to save Himself." Where is the pride of life now ? Do you, men, who are so anxious to shine for genius, for knowledge, for wisdom, for power, and for strength, and, perhaps, I will add, for sanctity of a certain kind, look on the face of Jesus Christ dying ! See how He has stretched Himself out upon the cross on our pride, on our vanity, and has come eye to eye with us, that, though His eyes closed in death, our eyes, like those of the child under the prophet, may open to the life eternal. But there remained the third evil which He discovered, and which He saw with such rude evidence brought before Him—the concupiscence of the flesh, my brothers. All holy as He was, the Son of God did not only come in contact with the avaricious and the proud, but He also came in contact, ay, and in rude contact, with the impure. Can anything be imagined more beautiful than the woman, a vile sinner, a woman loaded with her impurities, reeking with her sins, who rushed into her house on a sudden impulse ; for she has seen His face at a distance, and the sight of it has awakened her eyes to her own impurity and vileness ; and she tears off hastily the silks and satins, tears the bracelets off her fair and beautiful arms, drags the coronet off her head and lets loose the luxurious hair, snatches up a box of ointment and goes into the street to find Him. She is told He has gone into a certain house ; she goes into the house and steals around until she finds Him, takes His feet in her hands, presses the feet of the Son of God to her lips that only yesterday were quivering in the excess of her impure love.

Oh! how rude the contact between all that is highest in heaven and all that is most loathsome on earth. How still more so was the contact when the Pharisees, hard and senseless men, came in a crowd around Him, and suddenly the crowd separated, and there, standing close to the Son of God, so close that her very breath was almost felt upon His face, a woman caught in her iniquity, a woman taken in her adultery, a woman not even repentant—no tear in those eyes ! She was defiant ; no quivering of shame upon those lips, no remorseful tears in those eyes, no word of expiation from her mouth ; and yet He allowed Himself to come in contact with all this. And the hour comes when He is to outstretch Himself upon this last and most terrible wound of our dead nature. The child must be brought back to life, the child must be brought back to the life of purity as well as of humility and faith, and the only way the Son of God can do this is to render Himself completely, and surrender Himself into the hands of His enemies—to leave Himself altogether at their mercy, to give every single member of His body to them, to deny them nothing that they may wish to do with Him ; and, therefore, to cure our sensuality and fleshliness, our self-indulgence, our lustfulness, and our impurity, the Son of God said to them: "Behold me! now your hour is come, and the powers of darkness have me; do with me what you will." And accordingly in the early morning of Friday, having taken Him before Pilate, he receives the first portion of His sentence, and Pilate says to the soldiers: "Take Him, scourge Him." To the people he said: "Wait a while; I will bring Him back and you shall see Him again ; I will lay my hand upon Him, don't be afraid." For they were crying out for His blood. "His blood! His blood!" the mob of Jerusalem cried; "Shed His blood, we want His blood." Pilate said: "Wait; don't be afraid, I will shed His blood, *emendatum dimittam.* I swear to you I will not kill Him, for He is an innocent Man; but before I dismiss Him I will lay my hand upon Him; wait." The soldiers then took our Lord and brought Him out into a square court, enclosed by the Prætorium and the palace of Pilate. In the middle of the court was a short pillar, and to it was attached a chain. They brought our Divine Lord over to the pillar. They stripped Him naked in that early morning in March; they tied His arms behind His back to the pillar, and the company of Roman archers who had spent the night tormenting Him girded themselves up to their new work, to scourge Him. They had scourges, according to the Eastern tradition, scourges of new cord, scourges of iron, and scourges of green branches of a thorny tree, and each man armed with his scourge began to work upon the body of the Saviour. They tore Him from head to foot; they first blackened His flesh, raised livid welts all over Him ; presently the skin is broken, the flesh is broken, the blood begins to flow; one strikes Him across the face, another strikes Him full upon the head, until He begins to stream forth blood from every member of His sacred body. The blood flows down around Him, no part of Him is spared;

when the scourges are sodden with blood they are flung aside, and fresh arms of those stalwart soldiers come with fresh scourges to begin the flagellation again. When the branches of the thorny tree are worn out and have lost their bitterness fresh branches are brought. From head to foot, standing deep in His own blood, they scourge Him until they think He is dead, and when they cut the cords that bound Him to the pillar the Lord Jesus Christ falls lifeless in the midst of them, and He is raised up, and they have to wait a while until some signs of life return to Him. His garments are thrown hastily upon Him, and He is brought back to Pilate. But before they bring Him back one of the soldiers, perhaps out of the very fresh branches they had brought to continue the flagellation, plaited a crown of the thorns and forced it upon His head and opened seventy-three fresh wounds. And thus bleeding and dying He is brought to Pilate. Pilate beholds Him, and is horrified to see how completely, how awfully his own instructions have been carried out. He brings Him out upon the balcony of his house, and, turning to the Jews, he says only these words: "Behold the Man—behold Him! You have asked for His blood; go into the court of my house and you will find the blood upon the pavement. You have asked for His blood; behold! it is flowing from a thousand wounds." But the answer the Jews gave was: "We demand more than His blood, we demand His life"; and so Pilate gave Him up to them. He gave Him "into their hands," says the Evangelist, "to work their way upon Him." And in a few minutes the bleeding, fainting figure of our Lord is seen emerging through the crowd at Pilate's house, with a cross upon His shoulders, the other end trailing upon the ground, and heavy enough to bear on its uplifted arms the weight of a strong man.

With that cross on His shoulders He climbs the flinty sides of Calvary, falling three times upon that sad journey, and, arriving at the summit of the hill, He is stretched on the cross. His garments are taken from Him rudely, the cross is laid on the ground, and the prophet of God, the man of God goes a second time to the Sunamitess' son and stretches Himself out over the dead. He has healed the concupiscence of the eyes by His poverty; He has healed the pride of life by His excessive humiliation. He now heals the concupiscence of the flesh, for He lays His own flesh under their arms. The nails are laid upon the palms of His hands and upon the insteps of His feet, and the hammer comes upon them, and a sound is heard of iron driving—first through flesh, rending sinew, nerve. The hands, the fingers, involuntarily close round with their excessive agony. The nails come out at the back of the hand and sole of the foot, and strike into the hard wood, and then, with louder and more resonant blows, these huge spikes are driven in, until the executioners have satisfied themselves they are firm enough. And now the cross is slowly raised up; there are ropes upon the arms of it, and there are strong men pulling at these; and there are some holding the foot of the cross, and their hands are reddened from the blood flowing from the Man that is hanging there, and His blood flows upon their heads; it falls down in great drops, like the first drops of the summer's rain. And the cross sways in the air, and the people near and far have their eyes fixed on the raised figure, and slowly it rises—slowly it rises until at length raised to a perfect perpendicular. The body sways out, held on by the nails that keep His hands and feet. The awful head, crowned with thorns, the whole body, lacerated and bleeding, hangs out there, and the Man is still alive, and all the people behold Him. And for three long hours, hour after hour, from twelve o'clock in the day, when the cross was lifted up, until three o'clock in the afternoon, three long and terrible hours, He hangs; His heart is breaking, the tension of the nerves, the strain on the muscles, the loss of blood, the awful agony of every limb is breaking His heart slowly. There He is outstretched—stretched out upon us for the last time—and now the dead child that was only warmed in Bethlehem at the Incarnation must prepare to be quickened into life at the crucifixion. Seven times He spoke during these three hours—seven times He spoke, sometimes to God His Father, as when He said: "O Father! into Thy hands I commend my spirit"; sometimes to man upon the earth, as when He said to St. John: "Take my mother for thy mother," and to His mother: "Behold thy son"; sometimes to Himself, as when, as if communing with Himself, He said: "*Consummatum est*"—"All things are now accomplished, I have done." At the end of the third hour there was a sudden silence among the crowd; even those who were loudest in their hissings, even those who were most outrageous in their insults felt a strange feeling of fear come over them, and they held their peace. The Magdalene, who was weeping freely, ceased her weeping, and something more awful than the expression of sorrow came over her; the Mother of God stood silent at the foot of the cross; the Roman soldiers ceased their babble and their conversation; their centurion or officer rose up, and with an impulse that he could not account for commanded silence, and there was dead silence. And then, dearly beloved, the clouds came over the face of heaven until no ray of sunshine was seen, but a blackness like night came on. The third hour was approaching, it was close; the Man upon the cross seems so far dead and exhausted as to be unable to say another word. And suddenly the dying and drooping head was raised, the loving heart dilates and expands; the lips, quivering in the agony of death, are cleared for an instant; the eye, over which the film of death has come, becomes clear and bright as ray of noonday sunshine; a glory as of life eternal is upon the face of the dying, and a voice is heard ringing out from the heart and from the lips of the dying Jesus: "Father! Father! abandon me not. Into Thy hands I commend my spirit." The head fell upon His bosom and the spirit was gone; but the voice, the voice went out and swept round the slopes of Calvary and startled the dead in their graves—the voice went out and swept through the streets of Jerusalem and filled every house with terror, as when the Angel of Death went through the Assyrian camp of old—the voice went through the garden of Gethsemani, and the lofty trees shivered as in the throes of a tempest at its passing—the voice ascended the mountain of Olivet, and the great crags and mountains rocked on their bases, and the graves gaped open and the dead came forth, and strange voices were heard around. And the voice has stricken terror in every heart, and in the sounding of the word and the going forth of the spirit the humanity that was dead for four thousand years sprang up, like the Sunamitess' son, into life, under the death-groan of Jesus Christ.

Sprung into life! Behold the truth: the centurion, the Roman soldier that commanded the soldiers, the officer that was in command over them, snatched a lance, and he came and said: "I will test it; that cry could not be the cry of a mere man dying—that cry that has shaken the hills and covered the earth with darkness, and waked the dead out of their graves, and made the stones gape with fear. I will test it." He set his lance and drove it right through the breast of Jesus Christ; and, drawing back that lance, to his amazement, from the dead Man's heart came a stream of water, pure and limpid, and of blood. At the moment he saw that miracle he cast himself upon the earth. "Surely," he said, "Thou art the Son of God." And the Roman soldier adored his dead Lord. Surely the Sunamitess' son has arisen, the dead has spoken, the eyes that were darkened for ages have seen the light, and the darkness that reigned universal over man has sprung up into a glorious life by the death-cry of Jesus Christ. Who is the Sunamitess? When the prophet had raised the dead child to life he said to his servant, Giezi, in the text to which I invited your attention: "Go to the Sunamitess, and tell her to take her child?" Who is the Sunamitess? Who is the mother to take her child vivified by the death-cry of Jesus Christ." Ah! dearly beloved, He pointed her out to us just before He died. He told us her name, her sweet and blessed name, with His dying lips. He looked upon her with His dying eyes, and He said to John, representing all Christian men: "O son! forget the mother that bore thee. Behold thy Mother is here in Mary, who is my Mother." There is the Sunamitess. To the Sunamitess He said: "Behold thy son." The prophet said to his servant: "Call this Sunamitess and tell her to take her child who is brought back to life." And Mary opened her arms, at the foot of the cross, and our humanity, restored, regenerated, revivified, fell into the arms of Mary as the revivified child into the arms of his Sunamitess mother; and this was the last legacy of Jesus Christ to us. Dearly beloved, one word and I have done; for, in truth, the subject is a great one, and I fear that I have already trespassed upon your patience. My beloved, behold our Lord and Saviour —behold the Man of men—the true Man—the true Father and Brother of men! See how He has conformed to us— conformed to our misery, to our weakness, to our sufferings, to our death, upon the cross! See how stretched out those glorious arms of His are! Oh! see how the open heart is rent, and pouring itself out for you. Come—come with the Roman centurion—come every man of you, before you leave this church to-night—with the Roman centurion kneel down and confess Him; say, as Longinus said: "Oh! Thou art surely the Son of God." Open your arms—open your hearts, that you may be conformed to the outstretched arms and the open and rent heart of Jesus Christ; open your lips to the confession of faith with the Roman soldier; open your hearts, and rend them to sorrow for your sins; open your hands, and may the Lord of glory, who died for you, be impressed upon you in every action of your life; and so, dearly beloved, you shall rise from death unto the life of grace before the dying figure of Jesus Christ, your Saviour.

THE CROSS THE SIGN OF SALVATION.

THERE is no better argument on the theme here treated than can be found in this discourse, which was delivered by Father Burke in the Cathedral at Enniscorthy, Ireland, Sunday, April 12, 1874.

"*At that time:* When it was late that same day, being the first day of the week, and the doors were shut, where the disciples were gathered together for fear of the Jews, Jesus came and stood in their midst, and said to them: Peace be to you. And when He said this He showed them His hands and His side. The disciples therefore were glad when they saw the Lord. He said therefore to them again: Peace be to you. As the Father hath sent me, I also send you. When he said this he breathed on them; and said to them: Receive ye the Holy Ghost; whose sins ye shall forgive, they are forgiven them; and whose sins ye shall retain, they are retained. Now, Thomas, one of the twelve, who is called Didymus, was not with them when Jesus came. The other disciples therefore said to him: We have seen the Lord. But he said to them: Except I shall see in his hands the print of the nails, and put my finger in the place of the nails, and put my hand in his side, I will not believe. And after ei ht days again his disciples were within, and Thomas with them. Jesus cometh, the doors being shut, and stood in the midst, and said: Peace be to you. Then he said to Thomas: Put in thy finger hither, and see my hands, and bring hither thy hand, and put it into my side, and be not faithless, but believing. Thomas answered and said to him: My Lord and my God! Jesus said to him: Because thou hast seen me, Thomas, thou hast believed; blessed are they that have not seen, and have believed."

IT has been well said that we owe more to the disbelief of Thomas than to the faith of all the other disciples, because Thomas put Christ to the proof of the truth of His resurrection; and Christ, by proving it to Thomas, proved it to all the future generations of man. Even in his doubt there was a certain spirit of wisdom in Thomas when he made his appeal to the truth of the Divine sacrifice; for sin is the suffering of Jesus Christ. It was Christian instinct that made him say: "Show me the marks on His hands and sides, and I will believe in Him." Oh! wonderful wisdom and mercy of God, who even through the infidelity of Thomas has given us proof of His divine wisdom. You are right, O, Thomas! You are wrong in your unbelief, wrong in your doubts, but right when you say: "Let me see in His hands the mark of the nails, and I will believe in Him." Jesus comes before them eight days later in that upper chamber, the doors being closed for fear of the Jews, and He says to Thomas: "Come here; look at these hands; are they not pierced with the nails? See this bleeding side of mine; reach hither thy hand and thrust it into my side; and be not incredulous, but believe." When the apostle saw the terrible reality—when he saw Calvary and the grave overcome, and Jesus glorified—he knelt down and cried out: "My Lord and my God!" What did it mean? It meant that it was by the "stigmata" of Calvary that the world was not only redeemed but evangelized. It was through the cross of Christ that the preaching of the Gospel began. It was through the cross and its power and efficacy that the Gospel was propagated; and it was through the cross that all men must be saved. He "preached Christ crucified," and the Word of Christ. The Scripture tells us that "Faith comes by hearing, and hearing by the Word of God"; and therefore the apostle calls it "the Word of Faith which we preach." The very same Word, the Word of Christ—to those who are ready to perish in their own wickedness that Word is folly; but to those that believe it is "the power of God and the wisdom of God." It is well they should reflect on these things. His spouse, with tears in her eyes and the songs of lamentation on her lips, calling on us to kneel down and kiss the feet of the image of Him who was crucified for us! The economy and the wisdom of God explained it all; therefore, when He would recall Thomas from his infidelity He said: "Behold my hands and my feet; and be not incredulous, but believe." To this day the faithful man believed the cross was the power of God and the wisdom of God. From generation to generation the Church has carried the message to every land; and the burden of her message was the cross of Jesus Christ. The one and only mission for which the Church was established in the world—the one and only reason for which the Almighty God created her and put His Word upon her lips—was that she might be the light of divine truth and the messenger of divine grace; that Christ might be known to the minds of all men by divine faith, that He might reign in the hearts of all men by grace and divine love. Behold the mission of the Catholic Church! By that faith and grace the souls of men can be saved. Without that divine grace it was impossible to be holy and to be saved. He who demands more than faith and salvation demands more than the Church has a right to promise and more than she has a right to administer. Faith and grace come through Christ. He was the incarnation of the Holy Ghost, who was eternal, and of the Virgin Mary He was made man.

He was born in Bethlehem, matured to manhood in Jerusalem, but all tended to the cross. It was for the cross that He was born. It was for that He was prepared in the all-holy bosom of the Virgin Mary. It was for that cross that He grew apace under Mary's hand. It was to prepare the world for the cross that He preached three years in the towns and cities of Galilee and in the Temple of Jerusalem. It was on the cross on Calvary that the mission of the great Saviour was fulfilled in the redemption of mankind. It was there that was wiped away the curse of universal sin. He was not God only, not man only, but God and man united in Jesus Christ. He was God and man by the integrity of His manhood and the fulness of His divinity, so united as to become one Divine Person, never to be separated. The humanity of Jesus Christ is as much an object of our faith as His divinity. We are Christians by our full belief in Him as God and man united. He had put to the proof the reality of that humanity. We read of old that the angels of God took to themselves phantom bodies, that they might present themselves to man and thereby fulfil their mission. As, for example, the angels that came to Abraham in his tent took to themselves phantom bodies that they might appear to the bodily eye. Gabriel himself, when he came to earth, was obliged to take to himself a body; but it was while bearing the message from God, and when the message was once delivered the body disappeared and the spirit returned as it came. But when the Lord God came down from heaven it was not a mere verbal message He came to deliver. It was not a mere formal or phantom body He came to assume for the time. No; He came to do laborious work—a work that demanded all the true form of a true man. He alone of all the heavenly ones proved the reality of the nature that He took upon Him by shedding His blood, and after He had proved the terrible reality He burst the bonds of death. Therefore His sacred humanity was a great object of our faith—a humanity in which God Himself was present. Its reality was testified by the cross. It was the blood of the Sacred Heart of Jesus which flowed in the sevenfold channels of the sacraments; and when brought in contact with the unregenerate child of Adam, being tinged mystically with the blood of Christ, the child of nature became a child of grace, the heir of hell became a child of God. These were but the words of man falling from the lips of man, yet they were but the echo of words that fell from Jesus Christ in heaven. He said: "Behold my hands and my feet! Behold I am real! I am He who saved you. Receive the Holy Ghost; whosoever sins ye forgive, they are forgiven." These were the words of God, who was crucified, spoken in His sacred humanity. And to the eye another hand was visible—the hand that was nailed to the cross, still bearing the stigmata of its crucifixion. If the Catholic Church is simply and solely to enlighten the world by that faith that came from the cross, it follows that the main position of the Church of God was to proclaim the cross in every land, to lift it up, and hold it in honor and glory, to proclaim its significance and power, to place it hither and thither over the earth, to let it go before the face of the Lord ; for He said : "Ye shall behold the sign of the Son of Man in the clouds of heaven."

This was what the Catholic Church has ever done. No man could ever accuse her of being ashamed of the cross. "God forbid that I should glory," says the apostle, "save in the cross of the Lord Jesus Christ." How she gloried in it when Mary Magdalene would not be torn away by brutal hands from that cross on which our Lord was dying! Christians leant their heads against it and found there the consolation and comfort which upheld them in their sorrow. The Catholic Church has kept it, has followed it, and bowed down before it. For the first three hundred years of the Christian era the cross of Christ was a sign by which the Christians were known. The moment they were seen making that sign they were known as Christians ; and when they were sentenced by tyrants to cruel tortures and terrible deaths, when they opened their arms to receive their death-wounds, they made the sign of the cross—the cross of Jesus Christ. Those who denied the divinity of Christ said to those who upheld the cross: "How could this cross have saved the world? Many a man had been crucified before ; how could such good come from it?"

Then came those who denied the humanity of our Lord, and they said : "He could not be true man, or we know He could not be true God." To them, again, the Church upheld the cross, and said : "Did He not suffer here? Was He not suspended on this cross? Was He not nailed hands and feet to it? Could that have happened if He were not true man?" Then came Nestorius and his heretics, admitting His divinity and His humanity, but denying that Mary was the Mother of God. Then, again, the Church upheld the cross, and said : "Were not the merits of Him who died on the cross sufficient to wipe away the sins of the world? Were not His merits infinite? And how could they be infinite unless the person who suffered was divine?"

And so the enemies of Christ and the enemies of Mary fled before the triumphant cross of the Son of God. And so throughout the world every heresy has found in the upraising of that divine cross its defeat. The banner of the cross is streaming forth, and many a hillside is spread out under its rays. A short time ago the site of this cathedral was a chaos. Look at its spire to-day! It spreads its shadow over the fallow ground, over the broad and faithful field and meadow, over the regions around, that where it falls it may bring the benediction of Jesus Christ. Yes; the Church teaches the cross of Christ, not only by the lips of her preachers but by that silent and most eloquent of all speech to which the poet refers when he says: "There are sermons in the stones." Why does the Catholic Church take the form of the cross? Because salvation was accomplished on the Hill of Calvary. Why is the cross planted on that beautiful spire? Not merely because it is a thing of beauty; not because it is an object to catch the eye; not because it has been reared up strongly and carefully by the cunning hand of the artificer, stone after stone, each stone fitted into the other, till the whole structure rose into the complete realization of the architect's mind and the mind of the Church, in all its solemnity and grandeur and beauty, fit and worthy to uphold the symbol of the cross of Jesus Christ.

When we look upon the cross upon that magnificent spire we should look upon it with instructed eyes. We should be able to interpret what the spire teaches. And first we should remember that when the Church of God was established on the earth by her Divine Founder he planted it in the midst of the world which was already civilized. When the Church sprung up first a great messenger had gone forth. It was her mission to purify every art, to lift up every science of every form. When the Church was established pagan architecture was symbolical of a false religion—spacious colonnades, large courts, and great buildings, with lines running level with the earth, and as little as possible raised above the earth. There was nothing in them looking to heaven—nothing leading the imagination to God. But when society improved, then the Church of God rose to the height of her sacred mission—to cultivate the arts, to create the sciences once more, and, inspired by the highest Christian ideas, that which before was but a beautiful corpse received its living spirit from the inspiration of the Church of God.

Slowly but surely, under her care, came forth from the Church—consecrated by her monks, stealing back into the light—the arts which barbaric armies had spread over and destroyed. Forth came Science with new rays of beauty in her face; and from her mind came forth the magnificent institution of Gothic architecture. It was no level, horizontal line, spreading out and taking in large portions of soil; the new idea was to take in so much of the earth only as was necessary to raise up a structure which should be a "thing of beauty and a joy for ever"— a structure sufficiently broad to take a strong hold of the earth, and gradually narrowing to a point, as if it were an arrow shot from the Church and destined to meet the skies. It must rear its head somewhat more gracefully and more tenderly on its body, but sufficiently strong to bear aloft the cross of Christ. The mind and spirit which created this structure were entirely Christian and Catholic. It was peculiarly symbolical of the Incarnation of our Lord Jesus Christ. It represented that He who was highest in heaven—the eternal God who dwells in light inaccessible, true God of true God, who came down from the highest heaven—emptied himself of all His greatness for love of man ; that He came to earth to seek and save that which was lost ; that He took upon Him the fallen and corrupted nature of man.

He found mankind in the slough of four thousand years of sin, degraded in every element of his nature—intellectually degraded—with hearts debauched and depraved by sin ; the devil rampant and triumphant over fallen nature, incapable of everything great in thought, word, or action; and He, the incorruptible God, came down from heaven, took upon Him our nature, sanctified it by His own divinity, prepared it till it became fit for contact with God, and in Himself raised that which was highest on earth to be highest in heaven. This was the mystery of the Incarnation. This silent preacher lifts its head to-day crowned with the cross that proclaimed that Incarnation. It was the sign of our human nature exalted in Jesus Christ; and when we look upon that cross crowning that glorious spire we should think of the humanity of Jesus.

Again, that silent preacher will proclaim every day, pointing away into the skies, the great and mighty truth, that as a man aspires to heaven, in the same proportion he must recede from the baseness and sinfulness of his fallen nature. We see what a hold that spire has taken of the earth, going down to the rock on which it has firmly fixed itself, raised by inches into solid squares, and from the tower springing an edifice which tapers gradually to a point, as it proceeds towards Heaven, rising beautifully, diminishing in weight, diminishing in thickness, till it reaches the point, and then, and only then, touching and upholding the cross. Thus it is with the true Christian, who must aspire heavenward, leaving earth and its cares and sins behind him.

The time is not remote when a battle different from that which the Church is now waging was decided on an adjoining hill. Then the day was dark and gloomy; but the morning dawned on the opposite hill—the hill on which we are now assembled. The cross has been planted firmly on its summit, and its emblem floats triumphantly from the church which we are now assembled to inaugurate.

THE BEAUTY OF DIVINE WORSHIP.

This sermon was preached by Father Burke at the opening of the Cathedral at Ballina, Ireland, January 25, 1874. He has here pictured in all its beauty the most divine of all the enjoyments and duties of man.

IN the name of the Father, and of the Son, and of the Holy Ghost. Amen.

"I have loved, O Lord! the beauty of Thy house, and the place where Thy glory dwelleth."

These words, dearly-beloved brethren, are taken from the Book of Psalms, and if we ask ourselves what is the beauty of the house of God, which the Psalmist declared that he loved, I answer that it is the beauty of divine worship. Dearly-beloved brethren, the Almighty God has many claims upon man—upon our gratitude for the benefits we have received from Him, upon our sorrow for the misfortune of having offended Him. But amongst the many claims that God has upon us, the very first of all is the claim of adoration or worship. He is our God—our Creator. He is infinite in perfection, infinite in wisdom, infinite in power, mercy, and love. The very first thing that God demands of man is that we should admit and recognize these attributes of God, and, recognizing them, that we should bow down and adore them. Therefore, dearly-beloved brethren, the Holy Ghost tells us in Scripture that if any man wish to approach God the very first thing that is necessary is to know God as He is. This virtue is called religion, by which we recognize God in Himself, in His attributes, in His creatures; and the first act of religion is the act of adoration or worship. Now, the Psalmist who uttered these words had not yet beheld the glory of God, the Temple of Jerusalem. The Temple was not yet built, but was to be the work of his son, the great and wise King Solomon. But David saw it not, and yet he said: "I have loved, O Lord! the beauty of Thy house." He beheld it in the vision of his mind, he saw the stateliness of its grandeur, the majesty of its proportions, the richness of its material. He saw there the gold of Ophir, the scarlet twice dyed of Tyre, and the costly marbles taken out of the hearts of the hills, and he rejoiced, because all this was fitting for the house in which the glory of the Lord God was to dwell. But above all things, dearly beloved, he beheld in the vision then in his mind all the tribes of Israel coming to Jerusalem to worship in the Temple and adore their God. He beheld the beauty of adoration surpassing all other beauties of the house of God. He saw, as the vision extended before his prophetic eyes, the successive generations of true Israelites worshipping there, and he rejoiced; until at length he beheld the Virgin leading in that Child who was God into His own house. Then it was that in the fulness of his prophetic heart he exclaimed: "O Lord! I have loved the beauty of Thy house and the place where Thy glory dwelleth; for lo! the Lord God has sent down His only Son into His own mansion"; and then the vision extended until the prophet saw the fading glories of Jerusalem pass away. He saw the veil rent, and the holiness depart from the house of God, until the abomination of desolation was there. He saw the mercy-seat empty, but again He saw rise from out the ruins of the one Temple of Jerusalem ten thousand temples surpassing each other in beauty and loveliness. He saw the ten thousand temples of the living God spring up under the sky, and everywhere the altar of sanctification, the tabernacle of the Divine Presence. And the latter glories far exceeded even the former, and then it was that he again exclaimed: "I have loved, O Lord! the beauty of Thy house, and the place where Thy glory dwelleth." The zeal which made him rejoice in the beauty of the house of God sprang up again in another and a greater and infinitely holier heart than that of David—it burned in the heart of our Lord and Saviour Jesus Christ, who was so zealous for the honor and beauty of His Father's house that when He came, a strong man in the fulness and in the maturity of His manhood, into that Temple of Jerusalem, expecting to find the multitude in adoration—expecting to feast His eyes on the beauty of worship—and He only found the money-changers sitting at their tables, the merchants disposing of their wares, and no man engaged in adoration or prayer, then, at this sight, the fury of God beamed forth from the eyes of the meek and humble Jesus; then, with avenging anger, He took the cords, and, plaiting them into a scourge, lifted His right arm and whipped them out of the Temple, saying: "It is written, My house shall be a house of prayer, but you have made it a den of thieves." The zeal that was in the heart of the royal Prophet-King of Israel—the zeal that burned in the heart and was manifested in the action of the Lord God made man—that zeal and that spirit passed on into the Church of God; for it is written in the Scriptures: "Thus saith the Lord, My Spirit shall rest upon you, and I shall put my seal upon you."

Therefore, from the very first days of Christianity to this hour, and as it shall be to the last of the world's existence, the first thought of every true-hearted, right-living Christian man is the honor, the glory, and the beauty of the house of God, and the majesty of the place where His glory dwelleth. For this God-like and Christian purpose, and animated, dearly-beloved brethren, by this divine spirit, are you assembled here to-day around the bishop and pastor of your souls. The same thought occupies your mind that occupies his; the same love burns in your heart as in his; the same spirit animates you as him—that is, the zeal for the beauty, the honor, the majesty of the house of your God. You are assembled to offer unto God the instrument that shall resound for ever to His praise, and in His name alone you are assembled to perform this duty and pay this solemn feature of reverence to the house of God, to make it vocal with the voice of praise; and this is but one of a series of efforts which you are making to accomplish the beauty of the house of God. Sacrifices require to be made, and you are not afraid to incur them in so high and holy a cause as the beauty of the house of God.

And now let us reflect and consider in a more especial manner that feature of beauty which your zeal and your love have added to the house of God. I said that worship was the highest act of religion and the first duty that we owe to God. Now let us consider in what this worship consists. It consists partly in work of the mind, partly in adoration of the heart, partly in the homage and adoration of the whole man, both soul and body. Worship begins with the mind, the intelligence, believing and bowing down before the truths of divine faith—of a faith without which it is impossible to recognize the Almighty God, or form any adequate idea of His self-existent and necessary being. Secondly, however, the feeling must pass from the mind to the heart. Faith alone, dearly beloved, will never save us; be not deceived! The Scripture says if we have faith strong enough to move mountains, and we have not the charity of God, our faith avails us nothing. And did not our Divine Redeemer tell us that the devils also have knowledge and believe. The devils believe and tremble, but they have no love, therefore they can never approach to God. Divine charity, loving, purifying, whilst it absorbs the heart of man, is a pure offspring of faith, and this also belongs to divine worship. Besides the faith of the mind and the love of the heart, the Almighty God demands the homage of the exterior man. He demands from us external and palpable acts of worship, such as that which the blind man paid to our Lord Jesus Christ. He opened the eyes of that blind man, and, having opened the eyes of his body, He opened the eyes of his soul, saying to him: "Dost thou believe in the Son of God?" The blind man answered: "Lord, where is He, that I may believe in Him?" Christ answered: "I am He." The blind man answered and said: "Lord, I believe." And naturally and necessarily the external act followed the avowal of faith; for, says the Scripture, "falling down, he adored Him." It came naturally. He said: "Lord, I believe," and in the next moment he was down on his knees adoring Him with faith and believed. And I ask you if the blind man refused to kneel down and adore, how could we say that he was sincere in his belief? "Dost thou believe in the Son of God?" said our Lord, and the answer was: "Lord, I believe." If you believe in Him, you must adore and worship Him. The worship of the external man—the bowing down of the head and the bending of the knee—is the necessary consequence of faith, of the intelligence and love of the heart, and therefore it is that the Scripture tells us expressly by the mouth of the apostles that at the sound of the name of Jesus, which is above all names the name, the only one given to man whereby he may be saved—that at the sound of that name every knee shall bend, in heaven, on earth, and in hell. Worship, therefore, involves, dearly beloved, the mind, the heart, and the exterior man.

Now, when Jesus Christ instituted the Christian religion, and when He formed His Church, it was for the express purpose of perpetuating for ever amongst men the knowledge and love and the worship of the Almighty God. Therefore the Church of God is bound to appeal to the mind, is bound to appeal to the heart, is bound to furnish with solemn liturgy the exterior expression of her worship. She appeals to the mind, and that she might be able to make that appeal Christ, the Son of God, put upon her lips the word of truth that was never to fail—the word of truth that was the created faith in the mind and intelligence of men—the word of truth that was to be preached by the life of the Church to the end of time.

Therefore St. James tells us faith comes by hearing— hearing the Word of God. Therefore Christ our Lord said to His Church, Go preach the Gospel to every nation. If the Son of God, dearly beloved, wished or intended to create only intellectual religion, He would have stopped here. If He had intended to appeal only to the mind of man, He would have stopped at the tradition of the Word; but the intention of our Lord Jesus Christ in founding the Christian religion was to go farther and deeper than the mere intelligence. It was to strike home to the heart. It was to penetrate the spirit and to obtain possession of the whole man, and therefore He did not stop at the mere granting of the Word, creating light and faith, but He furnished His Church with every means by which she can appeal to the heart, move the spirit, bow down the head, and chasten and purify the body as well as the soul of man; and amongst the means with which God furnished His Church to reach the heart and to strike the spirit of man in His worship, one of the most direct, one of the most powerful is the appeal which is made by the music of the Church to the ear, and through the hearing to the heart of man. Church music—the voice of praise lifted up in melodious chords; the swell and the pealing of the organ bearing aloft the loud hosanna of adoration to God; the soft, low, tender notes that steal through the senses into the heart of man, and draw us away from ourselves until we are altogether before God; a mild strain that falls like the breathing of God's angels in its soothing influence on the troubled spirit, until we are truly called, lulled into that state of sacred rest that is necessary in order to hear the voice and realize the presence of God; the storm-rushing notes that proclaim in voice of praise some strong emotion of joy, some delightful surprise of revealed truth, some mighty mystery giving us triumph over the enemies of God—all this interpreted by the Church's music forms one of the most powerful appeals which she makes in her worship to man, not only to his intelligence, but it arouses the heart of man to the voice of the preacher, proclaiming revealed truth as an appeal to your mind. He appeals to you with his proofs, with his arguments, with his denunciations, in order to create in your souls that amount of knowledge without which it is impossible to please God; but the voice of the organ appeals rather to your heart. Deep in nature, deep in the nature of man, is the appeal. Perfect is the wisdom which the Church of God manifests, and deep her knowledge of human nature, when she brings to her aid through the ear an appeal to the heart of man by the powerful help of her ecclesiastical music; for, dearly beloved, there is, perhaps, no feature in our nature more interesting to the philosophical student than the strange mystery of the harmony of man's soul with song. Every emotion of the heart naturally finds its vent in some musical note. Thus, when the Almighty God created in the beginning, the spheres moved in harmony under His commanding voice. All nature took up its song, its melody of obedient praise and glorious thanksgiving to Almighty God. We have the authority of the Scripture for this: "The heavens tell the glory of God, and the firmament proclaims the work of His hands"; and in the Book of Job we find these beautiful words: "Where wert thou, O man! in the beginning when the Lord created the heavens and the earth, when the morning stars praised the Lord together, and all the sons of God made a joyful melody?"

All nature is epitomized in man, and the harmony that pervades the whole creation of God is re-echoed in the inner soul of man. The little infant, acting only according to the instinct of nature, announces a gleam of pleasure passing over its innocent spirit or the fleeting cloud of infant sorrow by a wail, which denotes the one, or the musical high note, which proclaims the other. And as the man grows into his manhood, the natural expressive note of music comes to him; it needs not the instruction of a master, it is there implanted by nature herself in his soul, that he should express joy or sorrow in a musical note. And so in like manner, when we come to consider God's dealings with man, as revealed to us, do we not find both in heaven and on earth that music is the language of sorrow or of joy? Thus, when the angels of God were created, it was to notes of angelic music they attuned their celestial voices, as we are told by the inspired one of Patmos, who had beheld the joyful scenes that took place before the throne of God: "And the voice I heard was as the voice of harpers, harping on their harps." The voice of praise in heaven, the angelic voice, has resounded on earth over and over again. The shepherds were keeping watch on that winter night in the midst of flocks, when suddenly in the darkness of the night they beheld strange forms of beauty, flashing like beams of light. It was the angels flitting hither and thither in their joy.

Then were heard many angels filling the midnight air with melody, until it trembled with their music, saying: "Glory be to God in the highest; peace on earth to men of good will." Christ died, and in two days after, when the sun of Easter arose, its beams were cast on an empty grave where the night before a dead man was lying; but when the women came in early morning they heard the angel's voice, and saw the angel clothed in white, who said: "Why seek you the living amongst the dead? Christ is risen. He is not here." Forty days after the Lord Jesus Christ was seen on the summit of Mount Olivet amongst the olive groves; and the apostles beheld Him as he rose up into the air, rising higher and higher, until they beheld but the wave of His hand giving His last blessing. Then they saw Him ascending higher and higher until bright clouds flashed only, as it were, with His reflected light. Presently they heard the angel's voice—"You men of Galilee, why stand you looking up to heaven? He is risen. He will come again! He will come again!" And they heard the glorious choirs of the angels singing: "He will come again! He will come again, even as you have seen Him rise!" And then the voice was silent until fifteen years later, when Mary, the Mother of Jesus, passed to her Son; and then we are told in the annals of the time that angelic voices proclaimed the glory of the Mother of God, and for three days and three nights the apostles heard the angels filling the air with their music.

Then their voices ceased, nor voice of angel was ever heard on earth since; but the song that is expressed in heaven, the worship that finds its expression in God's own angelic music, is taken up by the Church of God on earth, and it is her duty and her privilege to perpetuate the praise of her Divine Lord in the solemnity of her holy song. "I will put upon thy lips," says the Lord, "my words, and they shall not die from thy lips, and the voice of praise shall resound in thee until the end of time." So, dearly beloved, the Church of God started into her existence and began with music. She appealed to the pagan nations of old, not only by the voice of her preachers and the testimony of her martyrs, but also by that sweet musical liturgy which she established in the midst of them. So that even in the three centuries when the Church of God was persecuted—when no Christian man dared show his face, when they were only seen to be martyred—we read that in the dark, deep catacombs of Rome such strains of divine music were heard that the Roman pagan citizens walking the streets were astounded and amazed. It seemed to them as if the very atmosphere around them was laden with song. It was the Christian people singing the praise of their God in the caverns. It was Cecilia's voice, keeping time with her harp, which helped to bear along and sustain her in her angelic song of praise.

St. Augustine tells us that before he was converted from heresy and sin his heart was first deeply moved by the delightful music that came from the choir of the grand cathedral of Milan. Sweeter to the young pagan than the preaching of the gifted Ambrose; more entrancing than the enchanting strains which enlivened the Bacchanalian orgies of Hyppo or of Carthage; sweeter than all was the music of Milan; for the sweetness of that song was the sweetness of Jesus Christ and the glories of His saints. It is a singular and a significant fact, dearly-beloved brethren, that such is the peculiar constitution of man's nature, although we have within us an intellectual soul and spirit like to the angels, whose soul is thought, yet the soul of man can never be called into active existence until the senses are first appealed to, the eye or the ear bringing sensation to the soul. The soul of man is at the mercy of the body. Deprive that body of the senses, strike the infant eye with blindness, close the organ of hearing, remove the five senses, and the soul will indeed still live, but it will be incapable of one emotion of love—it will be without the intellectual thought or heart in the mission of life. The holy St. Augustine described the eye as the master sense, sight the first of the senses, blindness the greatest privation that could befall man. But, though the eye is the organ of the master sense, the ear is the most important; for it is by the hearing that faith comes—by hearing the Word of God—for it is through the hearing it comes to the heart. The sense of hearing appeals to the inmost soul. The eye may instruct the intellect, but the ear appeals direct to the heart. If the soul be troubled; if the dark clouds of despair darken it; if apprehension for the future overwhelm it; if pressure of fright disturb or scare it, then the most soothing power over it is the sweet strains of celestial song.

Thus when Saul was afflicted, and the demon of unquiet raged within his heart, and now unfounded apprehension, and now remembrances of the past, and now restless trouble afflicted him, the only way the king could be calmed in his tribulation was to get the young musician, David, who musically played his lyre, and the boy soothed the heart of the king, and his symphonies were like to the refreshing dews of God, and like a beam of light dissipating the clouds of despair, and bringing back to the hopeless, hope.

Again, when the chosen people of God were fleeing from the land of Egypt, and, under the leadership of Moses, were crossing the Red Sea, Pharao followed with his host, and the waters rushed in upon him and engulfed him and his chariots and horses. When the surging waves subsided, the people saw the mighty armament of Egypt floating in ruin upon the waters, and, seeing, they felt a mighty gratitude to their God and their Deliverer. How did they express it? Mary, the sister of Moses, swept the chords of her lyre and led the choirs of the daughters of Israel, whose voices mingled with the sons of the people, and raised a mighty song of prayer and praise, so naturally did this people give vent to their grateful emotions in song and harmony. The next great incident was the consecration of the temple, when all Israel, from Dan to Bersabee, came in their tens of thousands; and when the long procession passed over the tented plain, headed by the king, surrounded by a hundred and twenty priests blowing trumpets, to the entrance of the temple, they blew a blast of praise, and sackbut, and timbrel, and organ resounded with the song of joy, and thanksgiving, and supplication. Then did God give a sensible sign of His presence, for He was moved by their voice; and the people feared, for they felt that their God was among them. And so when the Catholic Church rose to the mission which was to enlighten, direct, purify, save, and strengthen human nature, and to raise man to the dignity which God intended—namely, to be worthy of the Son of God—it was quite right and natural that she should use the heavenly art of music to develop the purpose of her mission. Then we read that the liturgy of the Church was expressed in music. And even as in the time of Josue, the crusaders in their time went forth to battle to the sound of the music of the Church, which timed the tramp of mailed warriors to many an Eastern battle-field.

Reading the records of that holy and happy time, we are told how the chivalrous baron on his return, putting away from him the mail and chain armor, wandering into the church, knelt down and listened to the organ-notes skilfully touched by Benedictine hands; how his heart's cords were touched by the sacred strains of the organ, now whispering softly, now swelling out in majesty, until his proud heart, moved to the humility of Christian sorrow, rebounded, and from his swelling eyes flowed tears of repentance more grateful than the drops of blood which he shed in Palestine, on the sands of the East, doing battle for the Sepulchre of God. As time went on the Church created that prince of instruments, the organ, for her own purpose, and improved and made it perfect, until in our day it has become a solemn, grand, almost vocal messenger of praise and hope, the expresser of love—has come to be able to influence our souls and spirits as if the voice of God itself were upon its notes. The people entered into the church, the young thinking of pleasure and dissipation; the old discontented and thinking of the troubles and the infirmity that pressed upon them; the rich thinking of their ambition and power; the poor borne down by distraction and by the weight and burden of their poverty; each man thinking of himself in some way or other—they entered the church and knelt down before the altar, a motley and dissipated herd. The sounds of the organ came forth calling them away from their own selfish desires and separation. Presently the voice of music invites them, steals them, and leads them into the presence of Jesus Christ. Presently these grand hosannas and hallelujahs fill the house of God, and the air trembles with the wings of song. They come like the breeze that came to the prophet on the summit of Mount Carmel as he knelt down, for he knew that God was passing. So the organ brought them into the holy presence of their God. Proud men forgot their pride when there bowed down, the old their infirmity, the poor their poverty; every eye was moistened, every ear touched, and, every heart being moved, the great instrument had fulfilled its mission, for it had brought their hearts into the presence of Jesus Christ.

The organ is, therefore, one of the most necessary appendages and most useful of Catholic worship. It is formed, as you know, of a multitude of pipes, each one with its own particular note—some of them of the highest, some of them the deepest and most solemn, and some the lowest; each of them differing from the other, but all massed together and put under control to express one perfect note of praise. Out of diversity springs union; out of multiplicity comes harmony. Is it not so with the congregation that they represent? Have we not all fears, hopes, sorrows, joys, each one distinct from his neighbor, so distinct that the man by your side you might part with for ever and never miss him from existence? So springs one act of love and praise from the whole. No matter how diverse or different the people may be, when it is a question of praise, worship, and faith, they are all wholly one—the pulsation moves through them all. Thus the great instrument is the interpreter and the image at the same time of much of this. It is and will be a kind of angel, inanimate yet vocal, insensible yet powerful, proclaiming to you in its own way the great mysteries of faith and reproducing the life of Jesus Christ.

The Catholic Church reproduces in her festivals the life of Christ. She is nothing more than a representation of that life; and at each scene the organ takes an active and important accompanying part—at every scene save one. Christmas morning will come with its frosty air, and the altar will be lighted up and the people will be kneeling around, when suddenly and at the moment we are not thinking will peal out in glorious tones the happy invitation, "Come, let us adore him"; and at the sound of the voice we are transported with the shepherds to the newly-born Babe. Easter will come, and the tears shed for the Crucifixion will have been dried up, and in the ceremony of the time the organ will take a joyful part. I have said at every mystery save one shall the organ sound. On one day in the year shall the organ be silent; no note shall escape from it; it shall be as it were a being struck dumb. On that day the Church wears the black robe of grief; she stands at the feet of the crucified and overhanging figure of Jesus, even as did the Virgin Mother in the muteness of her sorrow on Calvary. Her heart is broken; her feelings are too deep for utterance. On that day the organ is silent—silent that every man may examine his heart, and may meditate what part he had in the death of our Lord. On Saturday, however, hope will come; and the organ will peal forth again, and there is no death, but triumphant resurrection. Thus would the organ interpret to them like the angel with a strong voice. A child is born to one amongst you; the organ will put forth its voice of praise. A man dies, and around his body as it lies before the altar surrounded by the lights the organ flings the incense of its suffrage. In all that appertains to the ceremonies of the Church it shall take part, and the great instrument shall be a joy and a comfort to you and to your children for future time. Therefore I congratulate you, not merely on the possession of a thing of beauty which is a joy for ever, but also on it as an aid to the fit worship of God.

Meantime, I need not tell you there have been improvements made, and there are yet many improvements to be made, in the church, and to effect them the bishops and pastors relied on that fund which had never failed for fifteen hundred years—namely, the great deep faith of the Irish heart. No sooner were the Irish people converted to the Church than tens of thousands of the consecrated voices awoke the echoes in the churches which were built, and night and day for full seven hundred years resounded the holy song of prayer and praise, so that the emperors of Germany sent their ambassadors for choirs of singers to Ireland, and in the monasteries of the wooded Glendalough, and in Arran thrust out in the Atlantic, in Mayo, and in your own Abbey of Moyne, were found in Ireland the best singers in the world. That holy voice was hushed in the clash of arms during the Danish invasion, and again it was silenced in after-years by persecution which all now regret—perhaps none more than the children of those who inflicted the persecutions—but to-day again a crown of glory rests upon the Church. Protestant as well as Catholic admits that that Church is an ancient and a venerable one; and though bearing the scars of many a well-contested field, and often uncrowned, never yet has she been disrobed. To-day, anew, the Church of Ireland rises, and the native song of praise—the song of Columb, and Kevin of Glendalough, of Monasterboice and Monasterevin—

sounds again through the length and breadth of the land. To-day the Church sings the praises of God as if never interrupted, and so she would continue to do on earth as is done in heaven, singing for ever and ever: "Holy, holy, holy, Lord God of Sabaoth, the heavens and the earth are filled with thy glory."

PUBLICATIONS
OF
P. J. KENEDY,
Excelsior Catholic Publishing House,

5 BARCLAY ST., NEAR BROADWAY, NEW YORK,
Opposite the Astor House

Adventures of Michael Dwyer................	$1 00
Adelmar the Templar. A Tale..............	40
Ballads, Poems, and Songs of William Collins...	1 00
Blanche. A Tale from the French............	40
Battle of Ventry Harbor.....................	20
Bibles, from $2 50 to	15 00
Brooks and Hughes Controversy............	75
Butler's Feasts and Fasts....................	1 25
Blind Agnese. A Tale.......................	50
Butler's Catechism...........................	8
" " with Mass Prayers...........	30
Bible History. Challoner....................	50
Christian Virtues. By St. Liguori............	1 00
Christian's Rule of Life. By St. Liguori.....	30
Christmas Night's Entertainments...........	60
Conversion of Ratisbonne...................	50
Clifton Tracts. 4 vols......................	3 00
Catholic Offering. By Bishop Walsh.........	1 50
Christian Perfection. Rodriguez. 3 vols. Only complete edition...........................	4 00
Catholic Church in the United States. By J. G. Shea. Illustrated.........................	2 00
Catholic Missions among the Indians.......	2 50
Chateau Lescure. A Tale....................	50
Conscience; or, May Brooke. A Tale........	1 00
Catholic Hymn-Book.........................	15
Christian Brothers' 1st Book................	13
Catholic Prayer-Books, 25c., 50c., up to	12 00

☞ Any of above books sent free by mail on receipt of price. Agents wanted everywhere to sell above books, to whom liberal terms will be given. Address

P. J. KENEDY, Excelsior Catholic Publishing House,
5 Barclay Street, New York.

Christian Brothers' 2d Book...............	$0 25
" " 3d "	63
" " 4th "	88
Catholic Primer..........................	6
Catholic School-Book....................	25
Cannon's Practical Speller..............	25
Carpenter's Speller.......................	25
Dick Massey. An Irish Story............	1 00
Doctrine of Miracles Explained.........	1 00
Doctrinal Catechism.....................	50
Douay "	25
Diploma of Children of Mary...........	20
Erin go Bragh. (Sentimental Songster.).....	25
El Nuevo Testamento. (Spanish.)..........	1 50
Elevation of the Soul to God............	75
Epistles and Gospels. (Goffine.)...........	2 00
Eucharistica; or, Holy Eucharist...........	1 00
End of Controversy. (Milner.)............	75
El Nuevo Catecismo. (Spanish.)..........	15
El Catecismo de la Doctrina Christiana. (Spanish Catechism)......	15
El Catecismo Ripalda. (Spanish)............	12
Furniss' Tracts for Spiritual Reading......	1 00
Faugh a Ballagh Comic Songster..........	25
Fifty Reasons.............................	25
Following of Christ.......................	50
Fashion. A Tale. 35 Illustrations...........	50
Faith and Fancy. Poems. Savage..........	75
Glories of Mary. (St. Liguori.)............	1 25
Golden Book of Confraternities...........	50
Grounds of Catholic Doctrine...........	25
Grace's Outlines of History..............	50
Holy Eucharist...........................	1 00
Hours before the Altar. Red edges	50
History of Ireland. Moore. 2 vols.......	5 00
" " O'Mahoney's Keating.......	4 00
Hay on Miracles	1 00
Hamiltons. A Tale........................	50
History of Modern Europe. Shea........	1 25
Hours with the Sacred Heart............	50
Irish National Songster...................	1 00
Imitation of Christ.......................	40
Catholic Prayer Books, 25c., 50c., up to	12 00

☞ Any of above books sent free by mail on receipt of price. Agents wanted everywhere to sell above books, to whom liberal terms will be given. Address

P. J. KENEDY, Excelsior Catholic Publishing House,
5 Barclay Street, New York.

Irish Fireside Stories, Tales, and Legends. (Magnificent new book just out.) About 400 pages large 12mo, containing about 40 humorous and pathetic sketches. 12 fine full-page Illustrations. Sold only by subscription. Only.................. $1 00

Keeper of the Lazaretto. A Tale...............	40
Kirwan Unmasked. By Archbishop Hughes.....	12
King's Daughters. An Allegory.................	75
Life and Legends of St. Patrick.................	1 00
Life of St. Mary of Egypt......................	60
" " Winefride...........................	60
" " Louis...............................	40
" " Alphonsus M. Liguori.............	75
" " Ignatius Loyola. 2 vols...........	3 00
Life of Blessed Virgin...........................	75
Life of Madame de la Peltrie....................	50
Lily of Israel. 22 Engravings..................	75
Life Stories of Dying Penitents.................	75
Love of Mary	50
Love of Christ..................................	50
Life of Pope Pius IX............................	1 00
Lenten Manual..................................	50
Lizzie Maitland. A Tale........................	75
Little Frank. A Tale	50
Little Catholic Hymn-Book.....................	10
Lyra Catholica (large Hymn-Book).............	75
Mission and Duties of Young Women........	60
Maltese Cross. A Tale..........................	40
Manual of Children of Mary....................	50
Mater Admirabilis...............................	1 50
Mysteries of the Incarnation. (St. Liguori.)...	75
Month of November.............................	40
Month of Sacred Heart of Jesus................	50
" " Mary................................	50
Manual of Controversy..........................	75
Michael Dwyer. An Irish Story of 1708.........	1 00
Milner's End of Controversy....................	75
May Brooke; or, Conscience. A Tale.........	1 00
New Testament..................................	50
Oramaika. An Indian Story....................	75
Old Andrew the Weaver........................	50
Preparation for Death. St. Liguori............	75
Catholic Prayer-Books, 25c., 50c., up to	12 00

☞ Any of above books sent free by mail on receipt of price. Agents wanted everywhere to sell above books, to whom liberal terms will be given. Address

P. J. KENEDY, Excelsior Catholic Publishing House,
5 Barclay Street, New York.

Prayer. By St. Liguori.................................	$0 50
Papist Misrepresented...........................	25
Poor Man's Catechism...........................	75
Rosary Book. 15 Illustrations..................	10
Rome: Its Churches, Charities, and Schools. By Rev. Wm. H. Neligan, LL.D.............................	1 00
Rodriguez's Christian Perfection. 3 vols. Only complete edition.............................	4 00
Rule of Life. St. Liguori...........................	40
Sure Way; or, Father and Son................	25
Scapular Book....................................	10
Spirit of St. Liguori.............................	75
Stations of the Cross. 14 Illustrations.......	10
Spiritual Maxims. (St. Vincent de Paul).....	40
Saintly Characters. By Rev. Wm. H. Neligan, LL.D...	1 00
Seraphic Staff...................................	25
" *Manual,* 75 cts. to........................	3 00
Sermons of Father Burke, plain................	2 00
" " " gilt edges.........	3 00
Schmid's Exquisite Tales. 6 vols.............	3 00
Shipwreck. A Tale................................	50
Savage's Poems.................................	2 00
Sybil: A Drama. By John Savage..............	75
Treatise on Sixteen Names of Ireland. By Rev. J. O'Leary, D.D...........................	50
Two Cottages. By Lady Fullerton.............	50
Think Well On't. Large type....................	40
Thornberry Abbey. A Tale......................	50
Three Eleanors. A Tale.........................	75
Trip to France. Rev. J. Donelan...............	1 00
Three Kings of Cologne........................	30
Universal Reader................................	50
Vision of Old Andrew the Weaver............	50
Visits to the Blessed Sacrament.............	40
Willy Reilly. Paper cover......................	50
Way of the Cross. 14 Illustrations............	5
Western Missions and Missionaries........	2 00
Walker's Dictionary.............................	75
Young Captives. A Tale........................	50
Youth's Director.................................	50
Young Crusaders. A Tale......................	50
Catholic *Prayer-Books,* 25c., 50c., up to	12 00

☞ Any of above books sent free by mail on receipt of price. Agents wanted everywhere to sell above books, to whom liberal terms will be given. Address

P. J. KENEDY, Excelsior Catholic Publishing House,
5 Barclay Street, New York.